STUDIES IN SLAVE AND POST-SLAVE SOCIETIES AND CULTURES

Series Editors: Gad Heuman and James Walvin

AFTER SLAVERY

STUDIES IN SLAVE AND POST-SLAVE SOCIETIES AND CULTURES

Series Editors: Gad Heuman and James Walvin

ISSN 1462-1770

Other Titles in the Series

Unfree Labour in the Development of the Atlantic World
edited by Paul E. Lovejoy and Nicholas Rogers

Small Islands, Large Questions
Society, Culture and Resistance in the Post-Emancipation Caribbean
edited by Karen Fog Olwig

Reconstructing the Black Past
Blacks in Britain 1780–1830
by Norma Myers

Against the Odds
Free Blacks in the Slave Societies of the Americas
edited by Jane G. Landers

Routes to Slavery
Direction, Ethnicity and Mortality in the Atlantic Slave Trade
edited by David Eltis and David Richardson

Popular Politics and British Anti-Slavery
The Mobilisation of Public Opinion against the Slave Trade, 1787–1807
by J.R. Oldfield

Classical Slavery
by M.I. Finley

Slavery and Colonial Rule in Africa
edited by Suzanne Miers and Martin Klein

From Slavery to Emancipation in the Atlantic World
edited by Sylvia R. Frey and Betty Wood

AFTER SLAVERY

Emancipation and its Discontents

Editor

HOWARD TEMPERLEY

University of East Anglia

FRANK CASS
LONDON • PORTLAND, OR

First published in 2000 in Great Britain by
FRANK CASS PUBLISHERS
Newbury House, 900 Eastern Avenue
London, IG2 7HH

and in the United States of America by
FRANK CASS PUBLISHERS
c/o ISBS, 5804 N.E. Hassalo Street
Portland, Oregon 97213-3644

Website: www.frankcass.com

British Library Cataloguing in Publication Data

After slavery: emancipation and its discontents. –
 (Studies in slave and post-slave societies and cultures; no. 10)
 1. Slavery – History. 2. Slaves – Emancipation – History
 I. Temperley, Howard, 1932–
 306.3'62

ISBN 0-7146-5022-6 (cloth)
ISBN 0-7146-8079-6 (paper)
ISSN 1462-1770

Library of Congress Cataloging-in-Publication Data

After slavery: emancipation and its discontents/editor,
  Howard Temperley. p. cm. – (Studies in slave and
  post-slave societies and cultures, ISSN 1462-1770)
  "This group of studies first appeared as a special issue of
Slavery and abolition, vol.21, no.2, August 2000" – T.p. verso.
  Includes bibliographical references and index.
  ISBN -0-7146-5022-6 (cloth) – ISBN 0-7146-8079-6 (pbk.)
  1. Slaves – Emancipation – History. 2. Freedmen – History.
  I. Temperley, Howard. II.
Slavery & abolition. III. Series.

HT1025 .A37 2000
326'.8'09–dc21   00-031783

This group of studies first appeared as a special issue of *Slavery and Abolition*,
Vol.21, No.2, August 2000, published by Frank Cass.

Printed in Great Britain by Antony Rowe Ltd.

Contents

Introduction   **Howard Temperley**   1

Emancipation in Haiti: From Plantation Labour
   to Peasant Proprietorship   **Carolyn Fick**   11

Abolitionist Expectations: Britain   **Seymour Drescher**   41

African-American Aspirations and the Settlement
   of Liberia   **Howard Temperley**   67

From Chattel to Citizen: The Transition from
   Slavery to Freedom in Richmond, Virginia   **Michael Naragon**   93

Fifty Years of Freedom: The Memory of
   Emancipation at the Civil War Semicentennial,
   1911–15   **David Blight**   117

Riots and Resistance in the Caribbean at the
   Moment of Freedom   **Gad Heuman**   135

'A Spirit of Independence' or Lack of Education
   for the Market? Freedmen and Asian Indentured
   Labourers in the Post-Emancipation Caribbean,
   1834–1917   **Pieter Emmer**   150

The Delegalization of Slavery in British India   **Howard Temperley**   169

The End of Slavery and the End of Empire:
   Slave Emancipation in Cuba and
   Puerto Rico   **Christopher Schmidt-Nowara**   188

Unfinished Business: Slavery in Saharan Africa   **David Seddon**   208

Slavery to Freedom in Sub-Saharan Africa:
   Expectations and Reality   **Suzanne Miers**   237

The Aborigines Protection Society, 1837–1909   **Charles Swaisland**   265

Comparative Approaches to the Ending
    of Slavery   **Stanley Engerman** 281

Notes on Contributors   301

Index   303

Introduction

HOWARD TEMPERLEY

The abolition of slavery is arguably the greatest humanitarian achievement of all time. It ended an institution that had existed throughout history and taken many different forms. It was all the more remarkable for the speed with which it occurred. In the case of Western chattel slavery it was accomplished in little more than a century – which is to say between the launching of the first British anti-slavery campaign in 1788 and the ending of Brazilian slavery in 1888. In Asia and Africa, where Western ideas of liberty were viewed with suspicion and slavery was deeply rooted in the culture, emancipation took longer and in some places is still not fully complete. But, wherever it happened, the transition from slavery to freedom met with strong resistance, not only from former owners but also from other groups that saw their interests threatened.

In theory, of course, slavery and freedom are polar opposites. To cease to be a slave is to become free. That, at least, was the assumption of those eighteenth- and nineteenth-century reformers who believed in the natural right of men and women to liberty. They campaigned against slavery because they saw it as an institution that not only denied men and women their freedom but turned some people into mere tools for satisfying the needs of others, thereby providing a fertile breeding ground for all the worst human vices. Because slaves were denied education and compelled to labour under the threat of punishment, their minds were as much in bondage as their bodies. Treated as if they were mere livestock, they actually became, to a degree, brutalized.

But, according to its opponents, slavery also brutalized owners by hardening them to the sufferings it entailed. Like other privileged groups, those who profited from the ownership of slaves took the advantages they enjoyed to be a matter of right. Some lived in patrician style and acquired aristocratic pretensions. Nevertheless, the powers they wielded and the methods they were obliged to employ affected their characters, rendering them as a class notoriously arrogant and domineering. In short, they presented to the world the spectacle of a privileged group deriving its wealth by trampling on what had increasingly come to be regarded as basic human liberties.

Slavery was also seen as anachronistic. Where it flourished economic development was slow and free labour had trouble competing. This could be seen by comparing the slave societies with the economically vibrant and rapidly industrializing societies of western Europe and the northern United States. Moreover, the restrictions required for its maintenance had a habit of impinging on the liberties of free people, as could again be seen in the case of United States where free citizens found themselves obligated to return runaways and were restricted in the range of subjects on which it was permissible to petition Congress.

This was all very much in contrast to the slaveholders' view of slavery as being both salutary and necessary. Far from being wrong or unnatural, it was as they saw it a time-honoured institution that had been accepted by all the great civilizations of the past. The Bible approved it. The Greeks built their democracy upon it. Plato made it a feature of his ideal society. All societies were of necessity hierarchical. As some were equipped to rule and others to be led, what could be more natural, then, than a division of functions based on that principle?

In communities where such views were dominant to protect the freedom of former slaves was bound to prove difficult. There was obviously more chance of its happening in places such as New England where only a few slaves had been held than in full-blown slave societies such as South Carolina and Jamaica, where slave labour had constituted the principal mode of production. But, whatever the attendant circumstances, to ensure that the freedom granted was genuine and not a mere exchange of one type of servitude for another was plainly not something that could be achieved by the stroke of a pen. More was required than a change in nomenclature. Even when laws designed to ensure the freedom of former slaves were adopted there was no guarantee that they would be equally enforced or that subsequent legislation in the form of vagrancy regulations would not render them obsolete.

Removing the prejudices and ingrained attitudes to which the master–slave relationship gave rise was bound to take time. Meanwhile, new working practices had to be established. Former slaves who failed to accept what they were offered were apt to find themselves evicted from their homes and garden plots. As always, when it came to bargaining, the advantages lay with the rich, propertied and educated rather than with the poor, homeless and illiterate.

Emancipation also had consequences for the wider community. Because slaves were classified as property, the act of freeing them represented a loss of capital. The ex-slaves remained as free workers, but the accumulated wealth they had represented, and which had often been used as collateral for raising loans and other purposes, vanished. Those most immediately affected were the owners, but so too, at one remove, were all those to whom they were financially obligated. How much of the £20 million compensation paid to planters by the British government was pocketed by the planters themselves and how much went to pay off their debts will probably never be known. Where compensation was not paid, as in the American South, the result was to create an acute shortage of investment capital that retarded the economic development of the entire region. This, in turn, affected the fortunes of free workers, already unhappy at the prospect of having to compete with the newly emancipated for employment.

Thus, in differing ways and to varying degrees, the ending of slavery affected the lives of people far removed from the farms and plantations where slaves were employed. To assess its success or failure is therefore a tricky business. As Stanley Engerman shows, much depends on the viewpoint adopted. The freedmen obviously saw emancipation from a different viewpoint from that of their former owners. Pleasing some meant disappointing others. The viewpoint of bankers was not necessarily the same as that of shippers, merchants and retailers. Consumers, who had been assured that slavery was an archaic and inefficient institution, had cause to think again when production fell and prices rose. It may, of course, be argued that the need to free the slaves was a matter of such moral urgency that the losses sustained by others were of little or no consequence. Nevertheless, it is pertinent to enquire whether the same, or better, results could have been achieved at a smaller cost.

One problem this raises is that of determining the criteria for measuring the success or failure of emancipation. From the point of view of those who regarded slavery as a sin in the eyes of God, the destruction of the institution was in itself evidence enough of success regardless of knock-on effects. But adopting a less fundamentalist viewpoint and assuming that the overriding aim of most supporters of emancipation was to improve the well-being of the slaves, one asks how far would living conditions have to be raised for the experiment to be judged a success? Would it be enough to show that they had been measurably improved or would it require that they be raised to a level where they became indistinguishable from those of the rest of the population?

To apply these criteria to the case of Haiti involves special difficulties because what happened there was so closely tied up with Haiti's struggle for independence. In one sense Haitian emancipation may be said to have been spectacularly – indeed uniquely – successful in that nowhere else in the entire history of the world has so large a body of slaves managed to free themselves by their own efforts. Having repelled all attempts at their re-enslavement, Haiti's ex-slaves were exceptional also in being spared the experience of having to live in a society still dominated by members of the former slave-owning class. Set against this, however, was their misfortune in having to pay a heavy price in terms of death, suffering and loss of freedom as a result of Haiti's long struggle for independence.

The ambition of most of Haiti's former slaves, as Carolyn Fick shows, was to become independent rural smallholders. However, as the leaders of the rebellion soon discovered, this was not compatible with the need to keep up the exports needed to finance the war. That meant reintroducing gang labour and the plantation system which, in turn, meant resorting to authoritarian methods. Workers were accordingly ordered back to their former plantations. Toussaint Louverture initiated the process by putting agricultural production on a military footing, requiring workers to perform their duties as if in the army and subjecting them to the same code of military discipline as military personnel.

Thus, instead of enjoying the fruits of their liberty, the mass of Haitians found themselves saddled with a ruthless black dictatorship bent on restoring production methods almost identical to those from which they had lately been set free. Although the use of the whip as a symbol of the former regime was now forbidden, the use of clubs was found to be equally persuasive. For want of investment capital sugar production never again reached eighteenth-century levels of production. Coffee, indigo and dyewood exports, on the other hand, fared better. But, with the danger of reconquest gone, the workforce recalcitrant and the plantation system in disrepair, the exertions required to maintain central control of the whole rickety system began to seem pointless. Even so, it was not until the 1820s and the 1830s that most Haitians achieved the goal to which they had all along aspired by becoming peasant proprietors.

To the rest of the world the sight of the richest colony in the Antilles first erupting into rebellion and then subsiding into isolation and poverty served as a caution and warning. Slaveholders interpreted it as proof of the foolishness of relaxing the iron discipline upon which slavery necessarily depended. Even loose talk of emancipation was dangerous. Abolitionists, in turn, pointed out that circumstances of the kind that had given rise to the rebellion in Haiti, which is to say those resulting from the collapse of colonial authority on account of the French Revolution, could not possibly recur and so could have no bearing on what could be achieved by adopting properly thought out measures. The likeliest cause of rebellion was an adamant refusal to contemplate change. Tactfully handled, slaves would gladly fall in with any measures that promised to ameliorate their condition. As for the claim that emancipation spelled economic ruin, was it not possible that a labour force made up of free workers would prove more efficient than one composed of slaves?

To Britain's West Indian planters this appeared an unlikely proposition. Nevertheless, evidence supporting it could be found in Britain's own recent experiences in the field of labour policy and in the writings of no less an authority than Adam Smith. In *The Wealth of Nations* Smith went so far as to argue that of all labour systems those based on the labour of slaves, because it was given grudgingly, were the least efficient. In Britain economic growth had gone hand in hand with a general loosening up of the labour market. Wholly new industries had arisen with the result that the country was richer than ever before. Liberty and productivity went together. Although such arguments were unlikely to impress planters, or anyone else with first-hand knowledge of the kind of coercion customarily employed in sugar production, a sufficiently plausible case was made out to persuade the public that the planters' protestations of impending ruin should not be taken too literally.

In the event, the planters were proved right to the extent that emancipation led to a flight of labourers from the plantations and a steep decline in exports, as a result of which British consumers found that they had to pay considerably more for their sugar. This was disappointing and naturally led to complaints that they had been misled. But as Seymour Drescher's contribution shows, the notion of improved efficiency, although useful as a debating point, had never been a motivating force in the campaign for emancipation. Adam Smith's statements, moreover, were not echoed by other economists, and when scrutinized can be seen to have more to do with his assessment of the kind of work carried on in workhouses and prisons rather than on any detailed knowledge of what went on in the sugar colonies. So far as the abolitionist leadership was concerned, the overriding issue was the need to end what they regarded as a cruel and immoral institution rather than the possible economic consequences, regarding which the better informed among them felt far from optimistic.

What slaves hoped to gain from their freedom, apart from a measure of relief from the drudgery of their daily lives, is not easily determined. Being illiterate, they had little opportunity to record their views. Presumably for the great majority the prospect of freedom, hedged about as it inevitably was by constraints and uncertainties, must have appeared very much a relative concept. A partial exception, however, can be made in the case of the settlers of Liberia. Like the Haitians, they were spared the experience of having to adjust to their new status in conditions largely dictated by their former owners. Unlike the Haitians, however, they did not have to fend off invading armies, although intermittent struggles with the surrounding tribes required the maintenance of an active militia. Allowance must also be made for the continuing influence of the American Colonisation Society and its several state affiliates to which the settlers continued to look for advice and financial support. Nevertheless, from the outset they had made plain their refusal to be dictated to and at one point even went so far as to stage an armed rebellion, expelling the Society's white agent from the colony. Thereafter they enjoyed a considerable degree of latitude in determining the character of what, in 1847, became Africa's first independent republic.

What most impressed visitors to Liberia was how American it was. The scheme's white sponsors had supposed that because the settlers' ancestors had come from Africa they would find ways of amalgamating with the local population. Scholars, too, have made much of the extent to which African culture survived in the New World. Evidence of such affinities, however, is singularly absent. Far from identifying with the indigenous populations, Liberia's settlers saw them as savages. Instead, they identified with the early settlers of North America. Like them, they saw themselves as representatives of an altogether more advanced civilization struggling against many adversities to build a better version of the society from which they had fled on account of persecution. Never for a moment did they doubt their right to possess the lands they were bent on seizing or the superiority of their culture to that of the African peoples they encountered. As is all too often the case, those who had been persecuted found themselves becoming persecutors in their turn.

Former slaves who remained in the United States encountered no such temptation. On the contrary, their problem was that, although nominally free, they were obliged to go on living as part of the same society in which they had lived as slaves and under arrangements weighted so as to favour the interests of their former owners. But, as Michael Naragon shows, the newly emancipated men and women in Richmond, Virginia showed their metal by asserting their political rights and invoking the aid of the Federal government. For a time this worked to their advantage, but eventually the government wearied of intervening and left them to struggle on as best they could under white majority rule.

Because they regarded their emancipation as less than complete, African Americans remembered the Civil War in a different way from whites. Both regarded it as a pivotal event in their own and their nation's history. With the passage of time, however, whites increasingly saw it as the culmination of struggles that had originated at the time of their nation's foundation and under which history had now drawn a firm line. With the arrival of its fiftieth anniversary, therefore, it seemed only natural to them to celebrate the reconciliation between North and South and indulge in the nostalgia evoked by memories of the songs, uniforms and heroic deeds of former times. African Americans, on the other hand, saw the Civil War as marking a beginning rather than an ending. As they saw it, the processes it had set in motion still had far to go. In their case, as David W. Blight shows, memories of the war evoked thoughts about how little had actually been achieved despite the promises made and the lives sacrificed. Southern intransigence and Northern indifference together had ensured that the reforms and adjustments initiated by the war would run into the sands, leaving the vast majority of African Americans labouring under a system of racial segregation scarcely less onerous than the slave system that it had replaced.

In the West Indies also the results of emancipation failed to measure up to their advance billing. Because blacks were relatively more numerous and economically important, and because social constraints were correspondingly weaker, many chose to take the path earlier taken by their Haitian counterparts by becoming peasant proprietors. Given their experience of plantation agriculture this is understandable. When the 1833 Emancipation Act ruled that former slaves should serve a period of apprenticeship during which they would accustom themselves to working for wages, their response, as Gad Heuman shows, led to riots and arson. Whatever else freedom may have meant, to most slaves it meant release from the backbreaking drudgery of gang labour.

Whether their flight from the plantations was in their own best interests is another matter. Eking out a livelihood, mostly on poor soils, without education or medical care, many found themselves living in worse conditions than before. Abolitionists blamed the planters for their exodus. Meanwhile, desperate for labour, planters began importing migrant workers from India and China. Abolitionists opposed this traffic, sometimes going so far as to describe it as a new slave trade. Historians, failing to take into account the conditions these migrants were fleeing, have also generally taken a critical view. Yet, as P.C. Emmer's contribution indicates, migrants showed sound economic judgement in choosing to go to the Caribbean, a view borne out by the fact that most decided to remain there on the expiration of their indentures. Despite its drawbacks, plantation agriculture remained the most dynamic sector of the Caribbean economy and Indian immigrants profited from the opportunities it offered. In contrast to the ex-slaves, they were familiar with the workings of a market economy and adept at accumulating capital, which they used to buy farms or set up small businesses.

While British planters were importing indentured labourers from Asia, their Spanish counterparts continued to import slaves direct from Africa. This gave them a competitive advantage, and it was not until 1867, largely as a result of Anglo-American pressure, that a stop was put to this traffic. The following year an anti-colonial rebellion broke out in Cuba. Aided by the growing abolitionist sentiments of the Spanish Cortes, the demands of the insurgents led to slavery's being first curtailed and then, in 1886, finally abolished. Cuban planters had never been totally dependent on slave labour. Partly for this reason, but also because the Cuban sugar industry was already highly capitalized, some of its plantations being among the largest and most mechanized enterprises of the age, emancipation did not have the same catastrophic effect on production that it did elsewhere in the Caribbean. Emancipation and the need to employ a diverse workforce, as Christopher Schmidt-Nowara shows, meant that ex-slaves developed common class interests with former free workers and played an important part in the subsequent struggle for Cuban independence. Because of the anti-racist ideology of the insurgents, many Cubans of colour became members of the officer corps. Although distinctions of race and class persisted into the early republic, giving rise to some violence and no small amount of political dissension, the Cuba that emerged from the years of nationalist struggle was more genuinely multiracial than was commonly the case in post-emancipation New World societies.

It might have been thought that in India and Africa, where slave status was not associated with distinctions of race, the integration of ex-slaves into the larger society on terms of equality would have been easier. In practice this was seldom the case. What might appear possible racially was apt to prove exceedingly difficult on account of cultural factors. Custom, tradition, institutions, tribal allegiance, family structure, religious practice and social hierarchy – ways of thinking and behaving – all constituted barriers. Nowhere were these obstacles more in evidence than in India.

How many slaves there were in India it is impossible to say as chattel slavery in the strictly defined Western sense scarcely existed there, but then neither did freedom. All Indians were subject to the restrictions imposed by the caste system. This meant that those belonging to the lower orders – the great majority – were effectively confined to certain occupations, in addition to which many, on account of debt, destitution, or hereditary status, laboured under other obligations. A proportion of the domestic and agricultural workforce, therefore, consisted of persons obliged to work for employers from whom they received little or no remuneration, while many more were effectively serfs bound to perform traditional services within the communities where they lived.

Anxious to save itself from the charge of condoning slavery but reluctant to interfere in the domestic arrangements of its Indian subjects, the British East India Company washed its hands of the matter by passing Act V of 1843 according to which any offence committed against a free man would be considered equally an offence if committed against a slave. Not least among the Act's advantages from the point of view of the Company's administrators was the fact that it required no active enforcement and may actually have relieved them of some of their former responsibilities, such as the duty of returning runaway slaves. It had little or no immediate effect on the lives of those held in bondage. In the long run, however, it loosened the traditional bonds tying workers to employers and to their places of origin, and to that extent helped to promote labour mobility.

It also became the accepted method adopted by European administrators the world over for dealing with indigenous forms of slavery. In Africa, as in India, colonial rule depended on the support of local elites whose allegiance was conditional on their being allowed to retain their traditional powers and privileges in so far as these did not conflict with colonial interests. Putting an end to slave trading was obviously necessary because it encouraged inter-tribal warfare and was likely to lead to disputes with other colonial powers. Interfering with slavery itself, however, was quite another matter. The distinction between slave and free status was not as clear cut as in the West. Exactly what freedom meant in the context of Africa's highly complex family and tribal structures was not easily defined, and even had the continent's new rulers been willing to adopt a more actively interventionist approach, the traditional character of African society set limits to what could be achieved.

For the most part, as Suzanne Miers and David Seddon show, Africa's new rulers genuinely wished to see slavery eliminated. This, however, did not prevent their turning a blind eye to much that went on around them or even employing slaves, as, for example, on communal development projects, when other forms of labour were unavailable. Many of the porters employed on exploratory expeditions were slaves. So far as most colonial administrators were concerned it did not do to enquire too closely into such matters.

Still less did it do to allow them to come to the attention of the Aborigines Protection Society or the British and Foreign Anti-Slavery Society, both of which took it as their remit to bring to public attention any deviation from the nation's declared mission to rid the world of slavery. Britain's commitment to ending slavery ws repeatedly cited as proof of the nation's benign intentions and in defence of her colonialist policies. This impressed Britain's rivals less than it did her own population, who were nevertheless surprised, having been told that parts of Africa were being taken over for the purpose of eliminating slavery, to discover not only that it still existed but was actually condoned. When such matters came to light, articles appeared in newspapers, questions were asked in Parliament and embarrassed officials found themselves called upon for explanations.

Yet, in spite of these efforts, slavery or practices akin to it survived the colonial period and are to be found in parts of Asia and Africa even today. Some of these are the remnants of traditional practices and are associated with distinctions of caste or lineage, but others are of more recent origin, the product of tourism, war or the demand for cheap products. Anti-Slavery International, the linear descendant of both the British and Foreign Anti-Slavery Society and the Aborigines Protection Society, reports regularly on such developments, as does the United Nations and the International Labour Organization.

Thus the Victorian belief that the last vestiges of slavery were destined shortly to disappear has been shown to be an illusion. It would be a mistake, moreover, to suppose that the persistence and recrudescence of slavery have been solely a Third World phenomenon, for if forced labour is counted as slavery, as it deserves to be, some of the most horrific twentieth-century examples of it have occurred in Europe. Although no country today will own up to having slavery, and some have proclaimed its abolition more than once, it has an uncanny habit of lingering on, and in some cases even where it has been eradicated of reappearing in a new guise and under another name.

Emancipation in Haiti: From Plantation Labour to Peasant Proprietorship

CAROLYN FICK

The ending of slavery in the French colony of Saint Domingue (present-day Haiti) was a unique event. Nowhere else in the New World, or for that matter in the history of world slavery, had armed slave rebellion, independently organized and self-directed, been successful. This made it an extraordinary and a historically unparalleled accomplishment. But the rebellion that was initiated by the slaves in Saint Domingue in 1791 and that culminated in emancipation in 1793 was also part of a larger and even more complex process of revolutionary change that had begun in France in 1789. The repercussions of those events had opened the way for the unfolding of a full-scale revolution in the colony that acquired a dynamic of its own. The course of the French Revolution in the end, however, saw the triumph of France's new bourgeois republic consolidated under the consular regime of Napoleon Bonaparte, who, in an attempt to restore slavery in the colony and to rebuild France's colonial empire, launched a military expedition against Saint Domingue in 1802. Resistance to the French invasion by the former slaves turned into a life-and-death struggle for independence. On 1 January 1804 Haiti became the second nation in the New World to establish its independence.

What most concerns us here, however, is first, what the mass of former slaves, tens of thousands of whom actively engaged in the insurrections that led to general emancipation in 1793, expected to get out of abolition; and, second, what they hoped for from independence. But before looking at these issues, a summary of the colony's situation at the eve of the revolution will help to explain why it was a revolution that resulted, rather than merely a contained or narrowly focused set of rebellions by the colony's three contending groups – the white planters, the free coloureds and the slaves.

Background to the Revolution

By 1789 Saint Domingue, with over 7,000 plantations, more than 3,000 of these in indigo, roughly 2,500 in coffee, perhaps 800 in cotton, another 50 in cocoa, and – the economic cornerstone of the colony and domain of the white plantocracy – nearly 800 plantations producing both raw and semirefined sugar, was by far the most fully developed and the greatest wealth-producing colony of its time.[1] In consequence of its tremendous expansion in sugar and, especially after the Seven Years War, of the rise in coffee cultivation, the slave population had grown at phenomenal rates, more than doubling between 1764, when slaves numbered just over 200,000, and 1789, when official census figures placed their numbers conservatively at 465,429, or roughly half a million.[2] By this time the annual entry of slaves into Saint Domingue through the French slave trade had reached an unprecedented average of between 37,000 and 40,000,[3] with the result that, by the eve of the revolution, at least two-thirds of the slave population of Saint Domingue had been born in Africa.[4]

Thanks to this expanding prosperity, and despite their subordination as a racial caste, the free coloureds had made significant strides. It was, in fact, during these last two decades of the colonial regime that the most substantial increases in both their demographic and economic preponderance took place, putting them at odds with their white planter counterparts as owners both of plantation property and slaves.[5] During this period, as well, their official numbers had practically quadrupled, from 7,000 in 1775 to roughly 28,000 by 1789, thus placing them in near demographic equality with the white population, which stood at somewhere just above 30,000.[6] Yet, because of their colour and slave origins, they were legally defined as an intermediary caste between whites and slaves and were thus prevented from acquiring full civil or political equality, whatever their economic standing.[7]

With the opening of the Estates General in France in 1789 and with news of the revolutionary position taken that summer by the Third Estate in the name of liberty and equality, both the white planters and the free coloureds began to organize parallel movements in the colony and the metropolis in order to put forward their particular grievances. The white colonists wanted free trade, an end to the economic constraints of mercantilism (the Exclusive) and freedom from the despotism, as they saw it, of the royal bureaucracy in the running of the colony's internal affairs. Factionalism within the planter elite over the political means by which to achieve these goals, however, soon pitted parties against one another in armed enemy camps, resulting in a total breakdown of authority.[8]

For the free coloureds the ideological slogans of liberty and equality embodied legitimate aspirations toward achieving the civil and political rights they were denied because of their African blood.[9] Given the specificity of the class and race relations that defined Saint Domingue as a plantation slave society, the attempt by the free coloureds to realize their goals through political mobilization inevitably clashed with the racial interests of the planters and by 1790 led to outbreaks of open violence. The responses of the French government to these incidents were mitigated by the need to balance the demands of the colonial bourgeoisie for local autonomy with those of the liberal revolution based on notions of citizenship and the Rights of Man. Each attempt by the government to address the problem of civil rights for free coloureds merely envenomed the situation, pushing the white planters toward greater intransigence and violence in defence of slavery and white supremacy and leaving the free coloureds with no choice but to resort to armed warfare in return.[10]

But how did the slaves, from their own perspectives and with aspirations of their own that derived, for most of them, as much from their recent African past as from the day-to-day realities of life under plantation slavery, interpret these events? How did they respond to the new ideas about liberty and equality that were circulating? And how, for that matter, did they view the assertive and audacious positions taken by their own masters with respect to metropolitan authority and by the free coloureds with respect to white authority? What, indeed, did liberty and equality mean pragmatically and substantively for the mass of African-born plantation labourers who strove daily to define for themselves a new identity under the harsh realities of their enslavement? And what did all of this mean for creole slaves who, by virtue of their knowledge of white society, greater freedom of movement in the cities and by their position of authority over their African counterparts as slave drivers, were well placed to act and to organize for change?

A Decade of Change

For one thing, the final decade of the colonial regime had provided some ground for hope among slaves that their conditions might improve. In 1784 and 1785 the French government had instigated a number of reforms to the seventeenth-century slave code, or *Code Noir* of 1685 – all bitterly opposed by the planters – that were intended to ameliorate working and living conditions. Hailed as humanitarian by the late-eighteenth-century Bourbon government, these measures reinforced earlier provisions of the *Code Noir* stipulating the exemption of work on Sundays and holidays for all slaves, as well as the reduction of workload and exemption from night work on sugar estates for pregnant women. For the first time metropolitan legislation placed restrictions upon the excesses of brutality that masters could inflict upon their slaves by limiting to 50 the number of lashes that could be administered as punishment and by forbidding mutilation and other forms of torture that might result in the death of a slave. Also for the first time, slaves were given the legal right to report any infractions of these regulations to the courts and thus the power to bring planters, overseers, and managers to trial.[11]

Particularly revealing in this respect is the often-cited case, in 1788, of Nicolas Le Jeune in the North Plain, in which a group of slaves brought their master's treatment of six of their co-workers suspected of poisoning – four of whom were put to death and two of whom died from the torture inflicted on them during their interrogation – to the attention of the courts. The evidence against the planter was overwhelming and clearly warranted his conviction. Although a common front of white solidarity and white supremacy ensured the planter's acquittal, the case none the less marked a turning point in master–slave relations.[12]

Another reform measure was the reiteration of the owner's obligation to provide the required plantation food rations for his slaves and the requirement that small plots, or kitchen gardens, be reserved exclusively for their personal use and individual profit. The slaves had, over time, come to consider these plots virtually as their own personal holdings and, although it was the owner's legal responsibility to feed his slaves, in practice more often than not slaves depended upon the scant produce of their own gardens for their survival, especially in times of drought or when shipments of staples were interrupted during times of war.[13] Meagre as they were, the slaves saw these plots as their own in a world in which they owned nothing else and, in the aftermath of emancipation, constantly sought ways to expand them or to increase the time they might devote to working them, always to the detriment of the owner's needs and the production of plantation crops.

Other factors, too, contributed to a vision of change. Rumours were circulating, not only throughout the colony but also much of the Caribbean, that slaves had been granted three free days per week by the king, but that their owners refused to implement the decree.[14] These rumours were, of course, false, but the belief, especially after the 1784 and 1785 reforms to the *Code Noir*, that the king might have issued a decree so freeing them, thus allowing them to devote nearly half the work week to their own gardens and to expand the scope of their free time, encouraged the belief that things were actually changing.

In the context of the revolt of their own masters, and then of the free coloureds, slaves began organizing themselves to enter the revolutionary process with an aim, at the very least, of gaining partial freedom. The rumours therefore provided a set of immediate goals, among them the abolition of the whip and the *cachot* (solitary confinement), as well. And so, in the midst of the political upheavals that their own masters had initiated, slaves began to see opportunities to push their consciousness to new limits, to 'test' as it were the chains of their bondage. But for them, the realization of any substantial change in their condition would necessarily entail an alteration in, if not the dismantling of, slavery as it existed. For that, they would have to draw upon their own capacities and initiatives and challenge the system as it stood.

The first articulate demands by slaves for their three free days occurred in January 1791 at Port-Salut near les Cayes, the principal city of the South province, anticipating by a full seven months the massive revolt of 22 August 1791 in the North Plain that swept tens of thousands of slaves into open rebellion.[15] A week before the latter outbreak, on the night of 14 August, a Sunday, roughly 200 members of the slave elite – slave drivers, coachmen, a few domestics and other trusted slaves of the plantations throughout the plain, and even a few free blacks – held a meeting on the sugar estate of Lenormand de Mézy in the North Plain parish to discuss the political developments in France and in the colony, and to set the plans for the revolt.[16] False documents were read to the effect that the king had granted the slaves partial freedom for three days a week, that the masters refused to consent and that royalist troops were on their way to enforce it. Were it actually the case, such a reform would have altered fundamentally the nature of plantation slavery both as a form of bondage and as a mode of labour by creating a condition of semi-freedom. It was on the basis of such expectations that, in the revolutionary turmoil that had been escalating for over two years, the slaves succeeded in launching the most spectacular and, in the end, the most extraordinary slave insurrection known to history.[17]

Yet it would require another two years of sustained insurrectionary activity throughout the colony's three provinces before emancipation could finally be achieved. During this time the slaves and their leaders adjusted their goals and demands pragmatically and strategically. Thus we find among their demands, once they were face-to-face with the authorities, requests for manumissions for their chosen leaders, the abolition of the whip and the *cachot* and, in one of the most massive rebellions of the South, in the mountainous region of Platons, territorial rights to the region they had conquered and occupied as a virtually autonomous maroon community, together with three free days per week for every slave throughout the plain.[18]

Freedom for the mass of insurgent slaves, if it was to be realized at all, was fundamentally intertwined with an independent claim to land. Work and labour for the profit of another or for the production of export crops on which the colony's existence depended was profoundly antithetical to their own vision of things. And so if we measure the post-emancipation realities and reactions of the ex-slaves, who were to remain as servile but legally free plantation labourers, against their self-defined aspirations and expectations, we can begin to see in embryonic form the essence of the agrarian problem that beset not only the French civil commissioners once they proclaimed the legality of general emancipation, but later Toussaint Louverture and the Haitian state itself under its post-independence rulers, Jean-Jacques

Dessalines (1804–6), Henri Christophe (1807–20) and Alexandre Pétion (1807–18).

Emancipation from Above

An overview of the circumstances in which the abolition of slavery occurred and the emancipation regime put into place by the French civil commissioners, Léger-Félicité Sonthonax and Etienne Polverel, in the summer of 1793 will help to elucidate the process of emancipation. What needs to be borne in mind is that freedom did not occur by virtue of a single, universal proclamation but was the outcome of a combination of mutually reinforcing factors that came into place at a critical moment. Not the least of these was the on-going reality of the independent, militarily-organized slave rebellions. By March 1793 France was officially at war with both Great Britain and Spain; the rebel slave leaders of the North, including Toussaint Louverture, formalized their tacit alliance with Spain and became ranking officers of the Spanish army, thus placing those parts of the North province that were already occupied by slave forces under Spanish control. Great Britain, for her part, was now moving toward an invasion that would be supported by secessionist colonists seeking refuge under British occupation from the revolutionary republicanism of France's two civil commissioners, who had been sent to the colony by the French Legislative Assembly the previous fall, armed with 'all the necessary powers' to restore order and impose respect for metropolitan authority.[19] In June the arrival of a new Governor-General, Thomas Galbaud, appointed by the French to fill the vacancy created by Sonthonax's arrest and deportation of his predecessor, created additional problems. The counter-revolutionary manoeuvres of Galbaud, who refused to recognize the superior authority of the civil commissioners, led to rioting by his supporters and outbreaks of arson in several quarters of Le Cap, the capital of the North, destroying two-thirds of the city. The commissioners now had only the city's free coloureds and some 10,000 slaves to rely upon in defence of the capital. Thus, with the mass of northern slave rebels fighting and occupying territory in the name of Spain and, in June, with the perceived threat of an imminent British invasion (which did, in fact, materialize),[20] Sonthonax, the commissioner for the North, was convinced that the defence of the colony itself depended utterly upon securing the military support of the slaves in the name of revolutionary France.

To give them a reason to fight for France the commissioners, in a joint proclamation of 21 June 1793 (in the midst of the Galbaud affair at le Cap), took their first step toward general emancipation by declaring that 'all Negro warriors who fight for the Republic against its internal or external enemies shall be free', thereby combining abolition with revolutionary republican virtue. The mechanisms to achieve these freedoms were put in place on 2 July, followed by the extension of freedom to the women and children of the 'men of 21 June', provided that they become officially married. On 25 July a further proclamation promised to ameliorate the lot of those blacks still remaining in slavery. Finally, in response to massive support for emancipation coming from the commune assembly of le Cap, Sonthonax took the final step on 29 August and proclaimed general emancipation and the universal rights of French citizenship throughout the North province.[21]

The 29 August proclamation of general emancipation, effective at this point in the North province only, thus declared free all persons who were still enslaved and ordered that the Declaration of Rights of Man and Citizen be printed and posted in all cities, towns and military camps throughout the province. But although the rights of French citizenship would be extended universally, these would be subject to the prescribed restrictions of a new labour regime.[22] The real problem, therefore, was to reconcile general emancipation, based on principles of individual liberty and universal rights of citizenship, with the pressing needs of a war economy that depended for revenues on sustained export-crop production and required the maintenance of the colonial plantation system. Plantation agriculture and 'free labour' would thus go hand-in-hand, and together they would have to be organized and regimented to meet the situation. Slavery would be abolished but the plantation regime and its requisite mode of labour would not.

First, the field labourers would remain on the plantations of their former owners for a minimum of one year, during which time they would continue to be engaged in agricultural work and could not, without the express permission of a justice of the peace, change plantations. A third of the plantation revenues, or the equivalent of one-quarter after the deduction of government taxes, would be divided according to rank and sex among the workers; one-third would constitute the owner's profits and the remaining third would be reserved for the maintenance and operating expenses of the plantation. Work foremen, or *conducteurs* (as the former slave drivers, or *commandeurs*, were now called) would receive three parts, secondary foremen two, all men over 15 years of age one part, women two-thirds of a part, children of both sexes between 10 and 15 one-half of a part, and women with children under 10 years a full part. All of this was contingent upon a full six-day working week, as under slavery, with only Sundays or holidays off and an allowance of two hours every day for families to tend to their gardens. The whip was formally abolished and replaced by the stocks (*la barre*) or, at the worst, by the loss of part or all of one's wages as a fine for an infringement of the work regulations or failure to obey the orders of a *conducteur*, the amount to be decided by the justice of the peace and paid into the collective revenues of the work force. All ex-slaves who were not attached to a plantation, who were not in the army or who were not working as domestics, were subject to imprisonment. Any unauthorized leave from the plantation was defined as vagrancy and warranted a prison sentence of one month for the first offence, three months for the second and a sentence of public works for one year for a third. Regular weekly inspections of plantations and reports by the justice of the peace were also required, while workers' wages, usually in the form of paper notes, were allocated by two assessors assisting the justice of the peace.

Sonthonax's proclamation and the prescriptions it contained affected only the slaves of the North, however, while in the West and the South only those that opted to join the French army were freed. Etienne Polverel, the commissioner for the West, was opposed at this point to universal emancipation and was preparing on his own the transition from slavery to general emancipation by a far more complex process. First, on 27 August, two days before Sonthonax's universal abolition in the North, and unaware of his colleague's intentions, Polverel issued a proclamation freeing those slaves who remained on the vacant plantations of emigre and deported planters whose property had been sequestered by virtue of a proclamation he issued on the 21st. These slaves, along with those already armed and freed in defence of the colony and the republic, would enjoy the right of 'co-ownership', although in the division of revenues, the soldiers, who 'risk their lives and expose themselves to far greater dangers' than the farm workers, would obtain a larger portion.[23] In this way he would extend the rights of property forfeited by traitors and émigrés to 'the universality of the workers of that plantation' and to the warriors collectively. Exactly *how* these plantations, comprising roughly only one-third of the plantations of the West, would be managed by the ex-slaves was never made clear. The notion of collective 'proprietorship' remained abstract and, in fact, meant little to the freed slaves of these estates who would still be required to labour as before under the alienating conditions of large-scale plantation production.[24] They apparently responded to Polverel's ideas with ridicule and laughter, as they jeered: '*Commissai Polvérel, li bète trop, li pa connaît ayen.*'[25] What Polverel intended, however, as he stated in the preamble to his 27 August proclamation, was to make citizens and landholders out of the ex-slaves. Knowing that they would never work industriously for the profit of others, he wanted ideally to make them worthy of their freedom by providing them with an incentive to work for themselves. For the ex-slaves, however, the one thing that would give their freedom significance, the break-up of the estates and the distribution of land to individual workers and their families, was not in Polverel's plans any more than it was in those of Sonthonax.

Moreover, these grants pertained to only one-third of the slaves in the West. As regards the slaves on those plantations where the owners or managers were still present, Polverel did not want to infringe upon the owners' property rights and was therefore more reluctant to free them unilaterally: these slaves would simply have to wait. He had received word of Sonthonax's proclamation of immediate universal emancipation on the 30th, three days after issuing his own, thus putting him potentially at cross-purposes with his colleague. In calmer times than these, Polverel's plans or some modified version of them might conceivably have been adopted. But events outpaced him. A uniform policy of emancipation was now obviously required, and it was the expediently designed model of Sonthonax that was adopted. The death on 27 September of the third civil commissioner, Olivier Delpech, settled the problem for the South. Jurisdiction over this province fell to Polverel, who, on 31 October, two full months after Sonthonax, imposed the Declaration of the Rights of Man and Citizen universally in both the West and the South, thereby freeing all the remaining slaves in Saint Domingue.[26] In order to ensure the continuance of production, however, he promised to follow his proclamation of general emancipation with his own code for the plantation labourers. Due to his subsequent illness, these regulations were not issued until 7 February the following year.

Reactions to Freedom

What, then, did emancipation mean for the slaves who had fought since 1791 to be free on their own terms? During the period of transition from slavery to the new system of wage-based labour, a period characterized by administrative chaos and, particularly on the vacant or sequestered plantations, little or no surveillance, the freed slaves took it upon themselves to establish the basis of their new freedom. In the South, where archival evidence exists to record acts of resistance to their emancipation on Polverel's terms, we find a fairly wide range of responses. To one degree or another, the workers actively imposed their own will as legally-free beings upon their situation and in so doing attempted ultimately to transform themselves into free smallholding peasants.[27]

And so we see during this period, roughly from October 1793 to April/May 1794, during which time Polverel's labour and police regulations for the farm workers were not yet fully operative, and especially on the plantations of émigrés or deportees, spontaneous acts of land appropriation to suit the needs of the newly emancipated. Most commonly, they expanded the size of the small plots or kitchen gardens provided for them by their former owners by cultivating additional plantation property as if it were their own. On some plantations they would collectively organize work brigades as under slavery, each brigade cultivating for itself that part of the plantation property to which it had been assigned and selling the products that were superfluous to its needs. On an abandoned coffee estate in the parish of les Cotteaux, a group of blacks (presumably coming from another plantation) had decided to settle by cutting down and burning the coffee grove in order to build houses for themselves. On others they stole surplus plantation goods such as syrup, sugar, coffee or indigo to sell at market, transporting these with a borrowed or stolen horse or mule; they gathered the uncultivated products of the land, such as wood for their fires or fodder for their pigs, and freely helped themselves to the plantation rations.

On those plantations where the owner or a manager was present and a regular work routine was imposed, and where they could not simply do as they pleased, the workers attempted none the less to exercise a measure of control over their work conditions and, by so doing, reserve an extra day per week for themselves and their own gardens. Here the most persistent aim was to limit their working week to five days, even though by Polverel's code it meant that their collective pay would be cut in half.[28] In the meantime, during the working week, they often did very little, arriving late in the morning, quitting early in the evening and working unproductively in between. The refusal to work altogether was apparently widespread, too, given the repeated incidence of this violation in the prison lists and administrative records for the period. Such refusals could involve individual workers, small groups or entire plantation labour forces. In order to lighten the pace and load of work, they constantly broke implements, destroyed sugar cane or refused to perform night work at the mill. Insolence, insubordination and threats toward their superiors were more often than not the rule. Women were no less vociferous than the men in this respect. They also wanted full pay and not the two-thirds they were allotted by Polverel.[29]

Vagrancy became common. In spite of their obligation to remain attached to the plantations of their former owners, workers went off to where the work discipline might be less severe or production schedules less demanding. Other farm workers left simply to join friends or kin on another plantation, or to hide out and not work at all. Still others slipped into the ranks of the Legion (as the military units of the freed slaves in the French army were called) to pass themselves off as legionnaires and take advantage of the more freewheeling lifestyle of the military camps. By the same token, legionnaires could also be found among family and friends on their former plantations, having decided, for one reason or another, to slip out of the ranks of the army.

These then were the attitudes and the aspirations of France's new army of free black labourers and soldiers upon whom the government depended to defend the colony and sustain the war against her foreign enemies, Spain and Great Britain, now in control of the better part of the colony. The expectations of freedom held by the newly-freed were thus frustrated and constrained in large part by the economic exigencies of war. As the commissioners saw it, without the diligent labour of the plantation workers the government 'would have neither the rations with which to feed the soldier nor the revenue with which to pay his salary'.[30] The agricultural labourers should therefore consider themselves the counterparts of their warrior compatriots, who, in defending France, were also defending general emancipation and would thus have to make themselves worthy of their freedom by submitting to the discipline and rigours of plantation labour. In the preamble to his 7 February work code, Polverel reminded those workers who thought that freedom might justify a personal claim to a plot of land that this was not the case and told them point-blank: 'This land does not belong to you. It belongs to those who purchased [or] inherited it from the original owners.'[31] Any notion of co-proprietorship, incomplete and tentative as it was in his 27 August proclamation, was now irrelevant, and the workers had to understand that their freedom meant regimented and regulated labour for others. He further justified the limiting of the size of their gardens to what it had been under slavery, arguing that, since the workers were now co-recipients of plantation profits, they no longer needed these, but, since he did not want to remove them altogether, they would remain as they were under slavery, 30 paces by 20 paces each.[32]

Although the actual administration of the new system varied from region to region, the responses of the black labourers were similar throughout the colony. In the north-west at Port-de-Paix, for instance, where an open revolt of farm workers broke out, their complaints centred on the fact that they were not paid what they were owed or were paid in worthless paper notes, and that they were harassed and forced to sell their chickens and pigs for a pittance when they went to town. Moreover, they complained: 'we are arrested by the police, put in prison without food, and we must pay to get out of jail'.[33]

So the period from emancipation in 1793–94 to the eventual consolidation of power by Toussaint Louverture and the emergence of a politico-military power structure dominated by indigenous black leadership in 1801 was one of transition. It is in this period that the aspirations of the former slaves toward establishing themselves as independent rural smallholders producing for subsistence or limited local markets (characteristic of the later nineteenth-century Haitian masses), emerged as manifest expressions of what freedom meant. New World colonial slavery, however, had never before been abolished, and in this both the revolutionary civil commissioners and the emancipated slaves were breaking new ground. But with the colony still in the grips of foreign powers, potential alternatives to the plantation mode of production could not be considered. Thus the post-emancipation regime of land and labour was characterized by an untenable policy which attempted to reconcile large-scale plantation agriculture with the universal right of the former slaves to be free French citizens. They took that right and gave it substantive meaning in their resistance to the coercive work codes and, where they could, in the seizure of land for their own purposes.

Slave Emancipation and the Emerging State

The problems Toussaint Louverture faced with respect to the economy and the labour force once he reached the pinnacle of power in 1801 were substantially the same as those of the civil commissioners, but much more complex, as the revolution in France after the fall of the Jacobin government in 1794 progressively moved toward political conservatism and, with respect to slavery, toward an eventual restoration of the old colonial regime.

The politics of the intervening period cannot be dealt with here at any length; however a summary of the events is necessary to an understanding of the contingencies confronting the black revolutionaries. In June 1794, after the French National Convention had formally abolished slavery by its law of 4 February, Toussaint deserted his Spanish allies and joined the French army in defence of the republic.[34] Over the next four years, he rose to new heights and defeated both the Spanish and the British occupation forces and personally negotiated the evacuation of the latter.

With the final defeat of the British, the colony was safely in the hands of France as regards international politics; internally, however, it left the situation wide open for a struggle for political supremacy between the colony's new indigenous elites, which derived in large part from the socio-racial stratification of the pre-revolutionary colonial structure of castes. On the one hand there were the upwardly mobile emancipated blacks who had risen, like Toussaint, to positions of status through the ranks of the military. On the other there were the light-skinned, former free coloureds, who, by virtue of their former free status, their education, their properties and by the fact that, as a class, they alone could claim both French and African parentage, saw themselves as the legitimate heirs to power in the new society, now multiracial and, in principle, egalitarian. A civil war ensued between the parties that left the mulatto forces of General André Rigaud and the coloured elite in the South bitterly defeated at the hands of Toussaint Louverture and the black generals, notably Dessalines, who was given military jurisdiction over the South. The end of the civil war thus neutralized Toussaint's potential political rivals and left him with virtually absolute and, for the time being, unchallenged authority. He proceeded to consolidate his position by ordering a military expedition to Santo Domingo (the eastern part of the island), which had been ceded to France by the Treaty of Bâle in 1795 but, until now, never brought under French administration. As commander-in-chief and governor of a unified Saint Domingue, Toussaint then promulgated a constitution in 1801 that formally sanctioned the abolition of slavery,[35] made him governor-for-life with powers to designate his successor and redefined the status of Saint Domingue as that of a virtually self-governing French territory.

Given the vagaries of a revolution in France that, by its own internal logic as a bourgeois revolution, had not initiated the abolition of slavery and only legitimized it once slavery was overthrown in the colony, Toussaint was charting a course that would place him and his people in direct opposition to the gathering forces of reaction under the Directory and, finally, under the consular regime of Napoleon Bonaparte. The outcome of that trajectory was threefold.

First, the type of society he was creating was dictated by the need to equip and furnish a strong military, without which the defence of emancipation would be compromised, and that depended upon plantation agriculture and exports to bring in foreign exchange revenues. This he accomplished, actually putting the economy on the road to recovery, but only by maintaining the large estates and by leasing these to the leading black generals, thus placing the workers under direct military supervision. Secondly, by leaving no room for French authority in his constitution and by placing Saint Domingue on an equal footing with the French government, Toussaint had virtually arrogated the powers of self-rule for the colony. This he did in order to safeguard the permanence of general emancipation while still remaining nominally French. The only possible outcome of such a situation, once the armies of Bonaparte arrived in 1802, was either defeat and re-enslavement under French rule or total moral and military victory over France and complete independence. Thirdly, what emerged out of all this was the unbridgeable gap between the state structure, which was a military one, and the rural agrarian base of the nation.[36]

First, let us look more closely at the type of society that emerged under the black governance of Toussaint Louverture. What was fundamental in Toussaint's mind was that only by re-establishing a solid economic base for Saint Domingue and combining it with colonial sovereignty under black governance could general emancipation ever be fully guaranteed in such a precarious environment as the late eighteenth-century Atlantic world, still dominated by the imperial powers of Europe. But in restoring the economy of Saint Domingue he recognized and accepted the fact that it was the agricultural prosperity of the colony and the exporting of its products that were the essential preconditions for its very existence. Knowing all too well the inextinguishable inclination of the black workers for independent smallholding, he also understood that the only way to make them work on the large estates, most by now sequestered and farmed out to his leading officers, and to produce crops for export, was through coercion. They were free, and Toussaint, 'a black like them', as he always put it, would never let them forget that; nor would he ever let them forget that it was the preservation of their emancipation which was paramount, no matter how harsh or incomprehensible his decisions may have seemed to the average worker. But for all that, plantation workers were to remain more or less in a state of serfdom.

Work discipline, therefore, was among the most pressing of Toussaint's concerns in attempting to stimulate and stabilize plantation production, and he addressed the problem in a series of labour and policing regulations. The first comprehensive one, basically an extension of the work codes of Sonthonax and Polverel, was his *Règlement de Culture* of 12 October 1800.[37] In lofty terms, he made it clear that he considered agriculture to be the basis of government, as it provides commerce and prosperity, and thus generates industry and the arts, while employing all members of society. However, for Saint Domingue, he likened the plantation and the agricultural labourers, the former slaves, to soldiers in an army unit. Just as the soldier cannot decide to leave his battalion for another without incurring severe punishment, so the farm workers would be bound to the same plantation and forbidden, without legal permission, to move about as they had latterly been accustomed to doing.

This had been particularly the case with the younger generation of blacks who were, on average, now between 20 and 25 years old and constituted the key demographic component of the plantation population by 1801.[38] They would have been no more than 10 to 15 years old when the revolution broke out a decade earlier in 1789–91; as such they would not have been fully integrated into the work gangs and so had never really known or endured plantation slavery at its peak. Their formative years were those of an entire decade of revolutionary upheavals in which their compatriots were the principal actors and in the course of which slavery had been overthrown. So, except on those plantations where a regular work routine had been maintained throughout the revolutionary years by the presence of the original manager or owner, these blacks had little regard for work. While the older ones might conform, more or less, to the work regime out of their past experience under slavery, the younger elements tended, by and large, to do as they pleased.[39] As Toussaint put it in his *Règlement de Culture*, 'they do not want to devote themselves to [plantation] agriculture, because, they say, they are free and spend their days running about, giving a bad example to the other workers'.[40]

Among the workers remaining on their plantations were those using the land for their own purposes, as they had done during Polverel's tenure as civil commissioner. For instance, on the Rossignol-Desdunes cotton plantation in the West, which had been sequestered and farmed out to a mulatto offspring of the former owner, it was found that 'the workers all had at their disposal a fairly considerable expanse of property for their own gardens, to which they devoted all their time, in spite of the prohibitions against these practices contained in the work regulations of the commander-in-chief, Toussaint Louverture'.[41] This expansion of peasant cultivation had evidently led to the development, under the prevailing wartime conditions, of internal regional markets representing a kind of 'economy within an economy', on which the colonists themselves partially depended.[42] Clearly for Toussaint, this state of things could not continue.

Therefore, all managers, *conducteurs* and workers would now be required to perform their duties, as would a soldier in the army, be subject to army discipline and the same severity of punishments. All farm workers who were not on a plantation and who could not prove to have been a domestic *before* emancipation or to have a trade or remunerative vocation and who might be living in towns and villages in order to abscond from work were required to return to the plantations of their former owners. The military commanders posted in these towns were required, on penalty of arrest and imprisonment or of being dismissed from their office, to search out and report any and all farm workers that might be found, thus putting an end to any occupational, residential or social mobility the average farm workers might have had.

In fact, at this time some cultivators had managed somehow to escape the reconstruction of the plantation economy and begun purchasing, either individually or in association, portions of estates that a few owners were already breaking up and selling off in small lots.[43] To bring an end to such practices, and to prevent the emergence of an independent peasantry, Toussaint promulgated a new law in May 1801 that explicitly prohibited all land transactions without special permits; such permits could only be granted for sales or purchases involving at least 50 *carreaux* (roughly 165 acres) and proof that the purchaser had sufficient financial resources to develop the land.[44]

Finally, in July 1801, when Toussaint promulgated his constitution containing a clause that authorized the governor to enact all necessary legislation relating to agriculture, the *Règlement de Culture* was in fact constitutionalized. Thus, with the exception that workers were no longer the property of their former owners and could not be whipped (but could be, and were, beaten), and now received small payments from one-quarter of the net plantation revenues, their lot was no different from what it had been under slavery. Freedom of choice was non-existent.

By placing the plantation regime under the supervision and control of the military, Toussaint's system not only allowed, but encouraged continual intervention by army officers in the actual running of the plantations, not to mention the daily personal lives of the workers. Toussaint's generals were themselves either the leaseholders of the sequestered plantations that had come into the national domain or owners of other property. Toussaint himself owned some coffee estates and real estate, while Christophe was reported, or believed, to be worth almost $250,000 in 1799. Dessalines rented some 32 plantations which yielded annually around 100,000 francs each in revenues.[45] As agricultural inspector for the South, where the severity of the work regime was the harshest, his supervision of the plantations was notoriously pitiless. Numerous contemporary writers bear witness to the tyrannical tours of inspection conducted by the black general. In the words of one, Pamphile de Lacroix, 'if a *commandeur* blamed the lack of productivity on the obstinate laziness of the workers, he would have to designate one by lot to be hanged' to pay for the rest. According to Lacroix, Dessalines reportedly got more work out of ten cultivators than 30 slaves would have done in colonial times.[46] The early nineteenth-century Haitian historian Thomas Madiou mentions that corporal punishments were still practised, and although the whip as a symbol of slavery had been legally abolished, chastisement was carried out using *lianes* or thick vines, as well as by clubs called *cocomacacs*. Executions apparently were carried out by bayonet.[47]

But even if these accounts were exceptional and pertained largely to the South, the militarization of agriculture under Toussaint was none the less extended throughout the colony and made the work gangs look more like army battalions at war, under the orders of a commanding officer, than an agricultural enterprise based on free labour. It was under such conditions that disaffection and opposition among the agricultural masses in the North were channelled into an organized revolt of farm workers throughout the North Plain parishes toward the end of October 1801. It was Toussaint's nephew General Moïse, who, as agricultural inspector for the North, was held personally responsible. It had been known that he opposed his uncle's regime. He disdained the use of physical violence that Dessalines encouraged and had apparently requested of Toussaint that he permit the parcelling and sale of state land to lower-ranking soldiers.[48] Personally he ensured that the workers received their quarter share of plantation revenues before the owners or managers received theirs. Regardless of Toussaint's measures, he could not, as he put it, 'bring [him]self to be the executioner of [his] colour.'[49] Given his close attachment to the workers under his supervision and his embodiment of their goals and aspirations for independent landholding, Toussaint charged him with inciting a revolt against his authority and, without trial, had him and a number of his aides shot by firing squad.[50]

Immediately thereafter, in November, Toussaint issued a decree reinforcing even more severely his earlier work regulations. The decree required military district commanders to prepare nominative lists of all farm workers on every plantation under their jurisdiction to be sent to the generals and forwarded to the governor. Everyone who was not a farm worker and could prove a vocation was now required to carry a passport; anyone found without a passport was arrested and thrown back into plantation labour. Moreover, soldiers were forbidden to mingle with the plantation workers, while any manager or *conducteur* who failed to report runaway workers from another plantation to the district commander within 24 hours was subject to eight days of imprisonment.[51]

Thus the intensity of labour, the severity of discipline and the harshness of working conditions, as well as the residential and occupational immutability of the workers constituted the legally defined and militarily enforced limits to their freedom. And in spite of resistance to these coercive measures and, in the North, of open widespread revolt, productivity and colonial exports did undergo a significant economic recovery.

The Economic Performance of the Louverture Regime

By taking 1789 as the base, and by comparing export levels in 1801 and 1802, at the peak of Louverture's reign, with those of 1795, when the economy of Saint Domingue was in a shambles and agricultural exports virtually non-existent, we are forced to recognize the fact that Toussaint's system, in spite of all the opposition it aroused and in spite of severe demographic decline in the middle-adult age group of the workforces, none the less proved to be, in the words of agrarian economist and Haitian specialist Mats Lundahl, 'remarkably efficient'.[52]

In 1795, after six years of political turmoil, half of which were consumed by armed slave insurgency and massive destruction of property throughout the colony, during which time the old colonial regime had been shattered, slavery overthrown and the new labour regime was barely enforceable, the colonial economy had, as Lundahl put it, 'become a closed one based on subsistence production and production for limited fragmented domestic markets'.[53] But by 1801, sugar exports were actually at 13 per cent of their 1789 levels, as compared to a mere 1.2 per cent in 1795. Similarly, in the same year coffee exports were at 57 per cent of their 1789 levels as compared with 2.8 per cent in 1795. Cotton was up to 35 per cent of 1789 levels from 0.7 per cent in 1795, while indigo declined only slightly from 0.5 in 1795 to 0.1 per cent of its 1789 volume. According to Lundahl, in 1802 the economic performance of these exports (with the exception of coffee, which declined by 12 per cent but still remained at 45 per cent of 1789 levels) was even more promising, with sugar reaching 38 per cent, cotton 58 per cent and indigo 4 per cent of their 1789 levels.[54]

Thus the economic recovery of the colony under Toussaint, limited though it was, still compared well with the state of devastation and abandon that had preceded his governance, and by 1801/2, compared with the years from 1789 to 1795, there was tangible growth. With this, Toussaint was able to build up fairly large reserves for, as he put it, *toute éventualité*, that is, primarily for defence, as the army alone consumed some 60 per cent of the colonial government expenditures in 1801.[55] To offset the labour shortages on the plantations, Toussaint also had established reserves with which he apparently would purchase fresh African labourers from slave-trading merchants, to be set free once inside Saint Domingue. Thus he managed to revive the plantation system at a critical moment in time when the universality of slave emancipation was coming under question by pro-slavery advocates and members of the Directory[56] and would be openly challenged militarily by Bonaparte. Such foresight and acuity on the part of Toussaint Louverture must be recognized. And yet, as he had embarked on the process of reconstructing the economy, building and consolidating a base of power within the colony and of redefining Saint Domingue's relationship to France, he did so at the cost of fundamentally alienating the overwhelming mass of black agricultural labourers who constituted the base of the emerging social and political pyramid. At this point, the bifurcation of the previously united forces that had made the revolution, had overturned slavery and the colonial regime and defeated France's enemies in the name of liberty was now definitive: 'State and nation were tied by the ideal of liberty, but the nation measured its liberty in Sunday markets and the right to work on garden plots. The Louverture party, on the other hand, embryo of the state-to-come and defender of this same liberty, was firmly attached to the plantation regime.'[57]

When Bonaparte's troops arrived in February 1802 under the command of General Victor-Emmanuel Leclerc, his brother-in-law, Toussaint had already lost the unconditional support of the masses and had only the loyalty of his generals to rely upon. The outcome of that struggle resulted in independence, but the devastation and cost in human lives and suffering were rendered far more extreme than they need have been, as the black leadership and the masses remained divided and fought in opposing camps for critical periods of the war against the French.[58]

Independence was declared on 1 January 1804 and the abolition of slavery was, of course, confirmed and reconstitutionalized, but the gap between the state and the people was also further reinforced. The fact was that, for the vast majority of former slaves – many of whom had been engaged in the armed rebellions and military engagements that propelled the emancipation struggles at every stage – independence was seen in terms of establishing an unhampered claim to the land they tilled. The harder fact, though, was that, for a country of ex-slaves in a world still dominated by the major slave-holding powers of Europe, national independence had to be defended. And for this Dessalines faced the same recurring problem of having to revitalize a war-stressed economy and to counter by coercion the strong popular tendencies toward smallholding in order to keep exports at levels sufficient to finance the military.

The Post-independence Haitian State

To rebuild the economy, therefore, Haiti needed new investments in capital and labour, both of which were severely lacking after the war of independence, which lasted from 1802 to 1804. Even though exports had not declined during those two years to anywhere near their 1795 levels, still, it has been estimated that it would have taken altogether some 95 million francs or £4 million to reconstruct and reactivate at full capacity the country's 793 sugar, the 3,000 or so coffee and the approximately 4,000 other plantations producing indigo, cotton and basic foodstuffs.[59]

By now, the ravages of 13 years of warfare had left the Haitian population decimated. The first census of the fledgling nation, taken in 1805, indicated that the population had declined a full 30 per cent from just over half a million in 1789 to a mere 380,000, with women outnumbering men by roughly three to two.[60] The army, moreover, which was estimated variously at between 15,000 and 37,000, thus claimed, at a minimum, one-tenth of the male population.[61]

Shortages in both labour and capital, combined with the changing composition of Haiti's agricultural exports that began under Toussaint, where only coffee really performed well against 1789 levels, were critical factors impeding any real economic take-off. The most labour- or capital-intensive exports, notably sugar (which never regained its former place among Haiti's exports and for which world prices were falling) but cotton and indigo as well, all declined. Realistically, the country could rely only on coffee and the small but growing sector of dyewood (*campêche*) and mahogany.[62] Thus the Haitian state embarked on independence without a national bourgeoisie, as all former French landowners were forbidden from ever setting foot in the country again as property owners;[63] with a colonial export-model economy that depended on the maintenance of large-scale agricultural production for it to generate revenue; and an over-exploited and numerically diminished mass of labourers for whom the meaning of independence was embedded in smallholding.

So long as Haiti was threatened, or perceived by her leaders to be threatened by reconquest and the restoration of slavery, the maintenance of what has been termed '*la grande culture*' in Haitian historiography, as opposed to '*la petite culture*' or smallholding, remained unquestioned by Haiti's first black independence leaders, Jean-Jacques Dessalines and Henri Christophe. For these men the most pressing and overriding imperative was to preserve independence, and they unquestioningly chose the path of rebuilding the large plantations.

In Dessalines's world, therefore, all citizens fell into one of two categories: either they were labourers or soldiers. Anyone who was without a recognized trade or who was not a soldier was automatically relegated to the field as an agricultural worker. As artisans and tradesmen were counted as labourers, albeit urban ones, only the tiny segment of government agents, clerks, tax collectors or plantation managers and overseers filled in the social structure. All of these functioned under the iron hand of Dessalines. Thus, the mastery of the state, a military one, over the collectivity of the nation, begun under Toussaint, was firmly entrenched by Dessalines in a society where one's economic task provided the sole criterion of one's social position: 'All people except soldiers', Dessalines decreed, 'must be attached as cultivators to a plantation.'[64] Male labourers, moreover, could be conscripted into the army at any moment.

On the plantations, the whip was banned, but, as under Toussaint, beatings with *lianes* or *cocomacacs* continued as overseers and managers exacted by coercion and physical abuse the maximum labour from their workers. And so, the mass of the population in the new nation had been returned in servitude to the same agricultural tasks they had known under slavery, with little tangible hope of ever achieving their aspirations.[65] With the emergence of the Haitian state it was a military mentality that defined the national consciousness at the state level, while the base of the population had, since the days of their kitchen gardens under slavery and throughout the revolution after emancipation, always demonstrated a pronounced tendency toward independent peasant smallholding.

But there were other discontented elements in the post-independence society under Dessalines, too. As all land held by French owners had been confiscated either during the revolution or by decree after 1803, and was run by the state as part of the national domain, the only class of people that remained outside Dessalines's rigid social and economic structure were those who had actually owned estates or other property in their own name during the colonial period *before* 1803; these were the former free coloureds, primarily in the South and the southern parts of the West. Since Dessalines had feared that, as the white owners fled the colony after the defeat of the French army in 1803, they would entrust their property to their mulatto offspring with the intention of later reclaiming it, all transfers of title after 1803 were subject to verification. Lands claimed by mulattos but previously held by whites were confiscated by the state. So Dessalines's land policy was as much anti-mulatto as it was anti-French or anti-white, a situation that exacerbated the tensions between Haiti's two emergent elites and led to a mulatto-inspired conspiracy that prompted his assassination in 1806.

Now the country's collective past and common struggles against colonial rule and racial subjugation forked in separate directions, splitting the country in two. The mulattos in the South had nourished expectations of their own after independence. Their struggles for civil equality had begun at the very outset of the revolution against the racial policies of the French and white colonial governments that denied them access to political office. They had fought and lost a civil war against Toussaint Louverture, and had now seen their aspirations once again frustrated under the closed autocratic rule of Dessalines, the former slave who crowned himself emperor in 1805 and declared: 'Moi seul, je suis noble'.[66] Thus they looked with apprehension at the eventuality of Henri Christophe, next in line among the black military leaders of independence, becoming Dessalines's successor as chief-of-state. They manoeuvred to prepare a new constitution that would effectively remove absolute powers from the presidential office and then proceeded to elect Christophe, who would reign as little more than a figurehead. Refusing to govern under such a constitution, Christophe led an army toward the South to impose recognition of his absolute authority, was met by armed resistance and the secession of the South. An ensuing civil war prolonged the division of the country until Christophe's death in 1820.

The division of the country into two distinct political units, the Kingdom of Haiti, under Henri Christophe in the North,[67] and the Republic of Haiti, under the mulatto president and southern revolutionary general Alexandre Pétion, also embodies, paradoxically, the contradictory and irreconcilable goals of the black leadership for large-scale export agriculture using servile labour, on the one hand, and those of the coloured elite, on the other, that favoured a *laissez-faire* political economy, land distribution to the masses, but exclusive mulatto rule in the political arena. A closer look at the two post-independence regimes may help to elucidate this paradox.

The Reign of Christophe

Under Christophe's governance of northern Haiti, no fundamental change in the quasi-feudal structure of plantation agriculture occurred. Government estates were farmed out on five-year leases to the highest bidder, usually high-ranking members of the military or of Christophe's self-created nobility. These were cultivated by permanent agricultural labourers who, as they had been since the days of Toussaint, were now still prohibited from leaving the plantation, usually the one on which they were born. More than that, in order to guarantee the permanent reproduction of plantation labourers, the *Code Henry*, which established relations between estate holders and farm workers, formally prohibited any non-agricultural worker from marrying a plantation labourer.[68]

The daily work routine, from Monday to Saturday morning, still demanded 10 to 12 hours of labour per day, and discipline was as strict as it had been under slavery. Families were given their small plots on which to cultivate their own food, and, as under all the regimes since 1793, the workers would receive, after taxes on plantation production were paid by the lessee, one-quarter of the profits of production collectively. Christophe therefore attempted to guarantee the productivity of the blacks through a wage incentive in cultivating cash crops: as market prices rose, so too would the value of their quarter share of the profits.

This, however, produced mixed results. On the balance sheet, the finances of the kingdom were solid. Christophe encouraged commerce, especially with Great Britain, and both welcomed and protected foreign merchants. He replaced all circulating coinage with gold and silver currency as the standard, raised an annual average of 3 to 3.5 million dollars in government revenue, apparently higher than it had been even in 1791, and, upon his death in 1820, left the treasury with a surplus of 6 million dollars.[69] Overall the economy under Christophe performed well enough for a country beset with all of the disadvantages and setbacks that accompanied her independence.[70]

As for the workers themselves, their preference for personal proprietorship was reflected in the increasing defections of plantation workers from Christophe's regime, either to the hills and mountains, where, as maroon peasants and squatters they could engage in subsistence crop cultivation, or toward the more tolerant regime of Pétion, where they might have a chance to realize their aspirations for land. These stratagems were, as we know, as old as slavery itself.

As the disaffection of the farm workers mounted toward the end of Christophe's reign, with two uprisings having broken out in the north-west,[71] Christophe tried to prevent the collapse of his system by allowing, for the first time, the partial parcelling out of government estates. In July

1819 he passed a royal edict that would grant rural property to soldiers and officers according to rank: 20 *carreaux* (66 acres) for a colonel and one *carreau* for a soldier.[72] These measures affected only members of the army, though, and did nothing to satisfy the aspirations of the vast majority of the coerced agricultural labourers. Clearly it was too little too late.

But other factors, too, may have pushed the farm workers of Christophe's kingdom to desert. The economic viability of cash-crop production, as opposed to peasant production, depends largely upon outside market forces. In spite of the maintenance of large-scale plantation production, sugar was never revived as a major export, and what little exported sugar Haiti was able to produce was in less lucrative raw sugar, which could not compete in a market where a parallel decline in prices for cane sugar was occurring, in part due to stiff competition from Cuba. Coffee, which alone held its own as Haiti's leading export, was still subject to market variations and had to compete against other coffee-producing countries or colonies. Thus the value of the Haitian farm workers' collective wage of one-quarter of their plantation's profits would have been subject to market fluctuations that could, in bad years, leave them all the more destitute and yearning for their own parcel of land on which to cultivate their crops and more freely define their own lives.

Whatever the reasons, it was the process of land distribution, or parcelling out, begun by Pétion in the South that sealed the demise of large-scale plantation agriculture in Haiti. This, however, was the outcome, not the explicit intent of Pétion's land policies.

The Demise of the Plantation

Pétion fully intended to meet the expectations of the coloured landed and commercial elite and began, in one of his first measures as president, by having the Senate restore to them, with compensation, all titles to properties of which they had been despoiled by Dessalines immediately after independence.[73] Other holdings as well that had come into the national domain under Dessalines were leased to leading military officers and government officials, who eventually became the legal owners. Finally, by 1812, nationalized properties were sold outright, but on the condition that half of the payment be made at the time of purchase and the other half within the year, thus ensuring that only those of substantial means could acquire estates.[74] To encourage large landowners further, his government abolished the one-quarter tax that had been levied by Dessalines and Christophe on plantation production, replacing it with a tax on coffee and, to stimulate large-scale sugar production, the removal of the tax on sugar exports. Planters were further subsidized by the government when the market values for these crops fell, as it bought up huge quantities of produce to compensate their losses.

In spite of these concessions aimed at restoring the prestige the coloured elite had lost under Dessalines and bolstering the economy, the plantation system was not revived. Agricultural workers in the South were not under the duress of military supervision as they were in the North. Planters therefore lacked the means by which to coerce their workers, who spent far more time on their own garden plots than on cultivating export crops. Individual large planters also lacked the capital, or access to credit,[75] with which to invest in the technology required for agricultural improvement, not to mention the restoration or replacement of sugar mills.

Economic decline rather than recovery set in, and as early as 1809 Pétion began a trend of parcelling out and distributing state land, starting with the non-active soldiers, who, in recognition of their contribution to independence (and in lieu of wages owed them by the government), each received 15 acres, with former officers receiving larger grants in proportion to their rank.[76] Land continued to be distributed in this way over the next decade, not only to high- and low-ranking members of the active military but also to civil servants, government administrators and even influential politicians in service to the state.[77] Although the best and largest grants of land had gone to the upper and the middle classes, who still concentrated on producing exports, a considerable area of land, approximately 400,000 acres taken from the older estates and broken up into smaller parcels, had gone out to some 10,000 recipients between 1807 and 1817.[78] In the end, the national domain was put up for sale at prices low enough for thousands of others to become property-owning smallholders. Many who could not afford to buy merely squatted and, over time, fixed their family names to the holdings they cultivated.[79]

By the 1820s and 30s, in the period of Pétion's successor Jean-Pierre Boyer (1818–43),[80] large landowners began to reconcile themselves to the poor returns from large-scale production and of refractory labourers, who spent more time cultivating their own crops than those of the owner. Moreover, any social prestige that might be derived from owning land and commanding labour was diminished by the fact that now practically anyone could own some land or have access to it. These landowners turned instead to more lucrative ventures in the commercial urban centres and in government, selling portions of their properties or, as absentee landlords, renting out or having the land worked under a system of relatively unsupervised crop-sharing known as *métayage* or *de moitié*, in which the workers kept the income from a half of the estate crop production entirely for themselves and spent the rest of their time cultivating their own gardens. In essence, they too had become virtual freeholders.[81]

The plantation system that had been the cornerstone of the former colony and the source of its tremendous wealth was now in irreversible ruin. Even Christophe, by the end of his reign, could not have kept it going much longer in the face of mounting resistance. But what this also meant was that Haiti was no longer a player of any significance in the Atlantic economy. And, although the parcelling of land that Pétion initiated in the early years of his presidency and that ended by defining the rural land structure of nineteenth-century Haiti may have helped to hasten the collapse of the plantation system and accelerate the economic decline of the country, it enabled the post-independence Haitian masses to realize what had been for them a long and bitter struggle to define their freedom. For the rural peasantry of Haiti it was the internal logic of the revolution from below that triumphed, even if it meant individual freedom in poverty.

NOTES

1. See G. Debien, *Les colons de Saint-Domingue et la révolution* (Paris: Armand Colin, 1953), p.50; H. Castonnet des Fosses, *La perte d'une colonie: la révolution de Saint-Domingue* (Paris: Faivre, 1893), p.8; and C. Frostin, *Les révoltes blanches à Saint-Domingue au XVIIè et XVIIIè siècles* (Paris: Ecole, 1975), pp.138–45.
2. Slave population figures covering the eighteenth century, taken from government sources, are found in Frostin, *Révoltes blanches*, p.28.
3. R. Stein, *The French Slave Trade in the Eighteenth Century: An Old Regime Business* (Madison, WI: University of Wisconsin Press, 1979), p.38; P. Pluchon, *La route des esclaves: Négriers et bois d'ébène au XVIIIè siècle* (Paris: Hachette, 1980), pp.19–20; for figures on slave imports by decade to Saint Domingue see D. Eltis, *Economic Growth and the Ending of the Transatlantic Slave Trade* (New York: Oxford University Press, 1987), p.249.
4. M.L.E. Moreau de Saint-Méry, *Description topographique, physique, civile, politique et historique de la partie française de l'île de Saint-Domingue*, 3 vols. (Philadelphia, PA: 1797; reprinted Paris: Société de l'histoire des colonies françaises, 1959), Vol.1, p.44.
5. During the late 1760s and throughout the 1770s and 1780s the free coloureds had participated in the rise and expansion of the coffee sector and possessed significant holdings in indigo, as well. On the rise of the free coloureds as planters see J. Garrigus, 'Blue and brown: contraband indigo and the rise of a free coloured planter class in French Saint Domingue', *The Americas*, 50, 2 (1993), pp.233–63. It had been said that, by the eve of the revolution, they owned one-third of the colony's plantations and a quarter, or well over 100,000 of its slaves. Castonnet des Fosses, *La perte*, p.11.
6. Figures for population growth during the hundred-year period from the 1680s to the 1780s in Saint Domingue and the rest of the French and the British West Indies are provided in Frostin, *Révoltes blanches*, pp.28–30. For a discussion of the accuracy of official census figures for the Saint Domingue free coloured population and of their demographic preponderance relative to their counterparts in the rest of the West Indies see C. Fick, 'The French Revolution in Saint Domingue: a triumph or a failure?', in D.B. Gaspar and D.P. Geggus (eds.), *A Turbulent Time: The French Revolution and the Greater Caribbean* (Bloomington, IN: University of Indiana Press, 1997), pp.71–2, nn.13, 14. One factor that probably contributed to their fourfold increase in official numbers between 1770 and 1789 was that now census takers were required to state the colour of the individuals on their lists: see Garrigus, 'Blue and brown'. On discrepancies in sources on the relative size of the white population, see C. Fick, *The Making of Haiti: The Saint Domingue Revolution from Below* (Knoxville, TN: University of Tennessee Press, 1990), p.278, n.14.

7. The policy of the French government regarding the status of the coloured populations in the French colonies was fixed in a memoir from the king to the *intendant* and governor of Martinique in 1777: 'The *gens de couleur* are either free or slave: the free are *affranchis* and descendants of *affranchis*: however far removed they may be from their [black] origins, they retain forever the imprint of slavery.' Cited in Fick, *Making*, p.20.

8. On divisions among the planters in the white ruling elite see especially C.L.R. James, *The Black Jacobins*, [1938] (London: Allison & Busby, 3rd edn, 1980), pp.59–84; also see Frostin, *Révoltes blanches*. On the position of the absentee planters in particular see G. Debien, *Les colons de Saint-Domingue et la révolution: essai sur le Club Massiac* (Paris: Armand Colin, 1953).

9. It was only in the last few decades of the colonial regime, however, in response to their demographic and economic strides, that the bulk of discriminatory legislation was passed. On changes in their social status over time and the emergence of social and legal discrimination see W. Cohen, *The French Encounter with Africans* (Bloomington, IN/London: Indiana University Press, 1980), pp.100–29; P. Boulle, 'In defense of slavery: eighteenth-century opposition to abolition and the origins of a racist ideology in France', in F. Krantz (ed.), *History from Below* (Oxford/New York: Blackwell, 1988), pp.219–46; J. Garrigus, 'Colour, class and identity on the eve of the Haitian revolution: Saint Domingue's free coloured elite as colons américains', *Slavery and Abolition*, 17, 1 (1996), pp.20–43; G.M. Hall, 'Saint Domingue', in D. Cohen and J.P. Greene (eds.), *Neither Slave nor Free: The Freedmen of African Descent in the Slave Societies of the New World* (Baltimore, MD/London: Johns Hopkins University Press, 1972), pp.172–92. For a detailed description of the *affranchis* on the eve of the revolution see in particular Moreau de Saint-Méry, *Description*, pp.25–111.

10. Full civil rights to all free persons of colour in the French colonies were finally granted by the Legislative Assembly on 4 April 1792. For an overview of the free coloured movements in the colony and in France in the context of the planters' revolts at this time see the works by James, *Black Jacobins*, pp.62–87; Robin Blackburn, *The Overthrow of Colonial Slavery: 1776–1848* (London/New York, NY: Verso, 1988), pp.172–98; C. Fick, *Making*, pp.76–88, 118–43. On these events see also the articles by R. Stein, 'The free men of colour and the revolution in Saint-Domingue, 1789–1792', *Social History*, 14, 27 (1981), pp.7–28, and J. Cauna, 'La révolution à Port-au-Prince (1791–1792) vue par un Bordelais', *Annales du Midi*, 101, 185–86 (1989), pp.169–200.

11. On the extent and consequences of the Bourbon slave reform measures, see Fick, 'French Revolution in Saint Domingue', pp.60–2.

12. The legal implications and contradictions in master–slave relations revealed by the Le Jeune case are critically treated in A. Gisler, *L'esclavage aux Antilles françaises* (Paris: Karthala, 2nd edn, 1981), pp.117–27. The full account of the case is found in P.de Vaissière, *Saint-Domingue: la société et la vie créoles sous l'Ancien Régime (1629–1789)*, (Paris: Perrin, 1909), pp.186–8.

13. On the role of the kitchen gardens in developing a sense of landholding among the slaves, especially in the South see the article by B. Foubert, 'Statut social et statut foncier dans la Plaine-des-Cayes sous la révolution: le rôle des places à vivres dans l'accession des esclaves à la liberté et la propriété individuelle', in M. Hector (ed.), *La Révolution française et Haïti*, 2 vols (Port-au-Prince: Société Haïtienne d'Histoire et de Géographie and Editions H. Deschamps, 1995), Vol.1, pp.71–9. On the evolution of the slaves' kitchen gardens in Saint Domingue and the distinction between these and the larger provision grounds see Fick, 'French Revolution in Saint Domingue', pp.72–3, n.21.

14. On evidence of the 'three-free-days per week' rumour throughout the Caribbean and its implication in slave revolts and conspiracies between 1789 and 1832 see D. Geggus, 'The Bois-Caïman ceremony', *Journal of Caribbean History*, 25, 1 and 2 (1991), p.53, n.18. On the spread of news and rumour generally throughout the Caribbean islands by way of sea and inter-island navigation and commerce see the study by J.S. Scott III, 'The Common Wind: Currents of Afro-American Communication in the Era of the Haitian Revolution', PhD thesis (Duke University: 1986) (Ann Arbor: University of Michigan Microfilms, 1989).

15. Saint Domingue was divided administratively into three provinces: the North, where the August 1791 slave revolt broke out, the West and the South.

16. On the composition of the participants in the 14 August meeting, see Fick, *Making*, pp.94–5.
17. The Haitian scholar Michel-Rolph Trouillot has argued convincingly that the Haitian revolution, even as it was happening, beginning with the slave insurrection of 1791 and continuing in subsequent phases, was inconceivable to European observers, because 'the framework within which proponents and opponents had examined slavery and colonialism in the Americas' denied the possibility that slaves could actually challenge the institution of slavery and succeed in overthrowing it as independent agents. In Trouillot's view, until recently, Western historiography, too, has tended either to silence the revolution by omitting it altogether, or to render banal the revolutionary content of the events to the point of trivializing them. See 'From planters' journals to academia: the Haitian revolution as unthinkable history', *Journal of Caribbean History*, 25, 1 and 2 (1991), pp.81–99.
18. On this see C. Fick, 'Dilemmas of emancipation: from the Saint Domingue insurrections of 1791 to the emerging Haitian state', *History Workshop Journal*, 46 (1998), pp.7–8 and *Making*, pp.141–6. In the North the rebel leader Jean-François did not attempt to negotiate the three free days with the authorities, concentrating rather on obtaining freedom for several hundred of the leaders, while the rank and file furiously demanded their three free days. See ibid., pp.114–17, 305, n.135.
19. R. Stein, *Léger-Félicité Sonthonax: The Lost Sentinel of the Republic* (London/Toronto: Associated University Presses, 1985), p.43.
20. D. Geggus has argued that the precariousness of France's position in Saint Domingue has been largely exaggerated by historians who have simply taken the Anglo-Spanish military threat for granted: 'From His Most Catholic Majesty to the godless Republique: The 'volte-face' of Toussaint Louverture and the ending of slavery in Saint Domingue', *Revue Française d'Histoire d'Outre-Mer*, 65 (1978), pp.491–4. However, on the threat of British invasion and the decision of Sonthonax to proclaim general emancipation, see Fick, 'French Revolution in Saint Domingue', pp.65–6, 74, n.39. By the end of the summer, at any rate, Great Britain would be in control of the Grande Anse districts on the extreme western peninsula of the South province, as well as Môle St. Nicolas at the western extremity in the North; before the end of the year, critical parts of the western coastal region would also be in British hands.
21. On the series of proclamations of the two commissioners and the circumstances leading to the 29 August 1793 proclamation, see the discussion in Stein, *Sonthonax*, pp.75–89.
22. The full text of the 29 August 1793 proclamation containing 38 articles is reprinted in A. Cabon, *Histoire d'Haïti*, 4 vols [1895–1919] (Port-au-Prince: Eds de la Petite Revue, 192?–40), Vol.3, pp.178–81. The following description of the labour regime is taken from these articles.
23. Cited in J. Cauna, 'Polverel et Sonthonax, deux voies pour l'abolition de l'esclavage', in M. Dorigny (ed.), *Léger-Félicité Sonthonax: La première abolition de l'esclavage* (Paris: Société Française d'Histoire d'Outre-Mer, 1997), pp.51–2.
24. Presumably the slaves, as any other owners, would pay the one-quarter government tax on production. The net remaining revenues would have to be divided somehow between those members of the plantation who chose to be in the army and those who chose to remain, with a portion remaining as operating expenses. Would the workers, however, be able to decide themselves who should get how much? Would the women be able to get their full part? Would the ex-slaves be able to choose their own manager, possibly one of their own? Judging from Polverel's own work code promulgated on 7 February 1794 (see below), one is inclined to answer in the negative. In any case events caused him to abandon the 27 August proclamation. In the 1794 work code, however, he did introduce the innovation of an elected administrative council. Fick, *Making*, p.169.
25. 'Commissioner Polverel is a silly fool; he doesn't know us at all.' Cited by M. Hector, 'Etat et Nation dans la période de transition: 1793–1820', in Hector (ed.), *La Révolution française et Haïti*, 2 vols (Port-au-Prince: Eds Deschamps and Société Haïtienne d'Histoire et de Géographie, 1995), p.126. Original citation in R. Lepelletier de Saint-Rémy, *Saint-Domingue. Etude et solution nouvelle de la question haïtienne*, 2 vols (Paris: A. Bertrand, 1846), Vol.2, pp.158–9. On the other hand, where workers were asked by the district military commanders to choose between Sonthonax's plans of immediate universal emancipation and

Polverel's plan of 27 August, with a vague promise that, in roughly six months' time, everyone would be free, many apparently chose the plans of Polverel, while others did not. Archives Nationales [Paris], DXXV 22, 216, 217, 219. A systematic examination of the *procès-verbaux* would need to be done to gain a clearer picture of slaves' attitudes toward the commissioner's plan, as the specific conditions in which slaves found themselves on one plantation or another would bear on their vote. Also, the manner and haste in which the *procès-verbaux* were conducted must be taken into account.

26. The reasons for Polverel's hesitations, stemming from his respect for the property rights of the owners that had not fled or were not deported, are discussed in Stein, *Sonthonax*, pp.90–4.

27. Unless otherwise noted, the following section will be based on the material presented in Fick, *Making*, pp.168–79.

28. When put to the workers as required by the work code, the choice of the five-day work week, from the evidence available, was not an uncommon or an unusual option. See ibid., pp.171–2.

29. For further elaboration on the resistance of women to Polverel's system of emancipation in the South see J. Kafka, 'Action, reaction and interaction: slave women in resistance in the South of Saint Domingue', *Slavery and Abolition*, 18, 2 (1997), pp.48–72.

30. Cited in Fick, *Making*, pp.178–9.

31. Cited in ibid., p.176.

32. These would have equalled approximately 600 to 700 sq m. See Foubert, 'Statut social', p.74.

33. Cited in P. Moral, *Le paysan haïtien: étude sur la vie rurale en Haïti* (Paris: Maisonneuve & Larose, 1961), p.16.

34. On the circumstances surrounding Toussaint's decision to desert the Spaniards and the timing of the turnabout see Geggus, 'Volte-face'.

35. The constitutionalization of general emancipation by Toussaint was necessary since the French Constitution of Year 8 (1799) of the consular regime of Napoleon Bonaparte, established immediately after 18 Brumaire (9 November 1799), stipulated that the colonies would henceforth be governed by 'special laws' that would take account of the particularities of each colony. Thus Saint Domingue would no longer be subject to the same laws as those governing French citizens in France. The transference of the constitutional universality of French citizenship for the colonial populations to 'special laws' was no doubt the first step toward the imminent restoration of slavery, and in this Toussaint read the cards correctly. As the Constitution of Year 8 made no mention whatsoever of general emancipation, the constitutional status of the abolishing of slavery on 4 February 1794 was effectively reopened. See in particular Y. Bénot, *La démence colonial sous Napoléon* (Paris: La Découverte, 1992), pp.15–31.

36. On this whole problem see the excellent study by M.-R. Trouillot, *Haiti: State against Nation: The Origins and Legacy of Duvalierism* (New York, NY: Monthly Review Press, 1990).

37. Extracts of the text of the *Règlement* are found in Cabon, *Haïti*, Vol.4, pp.96–8.

38. The middle-adult age group that would be between 25 and 40, and that would have been between 15 and 30 at the outbreak of the revolution, had essentially been decimated by the wars. See Cabon, *Haïti*, Vol.4, pp.88–92, 96–8, 190; and Moral, *Paysan*, pp.19–20.

39. See n.40.

40. In Cabon, *Haïti*, Vol.4, p.97.

41. M.E. Descourtiltz, *Voyages d'un naturaliste et ses observations sur les trois règnes de la nature*, 3 vols (Paris: Dufort, père, 1809), Vol.2, p.94. Cited and commented on in Moral, *Paysan*, p.19.

42. M. Lundahl, 'Toussaint Loverture and the war economy of Saint Domingue, 1796–1802', in H. Beckles and V. Shepherd (eds.), *Caribbean Freedom* (Princeton, NJ: Markus Weiner; London: James Curry; Kingston, Jamaica: Ian Randle, 1996), p.4; and by the same author, *Politics or Markets? Essays on Haitian Underdevelopment* (London/New York, NY: Routledge, 1992), p.160.

43. Fragmentary evidence is presented in Castonnet des Fosses, *La perte*, p.237, and is

commented on in Moral, *Paysan*, p.21. Other evidence of *de facto* land acquisition by former slaves on sequestered estates, in particular by *commandeurs*, who would be well placed to negotiate a piece of property with the resident manager behind the back of the owner, is presented in Foubert, 'Statut social', pp.76–7.

44. Lundahl, 'War economy', p.6; Moral, *Paysan*, p.21.
45. Cabon, *Haïti*, Vol. 4, p.114; Lundahl, 'War economy', p.6.
46. P. de Lacroix, *Mémoirs pour servir à l'histoire de la révolution de Saint-Domingue*, 2 vols (Paris: Pillet aîné, 2nd edn, 1820), Vol.2, p.47. Cabon, *Haïti*, Vol.4, pp.189–90.
47. In Cabon, *Haïti*, Vol.4, pp.189–90.
48. R. Dorsainville, *Toussaint Louverture, ou la vocation de la liberté* [1965], (Montréal: Eds CIDIHCA, 2nd edn, 1987), p.209.
49. Cited in James, *Black Jacobins*, p.275.
50. On the political repercussions of his execution, see ibid., pp.283–8; Fick, *Making*, pp.208–10.
51. The text of the proclamation is printed in Cabon, *Haïti*, Vol.4, pp.98–9; reference to the passport system is also cited in Moral, *Paysan*, p.19 and Lundahl, 'War economy', p.8.
52. In 'War economy', p.9.
53. Ibid., p.4.
54. Ibid., pp.4, 9.
55. Cabon, *Haïti*, Vol.4, p.195.
56. On Toussaint's perception of the political climate under the Directory and the question of slavery see James, *Black Jacobins*, pp.193–8. See also B. Gainot, 'Le Général Laveaux, gouverneur de Saint-Domingue député néo-Jacobin', *Annales historiques de la Révolution française*, 61, 4 (1989), pp.433–54.
57. Trouillot, *State*, p.44.
58. It is not the place here to discuss the dynamics of the war of independence. However, on the division between the leadership and the masses and the inability of Toussaint to master the situation by maintaining the loyalty of his own generals, who ended up defecting to the French, some of them even before he was captured and deported in June 1802, see James, *Black Jacobins*, pp.296–328. On the forces of indigenous popular resistance that erupted throughout the colony and, particularly in the South, which permitted the generals to abandon their positions in the French army and finish the war of independence in concert with the population see Fick, *Making*, pp.210–36.
59. In Lundahl, *Politics or Markets?*, pp.180–1.
60. J. Leyburn, *The Haitian People* [1941] (New Haven, CT/London: revised edn, 1966), pp.33–4; Lundahl, *Politics or Markets?*, p.181.
61. Ibid., p.176; Leyburn, *Haitian People*, p.36, n. 4.
62. Cabon, *Haïti*, Vol.4, pp.95–6; Moral, *Paysan*, p.27; Lundahl, *Politics or Markets?*, pp.184–5.
63. By 1806 the constitution declared: 'all property belongs to the Haitian state'. Moral, *Paysan*, p.28.
64. Cited in Leyburn, *Haitian People*, p.34.
65. While the two largest urban centres of the country, Port-au-Prince and Cap Haïtien (formerly Cap Français), had fewer than 10,000 inhabitants each and the army had somewhere between 15 and 37,000 in a population of 380,000, the overwhelming mass of Haiti's population remained rural and bound to the soil. Ibid., pp.36–7.
66. Cited in ibid., p.37.
67. Christophe actually preferred the anglicized spelling of his name and, upon his coronation in 1811, became known as Henry I.
68. Leyburn, *Haitian People*, p.45; Moral, *Paysan*, p.31.
69. Leyburn, *Haitian People*, p.51.
70. In 1818, two years before the end of his reign, the coffee crop was still close to 90 per cent of its 1805 level of £30 million and 34 per cent of its 1789 peak. Cabon, *Haïti*, Vol.4, p.95; Moral, *Paysan*, p.27, n.1.
71. These were at Gros Morne and Port-de-Paix. A. Dupuy, *Haiti in the World Economy: Class, Race and Underdevelopment since 1700* (Boulder, CO/London: Westview, 1989), p.88.
72. Moral, *Paysan*, p.33.

73. Leyburn, *Haitian People*, p.54; Dupuy, *World Economy*, p.89.
74. Dupuy, *World Economy*, p.89.
75. It must be remembered that neither Pétion's nor Christophe's Haiti had yet received political recognition of independence, while all ties had been severed with France. Access to metropolitan sources of credit was therefore virtually non-existent. See ibid., p.91.
76. Moral, *Paysan*, p.32; Leyburn, *Haitian People*, p.56.
77. Moral, *Paysan*, p.32; Dupuy, *World Economy*, p.89.
78. Dupuy, *World Economy*, p.90.
79. See Moral, *Paysan*, p.37.
80. After Christophe's death in 1820, Boyer ruled as the first president of a reunited Haiti.
81. Even smaller estates of 10 and 25 *carreaux* were parcelled out and sold along with others of 100 or 200 *carreaux* after 1820. See Moral, *Paysan*, pp.34–7. On the system of *métayage* see Leyburn, *Haitian People*, pp.76–7; 87. In the observations of John Candler, a visitor to Haiti in 1842, the crop-sharing arrangement on one estate in Furcy (in the West) provided the remaining 12 families with half the income from the 10,000 pounds of coffee the land yielded, but also:

> they appropriate to themselves almost the whole of the provisions which the land furnishes, sending down only a few of the rarer vegetables... to their master, for his table at Port-au-Prince, and supplying his need when he comes to reside for a few days in the country. This he knows very well, but has no alternative but to bear it quietly. (p.87.)

Abolitionist Expectations: Britain

SEYMOUR DRESCHER

Economic Development and the Abolitionist Perspective

Historians have had little difficulty in assuming a positive relationship between economic incentives and the rise of Atlantic slavery in the three centuries after 1450. Indeed, many of them have given slavery pride of place in accounting for European industrialization and world domination during two centuries after about 1750.[1] The successful functioning of the overseas slave systems was dependent upon a rigorous separation between metropolis and colony. While north-western Europeans consolidated their social and economic systems upon the principle of universalized civil freedom, they expanded their overseas tropical settlements based upon a broad range of coerced labour systems and statuses, including chattel slavery.

The continuity of such imperial systems depended upon an implicit or explicit rationalization of differences 'beyond the line' – economically, geographically, culturally and racially – usually some combination of these four.[2] Globally speaking, until the late eighteenth century it was western European freedom that was regarded as a 'peculiar' institution. As late as 1772 Arthur Young estimated that, of 775 million inhabitants of the earth, all but 33 million, residing in western Europe and the northern Anglo-American colonies, were slaves in one form or another. Adam Smith not only agreed with Young's proportion, but added that the unfree were likely to remain so for ages to come, if not forever.[3]

Against this background, the abolitionist political project, beginning in Great Britain in the 1780s, was simple and radical. Within a generation of its founding, it aimed at transforming the world overseas. As regards chattel slavery the world beyond Europe was to be realigned and the legal limits on dependency in western Europe were to become normative and universal.[4] Anti-slavery was faced with one enormous difficulty in engineering the fall of slavery. The positive relation of economic rationality to slavery in the Americas continued for the entire century of emancipations between the 1780s and the 1880s. Historians of slavery have been puzzled by this conundrum. For more than a century after the emergence of British abolitionism, they were reluctant to come to terms with the implications of this discordance. Instead, they followed the abolitionist strategy in labelling slavery as economically anomalous. In this perspective, anti-slavery somehow accorded with the dictates of progress.[5] During the last 30 years, however, an abundance of empirical research and theoretical analysis has forced a retreat from this older frame of reference. Increasingly, the point of departure for any study on abolitionist perspectives of emancipation must be that economic progress continued to sustain coerced labour, in a variety of forms, including slavery, throughout anti-slavery's triumphant long nineteenth century.[6]

In one sense, all the historians of British anti-slavery who have recently alternatively labelled its protagonists as revolutionary, imperialist, deconstructive or deceptive, pan-class or class-hegemonic are responding to the same paradox of political change against the grain of economic rationality. Looking back at one of the most successful social movements in world history, most are even inclined to overestimate the unity and hegemony of the British anti-slavery movement. Ironically, they echo the perspective of the Earl of Westmoreland, who, at the end of the eighteenth century, sarcastically referred to his abolitionist opponents in Parliament as 'these emperors of the world'.[7] British abolitionism is commonly presented, not only as an ideologically monolithic movement, but as one that epitomized the hopes, aspirations and expectations of the entire British nation, its ruling class and its culture during the era of the Industrial Revolution.[8]

On the contrary, once one shifts attention from abolitionism's dramatic transformation of British policy and mentality to the record of abolitionist expectations, it becomes apparent that their faith was uncertain. Its elite were deeply troubled by the same ecological contrast between European metropolis and overseas colonies that disturbed West Indian slave-holders and British policy makers. Moreover, there is striking evidence that abolitionist leaders never fully believed in the universality of one of the most fundamental articles of a world view, what historians have come to call the free labour ideology.

The most distinguished metropolitan source of this new world view was the economist Adam Smith. His *An Inquiry into the Nature and Causes of the Wealth of Nations*, published in 1776, supplied a distinctive economic argument to British abolitionists a decade later. For Smith, wealth and liberty ('opulence and freedom') were the two greatest blessings one could possess. The modern world was a world of commerce, creating a network of interdependence and resting upon the joint voluntary labour of a great multitude of workmen.[9] The opening theme of *The Wealth of Nations* was labour. In its productivity, its division and its maintenance lay the chief source of societal improvement. The optimum source of labour itself was the free action of the labourer. Ample rewards for free labour increased the activity, the diligence and the expeditiousness of the very population whose satisfaction and freedom, as both workers and consumers, was the true aim of an 'opulent and free' society.

In such a world slavery was not only morally objectionable but economically defective. Freedom for labourers was as beneficial for the masters as for the workers. Smith encapsulated the argument:

> The experience of all ages and nations, I believe, demonstrates that the work done by slaves, though it appears to cost only their maintenance, is in the end, the dearest of any. A person who can acquire no property, can have no other interest but to eat as much and to labour as little as possible. Whatever work he does beyond what is sufficient to purchase his own maintenance can be squeezed out of him by violence only, and not by any interest of his own.

The cost of the 'wear and tear' – of labour and its reproduction were at the expense of employers of both freemen and slaves. But the former cost the master less since the self-maintenance of the poor was generally more frugal and efficient than the management of masters.[10] Smith's formulation became a general article of abolitionist faith, ordaining the ultimate triumph of voluntary labour.

No subsequent formulation proved to be so straightforward or so compelling to anti-slavery advocates during the next three generations of political struggle against the Atlantic slave trade and Caribbean slavery. The whole world of historical experience was scoured to bear further witness that slave labour was 'in the end the dearest of any.' Smith's own demonstration was historical. The *Wealth of Nations* envisioned a succession of dominant modes of production in western Europe, corresponding to a series of economic stages from hunting and gathering, through ancient slavery, to modern voluntary wage labour. In this schema, of course, the New World presented a major problem.

If the western European sequence argued in favour of the superiority of wage labour, the reverse seemed to have been the case across the ocean, above all in the West Indies, where slavery had superseded indentured servitude. Before writing the *Wealth of Nations*, Smith himself had noted that bound labour was the prevailing form on the planet. Moreover, he anticipated that slavery was unlikely to disappear from the world for ages to come, if ever.[11] He offered two reasons for this contrast between free-labour optimality and bound-labour ubiquity. The first was a general, non-economic, human trait: love of dominating. This motive, of course, was not particularly helpful in explaining why the same western Europeans used one form of labour in Europe and another in the West Indies. The second reason was both economic and relevant to the paradox. It related to Smith's view of the generality of West Indian planters as agricultural profit-seekers, not feudal lords or rentier gentry.[12] The planters' choice of labour in the Caribbean was based more on profit than on pride or prejudice. Sugar was so valuable a product in Europe that the planter could afford the service of slaves. Indeed, the crop's profitability, with slavery, was greater than any other in the Atlantic world. In a book replete with policy assessments, the *Wealth of Nations* did not suggest that planters in the West Indies could increase their profits still further by emancipating their labour force.

If one read the *Wealth of Nations* less selectively than abolitionists were inclined to do, one could discover other serious qualifications to free labour superiority. But two relevant omissions from the book were as great a boon to future abolitionists as its formulation of free-labour superiority. In discussions of slavery in the Americas, Smith spoke of only two types of labourer – freemen and slaves. Aside from apprentices and miners in Britain itself, Smith seemed uninterested, to the point of total silence, in the existence and history of convict or indentured labour in America – especially the seventeenth-century displacement of British indentured servants by slaves in the sugar islands.[13] The process would receive short shrift in the debates over the British slave system before emancipation. During the age of abolition European freemen and Caribbean slaves would be juxtaposed in a stark dichotomy.

Smith's second omission was even more significant. It concerned his major hypothesis about the relative costs of 'wear and tear' – the reproduction of 'the race of journeymen and servants'.[14] When he turned to the New World for evidence of slave labour's dearness, Smith seemed interested in the urban clusters of North America, not the plantations of the West Indies, where the reproduction costs of the 'race' of servants were supported by the warren of Africa. Left to themselves, the choice of all New World sugar planters of all nations had been to replace all other forms of labour by African chattel slaves.[15]

From Abolitionism to British Emancipation (1787–1833)

For abolitionists who cited Smith the antithesis between the slave colonies and Britain was clearer than anywhere else in the world. James Ramsay, the first major polemicist against Caribbean slavery in the 1780s, casually invoked the principle of free-labour superiority against the existing system. Humanity could anticipate emancipation without qualms because 'he who can procure a freeman to work for him, will never employ a slave'. By a reckoning that was to be commonplace during the age of abolition, a free labourer doubled the output of a slave. Moreover, when the freeman died his place was supplied by 'natural' generation, not at 'enormous expense' from the slave market. Thomas Clarkson, the abolitionist movement's first national canvasser, boasted that sugar was already being raised by free men in Cochin China at one-seventh the cost of the British Caribbean product.[16]

Faith in the superior efficacy of free labour (or labour as free as it was in eighteenth-century Britain) did not depend on a reading of Adam Smith. The 'fruitlessness of compulsive labour' was proved 'every day in every workhouse in the kingdom. There is in proof too, the felons in the hulks, who produce not a fourth part of the ballast which is raised by the adjoining barges, where men are working on their own account.' The problem was always whether this experience could be transferred overseas. For generations to come such calculations elicited the rejoinder that the amount of labour extracted from the exploited and insecure freeman must therefore be far greater than what was being extracted from slaves. In this respect West Indian slaves must be better off than free English manufacturers and peasants. Ramsay's reply anticipated the general abolitionist response. Whether or not a European peasant reaped more of the necessities of life from his labour than a Caribbean slave, the free labourer's reward came from the 'charms of liberty itself'. Freedom softened his toil while it doubled his exertions. After work it secured him his own time, his family, his immunity from arbitrary cruelty. The putative attraction of lower costs of reproduction and security became articles of abolitionist faith.[17]

Another argument offered in opposition to major alterations of the British slave system was the universally acknowledged observation that freed slaves in the West Indies never remained in the cane fields. During the very early phase of the anti-slavery attack, when the slave trade was being targeted, abolitionists suggested hiring free blacks as domestics and returning slave domestics to the field as substitutes for forgone Africans.[18] Over the longer run, however, the abolitionists deployed the modernist's attack on slave labour's inherent servility and brutishness. West Indian free blacks did not work in the fields, and frequently remained idle, because planters demeaned labour. Slavery degraded labour, not the reverse. In a slave-tainted environment. No free persons would 'subject themselves to the driver's lash, who are not absolutely forced to submit to such a degradation'. The West Indian system's peculiar defect was 'its utter forgetfulness of *mind*' and motive in reducing humans to 'the vilest of brute species'.[19] If slavery polluted labour, every step towards freedom would restore the innate pride, intelligence and energy of labour.

From their first mass campaign against the African slave trade in 1788 to their agitation against colonial 'apprenticeship' 50 years later, abolitionists committed themselves to creating one world of labour relations. As William Wilberforce emphasized on the eve of the abolition of the British slave trade in 1807: '*the principles of justice are immutable in their nature and universal in their application; the duty at once, and the interest, of nations, no less than of individuals'.*[20] The supreme object and obligation of abolitionism was to dissolve 'the line'.

However, the abolitionist elite was far from comfortable about using the generic assertion of free labour superiority to guide policy making beyond the line. For decades, while theoretically armed with the good news of free labour superiority, most Parliamentary abolitionists opposed the immediate application of this immutable principle. Until well after the Napoleonic wars, and despite their creed of the unity of religion, justice and policy, abolitionists virtually ignored what historians have termed the 'free labour ideology' in its *economic* sense.[21] The principle of slave labour inefficiency was usually tucked modestly into the back pages of anti-slavery polemics.[22]

The abolitionist elite were even more circumspect in their direct appeals for popular action than in their tracts. Their major *Abstract of Evidence* on the slave trade in 1791 simply avoided the free-labour argument. The popular petitions reiterated this reticence. Fewer than one in twenty of the great mass petitions in 1792 referred to the inferiority of slave labour.[23] One rationale for this rhetorical reticence seemed to derive from the policy priorities of the abolitionist leaders between 1787 and their first major victory 20 years later. The abolitionists' first target was the African slave trade. In the West Indies slaves represented upwards of £50 to £100 millions of sunken British capital. Direct attacks on the Caribbean system would also evoke plausible challenges against the unconstitutionality of parliamentary emancipation. The planters could claim compensation for the confiscation of their legally sanctioned property. Finally, to attack slavery itself raised the spectre of overseas slave rebellion in response to public agitation for emancipation.[24]

Nevertheless, in arguing that an inevitable improvement would result from giving the 'blessings of freedom' to the West Indian slaves, abolitionists continually exposed themselves to the charge of hypocrisy in postponing emancipation. In response, abolitionist leaders declared that 'insanity alone could dictate' immediate emancipation.[25] In 1807 they demonstrated this conviction. As the slave trade abolition Bill reached its final stage in Parliament, a young MP introduced a motion requesting the immediate emancipation of all infants henceforth born in the colonies. Wilberforce immediately opposed this motion as unsafe and ruinous.[26]

The abolitionist rationale for delay was straightforward: too high a proportion of Caribbean slaves were African 'savages', debased by both superstition and enslavement. Slaves, as a group, required a long transition to absorb proper work habits, religion and civilization. Free labour would be superior only when, through gradual 'amelioration', the slow-growing plant of 'true liberty' overcame the slave's indolence and licentiousness. In his first writings on the subject Henry Brougham, later a parliamentary pillar of anti-slavery, could not even imagine testing the principle of free labour among uncivilized Africans, the 'common enemy of civilized society'.[27] What the *Wealth of Nations* seemed to affirm as a universal effect of free agency in labour was deemed disastrous as an immediate policy in the West Indian situation of 1807. That singular situation therefore left the free-labour ideology intact, because only 'truly' free men could test free labour's superiority.

Historians have tended to accept this formulation of abolitionist belief in free labour superiority as modified by the peculiar situation imposed upon the victims of the slave trade. The British elite as a whole has been widely characterized as adhering to the principle of free labour superiority until emancipation and beyond.[28] Was it just a peculiarity of the peculiar institution that rendered Caribbean slave labourers unfit to compete as free labourers, or did abolitionists themselves harbour deeper doubts about the ability of even never-enslaved free labour to compete with the contemporary slave system?

The more knowledgeable of the Saints in Parliament openly rejected the hypothesis of free labour superiority in the sugar islands. They knew, of course, from the beginning, that the least controversial way to end both the slave trade and the slave system of production was to supply sugar grown by free labourers at 'a *cheaper rate*'.[29] In the early 1790s they looked hopefully from one potential 'free labour' competitor to another: to the British East India Company, to North American maple-sugar extractors, to the new African colony of Sierra Leone.[30] By the time abolitionists finally succeeded in prohibiting the British slave trade, in 1806–7, all of the potential free-labour alternatives had foundered. New World slaves supplied more than 95 per cent of the north Atlantic's sugar.[31]

Before the 1820s the abolitionist strategy was to postpone agitation for emancipation to a vague and distant future. They occasionally referred to the 'consumerist' aspects of the free-labour argument. By focusing upon the acquisitive potential of self-motivated, free labourers, some contemporary political economists were turning public attention to the probable impact of an ever-broadening demand for amenities by labourers. Indeed, the mass consumption of slave-grown products – tobacco, sugar, coffee and cotton – was presumably already inducing British labourers to work more assiduously for these erstwhile luxuries. Voluntary labour not only increased the sufficient supply of worldly goods but the range and value of metropolitan demand.[32]

Yet, as applied to the West Indies, neither abolitionist arguments nor their policies tended to have a consumptionist orientation. In focusing upon the slave trade abolitionists initially emphasized the vast potential of Africa, not the Caribbean. Eliminating the internecine warfare inspired by slaving would rapidly transform 'one-third of the inhabitable globe' into a vast emporium for British commerce. In the Caribbean, on the other hand, abolitionists could only offer a gradual increase in colonial purchases of British exports, contingent upon the slow improvement of the still-enslaved bulk of the population.[33] Moreover, another aspect of abolitionist behaviour tended to depress, rather than to expand, the British consumption of West Indian produce. Beginning in 1791, an abolitionist consumers' mobilization launched a mass boycott against slave-grown sugar. The boycott's effect upon West Indian sugar producers was negligible, but it sometimes raised the cost of sugar to those consumers who purchased only ('free') East Indian sugar offered for sale in Britain.[34]

When slave trade abolition finally loomed in 1806, Joseph Barham, one of its few West Indian Parliamentary sympathizers, suggested that the time was ripe to venture beyond abolition of the trade and to challenge slavery itself economically. Barham suggested using Britain's recently acquired and undeveloped colony of Trinidad as an ideal laboratory for demonstrating the superiority of free labour. Barham wanted the British government to sponsor the migration of free Chinese labourers, famed for their good labour discipline. Wilberforce was initially inclined to support a project so favourably framed in favour of free labour. But the main author and strategist of the recent Foreign Abolition Bill of 1806 warned Wilberforce against supporting Barham's project. As the best-informed abolitionist on the West Indies, James Stephen foresaw nothing but disaster in such an experiment.

Stephen had already registered his anonymous opinion that slave labour had a decisive advantage over both free and other forms of involuntary labour in the sugar islands. He argued primarily from his knowledge of the results of emancipation in the French colonies of St. Domingue and in Guadeloupe during the previous decade. Stephen convinced Wilberforce that the experiment's failure would discredit all who sponsored it, including abolitionists. In print he again anonymously denounced the Trinidad free-labour project as preposterous. The case of Trinidad throws crucial light on early abolitionist assumptions. In 1802, when Trinidad's development as a slave colony with an unimpeded African slave trade still seemed likely, Stephen urged the exclusive importation of 'free negroes'. Even then, Stephen assumed that slave labour was the most profitable form of labour. Free (and even indentured) labour had to be permanently protected against slave labour. From the beginning of the century Stephen would not assent to a competitive situation.[35]

A few years later, as a Member of Parliament, Stephen himself successfully opposed a petition for a similar free-labour experiment, invoking the failure of the earlier Trinidad experiment as additional proof, that 'while slavery existed in the West Indies it was impossible that free labour could succeed in competition with it'.[36] When Stephen pronounced this conclusion, not a single abolitionist rose in Parliament to oppose or even soften this categorical dismissal of free labour superiority. Nor did any parliamentary abolitionist of the next generation ever suggest another pilot experiment.

Following peace with France in 1814 and the revival of the French Atlantic slave trade, Stephen added a detailed codicil to his evaluation of relative labour competitiveness. British slavery, now dependent exclusively upon natural reproduction, would henceforth, Stephen predicted, be undercut by the foreign 'buying' systems. Painful as he found it to confess this to a Prime Minister who had always opposed slave trade abolition, Stephen even parted company with some of his abolitionist colleagues' position that 'breeding' was cheaper than 'buying'. The British slave interest was unable to benefit politically from this private confession by their most knowledgeable and effective opponent.[37]

The abolitionist leadership launched a second major offensive against the British overseas slave system in 1823. They attacked British Caribbean slavery itself and requested Parliament to sponsor gradual legal emancipation. In attacking slavery abolitionists felt impelled to resurrect their long-muted free-labour ideology. Adam Smith was resuscitated and a search was undertaken to cull further support from economists. In view of the burgeoning authority of political economy the results were meagre. Few British political economists had bothered to reiterate, much less to elaborate, Smith's brief passages on slave and free labour. In the half century between the *Wealth of Nations* and the first campaign for gradual abolition there were probably fewer passages published comparing slavery and free labour by any major British political economist than had already appeared in the body of Smith's own work.

In the absence of academic mobilization, abolitionists reworked Adam Smith on their own, emphasizing his 'wear and tear' argument. They reinforced Smith by comparing British Caribbean population statistics with Malthusian population principles and the general propensity of human populations to procreate to the limit of available natural resources. The British Caribbean after 1807 offered the anomaly of a generally declining slave population.[38] The abolitionists had no compunction about comparing the West Indian slave population decrease to the high natural growth rate of slaves in the southern United States. West Indian defenders of their system countered by emphasizing the delayed effects of the slave trade abolition in accounting for declining slave populations. Their arguments were often statistically more sophisticated than those of the abolitionists, but they always carried the rhetorical burden of having to explain away the clear and simple fact of a declining number of slaves in the sugar islands within an Anglo-American world of otherwise rapidly expanding populations.

In appealing to their countrymen for political steps toward emancipation, abolitionists now insistently invoked the positive motives to labour as portrayed by the optimistic economics of the eighteenth century. Industry in a labour force implied a willing effort on the part of the worker. A free worker, like all others, sought to 'better his condition'. He became bonded to an ever receding threshold of amenities. Freed slaves would be doing more than exchanging hunger for the lash. They would be making the same 'voluntary sacrifices of time and ease... which influence other classes of mankind'. From Java to Mexico, abolitionists cited instance after instance of free men who were productively employed in the cultivation of tropical goods. These cases all presumably validated the hypothesis that the urge toward self-improvement offered more than sufficient security for the maintenance and even enhancement of West Indian sugar production after emancipation.[39]

No element of anti-slavery propaganda infuriated the West Indian interest as much as these sweeping assurances of improved labour performance after the ending of slavery. As far as the planters were concerned, abolitionists were propounding a general argument in defiance of transatlantic realities. The axiom of universal free labour superiority was extrapolated, not from a global plentitude of wage labour, but from a purely local experience. England was the European country where the desires for greater varieties of products yielded 'the greatest improvement of which human nature is susceptible'. The defenders of Caribbean slavery insisted that political economists were well aware of how few labourers possessed the incentives so requisite to this 'positive' motivation for labour. Moreover, insisted the West Indians, even in England's own industrial heartland, free men still alternated between working against hunger when destitute and for limited comforts and maximum leisure when well paid.[40]

From this perspective, the accumulation of leisure was a better way of 'bettering one's condition' than was maximizing one's income or consumption. Verification of labour's limited aspirations was demonstrated by the 'short week' favoured by many free British industrial workers. It was also apparent in the aversion to plantation labour demonstrated by all free blacks in the Caribbean. A world of waged labour based upon ever-increasing 'wants' remained more of a utopian future than a global reality. Anti-abolitionists empirically challenged

> the whole world to produce a single satisfactory precedent, where a similar ratio exists between population, capital and space, of slaves, in any numbers, who have been made free, executing the necessary

duties of tropical sugar labour for wages [or any equivalent income] consistent with the maintenance of the ... necessary and average profits of plantations...

They denied even *'the probability of such a result'*.[41] Planters' demands for both delay and compensation stemmed from this argument.

In the decade before British emancipation, the condition of Haiti was of great interest to those who debated the merits of slavery and the merits of gradual abolition. For abolitionists, Haiti's 'reproductive' performance was its principal asset. Although the numbers were hotly disputed, Haiti's official figures indicated a virtual doubling of the population from the outbreak of the slave revolution in 1791 to the 1820s. This increase stood in sharp contrast to the declining slave population of Britain's sugar colonies. Haiti appeared to conform to Malthus's principle of high natural increase in regions of low population density.

On the other hand, Haiti's economic performance was a boon to West Indian propagandists who wished to demonstrate the inefficiency of free labour in the Caribbean. There was no disputing the fact that slave Saint Domingue's position as the world's premier producer of tropical exports had long since vanished. By the 1820s Haiti had virtually disappeared as a producer for the north Atlantic sugar market. The case of Haiti was still more complicated by debates over the characterization of its population on the spectrum between free and coerced labour. If slavery had disappeared, Haiti's rural code allowed for deep infringements on personal liberties in the name of labour continuity. Was it the level of coercion that caused Haiti's low productivity and competitive failure, or had coercion preserved whatever was left of Haiti's productive and competitive capacity? When the British Colonial Secretary introduced the motion for immediate emancipation in 1833, he simply claimed that the San Domingo case was inconclusive and irrelevant. Many abolitionists and anti-abolitionists agreed with him.[42]

Neither the arguments of Smith and Malthus nor the relative performances of Haiti and the sugar colonies convinced the British government to accelerate emancipation. Two major abolitionist mass mobilizations and the post-Reform Act election of 1832, reinforced by the greatest slave uprising in the history of British colonization, forced emancipation on to the political agenda of the first Reform Parliament in 1833. No contemporary suggested that the efficiency of free labour was a significant motive in attracting any of the 1.3 million men and women who gathered at British public meetings to sign petitions for immediate emancipation.

Those responsible for the colonies had to be more concerned about the anticipated motivations and performance of slaves on the verge of freedom.

At the Colonial Office, James Stephen's son James feared the effects of the choices that would become available to the majority of labourers in the British Caribbean. Drawing upon the experience of Britain's other developing colonies, he and others concluded that as long as labour had the option of access to cheap land the cost of labour would remain high, probably too high for the full maintenance of the plantation system. Henry Taylor, the head of the Colonial Office's West India division, was dismissively sceptical about the doctrine that slave labour was dear in the Caribbean. Taylor, Stephen and Viscount Howick, a convinced supporter of both emancipation and of *laissez-faire* in political economy, mulled over various combinations of legal constraints on prospective freedmen. Without exception all were designed to maximize the continuity of plantation labour.

Empirically, Colonial Office social planners and the slave interest were not far apart. In parliamentary hearings before emancipation, the West Indian planters overwhelmingly testified that freed slaves never returned to the cane fields. Slave-holders inferred that freed slaves probably would not work at the prices offered to the owners of rented slave gangs during slavery. There was clearly a market for *non*-gang labour, which could be roughly reckoned at the prices of those slaves who were allowed to hire themselves out in other occupations. As for the field slaves themselves, there is no evidence that they had any interest whatever in their potential cost-effectiveness as free labourers for planters. No parliamentary committee requested their testimony. Some leaders of the Jamaica slave uprising of 1831 seemed to have envisioned freedom in terms of working for wages. Others imagined remaining as growers of sugar. Neither of these imagined futures (nor the destruction of crops and infrastructure occurring in so many uprisings) bespeaks a profit-and-production prospective among the planation slaves.

Some historians assume the general dominance of a universalized 'free-labour ideology' in Britain in 1833. However, the distinction between constraints upon labour in high- and low- density conditions was clearly assumed by all advocates of emancipation in the Colonial Office and in the Cabinet. They muted their public emphasis on the significance of the distinction for two reasons. Slave-holders were offering analogous arguments and would use them to argue for a delay in emancipation. Even after the House of Commons supported the government's general motion for immediate emancipation, such arguments could be used to maximize the coercive components in the detailed system of freed-labour regulation. Abolitionists feared that West Indian planters would use any institutional opening to recreate an approximation of the old constraints. In Parliament most abolitionists spoke in favour of reducing non-market constraints on ex-slaves to the absolute minimum that the majority would accept.

Outside Parliament abolitionist propaganda stuck to the idea of an exclusive choice between *Wages or the Whip*, backed by the Smithian generic pronouncement on slave-labour inferiority. There was no middle ground left between slave and free labour.[43] Emancipation, in the abolitionist formulation, would now vindicate the superiority of free labour. But what, as the slave interest protested, if it did not? We have only fleeting glimpses of how the abolitionist rank and file – those who attended abolitionist rallies and signed petitions – reacted to the pessimistic prognosis. Responding to West Indian predictions of falling production, Britain's most popular anti-slavery lecturer resolved the issue of post-emancipation production in a cascade of contempt. So what if Haitian exports were already down by two-thirds, and so what if the West Indian consumption of British exports were also to decrease? Would Ireland be worse off if she too exported less, keeping her produce 'for home consumption'? The only reported response was '*Loud Cheers*'. Even Haiti and Ireland, contemporary bywords for economic failure, could not deter cheering anti-slavery gatherings.[44]

From British Emancipation to American Emancipation

Between them, the great mass campaigns of 1831–33 and the Jamaica slave uprising of 1831 convinced Parliament and the government that there was no longer any middle ground between slavery and immediate legal emancipation. Members of the government and of Parliament, however, were not so sanguine about the potential outcome as were abolitionist crowds. The administration was deeply worried about the continuity of labour under a regime of wages. The Colonial Secretary, introducing the Emancipation Bill of 1833, called it a 'mighty experiment'. The notion stuck, and for a generation thereafter emancipation was referred to as 'the great experiment'. Radicals such as Daniel O'Connell were prepared to express total confidence in the success of an immediate transition to wage labour, without either transitional limitations or monetary compensation. The abolitionist leadership, which had emphasized the need for special transitional measures in the Caribbean for 40 years, also reversed itself. Responding to demands and priorities from out-of-doors, they moved successive amendments to minimize the delay in arriving at complete freedom of contract.

However, for the majority of the political nation, the government, the colonial bureaucracy, the overwhelming majority in Parliament and the West Indian commercial interests continuity of sugar production was of vital importance. The final Act reflected their deep uncertainty that free labour plantations would sustain, much less increase, their previous level of production and thereby undercut slave labour competitors.[45] The Emancipation Act provided for a huge compensation package of £20 million. Masters were allotted up to six years of mostly unfree labour ('apprenticeship') from their ex-slaves. Above all, protective duties were continued in favour of British colonial sugar. In one sense, the maintenance of protection was a remarkable commentary upon anti-slavery propaganda. For a decade abolitionists had taunted the West Indian interest for clinging to protective duties in favour of their own slave-grown sugar. This presumably showed that 'monopoly' shielded 'a forced cultivation' from competition with free (that is, East Indian) sugar. If West Indian slave labour in the colonies was more productive than free labour, how did it happen 'that in the case of the West Indies all the recognized principles of political economy should be thus strangely reversed?' What could better demonstrate that free labour competition would eliminate slavery? Yet at their moment of triumph, the abolitionists fell strangely silent about the possibility of realigning the West Indies with 'all the recognized principles of political economy' and about convincing slave Cuba and slave Brazil of the inefficiency of slave-based 'forced cultivation'. Freely opposing the government on both the length of apprenticeship and on the terms of compensation, abolitionists silently consented to the continuity of protection.[46]

British legislators thus anticipated, although they underestimated, the 'wear and tear' on the labour supply and discipline that would result from the transition. A 'cushion' of West Indian surplus sugar for British domestic consumption had characterized British colonial production since the beginning of the nineteenth century. During the apprenticeship period (1834–38) the quantity of sugar exported from the British West Indies to the United Kingdom fell by 10 per cent, while the London sugar price rose 40 per cent.[47] Another wave of popular pressure forced the early termination of apprenticeship in 1838. West Indian production fell again. It now met less than two-thirds of British consumption.

The government erratically responded to pressures and counter-pressures from West Indian proprietors, freedmen, consumers, abolitionists and an increasingly powerful free trade movement. For the first time since 1807 British governments cautiously began to open the ex-slave colonies to transoceanic migrant workers: to voluntary and unencumbered labour from the Americas and Europe; and to indentured contract labour from Africa and Asia. The flow of free labour from the Americas and Europe proved to be both insufficient in numbers and ineffective in performance. The flow of indentured labour from Africa and Asia was also initially hampered by the still-powerful abolitionist lobby, which denounced indentured labour as a new system of slavery.[48] The government also attempted to encourage the expansion of free labour sugar plantations in Africa and Asia. Its major African venture – the Niger expedition of 1840–41 – was a complete disaster. Further East the effort was more successful, but mostly in areas where one or another form of coerced labour system was introduced – indentured Indian labour in British Mauritius and the 'Cultivation System' in Dutch Java.[49]

In terms of commercial pressures, the shortfall in Caribbean production combined with high metropolitan consumer prices to put both British colonial sugar producers and abolitionists on a collision course with the rising British free-trade movement. A potential conflict had existed from the beginning of the abolitionist movement, when Dean Tucker had cautioned Ramsay that the Atlantic slave system would never really be undermined until sugar could be produced more cheaply by free men than by slaves. Tucker was totally wrong. Between 1788 and 1838 anti-slavery scored one victory after another over the British Atlantic slave system. Yet during the entire half century between Tucker's warning and British emancipation sugar produced by free labour made little headway against slave-produced sugar. Anti-slavery's victories were achieved without the aid of any grand coalition of new economic interests. Before emancipation all metropolitan abolitionist attempts, such as those of the merchant James Cropper, to form a coalition of East Indians, British Industrialists, free traders, consumers and abolitionists against the plantation slave system monopoly fell far short of abolitionist hopes or expectations.[50]

The economic reason was clear. Almost as soon as political abolitionism got under way British colonial sugar had virtually ceased to be effectively raised above world-market levels by the old British mercantilist legislation. From the 1790s until emancipation 'it was the world price which largely determined the remuneration which West Indian producers received... Had foreign sugar been admitted at the same rate of duty it would not have affected the consumers by more than a few percentage points'.[51]

If emancipation brought a sharp reduction in the exports of sugar and coffee to the metropolis from the British Caribbean, the first results seemed far more satisfactory from the perspective of the ex-slaves. Exports of sugar from the West Indies to Britain fell by nearly 30 per cent in the decade after the end of apprenticeship, but retained imports of clothing from Britain to the West Indies rose by more than 50 per cent between the years immediately before emancipation (1832–34) and the years following the abolition of apprenticeship (1839–44). Even more impressive was the sharp rise in West Indian wheat consumption. Wheat flour had never been more than an occasional luxury for most slaves, handed out to gangs assigned to hard labour or as part of special Christmas rations. Given that basic tropical foods grew in abundance, imported flour and flour products were obvious post-emancipation indulgences. Imports of wheat flour to the British West Indies more than doubled from just before emancipation to just after apprenticeship.[52]

As emancipation loomed, West Indian planters had attempted to make the most of the earlier abolitionist concession that slaves did not yet have enough of civilized labourers' 'artificial wants'. In this sense the slave-owners' fears proved to be completely unfounded. Ex-slaves used their new wages and independent earnings to purchase riding horses, gigs and conspicuously fine clothes. By the time of emancipation 'an adult British West Indian slave's material state, measured by quantity of food eaten and yards of cloth worn at least matched that of many British workers', and the standard of living of many ex-slaves must briefly have risen above that level. One of the major missionary champions of emancipation in the colonies happily testified to Members of Parliament that freedmen in the islands 'were decidedly better off than English workmen ...' A magistrate in British Guiana asserted that 'the peasantry, as a body ... can boldly challenge comparison with the happiest and best paid labourers of the most fertile districts in England'.

The consumerist aspects of freedom now featured prominently in abolitionist writings. References to the 30 to 40 per cent decrease in British West Indies sugar could be countered by noting the sharp rise in the ex-slaves' standard of living and the stimulus this gave to British manufacturers. Wages were high, new villages were founded and educational opportunities expanded. At the end of apprenticeship even West Indian vagrancy and contract laws had to be made more lenient than they were in England. This legislation was rolled back in the 1840s, but only to the extent that it was made identical with British metropolitan labour statutes.[53]

The abolitionists' involvement tended to go well beyond material consumption. Immediately after the end of apprenticeship, Joseph Sturge founded the West Indian Land Investment Company. Its target was £100,000, to be used for the development of free and independent villages, although it was blocked by the property-acquisition rules laid down by the government. Sturge also helped to found the Jamaican Education Society and female anti-slavery organizations, funding missionary-run schools on the island. A legal-aid fund was established to defray expenses of judicial oppression. It is quite possible that in the immediate aftermath of apprenticeship many ex-slaves momentarily enjoyed an array of support services unavailable to workers anywhere else in the Empire.

The cost of these results, however, elicited a rising crescendo of hostile propaganda from consumer and free-trade advocates in Britain. Emancipation dragged the question of free trade into the centre of the debate over colonial sugar. The termination of colonial apprenticeship coincided with the re-emergence of free trade as an urgent public issue. Two protected interests were quickly fused as a political target: West Indian sugar and English corn.

The limits of the free labour ideology in abolitionist circles were again demonstrated at the Second World Anti-Slavery Convention in 1843. A free-trade group had attempted to amend the slave-grown sugar exclusion plank of the first Convention in 1840. Now, in 1843, they pushed for revision on the grounds of free labour superiority, which the previous Convention had also unanimously affirmed. But the chairman refused to accept free labour superiority as the basis for a change of policy. He was convinced by the acrimony to move the previous question. Abolitionist opponents of free trade found themselves in the uncomfortable position previously occupied by slave-holders on the population question. Those who sought to protect the produce of West Indian ex-slaves had to deploy a series of complex distinctions: between slave labour production in Cuba and 'free' labour production in Java; between African-fed slave labour plantations in Brazil and native-born slave plantations in the United States South. It was the free trade advocates who could argue from the clear and simple fact of metropolitan consumer interests.

The campaign for ending protection for free labour sugar came to a climax in 1846. Abolition of the British Corn Laws was swiftly followed by the progressive reduction of protective duties favouring British colonial sugar. The debate leading up to this change had disoriented the abolitionist rank and file, sharply reducing their leadership's former ability to mobilize the larger public. Some abolitionists believed that the demise of plantation sugar would result in the expansion of smallholding and the 'peasant option', or at least a combination of wages and subsistence farming satisfactory to the ex-slaves. Others feared that stagnant sugar production would be followed by a declining standard of living among free labour within the colonies and a negative assessment of the great experiment by other slave-holding societies. The latter tended to realign themselves with British West Indian planters in favour of continued protection. Free trade sympathizers countered that heavily protected sugar was already useless as evidence of free labour's superiority. The split fragmented the unified abolitionist movement in the mid 1840s.[54]

Within Parliament even Members who most strongly regarded the well-being of the ex-slaves as the great experiment's principal concern could not ignore the government's general criteria of political and economic success. A dwindling number of die-hard abolitionists were reduced to fighting rearguard actions in favour of differential duties on sugar grown by 'free labour'. As the victory of world free trade over protected imperial free labour became imminent, its most ideologically interesting effect in

Parliament was the unanticipated revival of James Stephen's overt argument against free labour superiority. In 1833 no one could have imagined that William Wilberforce's own son would announce in Parliament, just 13 years after emancipation, that West Indian free labour could not compete with slaves. Samuel Wilberforce was as unequivocal in his pronouncement as the elder Stephen had been 35 years earlier: slave labour in the Caribbean was 'absolutely cheaper' than free labour in raising sugar.[55]

British sugar production stabilized and slowly revived after the crisis of trade liberalization. However, the revival came at the price of a shift in the terms of labour – the expansion of the market in East Asian indentured servants. What abolitionists in Parliament and in the Colonial Office had once denounced as a 'new system of slavery' was institutionalized as voluntary indentured migration to the British colonies. During the 1850s the magnitude of this new source of labour surpassed the transatlantic flow of African slaves, now reduced by aggressive British diplomatic and naval action. In contrast to the first four decades of the century, the British colonies recaptured the major share of labour flowing to the plantation Americas. While densely populated Barbados could expand production without recourse to the new bondsmen, the recovery of sugar in sparsely populated Trinidad and Guyana depended heavily upon them. Jamaica, with lower fertility and less recourse to migrant labour than Trinidad and a far lower population density than Barbados, stagnated.[56]

Planters beyond the line were uniformly unimpressed with the great experiment. Even in relatively undynamic slave colonies, whose imperial governments were vaguely committed to eventual emancipation, slave-holders preferred the coercive discipline of their slave plantations to the results they observed in the British free-labour colonies. In contrast, in Brazil or Cuba, where planters could still acquire fresh slaves for fresh land, they preferred to buy. Even where part of the slave force had become superfluous, as in the Dutch Antilles, when planters were asked to participate in planning for emancipation, they balked. In Britain the debate over the merits of free and slave labour now shifted from sugar to cotton. As the United States' sectional crisis deepened, the British metropolitan cotton interest vainly requested government encouragement for further experiments in free labour for producing a product, almost 90 per cent of which remained dependent upon slave labour. Former free-trade industrialists of Manchester found themselves in the embarrassing position of pleading for political help in developing alternatives to American agriculture. During the American Civil War they were concerned about enhancing the level of production in the cotton-growing systems of India, Egypt, Algeria and Brazil, asking no questions about their levels of labour coercion or standards of living.

At home, abolitionist propaganda abstractly valorized free labour. Yet the superiority of free labour, endlessly restated, never became the centrepiece of the abolitionist argument – or even one of its high rhetorical priorities. The coincidence between coerced labour and New World sugar production, right down to British emancipation, was simply too close to overcome the doubts of planters and governments.

Abolitionist leaders were themselves divided over the ability of free labour to sustain sugar cultivation competitively in the West Indies. Therefore British abolitionists tended to argue piecemeal and not always consistently from one measure to the next. Until slave trade abolition in 1807 they argued that 'breeding' would prove to be more profitable than 'buying'. Between abolition and emancipation in 1833 they argued that wages were more effective than whips. The main point was always to limit the slave-holders' options: prohibiting transatlantic imports and constricting intercolonial imports (1788–1834); constraining planters' abuse of labourers (1823–8); limiting apprenticeship and legal coercion (1834–38); and increasing the constraints on importing indentured labour (after 1838).

During the 1830s and the early 1840s abolitionists, at the height of their political influence, continued to narrow planter options, to denounce vagrancy laws and other modes of employer discipline and to counteract planter political domination. Some fought to maintain the briefly rising standard of living of the freedmen and to protect their bargaining position as workers against both metropolitan free traders and employers of indentured labour.[57] Over the long term, however, they could not persist in securing more protection for Caribbean free labourers than was available to metropolitans.

A century of debate over the relative merits of free vs. slave labour had been started by a mass movement to eradicate the differences between the conditions of labour in Britain and in her slave colonies. The superiority of free labour, proclaimed by Adam Smith and exemplified in the history of western Europe, was projected 'beyond the line' in order to extend the benefits of freedom throughout the British Empire and the entire world. After three generations of intense debate the discussion began to break out of the dualistic frame of reference in which both the abolitionists and their opponents had conducted it.

Conclusion

What, then, of the 'great experiment' in the British West Indies? The results were mixed, and especially disappointing to those who had held out the brightest hopes for simultaneous increases in commercial productivity and in the ex-slaves' standard of living. One great target audience of the experiment, the planters and governments of other slave societies, seemed particularly unimpressed. Although British Caribbean labourers in 1860 still seemed remarkably orderly in comparison with their European counterparts, few ex-slave colonies had demonstrated an ability to expand or even sustain production without the further aid of compulsory labour. Exemplary successes, like Barbados, were not frontier societies like the United States, Cuba and Brazil. Compared with the 'triumphant progress' of free labour communities in North America or in the southern Pacific; or to the 'scarcely less brilliant, though sinister and insecure prosperity of Cuba and Louisiana', the British Caribbean colonies in 1860 seemed 'stationary at best, subsisting but not accumulating'.[58] They matched neither their American free-labour brethren in their standard of living nor their Cuban slave labour brethren in productivity. They were already assuming the status of the less-developed societies that would be theirs over the following century.[59]

For British consumers the results were of diminishing significance. A decreasing proportion of their sugar came from the British West Indies. By 1860 the literature comparing free labour in Britain and in the British Caribbean was also diminishing. In general, the British Caribbean was a place 'where no marked improvement strikes the eye, even where there are no signs of absolute decay'.[60] 'Race' subtly gained credence as an explanatory device. From his chair in political economy at Oxford, Herman Merivale vigorously defended black workers against 'the common' representation of them as destitute of the ordinary capacity of workers. In densely populated Barbados they were 'as regular in their daily labour as the operatives of the old communities of Europe'. Even there, however, their numbers made the planters less anxious to innovate. No ex-slave colony received an evaluation as clearly progressive.[61]

The imaginary line between free and slave labour that ran between north-western Europe and most of the rest of the world when the *Wealth of Nations* was published had shifted a century later. Political action had ended or provided for the gradual ending of slavery throughout the zones of expanding European settlement. However, bound labour continued to be the dominant form of labour in the production of commercial crops in the tropics. With the repositioning of the line between free and unfree labour, race loomed larger than ever as a dividing line in determining the migratory flow of labour.

The great debate over the relative merits of free and slave labour ended with the return of the excluded middle. In this sense the battle between advocates of slave and free labour in the Atlantic system was a dramatic interlude between periods of more nuanced assessments of the performance of labour under various regimes of constraint and choice. At the height of abolitionist influence political economists were probably more wary of offering deflationary assessments of free labour superiority than either before or after. However, there never seems to have been a moment when faith in the free-labour ideology was consensual in Britain – not even among the abolitionist leadership.[62] It was still less so among other European, African and American elites.

As for the rank and file of popular abolitionism, it is difficult to tell whether they were more convinced of free labour's superiority than their leaders. They may have been impressed by the substantial quantity of British West Indian sugar re-exported from the metropolis before emancipation. In any event, it is difficult to imagine that they cheered politicians pledging to support emancipation or approached a petition signing table while carefully weighing the risks of Caribbean free-labour efficiency against the sense of helping a segment of humanity pass from servile degradation to independent dignity. Ascribing anticipated economic gains as a prime motive for the passage of emancipation was too absurd and contrived an accusation to require elaborate refutation. Yet perhaps, in the decade before emancipation, a casual popular assumption of free labour superiority made it easier to dismiss the well-grounded West Indian arguments as too self-interested to warrant serious consideration.[63] The same assumption would also explain why the protests against the supporting of protective sugar duties poured in from the provinces during the 'hungry forties'. From the industrial heartland of abolitionism came the cry that high duties put sugar 'nearly beyond the reach of our actually *famishing* population at *home* where our charity should begin ... [it was] *destructive* of the lives of our *labouring* fellow countrymen'. The problem of ensuring the continuity of labour, so effectively dismissed or marginalized in the era of slave-grown sugar, became the nemesis of anti-slavery.[64]

I have always wondered why the most famous positive assessment of anti-slavery was worded with peculiar reticence. In 1869 the historian W.E.H. Lecky hailed his countrymen's 'unostentatious and inglorious' crusade against slavery as 'among the three or four perfectly virtuous acts recorded in the history of nations'. Why 'inglorious?' Surely being placed among the top four perfect collective acts in history is more than slightly above average glory. Only in the light of some deep sense of disappointment does Lecky's adjective make sense. The great experiment, proceeding from great expectations, had entailed too many great disappointments.

In cultural terms, the true measure of the abolitionists' achievement lay less in a national conversion to a belief in free labour's universal superiority than in the psychological 'wear and tear' of their moral and political agitation against the doubters. The overwhelming asymmetry of mass opinion that slavery had to come to an end may have caused a brief suspension of disbelief in the high risk of commercial disaster. Colonial slavery did not, however, come under massive and sustained attack in Britain because it was incompatible with capitalism. Still less was it brought to an end because it was a defective form of capitalist labour. Anti-slavery mobilized against those general characteristics of chattel slavery that most distinguished it from contemporary legal and social relations in western Europe.

Viewed from Britain, New World slavery rested upon an extraordinary, and extraordinarily brutal, exercise of power. It was institutionally, if not always empirically, indifferent to the dignity, the bodies and the relationships of the enslaved. Masters could claim nearly absolute property rights in the persons they bought or inherited. Such claims extended well beyond the demand for 'ordinary labour service' as even the most dependent labourer in Britain understood that service. Masters routinely escaped public punishment for acts that would have cost them their liberty or their lives in the metropolis. In this sense the supreme achievement of the abolitionists was to have shifted the context of the debate over the terms of colonial labour by eliminating chattel property from the range of options available to employers. In a process drawn out over three generations the attack upon slavery also set in motion a series of changes that altered the terms of labour in other parts of the globe as well.[65]

NOTES

An earlier version of this essay appeared in Stanley L. Engerman (ed.), *The Terms of Labour: Slavery, Serfdom, and Free Labour* (Stanford, CA: 1999), pp.50–86.

1. I use 1750 as the rough demarcator for the beginnings of industrialization and European imperialism because the acceleration of both British industrialization and British global power, as proxies for European expansion, especially into Africa, Asia and Oceania, is usually dated during the second half of the eighteenth century. Two centuries later the most rapid deceleration of European political power and the rapid reduction of Europe's industrial lead over all other areas of the globe also occurred in the half century after World War II. On the debate over slavery and European economic growth see Immanuel Wallerstein, *The Modern World System*, Vol. I (New York, NY: Academic Press, 1974). For a recent focus upon British slavery as a cause of industrialization see Robin Blackburn, *The Making of New World Slavery: From the Baroque to the Modern* (London: Verso, 1997), Ch.12. Compare P.K. O'Brien, 'European economic development: the contribution of the periphery', *Economic History Review*, 2nd ser., 35, 1(1982), pp.1–18. On the contribution of slavery and the peripheries in general to economic growth and industrialization see also Stanley L. Engerman, 'The Atlantic economy of the eighteenth-century: some speculations on economic development in Britain, America, Africa and elsewhere', *Journal of European Economic History*, 24, 1 (Spring 1995), pp.145–75.

2. See, *inter alia*, Seymour Drescher, *Capitalism and Antislavery: British Mobilization in Comparative Perspective* (London/New York, NY: Macmillan Press/Oxford University Press, 1986), Ch.1; idem, *From Slavery to Freedom: Comparative Studies in the Rise and Fall of Atlantic Slavery* (Houndmills, Basingstoke/New York: Macmillan Press/New York University Press, 1999), Ch.1; David Eltis, 'Europeans and the rise and fall of African slavery in the Americas: an interpretation', *American Historical Review*, 98 (1993),

pp.1399–423; S. Drescher, 'The long goodbye: Dutch capitalism and anti-slavery in comparative perspective', *American Historical Review*, 99 (1994), pp.44–69; David Brion Davis, *Slavery and Human Progress* (New York, NY: Oxford University Press, 1984), Pt I; Robin Blackburn, *The Making of New World Slavery: From the Baroque to the Modern, 1492–1800* (London: Verso, 1997).

3. Arthur Young, *Political Essays Concerning the Present State of the British Empire* (London: W. Strahan and T. Cadell, 1772), pp.20–1; Adam Smith, *Lectures on Jurisprudence*, ed. R.L. Meek *et al.* (Oxford: Clarendon Press, 1978), pp.186–7. In the famous Somerset case, argued before Lord Mansfield, counsel for the Master opened his argument with the observation that slavery was widely sanctioned in three-quarters of the world and even in much of Europe.

4. Davis, *Slavery and Human Progress*, Pt II.

5. For the most explicit statement of this hypothesis in the British case see Lowell J. Ragatz, *The Fall of the Planter Class in the British West Indies* (New York, NY: 1928; reprinted New York: Octagon Books, 1963); Eric Williams, *Capitalism and Slavery* (Chapel Hill, NC: University of North Carolina Press, 1944; report 1994). Compare Williams's view with Seymour Drescher's in *Econocide: British Slavery in the Era of Abolition* (Pittsburgh, PA: University of Pittsburgh Press, 1977). See also '*Capitalism and Slavery* after Fifty Years', *Slavery and Abolition*, 17, 3 (1997).

6. See, *inter alia*, Robert W. Fogel *et al.*, *Without Consent or Contract: The Rise and Fall of American Slavery*, 4 vols (New York, NY: W.W. Norton, 1989–92); David Eltis, *Economic Growth and the Ending of the Transatlantic Slave Trade* (New York, NY: Oxford University Press, 1987); P.C. Emmer, 'European expansion and unfree labour: an introduction', *Itinerario*, 21, 1 (1997), pp.9–14; in *Fifty Years Later: Anti-slavery, Capitalism and Modernity in the Dutch Orbit*, ed. Gert Oostindie (Leiden/Pittsburgh, PA: University of Pittsburgh Press, 1995/1996).

7. See, *inter alia*, David Brion Davis, *The Problem of Slavery in the Age of Revolution 1770–1823* (Ithaca, NY: Cornell University Press, 1975), Ch.7–8; Howard Temperley, 'Anti-slavery as a form of cultural imperialism', in Christine Bolt and Seymour Drescher (eds.), *Anti-Slavery, Religion, and Reform: Essays in Memory of Roger Anstey* (Folkestone, Kent/Hamden, CT: Dawson/Anchor, 1980), pp.335–50; David Eltis, 'Abolitionist perceptions of society after slavery', in *Slavery and British Society 1776–1846*, ed. James Walvin (London: Macmillan Press, 1982), pp.195–213; Thomas C. Holt, *The Problem of Freedom: Race, Labour, and Politics in Jamaica and Britain, 1832–1938* (Baltimore, MD: The Johns Hopkins University Press, 1992), pp.13–33, *The Antislavery Debate: Capitalism and Abolitionism as a Problem in Historical Interpretation*, Thomas Bender (ed.), (Berkeley, CA: University of California Press, 1992); S. Drescher, 'Review Essay: *The Anti-slavery Debate*', *History and Theory*, 32 (1993), pp.311–29; David Brion Davis, 'Capitalism, abolitionism, and hegemony', in *British Capitalism and Caribbean Slavery*, ed. Barbara L. Solow and Stanley L. Engerman (New York, NY: Cambridge University Press, 1987), pp.209–27. The quotation by the Earl of Westmoreland is noted in Seymour Drescher, *Capitalism and Antislavery*, p.268n.

8. Howard Temperley, *British Antislavery 1833–1870* (London: Longman, 1972); David Eltis, 'Abolitionist perceptions'; Davis, *Slavery and Human Progress*, pp.220–3.

9. Adam Smith, *Lectures on Jurisprudence*, ed. R. Meek, D. Raphael and P. Stein (Indianapolis, IN: 1982), p.185; Smith, *Wealth of Nations*, ed. R.H. Campbell, A. S. Skinner and W. B. Todd (Indianapolis, IN: Liberty Classics, 1981), pp.22–3.

10. Smith, *Wealth of Nations*, pp.387–8, 98. Abolitionists later frequently alluded to the high overhead costs of managing slaves. In an evaluation of plantation costs in 1833, however, one of the Colonial Office policy architects dismissed the 'managerial-costs' argument with a single sentence: 'What capitalist in any country carries on a manufacture with fewer hired superintendents for every hundred of labourers than the sugar planter?' [Henry Taylor] 'Colonial Office, Jan. 1833. Memo. for the Cabinet', C0884/1, 58. [Hereafter, Taylor 'Memorandum'].

11. Smith, *Lectures*, pp.186–7.

12. Smith, *Wealth of Nations*, p.70.

13. *Adam Smith's An Inquiry into the Nature and Causes of the Wealth of Nations: A*

Concordance, Fred R. Glahe (ed.), (Lanham, MD: Rowman & Littlefield, 1993). Early abolitionists mentioned the presence of indentured labourers to refute the idea of the impossibility of using European field labour in the Caribbean. They were less anxious to discuss its subsequent yielding to slave labour.

14. Smith, *Wealth of Nations*, p.98.
15. Ibid., p.99. Defenders of the slave trade confidently appealed to the authority of Hume and Smith in defence of their system.
16. James Ramsay, *Objections to the Abolition of the Slave Trade, with Answers* (London: James Phillips, 1788), p.8; Thomas Clarkson, *An Essay on the Impolicy of the African Slave Trade* (Philadelphia: Francis Bailey, 1788); Clarkson, *The History of the Rise, Progress and Accomplishment of the Abolition of the African Slave Trade by the British Parliament*, 2 vols (London: Longman, Hurst, Rees and Orme, 1808), Vol.I, p.86.
17. See *Morning Chronicle* 15 Sept., 3 Oct. 1785; *London Chronicle* 29 Sept., 4 Oct. 1785; Ramsay, *Objections*, pp.8–9.
18. Ibid., p.104
19. William Wilberforce, *A Letter on the Abolition of the Slave Trade* (London: T. Cadell and W. Davies, 1807), pp.144, 210.
20. Ibid.,p.104 (original emphasis).
21. See, *inter alia*, Stanley L. Engerman and David Eltis, 'Economic Aspects of the Abolition Debate', in Bolt and Drescher (eds.), *Anti-Slavery*, pp.284–5; Jonathan A. Glickstein, *Concepts of Free Labour in Antebellum America* (New Haven, CT: Yale University Press, 1991); David Brion Davis, *The Problem of Slavery in the Age of Revolution, 1770–1823* (Ithaca, NY: Cornell University Press, 1975), pp.346–54; Howard Temperley, 'Capitalism, slavery and ideology', *Past and Present*, 75 (1977), pp. 94–118; id., 'Anti-slavery', in Bolt and Drescher, *Anti-Slavery*, pp.335–50; Eltis, *Economic Growth*, pp.20–4.
22. See, e.g., Wilberforce, *Letter*, p.254.
23. Seymour Drescher, 'People and Parliament: the rhetoric of the British slave trade', *Journal of Interdisciplinary History*, 20 (1990), pp.561–80.
24. Roger Anstey, *The Atlantic Slave Trade and British Abolition, 1760–1810* (Atlantic Highlands, NJ: Humanities Press, 1975), p.256. For the various valuations of capital invested in the British West Indies see Drescher, *Econocide*, pp.22–3.
25. Wilberforce, *Letter*, p.257.
26. *Hansard's Parliamentary Debates*, 1st Ser., 9, 17 March 1807, col.142–6.
27. H. Brougham, *An Inquiry into the Colonial Policy of the European Powers*, 2 vols (Edinburgh: E. Balfour, 1803), Vol.II, pp.60–140, 310–14; and Wilberforce, *Letter*, p.259.
28. See, *inter alia*, Eltis, *Economic Growth*, p.22; David Brion Davis, *Slavery and Human Progress*, pp.189–91.
29. Dean Tucker, *Reflection on … Great Britain and Ireland* (London: 1785), quoted in Folasin Shyllon, *James Ramsay: The Unknown Abolitionist* (Edinburgh: Canongate, 1977), p.77.
30. Drescher, *Econocide*, pp.114–19.
31. Ibid., pp.76–83.
32. See Eltis, *Economic Growth*, p.20; and Sidney W. Mintz, *Sweetness and Power: The Place of Sugar in Modern History* (New York, NY: Viking Penguin, 1985), pp.61–73.
33. See, e.g., Wilberforce, *Letter*, pp.262–4.
34. Drescher, *Capitalism and Anti-slavery*, pp.78–9; Clare Midgley, 'Slave sugar boycotts, female activism and the domestic base of British anti-slavery culture', *Slavery and Abolition*, 17 (1996), pp.137–62.
35. Drescher, *Capitalism and Antislavery*, p.243; James Stephen, *Crisis of the Sugar Colonies* (London: 1802), pp.185–9. Stephen's estimates of St. Domingue's production under Toussaint L'Ouverture are still regarded as reliable. See also Mats Lundahl, 'Toussaint L'Ouverture and the war economy of Saint-Domingue, 1796–1802', *Slavery and Abolition*, 6, 2 (1985), pp.122–38.
36. *Hansard's Parliamentary Debates*, 19, 4 April 1811, col.710.
37. Drescher, *Econocide*, pp.156–9.
38. B.W. Higman, 'Slavery and the development of demographic theory in the age of the industrial revolution', in Walvin (ed.), *Slavery and British Society*, pp.164–94.

39. See, *inter alia, The Petition and Memorial of the Planters of Demerara and Berbice on the Subject of Manumission, Examined* (London: Society for the Mitigation and Gradual Abolition of Slavery, 1827), pp.21–48.

40. Sir J.R. Wilmot Horton, *Speech in the House of Commons, 6 March 1828, with notes and appendix* (London: John Murray, 1828), App.B, p.73; Alexander MacDonnell, *Considerations on Negro Slavery* (London: Longman, Hurst, Rees, 1824), pp.62–8. While some historians assume that the 'consumer revolution' was well under way by the eighteenth century, others date its spread to the working classes after 1850. See E. Hobsbawm, *Industry and Empire* (Harmondsworth: 1968), p.74.

41. MacDonnell, *Considerations*, pp.63, 69; Horton, *Speech*, p.73; Gilbert Mathison, *A Critical View of the West India Question ... In a letter addressed to the Right Hon. Robert Wilmot Horton* (London: Smith, Elder and Co., 1827), pp.77–8.

42. See David Geggus, 'Haiti and the abolitionists: opinion, propaganda and international politics in Britain and France, 1804–1838', in *Abolition and Its Aftermath: The Historical Context, 1790–1916*, ed. David Richardson (London: Frank Cass, 1985), pp.113–40; Eltis, 'Abolitionist perceptions', pp.195–213.

43. Drescher, *Capitalism and Antislavery*, Ch.5–6. See also Harriet Martineau, *Tale of Demerara, Illustrations of Political Economy* (London: Charles Fox, 1832); Josiah Conder, *Wages or the Whip* (London: G. Woodfall, 1833); discussed by Patricia Hollis, 'Anti-slavery and British working-class radicalism', in Bolt and Drescher (eds.), *Anti-Slavery*, pp.294–315. See also Davis, *Slavery and Human Progress*, pp.189, 214–22; and Thomas C. Holt, *The Problem of Freedom: Race, Labour, and Politics in Jamaica and Britain*, pp.48–53. On slave motivations see Michael Craton, *Testing the Chains: Resistance to Slavery in the British West Indies* (Ithaca, NY: Cornell University Press, 1982), pp.300–4. Before British emancipation, the French Revolutionary colonial experience also indicated a high probability of partial or total withdrawal from plantation agriculture unless limited by coercive restraints.

44. George Thompson, *Speech on Colonial Slavery ... at ... Manchester*, 13 Aug.1832, quoted in Drescher, *Capitalism*, p.266, n.1. For Henry Taylor, at the Colonial Office, the strength of popular demands was such that immediate emancipation without any compensation seemed to be a real possibility by the beginning of 1833. The West Indians' only hope lay with those classes and politicians who valued property, legality and political economy. See Taylor, 'Memorandum', pp.62–3.

45. On the Bill's development and passage see Holt, *Problems of Freedom*, pp.42–50; and William A. Green, *British Slave Emancipation: The Sugar Colonies and the Great Experiment 1830–1865* (Oxford: Clarendon Press, 1976), Ch.4. Thomas Fowell Buxton specifically invoked the automatic and immediate efficacy of wages among free men as insuring adequate labour. See *Hansard's Parliamentary Debates*, 3rd Ser., 10, 10 June 1833, col.517.

46. For the abolitionists on sugar protection, see *inter alia, Second Report of the Committee of the Society for the Mitigation and Gradual Abolition of Slavery* (London: 1825), pp.26–33; *Anti-Slavery Reporter*, 12 (31 May 1826), pp.185–7.

47. J.R. Ward, *British West Indian Slavery, 1750–1834: The Process of Amelioration* (Oxford: Clarendon Press, 1988), p.249.

48. Green, *British Slave Emancipation*, Ch.9; Hugh Tinker, *A New System of Slavery: The Export of Indian Labour Overseas, 1830–1920* (London: Oxford University Press, 1974); David Northrup, *Indentured Labour in the Age of Imperialism, 1834–1922* (New York, NY: Cambridge University Press, 1995); P.C. Emmer (ed.), *Colonialism and Migration: Indentured Labour Before and After Slavery* (Dordrecht: M. Nijhoff, 1986).

49. Howard Temperley, *White Dreams, Black Africa: The Anti-slavery Expedition to the Niger, 1841–1842* (New Haven, CT: 1991); Pieter Emmer, 'The ideology of free labour and Dutch colonial policy, 1830–1870', in Oostindie (ed.), *Fifty Years Later*, 207–22. The 'cultivation system' required labourers to cultivate export crops for a certain number of days each year.

50. Davis, *Slavery and Human Progress*, pp.179–81, 199; and Roger Anstey, 'The pattern of British abolitionism in the eighteenth and nineteenth centuries', in Bolt and Drescher (eds.), *Anti-Slavery*, pp.19–42, especially p.25 and note.

51. Drescher, *Econocide*, pp.127–9, 174–7; Howard Temperley, 'Eric Williams and abolition: the birth of a new orthodoxy', in Solow and Engerman (eds.), *British Capitalism*, pp.229–57.

52. See Ward, *British West Indian* Slavery, pp.249ff.
53. Ibid., p.263; and William A. Green, *British Slave Emancipation*, pp.165, 306. Green emphasizes British anti-slavery's radicalization after emancipation, in its placing the 'highest emphasis on the protection of freedmen's liberty, not the maintenance of export levels.' See also Green, 'Was British emancipation a success?', in *Abolition and its Aftermath*, ed. D. Richardson, pp.183–202, especially p.199, n.36.
54. See Temperley, *British Anti-*slavery, pp.137–67; and Ruth Dudley Edwards, *The Pursuit of Reason: The Economist 1843–1993* (London: Hamish Hamilton, 1993), pp.19–20; and C. Duncan Rice, '"Humanity sold for sugar!" The British abolitionist response to free trade in slave-grown sugar', *Historical Journal*, 13 (1970), pp.402–18. Rice notes that sugar free traders always remained a minority in the movement (p.416), but Temperley correctly concludes that the split depreciated the once formidable powers of popular mobilization (*British Anti-slavery*, p.161).
55. *Hansard's Parliamentary Debates*, 3rd Ser., 88, 13 Aug. 1846, col.662.
56. Northrup, *Indentured Labour*, p.21, Fig.2.1. In the 1850s the British colonies received 61 per cent of indentured servants.
57. Temperley, *British Anti-slavery*, pp.141–51, Ward, *British West Indian Slavery*, p.263.
58. Herman Merivale, *Lectures on Colonization and Colonies* (London: Longman, Green, Longman and Roberts, 1861), pp.336–7. By the end of the 1850s British West Indian sugar exports had virtually regained their pre-emancipation levels (see Green, *British Slave Emancipation*, p.246). Charles Buxton, recalculating from the low point of the early 1840s, viewed the post-1846 rise in exports as a vindication of the decisive success of *two* 'great' experiments: British slave emancipation and British free trade, see Charles Buxton, *Slavery and Freedom in the West Indies* (London: 1860). *The Edinburgh Review* illustrates the continued volatility of assessments of free vs. slave labour in the 1860s. See Meadows Taylor, 'Cotton Culture in India', *Edinburgh Review*, 115 (1862), pp.478–509; Harriet Martineau, 'The negro race in America', ibid., 119 (1864), pp.203–42; P.W. Clayden, 'The reconstruction of the American union', ibid., 123 (1866), pp.524–56. On the outcome of free labour 'experiments' by Northern capitalists and abolitionists see Richard H. Abbott, *Cotton and Capital: Boston Businessmen and Anti-slavery Reform, 1854–1868* (Amherst, MA: University of Massachussetts Press, 1991), pp.87–8.
59. See Frank McGlynn and Seymour Drescher (eds.), *The Meaning of Freedom: Economics, Politics and Culture after Slavery* (Pittsburgh, PA: University of Pittsburgh, 1992).
60. Merivale, *Lectures*, p.337.
61. Ibid., p.340. From the perspective of many economic historians of the American South, a central theme 'remains the failure of the free-labour system to live up to the hopes of either its Republican spokesmen or the freedmen themselves.' (See Peter Kolchin, 'The tragic era? interpreting Southern Reconstruction in comparative perspective', in McGlynn and Drescher, *The Meaning of Freedom*, pp.291–311, especially pp.293–94).
62. The line between slave and free labour has blurred in slave historiography. See, *inter alia*, Mary Turner (ed.), *From Chattel Slaves to Wage Slaves: The Dynamics of Labour Bargaining in the Americas* (Kingston, Ont: Ian Randle, 1995), p.11; Mark D. Smith, 'Old South time in comparative perspective', *American Historical Review*, 101 (1996), pp.1432–69. Non-economic historians now seem as sceptical about Smith's view of the universal superiority of free labour as was Merivale. See, e.g., Michael Twaddle, 'Visible and invisible hands', in *The Wages of Slavery: From Chattel Slavery to Wage Labour in Africa, the Caribbean and England*, a special issue of *Slavery and Abolition*, 14 (1993), pp.1–12, especially pp.10–11.
63. See Alexis de Tocqueville, 'On the emancipation of slaves', in *Tocqueville and Beaumont on Social Reform*, in S. Drescher (ed.), (New York, NY: Harper and Row, 1968), p.150.
64. Temperley, *British Anti-slavery*, p.147, letter of Richard Caton, of the Bradford Anti-Slavery Society to J.H. Tredgold of the British and Foreign Anti-Slavery Society, 19 June 1841.
65. On the relation of the abolition of slavery to the abolition of other unfree labour systems see, *inter alia*, Stanley Engerman, 'Emancipations in comparative perspective: a long and wide view', in Oostindie (ed.), *Fifty Years Later*, pp.223–41; and Drescher, 'Reflections', in ibid., pp.243–61, especially pp.254–59. For an extensive overview of the complex impact of British emancipation on European consciousness see Davis, *Slavery and Human Progress*, pp.168–226.

African-American Aspirations and the Settlement of Liberia

HOWARD TEMPERLEY

What would have happened if a sizeable group of African Americans had actually managed to acquire a country of their own? Suppose, for example, that in the early nineteenth century a number of them – rather more than half former slaves, the remainder free-born – had emigrated to a distant land and there resettled themselves with the assistance of the US Navy and grants from the US Treasury and assorted well-wishers. And let us assume further that after they had become established this assistance had been withdrawn and they had been recognized as a sovereign state, an independent, black republic responsible for running its own internal and external affairs. What sort of a society do we suppose they would have created? We know that blacks were oppressed in America. What would they have learned from that experience? How would they act towards others less powerful than themselves? And, what, if anything, would their actions tell us about the character and aspirations of blacks in America?

Origins of the Republic of Liberia

In fact something very much like what I have been describing did happen with the settlement of Liberia.[1] The American Colonisation Society was founded in 1816 and attracted widespread support from whites in both the North and the South. Its aim was to return free blacks, and, in due course, as many of its supporters hoped, an increasing number of former slaves, to Africa.[2] The initial response of the free black community, fearing forced deportation, was mixed. Some condemned it out of hand; others saw it as having positive attractions.[3] In 1819 the United States government, needing to find somewhere to relocate Africans illegally introduced into the United States or freed by the US Navy in its efforts to suppress the slave trade (so-called 'recaptives'), agreed to underwrite the plan and appointed agents to oversee its execution. After a hesitant start, a tract of land was acquired in the area of what eventually became Monrovia, and this was gradually extended as more immigrants arrived. Meanwhile other settlements were being planted, some by the Society itself, others by independent state bodies, so that within a generation some 400 miles of the Grain Coast, extending from Cape Mount in the north to Cape Palmas in the south, was dotted with tiny African-American settlements.

Most of the early settlers were free men and women, some having been born free, others having amassed capital and purchased their freedom. At first many went with high aspirations, intent on missionary endeavour or commercial enterprise. Common to all was their belief that the United States offered little or no prospect of black men and women living on terms of equality with whites. But as news of the high mortality rates among new arrivals in Africa and the primitive conditions filtered back to America, the number of free volunteers declined. Many were influenced too by abolitionist attacks on the whole concept of colonization with the result that from 1830 onwards the majority of settlers were former slaves, many of them obliged to emigrate as a condition of being freed, a practice which became increasingly common as states tightened their restrictions on manumission and residence. All told, some 12,000 African Americans migrated to Liberia during the antebellum years, over 90 per cent of them from the South.[4]

The number of freed Africans in the settlements was initially small, amounting to no more than a few hundred. Most were parcelled out to established colonists as apprentices and ultimately absorbed into the settler community. Their influence on the character of the early settlements was therefore minimal. What made their presence significant was the virtually limitless scope it provided for making claims on the US Treasury. In the often chaotic conditions of the early years, strict accounting proved impossible. In such circumstances no clear distinction could be made between those expenditures that were necessary for the resettlement of freed Africans and those designed to benefit black colonists from America. It was, therefore, with a sense of shock that Amos Kendall, the Auditor General, reported to Congress in 1830 that in the ten years since the United States agreed to support the scheme the Treasure had spent over a $¼ million settling fewer than 260 recaptives at a cost of approximately $1,000 a head. 'It requires', he noted, italicizing his comments so as to convey his sense of alarm,

> a broad construction to find a grant of authority to *colonize them, to build houses for them, to furnish them with farming utensils, to pay instructors to teach them, to purchase ships for their convenience, to build forts for their protection, to supply them with arms and munitions of war, to enlist troops to guard them, or to employ the Army or Navy in their defense.*[5]

As the British had already discovered in the case of adjoining Sierra Leone, the resettling of former slaves in Africa was apt to prove expensive.[6]

One issue that remained unresolved for many years was the constitutional status of these settlements. Were they colonies of the United States? Attempts to have them recognized as such were resisted by Congress. Were they colonies of individual states? The right of states to maintain colonial establishments overseas was by no means clear. Originally the question was largely theoretical, the assumption being that the settlements would be governed by agents of the US government and of the Colonisation Society and that, generally speaking, the principles of American common law would apply. At first it was claimed that this arrangement sprang from the so-called *Elizabeth* Compact of 1820, by which the first settlers, on the eve of sailing, had agreed to accept the Society's authority.[7] In 1823–24, faced with a rebellion by the settlers, a more liberal regime was instituted allowing for the day-to-day administration of affairs to be conducted by popularly-elected officials chosen from among the body of the colonists.[8] This, in turn, was superseded by the Constitution of 1839, known as the Constitution of the Commonwealth of Liberia, by which all the settlements, apart from that belonging the Maryland State Colonisation Society, were brought together under arrangement allowing authority to be shared between a locally elected council and a governor appointed by the Colonisation Society in a manner reminiscent of the practice in Britain's former American colonies.[9]

That did not, however, solve the problem of Liberia's international status. Was a private philanthropic body entitled to maintain a colony and claim rights normally accorded only to sovereign states? This became an issue when foreign merchants, accustomed to trading along the coast, objected to paying docking fees, customs duties and otherwise having their operations interfered with, and prevailed on their own governments to make representations on their behalf.[10] The United States, although prepared to offer a measure of support to the colonists in their struggles with indigenous Africans, was unwilling to become involved in imbroglios with foreign powers. The Liberian Council, the colony's elected ruling body, therefore determined to pursue the only course open to it and issue a declaration of independence 'in the name and behalf of the people of the Commonwealth' proclaiming 'a Free, Sovereign and Independent State, by the name and style of the Republic of Liberia'.[11] At the same time a convention was summoned to draft a new constitution. This body, presided over by Samuel Benedict, a former slave from Georgia, was made up of delegates from each county. Taking as their basis for discussion a draft by Professor Samuel Greenleaf of Harvard, the Convention came up with a text modelled on that of the Constitution of the United States but containing a number of significant variants, among them clauses forbidding slavery, protecting the property rights of women and restricting citizenship and property-holding to 'persons of color'.[12] This version was duly ratified by popular referendum on 27 September 1847.[13] The following month the sitting Governor, J.J. Roberts, a freeborn black from Norfolk, Virginia, became Liberia's first elected President.

Rebellious Settlers

Even when thus described in broad outline, there is no mistaking the extent of Liberia's reliance in so far as constitutional matters were concerned on American ideas and precedents. In part, of course, this was due to the tutelage of the American Colonisation Society, which remained an important factor at least up to the time of independence. But to attribute the outcome *entirely* to white influence is to ignore the active part played by the settlers themselves, who, from the start, had demonstrated their independent-mindedness. Any notion that they would, out of gratitude, accept the Society's benevolent tutelage without question was quickly dispelled. Instead, they proved quarrelsome and uncooperative. Meanwhile, the turnover of white agents appointed by the Society and the US government was rapid. Often they had to substitute for one another. Many died within weeks of their arrival; most of the rest, their health impaired, fled back to America.[14] There were times when there were no white agents at all in the colony. While they were there, they had no military force or other means of coercion at their disposal. They would no doubt have been only too happy to do as they had been instructed and govern by executive decree, but, in practice, as they soon discovered, their authority depended on the willingness of the colonists to cooperate. There was simply no way that they could impose their will on the settlers where there was any disposition to resist.

This was conclusively demonstrated during the troubles of 1823–24. Jehudi Ashmun had come to Liberia with missionary aspirations. On arrival he found himself, the other whites having died or departed, cast in the role of civil governor and military commander-in-chief. It was his generalship that had enabled the settlers of Monrovia to survive attacks by the combined forces of the indigenes on 11 November and 1 December 1822 when for a time there was a serious possibility that the entire colony would be wiped out. This achievement, impressive as it was, had the effect of confirming him in his already autocratic views. Having established himself as the Liberian equivalent of Jamestown's Captain John Smith, he proceeded to rail against his charges for their refusal to accept the essentially feudal regime, based on the notion of the need to promote self-sustaining agriculture, that had been devised for their benefit. As a result, a group of armed rebels, led by the Reverend Lott Cary, a Baptist minister and former slave from Richmond, Virginia, seized power, compelling Ashmun to flee the colony. He returned five months later accompanied by the Colonisation Society's Secretary R.R. Gurley. After listening to the rebels' complaints they agreed to adopt a system of government that allowed the settlers a significant degree of control over their own affairs. The effect, according to Ashmun, was astonishing. Given authority, the dissidents became responsible citizens. Encouraged by his reports, the Colonisation Society reluctantly gave its approval to the new arrangement. In 1826 Cary was elected Vice-Agent and two years later became Acting-Agent, following Ashmun's departure for the United States.[15] As on many later occasions, a characteristically American approach was adopted, not because it was the one the Colonisation Society's managers preferred (which in this case it emphatically was not), but because it accorded with the wishes of the colonists.

Conflicting Aims

The notion that settlement overseas would transform the mental attitudes of America's blacks had, of course, been implicit in the idea of colonization from the outset. Being obliged to shift for themselves, it was argued, the colonists would need to develop their own latent skills, the discovery of which would, in turn, contribute to their self-confidence and sense of personal worth. Pride in their achievements would engender a sense of community and encourage individual enterprise. The Reverend Dr Robert Finley, one of the scheme's principal instigators, had waxed eloquent on the subject in this *Thoughts in the Colonization of Free Blacks* (1816), copies of which he circulated to Congressmen in advance of the Society's inaugural meeting. Blacks would, of necessity, learn self-help. 'At present,' he noted, 'they have few incentives to industry and virtue', but translated to a land of their own 'their contracted minds will then expend and their notions rise. The hope of place and power will soon create the feeling that they are men. Give them the hope of becoming possessed of power and influence, and the pleasure of their invigorated minds will be similar to ours in like circumstances.'[16]

There were, needless to say, many other and distinctly less altruistic reasons given for advocating colonization, and early reports from Africa, particularly those concerning the high death toll among new arrivals, were far from encouraging. Nevertheless, after a decade of experience it could be claimed that, in this respect at least, the scheme's aims were being realized. The settlers had become active agents in determining their own destiny. Henry Clay, looking back in 1829 on what had so far been achieved, paid tribute to the 'skill, bravery and power' they had displayed in withstanding tribal attacks, electing their own officials and helping to fashion their own system of government. As a result, the colony was now very much a going concern with its own schools, churches, a printing press and a public library of 1,200 volumes. Exports to the United States were valued at $60,000 a year. It all went to show that the vices commonly ascribed to American blacks 'do not spring from any inherent depravity in their natural constitution, but from their unfortunate situation'. The situation was not of their making; it existed because of the 'invincible prejudices' of the white population. It was idle to imagine that these white prejudices could ever be overcome. Regardless of the moral issues involved, blacks in America would remain victims. But, translated to Africa, settled in a land of their own, they would 'stand redeemed, regenerated and disenthralled by the mighty spirit of universal emancipation'.[17]

This was going a good deal further than the evidence justified and was certainly at odds with much of what was known about conditions in the colony. One way of persuading American audiences of the validity of such claims, however, was to compare African settlement with the experiences of their own forebears. The settlers of Jamestown, it could be pointed out, had suffered even greater losses. Americans, of all people, should be receptive to the notion of men and women trying to improve their lot by seeking asylum overseas. There was nothing unusual or peculiar about overseas migration. The world was dotted with colonies belonging to one European power or another. Americans' own ancestors had fled lands of oppression. What was different in the present instance was that the land of oppression was the United States. But who could deny that blacks in America were oppressed? Elias B. Caldwell, the Colonisation Society's first secretary, addressing its inaugural meeting, put the case forcefully:

> What was it that brought out ancestors to these shores? ... They left the land of their nativity, the sepulchres of their fathers, the comforts of civilized society, and all the endearments of friends and relatives ... to clear the forests, to encounter all the hardships of a new settlement, and to brave the dangers of the tomahawk and the scalping knife. How many were destroyed? Sometimes whole settlements cut off by disease and hunger, by the treachery and cruelty of the savages, yet were they not discouraged.[18]

Were blacks not men? They would, he asserted, be drawn on by the self-same impulses that yearly brought immigrants in their thousands to the United States – a desire to stand on an equal footing with other men. At meeting after meeting the message was hammered home that Liberia's immigrants were engaged in a heroic undertaking comparable to the first settlement of Virginia and Massachusetts Bay two centuries earlier.

According to Archibald Alexander, the author of the first comprehensive history of the settlements, the benign Providence that had so far ensured their success was identical to the one that had presided over the European settlement of North America. Just as those 'few feeble colonies' had grown to be 'one of the most powerful nations on earth' so it was to be anticipated that 'this little free republic' would prove 'the germ of a great and flourishing empire'.[19]

Such empyrean dreams were not peculiar to white colonizationists. Black spokesmen for the movement conjured up similar visions. On the eve of his departure from the United States in 1850, West Indies-born Edward Wilmot Blyden, destined to become Liberia's leading intellectual statesman, looked forward to a day when Liberia would extend its enlightened rule over the whole of West Africa.[20] Like other black separatists over the years, he saw himself as representing the truly radical cause and integrationists as dupes and temporizers. On returning to the United States in 1862 as Liberian Commissioner, he toured the country impressing on black audiences the contrast between the indignities from which they suffered in America and the opportunities that awaited them in Africa. After an absence of 12 years he found the experience living in America more than ever depressing.

> All the way to Washington a feeling of degradation held possession of me ... I thought how sad it was that so many coloured people seem disposed to cling to this land – fearing to go to Liberia lest they die of fever. But are they *living* in this country ...? A whole race in degradation! The idea is horrible! If they all went and died it would be a noble sacrifice for liberty![21]

Had not Patrick Henry said 'Give me liberty or give me death?' It was idle to expect whites to change. Prejudice permeated the entire culture. Whatever the outcome of the Civil War Whites would never accept blacks as equals. For that reason blacks had no cause to feel loyal to the United States, still less an obligation to go on investing their labour in its development. On the other hand, they did have a duty towards Africa, for until Africa was redeemed from its present state of backwardness their race's contribution to mankind's development would go unrecognized while their own achievements would continue to be ignored or belittled.[22] In due course Blyden became the first exponent of the notion of black Egypt's contribution to Western civilization and much else that was to influence twentieth-century African-American thinking.[23] In the 1860s, however, his main concern was with the personal benefits that would accrue to blacks through emigration. 'As soon as a black man of soul lands in Liberia', he declared, 'he feels himself a different man ... A consciousness of individual importance, which he never experienced before, comes over him ... In short he comes a full man ...' The choice was between true manhood and struggling on manfully in America.[24]

Why, then, were American blacks so reluctant to emigrate? In part, Blyden concluded, because of the false notions put about by white abolitionists who had represented colonization as a self-serving scheme got up by planters for the purpose of ridding America of free blacks, thereby removing a possible threat to their slave investment. That many had supported colonization for precisely that reason was undeniable. Planters had long seen free blacks as an anomalous and troublesome group whose very existence was a menace and a reproach. Many whites found their presence in northern cities disturbing. Since the War of Independence their numbers had markedly increased. Their allegedly criminal propensities were commonly cited as an argument in favour of colonization. In his *Thoughts on African Colonization* (1832) William Lloyd Garrison found no difficulty in demonstrating the pro-slavery and anti-free black tendencies of the movement. It was nourished by fear and selfishness. Above all it represented a betrayal of American ideals. Its advocates were incapable of imagining an America in which all races enjoyed equality of opportunity and laboured for common goals. They began with the proposition that racial prejudice was so closely woven into the fabric of society that it could never be eradicated. Theirs was a doctrine of despair. As he had told black audiences the previous summer:

> Now, to these promulgators of unrighteousness, with the Declaration of Independence in one hand and the Bible in the other, I fearlessly gave battle. Rich and mighty and numerous as they are, by the help of the Lord I shall put them to open shame. They shall not libel me, they shall not libel my country, with impunity. They shall not make our boasted republicanism a by-word and a hissing among all nations ...[25]

Because of its failure to honour its own proclaimed ideals the United States had become a pariah among nations. It pained his very heart and bowels![26]

Radical though *Thoughts on African Colonization* appeared, it was essentially a reaffirmation of traditional American beliefs and prejudices: America was a land of freedom, of 'light effulgent', Africa 'a strange land – a land of darkness and cruelty, of barbarism and woe'. This was not much different from what colonizationists were saying. Where Garrison's account differed unequivocally from theirs was in his confidence that blacks would eventually be allowed to enter the mainstream of American life, in other words that *white* attitudes could be changed, although how this was to be achieved, apart from securing the overthrow of slavery, he did not pause to explain. African Americans were Americans, as they had persuasively demonstrated whenever they had been allowed the opportunity, and the place for Americans was in America. Garrison, however, had little faith in the superior virtue of the oppressed. Translated to Africa, a quite different side of their characters would be revealed. Being 'a population degraded by slavery, and, to a lamentable extent destitute of religious and secular knowledge' they would treat others as they themselves had been treated by seizing 'every opportunity to overreach and oppress as interest or ambition shall instigate'. In a land without morals they would give free rein to their 'evil propensities' so that vice would 'preponderate over virtue, intemperance over sobriety, knavery over honesty, oppression over liberty and impiety over godliness'.[27] Such behaviour would provoke retaliation. Bloody conflicts would ensue from which the colonists would emerge victorious but this would only increase the enmity of the native Africans and so perpetuate the murderous cycle of oppression and rebellion. Nothing good would come of sending blacks to Africa. If colonizationists were anxious to have the continent redeemed, they would be better occupied bringing Africans to the United States for instruction.[28]

For those who rejected Garrison's integrationist assumptions, however, all this was beside the point. There simply *was* no future for blacks in the United States. So far as Edward Blyden and other separatist spokesmen were concerned it did not matter one whit what led white Americans to support the emigration of blacks to Africa just so long as they gave it their backing. What mattered was the future of the African race, not the moral conscience or ideological consistency of the United States. Garrison's heart and bowels were not their responsibility. Creditable or discreditable, it made no difference what the *motives* were as compared with the willingness of whites to further the cause by helping to create a free black republic in Africa.[29] Important as it was to secure the overthrow of American slavery, Blyden explained in *A Voice from Bleeding Africa* (1856), it needed to be viewed in the context of redeeming Africa and elevating the black race as a whole:

> Let colored men, then, of every rank and station, in every clime and country, in view of the glorious achievement of African Colonization, lend it their aid and influence. Let them look at the cause and not the instruments: let them behold and contemplate *results*, and not form conjectures concerning *motives* and *intentions* ...[30]

Abolitionists were utopians; they imagined that once slavery had gone all would be well. They had failed to grasp that slavery was merely symptomatic of an attitude that permeated the whole of white society. One had only to look at the condition of blacks in the free states to see that the ending of slavery offered no solution to the problem. Only by leaving the United States could African Americans feel truly liberated.

From Black Refugee to Expatriate American

That many of those who went to Liberia did indeed feel liberated is evident from their correspondence. In 1844 Abraham Blackford, a former slave, writing to friends in Virginia, described the pleasure he felt on visiting a white doctor in his surgery and being addressed as 'Mr Blackford'. Liberia was a black man's country. Whites in Liberia lived on sufferance and so were obliged to treat him with respect. When he encountered them on the streets 'they steps one side of the pavement and touch their hats'. Some invited him into their homes. It was much better, he concluded, 'than to be in the state for them to call you Boy'.[31] Other former slaves experienced similar feelings. James Cephas Minor, who arrived in Liberia in 1829, became a staff writer for the *Liberia Herald* and ultimately Judge of the Quarter Sessions for Montserrado County. In his view it was futile for blacks to seek liberty anywhere other than in Africa. 'Africa is a land of freedom. Where else can a man of color enjoy temporal freedom?' Thomas Jefferson had been right, he observed, in arguing that it was necessary that whites and blacks put an ocean between them.[32]

The same feelings also found expression in colonists' accounts of their day-to-day lives. Churches were being built, schools opened, new towns established. Many took pride in their farms and cottages and in listing their livestock and their crops under cultivation. Their letters also contain stirring accounts of battles with slave traders and local tribes. 'Since I been here I have been in three wars', writes John M. Page, 'but the last was indeed the hardest. We were in combat three hours before we could take the barricade.'[33] Sion Harris, describing an African attack on the mission station at Heddington, tells how he brought down the tribal chief Goterah with a charge of buckshot and afterwards presented his head to Governor Russwurm. Both he and Solomon S. Page write exultantly of the colonists' success in destroying the Spanish slave-trading establishments at New Cess and Trade Town and the release of the slaves held there. Authorities in the United States had doubted the colonists' ability to mount such a campaign, involving the mobilizing of some 350–400 militia, but they had been proved wrong. 'We mean to stand our ground and contend for our rights until we die', declared Harris. 'O if my cullarred friends would only believe and feel the love of liberty they would not stay in the United States.'[34]

By no means all the letters from former slaves were so affirmative. Many contained news of the loss of family and friends. Some correspondents had become the victims of war and seen their settlements destroyed, suffered crop failures, had their livestock carried away by leopards or experienced other mishaps. Often the reason for writing was to beg favours. Some, addressing former masters and mistresses, were embarrassingly obsequious. Few, however, expressed a wish to return to their former condition, although many would have liked to visit America to see those whom they had left behind. The case for believing that the colonists had improved their lot by settling in Africa was strengthened by the testimony of white witnesses. Captain Horatio Bridge, who spent a year cruising the Grain Coast with the US African Squadron, took the view that the colonists were 'more independent, as healthy, and much happier' than their counterparts in America. The general message was that Africa was a land which offered opportunities for those who worked hard and survived its acclimatizing fevers. There African Americans could achieve a status as independent farmers, traders or government officials that would have been impossible in the United States or anywhere else.[35]

The notion that the establishment of the Republic of Liberia represented the conscious and deliberate choice of former slaves and their descendants is most clearly spelled out in its 1847 Declaration of Independence. Drafted by Hilary Teague, a free-born black who had migrated from Virginia in 1821, it identified the 'people of Liberia' as having been originally 'inhabitants of the United States' who had left their 'native land' to pursue their destinies on a 'barbarous coast'. Besides their hope of finding refuge they also wished 'to evince to all who despise, ridicule and oppress our race that we possess with them a common nature ...' Much of the document is taken up with specific grievances:

> We were everywhere shut out from all civil office.
> We were excluded from participation in Government.
> We were taxed without our consent.
> We were compelled to contribute to the resources of a country that gave us no protection.
> We were made into a separate and distinct class, and against us every avenue of improvement was effectively closed.
> All hope of a favourable change in our country was thus wholly extinguished in our bosoms, and we looked with anxiety abroad for some asylum from the deep degradation.[36]

The settlers, in other words, were expatriates. Their 'country' was the United States. They were not, like Jews who fled to Palestine, children of the Diaspora who were returning to the land of their ancestors, a view more cherished by white than black exponents of colonization. Rather they saw themselves as being, like the original settlers of North America, engaged on an errand into the wilderness, seeking to find on a remote shore the rights, opportunities and personal respect denied to them in the land of their birth.

Two further points are worthy of note. The first and most obvious is that the document is closely modelled on the American Declaration of

Independence. It makes plain that what Liberians took exception to were not America's proclaimed ideals, to which, on the contrary, they fully subscribed, but the refusal of white Americans to apply these to men and women of African descent, who were seen as belonging to a distinct group or category debarred from citizenship and other rights and privileges accorded to whites. Admirable in theory, the universal and self-evident truths on which Americans claimed to base their system of government had in practice been applied in ways that were neither universal nor self-evident.

The second point concerns the term 'people of Liberia'. As used in the document it relates strictly to former 'inhabitants of the United States'. Nowhere is there any hint that it might apply to the vast majority of those living within the republic's borders, namely the indigenous Africans. The idea that it might do so seems not to have crossed anyone's mind. In this respect the Declaration reflects the general trend of settler thinking since the earliest days. The original *Elizabeth* Compact of 1820 had decreed that everyone migrating to or born within the Colonisation Society's territories should be entitled to the full range of rights and privileges enjoyed by citizens of the United States.[37] Like the *Mayflower* Compact of 1620, this was an agreement between individual settlers concerning the form of society they intended to establish. In neither case were the indigenous peoples of the areas concerned parties to the arrangement. In any case it was scarcely to be expected that peoples unacquainted with Western practices could readily be incorporated into the kind of society envisaged. Who could tell what would happen in the long run?

This was a question to which the exponents of African colonization, white and black alike, had given little thought. To those whites whose concern was simply to rid America of a troublesome presence the answer scarcely mattered. Others, more benevolently motivated, indulged in wishful thinking. It suited the interest of both groups to present the public and intending colonists with an outcome favourable to all parties. This required little exercise of the imagination since the necessary ingredients were already present in the minds of Americans. Africa was a barbarous place, a Dark Continent, into which the light of civilization had yet to penetrate.[38] The United States, by contrast, was a Christian and civilized nation, possessed of the most advanced system of government yet devised by man. Blacks returning to Africa would be missionaries, carrying the seeds of enlightenment and implanting them in that part of the world where they were most needed. Being of African race, they would be welcomed as returning exiles by their fellow Africans who would soon come to appreciate the superiority of their knowledge and skills. They would become Africa's natural leaders. As a result of their efforts a new black nation, modelled on the United States and dedicated to the pursuit of American ideals, would arise.

Attitudes to Africans

Such arguments continued to be heard up to the 1860s and beyond, although how far they were believed it is impossible to say. In one respect, however, they had from the first been shown to be inaccurate. Africans did not think of themselves as Africans, at least not in a way that would lead them to welcome those they saw as American interlopers. The first attempt at settlement ended disastrously when the chiefs of Sherbro Island refused to grant land to the colonists. Cape Montserrado, where Monrovia was established, was ceded reluctantly, Lieutenant Robert F. Stockton at one point holding a pistol to the chief's head.[39] Other tribes in the vicinity disputed the right of the chief in question to dispose of the land and joined forces to compel the settlers to withdraw. If the Americans were really peaceful settlers, the chiefs argued, why were they not prepared to put themselves under the authority of the traditional rulers of the area? Why did they insist on behaving as if they were conquerors?[40] The tribesmen's spears and knives, however, proved no match for the colonists' muskets and canon and after sustaining heavy losses they were obliged to come to terms. Under fire the settlers behaved with remarkable coolness and determination. No regrets were expressed over the loss of African lives. 'Our settlement,' Ashmun reported, 'was established in blood. The struggle on our part, the effort on that of the natives, were severe and violent, but the issue was such as to terminate their hostile machinations it is believed totally and for ever.'[41]

While this proved to be the case so far as Monrovia and its immediate vicinity were concerned, it did not apply to other areas of settlement where intermittent wars between colonists and tribespeople continued for the rest of the century and beyond. Many, although by no means all, were minor affrays and the issues were seldom as straightforward as in the case of Monrovia. Sometimes slave traders were involved, at other times intertribal rivalries, but underlying virtually all was that bitter sense of resentment which, as Garrison had predicted, Africans felt on finding an alien presence in their midst.[42]

The colonists appear never to have doubted their right to the lands they occupied. Like the settlers of North America two centuries before, they believed that Providence was on their side. They were the agents of civilization. Those who opposed the march of progress were 'savages'. As one former slave commented in relation to the Battle of Heddington:

> It is something strange to think that these people of Africa are called our ancestors. In my present thinking if we have any ancestors they could not have been like those hostile tribes in this part of Africa, for you may try and distil that principle and belief in them and do all you can for them and still they will be your enemy.[43]

Caught in a complex net of historical and racial ironies African Americans had become the bearers of the white man's burden. Native Africans were cruel and treacherous. James Cephas Minor commended the efforts of Liberia's Governor Thomas Buchanan, brother of the future American President, to subdue 'the ruthless and turbulent tribes around us'. Buchanan's successor, J.J. Roberts, originally from Norfolk, Virginia, and Liberia's first black Governor, noted 'the incalculable good that will accrue to the aboriginal inhabitants' on being brought 'into a more immediate connection with the colony, which will enable the government to exercise a salutary control over them; by which means, habits of civilization can be more readily introduced among them, and many of their cruel customs at once abolished.' He was happy to report that a number of tribes had lately agreed to cede land and put themselves under government protection on these terms.[44]

As with the Indians of North America, force was not always necessary. Many were only too happy to receive protection. Before the establishment of Monrovia the coastal peoples in that area had lived in fear of being seized by one of their more powerful neighbours and sold to Spanish slavers. Even the larger inland tribes, however, were impressed by the colonists' superior discipline and firepower. 'Such is the terror we have inspired,' noted Dr Joseph Mechlin, the US Government Agent, in 1829, 'that they will not molest any belonging to the colony.' When Bushrod Island was incorporated into the Monrovia settlement its inhabitants were reported to have danced for joy. They were duly instructed to think of themselves as Americans. In accordance with American anti-monarchist principles, their ruler, King Long Peter, was quietly demoted to the position of headman. Nevertheless, other rulers in the vicinity, according to Mechlin, were not merely willing but positively anxious to give up their independence in return for protection.[45]

Such arrangements brought other advantages. Closer ties facilitated trade, thereby benefiting both groups. Virtually all of Liberia's exports, from which Monrovia's leading families derived their not inconsiderable fortunes, came from trade rather than agriculture. Along the St. Paul river and elsewhere away from the coastal settlements colonists laboured on the land; but the notion of their becoming yeomen farmers in the Jeffersonian mould was soon shown to be illusory. Africans, it was discovered, were prepared to work for much less than Americo-Liberians. Although poor in many things, West Africa was rich in labour and wages were set accordingly. Sometimes Africans would work for nothing at all, as when country people were obliged to work on the roads or to assist with other communal projects; others laboured merely for board and lodging, as when tribal youths were taken into settler families as apprentices. Male settlers were not averse to taking African women as concubines although seldom prepared to accept them as wives. Sometimes the 'out children' born of these unions were absorbed into settler society. Any notion, however, that the two populations would amicably coalesce, as if by some magic alchemy of race in the manner envisaged by white Americans, was quickly dispelled. From the first the settlers saw themselves as a group apart, Americans in exile. That the passage of time had done little to alter this view is evident from the new republic's choice of motto: 'The Love of Liberty Brought Us Here'. Like the American Pilgrims, they were refugees in a barbarous land.[46]

In one respect, of course, the Liberian experience was totally unlike the American. Except during the very earliest days of settlement, or occasionally on the frontier, European settlers had never lived surrounded and outnumbered by Indians. Even in the immediate areas of settlement, however, Americo-Liberians generally represented only a minority of the population. Taking Liberia as a whole, it is unlikely that they ever constituted as much as 10 per cent of the total. When, in his inaugural address to Congress in 1863, President Daniel B. Warner estimated that the population had risen to between 12 and 14 thousand, he did not include in that total the 200,000 or so Africans living within the republic's borders.[47] So far as preserving the settlers' physical security was concerned this clearly represented a challenge. In other respects, however, colonists found little difficulty in adjusting to their situation by evoking the same principles employed, not only by the settlers of North America, but by Westerners the world over. They too believed in the superiority of Western over 'savage' culture, of Christianity over paganism, of machine-made products over handmade African artefacts. The eagerness with which Africans sought to acquire Western goods and their willingness, when not actively hostile, to learn English and otherwise adapt themselves to the colonists' needs merely confirmed the correctness of this view. The Africans, for their part, viewed the settlers as representatives of a powerful capitalist culture; 'they see', observed Jehudi Ashmun, 'the superior perfection of our fabrics, our arts, our jurisprudence, our mental culture, and ... almost wish themselves white or civilized men.'[48] In Kru the word used to describe the settlers, *Kwi*, was the same as that used to describe whites. Well into the twentieth century Monrovia continued to be referred to as 'the white man's town'.[49] Many of Monrovia's leading figures were, in fact, mulattos. Nevertheless, it was 'civilization', which in this context meant an American lifestyle, rather than pigmentation that set the colonists apart from the 'natives' and, within the settler community itself, distinguished the families of traders and government officials from those of the former slaves and their descendants in the outlying settlements. In Liberia it was culture, not race, that counted.

This was a view shared by both settlers and native Africans. Over the years the relationship between the two gradually evolved. It happened in a piecemeal way as additional areas were brought under government control and new trading patterns were established. Liberia's indigenous population consisted of some 16 tribal groups, each subdivided into several chiefdoms. Those with whom the settlers first came to terms lived along the coast in what eventually came to be called the 'constitutional zone', while those in the interior remained outside government control until late in the century and, in some cases, even beyond.[50]

Liberian expansion eastward thus had something in common with American expansion westward. Liberia's settlers, too, believed in 'Manifest Destiny'. Initially African chiefdoms, like Native American tribes, were seen as independent nations with whom it was appropriate to negotiate and make treaties as if between sovereign states. Once the settlers had become firmly established, however, this approach was replaced by one more along the lines of Chief Justice John Marshall's view of American Indians as 'domestic dependent nations'. The new attitude was aptly captured in Article 5, Section 15 of the 1847 Constitution which noted that:

> The improvement of the native tribes and their advancement in the arts of agriculture and husbandry, being a cherished object of this government, it shall be the duty of the President to appoint in each county some discreet person whose duty it shall be to make regular and periodical tours through the country for the purpose of calling the attention of the natives to these wholesome branches of industry.[51]

Africans, it seemed, were even in need of instruction on how to grow crops. In 1868, following the establishment of the Department of the Interior and the appointment of District Commissioners responsible for native affairs, Africans effectively became wards of the state, their taxes, employment, right of movement, form of dress and qualifications for residence being subject to regulations laid down by the government and administered by district commissioners through the agency of appointed tribal chiefs in the manner later adopted by white colonizers.[52]

Not least among the ironies of the situation was the Liberian state's classification of native Africans as 'aliens'. This had effectively been the view from the first but it was given official status by an Act of 1841 which provided that in the case of Africans citizenship was conditional on three 'creditable and disinterested persons' being prepared to swear that they had, over a three-year period, 'abandoned all the forms, customs and superstitions of heathenism … and conformed to the forms, customs and habits of civilized life'.[53] Such provisions, needless to say, did little to lessen the divisions between the two groups. The Liberian Constitution, while paying elaborate homage to liberal principles, virtually excluded Africans from the republic's political process by limiting voting and government office to male, land-holding citizens.[54] This constituted a double barrier, for, besides not being classified as citizens, they were also debarred from owning real estate by virtue of belonging, at least in theory, to groups whose practice it was to hold property in common. Occasionally some did manage to surmount these barriers, but only at the expense of renouncing tribal membership along with virtually everything else that made them distinctively African, becoming, in effect, African Americans. Those who succeeded in 'passing' in this way were mostly apprentices or the illegitimate offspring of settlers. Not until 1905, and then only in a notional sense, was citizenship extended to the great mass of Liberia's inhabitants. Given that Liberia's original two-party system had by that time been replaced by one-party rule, voting was, in any case, something of a formality.[55]

Conservative Attitudes of the Americo-Liberians

How Liberia's colonists would have behaved had they landed on some unpopulated shore it is impossible to say. Conceivably they would have created a form of society more reflective of their African origins, from which in many cases they were presumably only one or two generations removed. But what is noteworthy about the settlers of Liberia is the lack of evidence to show that they were influenced by, sympathetic towards or, indeed, anything other than wholly hostile to the beliefs, customs and general way of life of their African ancestors and of the peoples among whom they found themselves situated. It is almost as if a suspicion that they did not legitimately represent the culture on behalf of which they purported to speak had created in them a special need to observe its outward forms. In part, no doubt, this arose from a fear that anything other than a punctilious regard for Western norms would bring discredit on the colony. When Liberian leaders spoke of their republic as the great hope of the black race, one of the things they evidently had in mind was demonstrating that African Americans were no less capable than other Americans of upholding Western standards of behaviour. The fear of 'going native' and so losing status was one familiar to all colonizers, but it was one that, given their history, appears to have operated with peculiar force on the minds of Americo-Liberians. As Americans in exile, and more particularly, perhaps, as black southerners, which for the most part they were, they had already experienced enough humiliation at the hands of whites to make them fearful of doing anything that might expose them to further scorn.

    Some such explanation is plainly needed to account, among other things, for Liberians' dedication to preserving American political rituals. When, in

1847, Joseph John Roberts became Liberia's first President not only were the celebrations attending his inauguration reminiscent of the way American presidents were inaugurated, they were, as near as circumstances allowed, an exact copy. Soldiers marched, dignitaries processed, bands played, choirs sang, prayers were said and an oath of office was administered. In his augural President Roberts addressed his audience as 'fellow citizens'. It was, he said, an historic moment. He reminded them of the struggles of their forbears 'adventurers, inspired by the love of liberty and equal rights, supported by industry and protected by Heaven ... inured to toil, to hardships and to war.' Those had been heroic days. He recalled the bloody early battles when the combined forces of the indigenes had sought to drive the settlers into the sea.

> At a time when they were almost without arms, ammunition, discipline, or government – a mere handful of isolated Christian pilgrims, in pursuit of civil and religious liberty, surrounded by savage and warlike tribes bent on their ruin and total annihilation – they determined in the name of the 'Lord of Hosts' to stand their ground and defend themselves to the last extremity against their powerful adversary.[56]

He did not need to remind his listeners how God had come to their rescue. They were refugees from the land of oppression, but they should put aside all feelings of bitterness. It was their destiny to redeem Africa 'from the deep degradation, superstition and idolatry in which she has so long been involved 'by shedding on her inhabitants' 'the light of science and Christianity'.

Similar expressions of sentiment continued to be heard on formal occasions well into the twentieth century. Thus Liberia's rulers, following the American example, justified their exercise of authority, not only in terms of their dedication to libertarian principles but also by evoking a powerful myth concerning the heroism and sufferings of their nation's founders. As late as the 1950s one of Liberia's national holidays was Maria Newport Day, named in commemoration of one of the defenders of Monrovia who, by knocking out the coal from her pipe, touched off a canon thereby slaughtering the attacking tribesmen and turning the tide of battle. Another legendary figure was General Elijah Johnson, the founder of one of Liberia's principal dynasties and a veteran of innumerable native wars. On one famous occasion, offered assistance by a British man-of-war in return for a small piece of land on which to raise the Union Jack, he is reported to have uttered the words later taught to every Liberian schoolchild: 'We want no flagstaff put up here that will cost us more to get it down again than it will to whip the natives.'[57]

No less American in character were the sentiments expressed by Liberian presidents in their annual messages to Congress. In terms of the values evoked they were virtually indistinguishable from the addresses of the American presidents of the period: the need for enterprise, the special destiny to which Providence had committed the nation, the great strides that had already been made, and above all the need to maintain the momentum of progress. As President Warner informed a joint meeting of the two houses of the Liberian legislature in 1866, 'This progress should be continued; every step we take in it should be onward and upward: the object aimed at should be the elevation of the Negro race to the highest attainable point of improvement and excellence.' Liberia did not yet have the railway, the telegraph or great buildings such as those in more developed countries, but she had much to be proud of nevertheless.[58]

Visitors to Liberia seldom failed to express astonishment at the American feel of it all. A British naval expedition that called at Monrovia in 1841 found numerous places of public worship, competing religious sects and a printing press from which emanated two newspapers representing rival religious and political factions.[59] Sir Harry Johnston, the African explorer, whose two-volume study of the republic appeared in 1906, was impressed by the zeal with which colonists clung to the standards and practices of an America that had already ceased to exist. Their religious beliefs, prudery and social habits reminded him of a bygone era:

> The Americo-Liberian still worships clothes as an outward and visible manifestation of Christianity and the best civilization; that is to say the European clothes of the nineteenth century. He shares with our fathers the religion of the tall hat and frock coat.

Regardless of heat and humidity, no self-respecting Americo-Liberian man would dream of attending a social function or being seen on a Sunday unless so attired, nor would an Americo-Liberian woman think of putting on the beautiful clothes worn by Mandingo women. Why did the settlers worship such 'hideous idols'? Liberians' values were, he concluded, 'pitifully Anglo-Saxon'.[60] A generation later, Elizabeth Dearmin Furbay, viewing the morning-coated throng at President Edwin Barclay's inauguration, had to remind herself that she was not still in the United States. They were, it occurred to her, 'the African equivalent of the DARs and the my-ancestors-came-over-in-the-*Mayflower*-Americans', contrasting sharply with the robed figures on the tribal benches opposite. What, she wondered, passed through the minds of those Africans as they sat there 'with respectful yet uncomprehending attentiveness'? Many, she reflected, would be kings and princes had not the Americo-Liberians deprived them of their royal rights.[61] Carl Meacham, a black Peace Corps volunteer who worked in Liberia in the 1960s, was shocked by the Americo-Liberians' exploitation of peoples such as the Kru and Grebo and their assumption that, as an American, he would share their view of Africans. 'The discriminatory system in Liberia', he reported, 'reminded me of segregation in Alabama'.[62]

Liberia's Continuing Cultural Divisions

It was such attitudes, together with his very different experiences in Sierra Leone, that led Edward Blyden in his later years to despair of the Liberian experiment. Sierra Leone was a Crown Colony whose British officials saw themselves as responsible for protecting the interests of the indigenes from being encroached on by settlers. The composition of the settler population was different too, the overwhelming majority, some 74,000, being Africans released from slave ships by the Royal Navy as compared with a mere 3,000 American and West Indian blacks.[63] As a result, social and ethnic divisions there were much more varied. Liberia had lost her way, Blyden believed, because 'Owing to our false training we have been legislating as Americans in America for Americans.' As an early black separatist he had seen Liberia as an inspiration to blacks everywhere; now, as a Pan-African Nationalist, he saw that physical separation had failed to break the settlers' dependence on the beliefs and aspirations of white America. Intellectually Americo-Liberians had remained unemancipated: 'Liberia is a little bit of South Carolina, of Georgia, of Virginia – that is to say of the ostracized, suppressed, depressed elements of those states – tacked on to West Africa, a most incongruous combination.'[64] Liberia's settlers, he believed, had failed to see the inappropriateness of the social, economic and religious assumptions they had brought with them. At heart they had remained incorrigibly American.

According to Blyden, Liberia had failed for two principal reasons, both unconnected with the objections commonly expressed by the scheme's American critics. One was the colonists' unquestioning belief in the superiority of everything American, in spite of their own experiences and all the evidence demonstrating that social division, economic exploitation and political instability were the necessary concomitants of Western capitalism. Europe and America were already staggering under the burden of problems of their own making, yet Liberia's settlers had been beguiled into taking it upon themselves to carry this deeply-flawed and discredited system, the product of distant lands and alien cultures, and imposing it on peoples for whom it was manifestly unsuited. In agriculture they had adopted the gang system because that was what they had been taught in the Old South with the result that Liberian society was now characterized by discrepancies of wealth and power resembling those in the society they had fled.

The second reason for Liberia's failure was that settlers had cut themselves off from the 'bedrock' on which any stable African state must necessarily be based, that is to say, by gaining the support of the Africans themselves. Put another way, they had attempted to found a black nation on American principles rather than on the basis of a sympathetic understanding of African needs and culture. In so doing they had acted in ways contrary to the interests of the great majority of the inhabitants of the republic, with results that were bound in the long run to prove contrary to their own interests too. 'The race in its integrity is in the interior', he concluded. 'We are but fragments of it; and without the rock whence we are hewn we are but vanishing fragments.'[65]

Blyden's criticism was both penetrating and prophetic. He did not, however, propose any solution to Liberia's problems likely to impress the republic's rulers. He was one of the first Western-educated blacks to express a sympathetic interest in Islam.[66] He also drew attention to the virtues of African work methods, the communal structure of tribal society and the absurdity of wearing European clothes in the tropics. His later writings show an open-mindedness on a wide variety of issues relating to race, religion and African culture. But things had gone too far. Americo-Liberians, while admiring his intellect, had always regarded him as a maverick. From their point of view it was hard to see what they were now to do, or, indeed, how it would have been possible for their predecessors to have behaved much differently in the past. Their problems were the accumulated detritus of history. Moreover, like antebellum Southerners, whom in more ways than one they had come to resemble, Liberia's ruling elite found it hard to believed that such privileges as they enjoyed – hardly excessive by Western standards – were not their due.[67] In America their ancestors had been exploited and humiliated. In the process of removing to Africa they had borne more than their share of hardship and suffering. It was not their fault that so few black Americans had chosen to follow their example. In the early days of settlement Liberia had been described as 'a nation in the bud – a coloured America on the shores of Africa'.[68] Few as they were, that was what they had established. What more was expected? They had gone to Africa in order to become Americans and that, so far as circumstances allowed, was precisely what they had become.

The irony of Liberia's history is that the descendants of American slaves found themselves in a role performed elsewhere in Africa by white colonizers. It is doubly ironical in the sense that the nation whose values they purportedly represented regarded itself as anti-colonialist. In practice, of course, the United States' own conduct in that respect was open to question, at least in so far as the settlement of North America was concerned. Nevertheless, it was a belief that few Americans were inclined to doubt, given their numerical preponderance and the tendency of Native Americans, once brought under government control, to disappear, whether through removal, disease or a combination of the two. Native Africans, however, showed no such propensity. On the Grain Coast Liberian settlers encountered peoples far more numerous and robust than the tribes of North America. In their public rituals and acts of legislation they behaved as if they were a settler society much like the United States. In fact, their situation was analogous to that of later European colonizers of Africa and closest of all, perhaps, to that of South Africa's Boers, another lost tribe laying claim to the special guidance of Providence and obliged to live alongside a numerically superior, indigenous population viewed as alien, threatening, yet also available for exploitation as a labour force.

Like all history, the settlement of Liberia can be interpreted in a number of ways. In terms of the colonizationists' grandiose ambitions the results were plainly disappointing: America's domestic problems were not solved, the settlers were not welcomed as returning exiles, Africa was not redeemed. Exponents of black achievement might, nevertheless, find much to celebrate. Among Liberia's leaders were men of genuine distinction.[69] Long before the Massachusetts 54th Regiment had its moment of glory in the American Civil War or the Sea Island settlements were organized, African Americans were demonstrating their resourcefulness and courage in ways unavailable to them in the United States. Their correspondence bears witness to their determination, enterprise and love of freedom. They established Africa's first independent black republic, maintaining their political sovereignty while the rest of Africa succumbed to white domination.

Americo-Liberian rule ended abruptly with the bloody coup of 1980, the murder of President Tolbert and the execution of many of his ministers. These events were hailed by native Africans as a liberation from colonial rule. In the course of the disturbances that followed, many Americo-Liberians fled, some to Sierra Leone, others to Europe and the United States. A second exodus occurred in 1990 with the collapse of President Samuel Doe's People's Redemption Council and the onset of the civil conflicts that have persisted up to the present in spite of the intervention of a West African peacekeeping force.[70]

In retrospect, it is plain that these tragic events had been long in the making. In spite of belated attempts to gain the support of Liberia's tribal peoples, the country had remained a colony both in the sense of being financially dependent on the United States and by virtue of being governed by a small, culturally-distinct elite of non-native origin who led lives far removed from those of the vast majority of the population. The hostility with which they were regarded was aptly summed up by a Kpelle student in an interview with the anthropologist Merran Fraenkel in 1959:

These people are too hard in their hearts, they cannot change … There will be civil war. They think so much of themselves, and who are they? You know, they think they are so much better than us, but they are all sons of slaves – they were slaves here in Africa before they went to America; that is how they were sent.[71]

When told that this was disputed he replied with remarkable frankness, 'Yes, I know, but when someone hits you, you look for weapons to hit back.' Garrison, although wrong in many respects about colonization, was right in his prediction that it would provoke resentment and end in bloodshed. This was also what caused the despairing Blyden in later years to criticize Liberia's rulers for their rigidity and short-sightedness.

So what, it may be asked, does the history of these events reveal about the character and aspirations of African Americans? Most obviously, perhaps, their sheer 'Americanness'. Their experience had provided them with no alternative system of values to set against those of the United States. Rejected, denounced, exiled, there was no more dedicated group of Americans than the black settlers of Liberia. The corollary of this was their condescending and often arrogant attitude towards native Africans and the cultures they represented. While it would be unfair to hold Liberia's founders responsible for events that were to occur a century-and-a-half later, it is possible to see in their attitudes the genesis of at least some of Liberia's later troubles. Arguably the task they had set themselves was always a lost cause. Liberia is not the only African state to have imploded. Sierra Leone, in spite of the different policies pursued by its nineteenth-century founders, has fared scarcely better. Perhaps no settler group, however adaptable or well intentioned, would have succeeded in reconciling its own interests with those of the indigenous population. All the same, it has to be admitted that, as Americans, for the most part sons and daughters of the Old South, the task they faced was one for which they were singularly ill-prepared.[72]

NOTES

1. The best account of the American aspects of the movement is still P.J. Staudenraus's *The African Colonization Movement, 1816–1865* (New York, NY: Columbia University Press, 1961). For information on Liberia see C. Abayomi Cassell, *Liberia: History of the First African Republic* (New York, NY: Fountainhead, 1970); Yekutiel Gershoni, *Black Colonialism: The Americo-Liberian Scramble for the Hinterland* (Boulder, CO/London: Westview, 1985); J. Gus Liebenow, *Liberia: The Evolution of Privilege* (Ithaca, NY/London: Cornell University Press, 1969) and *Liberia: The Quest for Democracy* (Bloomington, IN: Indiana University Press, 1987); Tom W. Shick, *Behold the Promised Land: A History of Afro-American Settler Society in Nineteenth Century Liberia* (Baltimore, MD: Johns

Hopkins University Press, 1980). For official documents relating to Liberia's development see Charles Henry Huberich's two-volume *The Political and Legislative History of Liberia* (New York, NY: Central Book Co., 1947).

2. Robert Finley, 'Thoughts on the Colonization of Free Blacks,' in *Report of Mr Kennedy of Maryland on African Colonization* (House of Representatives, 27th Congress, 3rd Session, Rep. No.283, Washington DC, 1843), p.169 (henceforward referred to as *Kennedy Report*).
3. The notion that free blacks were unanimously opposed to colonization from its inception is false. See Marie Tyler McGraw, 'Richmond free blacks and African colonization, 1816–1832', *Journal of American Studies*, 21 (Aug. 1987), pp.209–11; Katherine Harris, *African and American Values: Liberia and West Africa* (Lanham, MD: University Press of America, 1985), pp.3–4; William Loren Katz, 'Earliest responses of American negroes and whites to African colonization', in William Lloyd Garrison, *Thoughts on African Colonization* (New York, NY: Arno Press/New York Times, 1968), pp.i–xi. Apart from the resolutions passed by the blacks of Philadelphia in 1817, the background to which, as Katz explains, is complicated, all of Garrison's evidence for black opposition comes from the period after 1831. See ibid., Pt II, 'Sentiments of the people of color'.
4. McGraw, 'Richmond free blacks', p.210; Merran Fraenkel, *Tribe and Class in Monrovia* (London: Oxford University Press, 1964), p.6. Of the 12,790 African Americans who migrated to Liberia before 1867, 11,703 were from the South and 1,087 from the North (American Colonisation Society, *Fiftieth Annual Report*, 1867, p.190.
5. *Kennedy Report*, p.457. For information on the number and treatment of African recaptives see Shick, *Behold the Promised Land*, pp.68–72.
6. Christopher Fyfe, *A History of Sierra Leone* (London: Oxford University Press, 1962), pp.134, 141–3, 154–5; Harris, *African and American Values*, p.35.
7. Huberich, *Political and Legislative History of Liberia*, Vol.I, pp.145–52.
8. Ibid., pp.331–40.
9. The text is in the *Kennedy Report*, pp.923–7. Maryland in Africa eventually became part of Liberia in 1857. The Maryland colony at Cape Palmas was the most ambitious of the state settlements. For details see Penelope Campbell, *Maryland in Africa: The Maryland State Colonisation Society 1831 to 1857* (Urbana, IL: University of Illinois Press, 1971).
10. Huberich, *Political and Legislative History of Liberia*, Vol.I, pp.774–8, 788–800.
11. Cassell, *Liberia: History of the First African Republic*, p.136.
12. Ibid., pp.415–30.
13. Ibid., pp.135–9; Huberich, *Political and Legislative History of Liberia*, Vol.I, pp.821–46.
14. The agents and their periods of office are given in Huberich, *Political and Legislative History of Liberia*, Vol.I, pp.705–9.
15. Ibid., pp.368–75; Staudenraus, *African Colonization*, pp.88–97; Ralph Randolf Gurley, *Life of Jehudi Ashmun* (originally published, 1835, reprinted New York, NY: Negro Universities Press, 1969), pp.165–250; Shick, *Promised Land*, p.38.
16. *Kennedy Report*, p.170.
17. Henry Clay, 'Address to the Colonisation Society of Kentucky, 1829', in Archibald Alexander, *History of Liberia*, pp.302–32. The quotations are taken from pp.319 and 322–3.
18. Quoted in ibid., p.86.
19. Quoted in ibid., p.9.
20. Hollis R. Lynch, *Edward Wilmot Blyden, Pan-Negro Patriot, 1832–1912* (London: Oxford University Press, 1967), p.6.
21. Letter to the *Liberian Herald*, 5 July 1862, in Hollis R. Lynch (ed.), *Black Spokesman, Selected Published Writings of E.W. Blyden* (London: Frank Cass, 1971), p.22.
22. 'The Call of Providence to the Descendants of Africa in America', in Lynch, *Black Spokesman*, pp.25–33.
23. Lynch, *Pan-Negro Patriot*, pp.54–8.
24. 'Address to the Maine State Colonisation Society, 1862', in Lynch, *Black Spokesman*, p.12.
25. Garrison, *Colonization*, p.14.
26. Ibid., p.141.
27. Ibid., pp.24–33, 124, 129.
28. Ibid., pp.35–7.

29. Lynch, *Pan-Negro Patriot*, pp.8–9.
30. Lynch, *Black Spokesman*, p.10.
31. Abraham Blackford to Mary B. Blackford, 9 Sept. 1844, in Bell I. Wiley (ed.), *Slaves No More: Letters from Liberia, 1833–1869* (Lexington, KY: University Press of Kentucky, 1980), pp.11–22.
32. James Cephas Minor to John Minor, 11 Feb. 1833, in ibid., pp.14–17.
33. John M. Page to Charles W. Andrews, 1840, in ibid., p.104.
34. Sion Harris to William McLain, 20 May 1849, in ibid., p.227. For other accounts of this particular campaign see ibid., pp.106–8, 323.
35. Ibid., *passim*; [Horatio Bridge], *Journal of an African Cruiser ...by an Officer of the US Navy* (New York, NY/London: Wiley/Putnam, 1845), p.43.
36. Declaration of Independence, Huberich, *Political and Legislative History of Liberia*, Vol.1, pp.828–32. See also the commentary on the Declaration in Fraenkel, *Tribe and Class*, pp.8–9.
37. Huberich, *Political and Legislative History of Liberia*, Vol.I, p.149.
38. For American attitudes toward Africa at this time see Michael McCarthy, *Dark Continent: Africa as Seen by Americans* (Westport, CT: Greenwood, 1983), pp.145–53.
39. Lt Stockton's graphic account of this episode will be found in: Colonisation Society of the City of Newark, *A Sketch of the Colonization Enterprise* (Newark, 1825), pp.2–3.
40. The Africans' case against the settlers is set forth in Capt Robert T. Spence to the Secretary of the Navy, 27 June 1823, *Kennedy Report*, pp.818–19. See also Huberich, *Political and Legislative History of Liberia*, Vol.1, pp.282–3.
41. Gurley, *Life of Jehudi Ashmun*, p.146 and App.3, pp.29–30.
42. For a brief account of some of these wars and their causes see Lynch, *Black Spokesman*, pp.99–110.
43. Peyton Skipwith to John H. Cocke, 22 April 1840, Wiley (ed.), *Slaves No More*, p.53.
44. Wiley (ed.), *Slaves No More*, p.19; Huberich, *Political and Legislative History of Liberia*, p.800.
45. Archibald Alexander, *A History of Colonization on the Western Coast of Africa* (Philadelphia: William S. Martien, 1846), p.335.
46. Cassell, *Liberia: History of the First African Republic*, p.166; Huberich, *Political and Legislative History of Liberia*, Vol.I, p.836. The family and business connections of Liberia's nineteenth-century trading elite are described in Shick, *Promised Land*, pp.44–50. On the question of compulsory labour see Liebenow, *Privilege*, pp.54–5, 58, 66–70, 208–9, 213–14. Liberia's prohibition of slavery did not cover compulsory labour, pawning and other slave-like practices, Huberich, *Political and Legislative History of Liberia*, Vol.II, pp.896–9, 915, 1491.
47. Cassell, *Liberia: History of the First African Republic*, pp.236, 247.
48. Gurley, *Life of Jehudi Ashmun*, App.3, pp.29–30.
49. Capt Charles H. Bell to Revd Alfred Chester, 3 April 1840, *Kennedy Report*, p.824; Fraenkel, *Tribe and Class*, p.196.
50. See Liebenow, *Privilege* and Gershoni, *Black Colonialism*, *passim*.
51. The full text of the Constitution will be found in Cassell, *Liberia: History of the First African Republic*, pp.425–30 and Huberich, *Political and Legislative History of Liberia*, Vol.2, pp.852–62.
52. Liebenow, *Privilege*, pp.53–9.
53. Huberich, *Political and Legislative History of Liberia*, Vol.II, pp.866, 1030.
54. See Article I, Section 11 and Article V, Section 12.
55. Fraenkel, *Tribe and Class*, pp.27–8, 119–20; Liebenow, *Privilege*, pp.25–9 and 'Liberia' in Gwendolen M. Carter (ed.), *African One Party States* (Ithaca, NY: Cornell University Press, 1965), pp.325–94.
56. Cassell, *Liberia: History of the First African Republic*, pp.143–4, 146.
57. Fraenkel, *Tribe and Class*, p.10; Huberich, *Political and Legislative History of Liberia*, Vol.I, p.226. For the Johnson family genealogy see Shick, *Promised Land*, p.48.
58. *Address of President Daniel Bashiel Warner to the Joint Meeting of the Liberian Congress, 1866* (Monrovia, 1866).
59. William Allen and T.R.H. Thomson, *Narrative of the Expedition to the River Niger in 1841*,

2 vols (London: Richard Bentley, 1884), Vol.I, pp.87–8. These religious and political feuds are described in Shick, *Promised Land*, pp.39–40.

60. Sir Harry Johnstone, *Liberia*, 2 vols (London: Dodd Mead, 1906), Vol.I, pp.354–6.

61. Elizabeth Dearmin Furbay, *Top Hats and Tom-Toms* (London: John Gifford, 1946), p.54.

62. Jonathan Zimmerman, 'Beyond double consciousness: black Peace Corps Volunteers in Africa, 1961–1971', *Journal of American History*, 82 (Dec. 1995), p.1020.

63. Michael Banton, *West African City: A Study of Tribal Life in Freetown* (London: Oxford University Press, 1957), pp.3–4.

64. Lynch, *Black Spokesman*, p.119.

65. Blyden's views on Liberia's errors are fully set out in 'The Three Needs of Liberia', a lecture delivered at Lower Buchanan, Grand Bassa County, in 1908 and reprinted in ibid., pp.119–25. The quotation is from p.124.

66. Ibid., pp.xxii, 273–311.

67. Liebenow, *Privilege*, p.15.

68. *African Repository*, 1828, quoted in McGraw, 'Richmond free blacks', p.215.

69. Brief biographies of Liberia's leading figures together with suggestions for further reading may be found in D. Elwood Dunn and Svend E. Holsoe (eds.), *Historical Dictionary of Liberia* (Mestuchen, NJ: Scarecrow Press, 1985).

70. Liebenow, *Democracy*, pp.153–96; David Lamb, *The Africans* (New York, NY: Random House, 1983), pp.124–33; Anthony Daniels, *Monrovia Mon Amour: A visit to Liberia* (London: Murray, 1992); Lynda Schuster, 'The final days of Dr Doe', *Granta* 48 (Autumn 1994), pp.39–95.

71. Fraenkel, *Tribe and Class*, pp.225–6.

72. This was pointed out by black as well as white critics. See 'Walker's Appeal to the Coloured Citizens of the World' (Boston: David Walker, 1830), in Sterling Stuckey, *The Ideological Origins of Black Nationalism* (Boston: Beacon Press, 1972), pp.94–5.

From Chattel to Citizen:
The Transition from Slavery to Freedom
in Richmond, Virginia

MICHAEL NARAGON

Emancipation, military defeat and Reconstruction worked a revolution in political relations and institutions. Sally Anderson, an African American from Henrico County, Virginia and her lawyer C.S. Bundy hoped to use this to their advantage. In early 1868 county officials convicted Anderson of arson and sentenced her to hang. Anderson and Bundy challenged the legality of the proceedings. Before US Circuit Court Judge John Underwood, Bundy produced evidence that at least one county magistrate, the prosecuting attorney and the court clerk had sworn fidelity to the Confederacy, thereby rendering the court and its decisions illegal under the Fourteenth Amendment to the US Constitution. The Virginia Attorney General urged Underwood to turn a deaf ear to such appeals. If applied, these standards of loyalty and legality promised to undermine every court in the state. Unconvinced, Underwood, a leading founder of the Virginia Republican Party, freed Anderson.

White Richmonders reacted with predictable outrage. Newspapers denounced 'Radical Justice' which endangered 'the order, industry, energy, and general well-being of the Virginia people…' Mayor George Chahoon ordered the city police to rearrest Anderson. Chahoon's view was that the judge's decision applied only to the legality of the court, not to Anderson's established guilt. The police had difficulty executing this task when a crowd of African-American men and women surrounded them and 'threatened a rescue'. They succeeded in arresting Anderson only after reinforcements came to their aid.

In the Mayor's Court, Anderson and Bundy claimed that the US Circuit Court's jurisdiction superseded the Mayor's Court's and that, since Congress still exercised control over the defeated Confederacy, only an appointed, military commission could retry the case. Chahoon quickly penned two letters, one asking district commander General Stoneman 'to secure a legal trial for all persons charged with crime', the other asking Henrico County magistrates to assume custody of Anderson. Stoneman declined, and the commonwealth attorney informed the mayor that Henrico officials no longer sought Anderson. To retry Anderson without violating the rule of double jeopardy meant admitting that her first trial had been conducted illegally. According to the commonwealth attorney, this was something to which Henrico County Courts would never agree. Apart from 'any consideration of self-respect', such a decision by a state court would be most disastrous in its consequences. County magistrates 'deeply deplore[d]' Anderson's freedom, but her 'punishment sinks into comparative insignificance' when weighed against the cost of undermining the state justice system.[1]

Anderson's victory highlights a much broader struggle occurring in postbellum Richmond and across the American South. Slavery had yielded to freedom. The abolition of slavery upset the entire edifice of economic and legal privilege and status that it had sustained. Woven into the cultural fabric of antebellum Southern politics, slavery could not – in the words of Stephanie McCurry – 'be disentangled from other relations of power and privilege'.[2] Emancipation none the less dissolved the sovereignty of masters over slaves but left unresolved the question of what citizenship would mean. A study of Richmond, the capital of Virginia and of the Confederacy, illustrates how emancipation corroded established patterns of political subordination and authority.

In Richmond emancipation and democratic reform sparked the creation of new political institutions, new forms of political mobilization and new habits of political thought. Begrudging acceptance of emancipation by former slaveholders and other whites did not imply a willingness to countenance any significant shift in African Americans' legal subordination. City whites, with the initial support of the US military, tried to maintain customary patterns of racial deference and legal inequality. In 1865 and 1866 African Americans responded by organizing a mass reform movement to press municipal authorities for rights and public services. Defying the political authority of former slaveholders and Confederates led some, like Sally Anderson, to turn to Federal law and the United States military. Others, such as Anderson's would-be rescuers, used mass mobilization to push demands for legal equality and citizenship rights. The disenfranchised crowded court dockets and marched in city streets hoping to establish a freedom unqualified by racial distinction. In response, those who hoped to re-establish social principles fashioned under slavery stridently resisted, turning to the local police and courts to dampen the revolutionary expectations unleashed by emancipation.

The Military Reconstruction Act of 1867 transformed the way disputes over political rights and freedom unfolded. The Act guaranteed universal male voting rights, and a great number of new voters, primarily African Americans, joined the Republican Party. At the same time, old partisan rivals united as former Whigs joined Democrats in a self-proclaimed 'white men's' Conservative Party.[3] Thus former slaves now battled former Confederates at the polls. Even after Federal Reconstruction ended in Virginia in 1870 these new alignments persisted and revolutionized the style and content of local civic culture. The informal, republican style of contesting local elections, which had characterized the 1850s, gave way to vitriolic partisan competition for council seats, the mayor's office and other elective positions.[4] The local party system that emerged was a by-product of efforts, such as those being waged throughout the Atlantic world, by people seeking power and searching for new understandings of citizen and state to replace the ones shattered by the abolition of slavery.

African Americans Take to the Streets

After the guns fell silent, the task of governing the city fell initially to Unionist Governor Francis Pierpont, the Army, and the Bureau of Refugees, Freedmen and Abandoned Lands, created by Congress on 3 March 1865. During the war, Pierpont had been Governor of restored Virginia, 'a shadow state recognized by President Lincoln that controlled only a small part of northern Virginia.' Within a month of Lincoln's death, President Andrew Johnson reaffirmed Federal support for Pierpont.[5]

The rebuilding of Richmond's polity occurred in a context of demographic change, industrial recession and relative commercial decline. Between 1860 and 1870 the city's population grew from 37,910 to 51,038, an increase of 35 per cent. Although the population had increased steadily before the war, this upswing was part of a fundamental shift in the city's social structure. European immigration fell by 25 per cent during this period while black migration swelled. African Americans accounted for two-thirds of the city's new residents, and by 1870 totalled 45 per cent of the entire population.[6]

The city's commercial sector recovered slowly from the war, but the number of small shops and factories grew rapidly. The total number of manufacturing establishments doubled between 1860 and 1870, but in 1870 they employed on average only half as many workers. Metalworking, tobacco fabrication and wheat and corn milling remained at the core of the city's industries and accounted for 85 per cent of all products manufactured in 1870. Of these, only the ironworks increased the value of its products. Tobacco manufacturers and flour merchants, in contrast, slipped behind the tobacco firms of North Carolina and the Midwestern and Western millers. Between 1860 and 1870 the number of tobacco factories declined by 24 per cent, while the market value of processed tobacco dropped 20 per cent. Merchants, who from 1855 to 1861 had traded an annual average of 600,000 barrels of flour, exchanged only 111,426 in 1867 and 164,861 in 1868.

Because of the difficulties facing tobacco manufacturers and flour millers, the total value of manufactured product in 1870 fell 15 per cent below that of 1860. Emancipation only intensified these economic difficulties. Abolition had raised questions about labour mobility and power that former masters and slaves alike expected the political system to settle.[7]

Responsibility for reviving the city's infrastructure fell initially to the Republican Party. Governor Pierpont desired a bloodless reconstruction. He thought that defeated Southerners had learned the value of humility, and he hoped that by showing leniency he would broaden the appeal of the fledgling Republican Party in Virginia. By mid-June 1865 he had restored all of Richmond's wartime city officers to power, including the ardent secessionist Joseph Mayo, who once again became Mayor. They, with the support of military officials, promptly set about restricting African Americans' mobility and independence through elaborate pass and curfew systems. These Black Codes, buttressed with freelance violence, aimed to restore the vestiges of servility. As Richard Lowe tells us, 'ex-Confederates could hardly have hoped for easier terms or a more lenient governor'.[8]

But hope for an easy political reconstruction quickly faded as African-American men and women fought the reassertion of antebellum values. A committee of black ward leaders singled out Mayor Mayo for special condemnation, attacking him and others for using the 'old negro laws' and the rights 'that free people of color have heretofore had in Virginia' to define the citizenship of free men and women. They further claimed that Mayo 'and his administration has been marked by cruelty and injustice to us, and the old Rebel police now and again in power have been our greatest enemies'. Appeals to military officials for protection and redress failed, and so the protestors drew upon their new and most potent resource: mass mobilization. Well before enfranchisement, a grass-roots reform movement took shape as African-American men and women used rallies, popular celebrations and mass rescues of police prisoners to claim rights and to reshape the political process.

During the spring of 1865 a committee of African Americans canvassed Richmond investigating claims of physical abuse and economic discrimination. Over 3,000 packed the First African Baptist Church on 10 June to hear its findings, which painted a stark picture of systematic racial oppression committed by former masters, the military, Mayor Mayo and city police officers.[9] Building on these grievances, the meeting stitched together a memorial calling on Governor Pierpont and President Johnson to extend real freedom to African Americans. A delegation financed by the African-American churches of Richmond and neighbouring Manchester delivered copies of the petition to Governor Pierpont in Richmond and President Johnson in Washington.[10] This produced immediate results.

Pierpont dissolved the city council, formally stripping Mayo of power and appointing a provisional city manager to govern until new elections had been held. Military officials reassigned the commanders of the Department of Virginia to the Far West and placed Richmond under the care of General Terry. Politically mobilized and articulate African Americans thus found it possible to use the power of the national government to influence local politics. Ultimately it was their actions that circumscribed efforts to reconstruct social relations associated with enslavement.[11]

Pierpont remained convinced that only the rapid restoration of civil authority would win supporters to the Republican fold. He further believed that many former Confederates had been humbled by military defeat and were antagonistic to the party of secession, the Virginia Democracy. Responding to pressure from military officials and Pierpont's party-building schemes, the General Assembly scheduled elections across Virginia for 25 July 1865.[12]

The campaign for local offices began much as in former times. Voters and friends informally nominated councilmen and aldermen of solid character devoted to the public good. Editorials warned voters to avoid old political loyalties and ignore former fire-eaters. Richmond's incumbent wartime political leaders faced little organized opposition. Although military officials persuaded Mayo to abandon his re-election campaign most of the other wartime politicians remained in the field.

The election quickly became a referendum on wartime loyalties and most Richmonders voted as they had shot.[13] Unionists were disappointed. Eighty per cent of the selected councilmen and 93 per cent of the aldermen had held wartime or antebellum seats.[14] Charges of fraud and intimidation soon surfaced. Returning Virginia Unionists complained that election officers had refused their ballots on the grounds of their failure to meet residency requirements. All but one city newspaper, the *Richmond Republic*, refuted what were described as 'the claims of a few disappointed office hunters'.[15]

General John Turner, who directly supervised affairs in Richmond, deplored the election of those who 'have been prominent and conspicuous in inaugurating and sustaining the rebellion'. Union sacrifices had been too great and Confederate treason too blatant for Turner to allow the results to stand. Three days after the polls closed he voided the results as a measure of 'justice to the thousands who have fallen on the battlefield or by disease....'[16]

The daily intricacies of governing quickly overwhelmed Turner, and he turned to experienced politicians for help. He appointed D.J. Saunders, former city council president and representative to the Confederate House of Delegates, to act both as the city's provisional manager and to exercise 'all powers and authority vested in the City Council under the charter of the City of Richmond',[17] although his decisions and appointments required Turner's approval. Regulating the market square, filling positions in the city's utilities and collecting taxes consumed increasing amounts of Turner's time. Federal demands that re-established local governments should resume the cost of poor relief and law enforcement further compounded his difficulties. Under mounting bureaucratic and financial pressure he eventually allowed all but two of the July winners to assume office.[18]

In April 1866 a slate of reform candidates eagerly awaited the impending races for city council; but when the polls closed voters had overwhelmingly endorsed familiar leaders and incumbents. Joseph Mayo won the mayoral race, while William Macfarland, former city representative to the secession convention, and six other wartime councilmen, went to city hall.[19] The election's significance lies more in what it reveals about urban Reconstruction than the strength of governmental reform. This time the military authorities let the results stand. Few at the time knew how the battle between President Johnson and congressional radicals might be resolved, but divided authority in Washington plainly lessened the military's willingness to intervene in local elections. To judge from the results, Richmond voters assumed that Reconstruction would be controlled locally and turned confidently to men with political experience. If the April 1866 city elections revealed the extent of political change expected to follow emancipation, Richmond voters were destined to be gravely disappointed.

Even before Johnson's rift with Congress became chronic, city councilmen found their control over local politics and the political culture of the Old South challenged once again, this time by the city's newest citizens. African Americans broadened their attacks upon slavery's legal heritage, which they had begun in the spring of 1865, by marching through the city streets. During the slavery era white Southerners had relied on public ceremonies and law to etch lines of racial oppression on to civic spaces.[20] Now African-American men and women paraded through once forbidden civic spaces in observance of four civic holidays: 1 January, 22 February, 3 April and 4 July.[21] This new but hotly contested political calendar commemorated significant events for African Americans.[22] Most white Richmonders refused to share Washington's birthday (22 February) or American Independence Day with African Americans, preferring to leave the city to celebrate in surrounding counties. They found it harder to ignore emancipation day festivities. White Richmonders lacked a standing tradition to distract them and the day's political message unsettled former Confederates, who found the topic of emancipation distasteful. But it was the day selected for its commemoration that really angered them. Some African Americans marked 1 January, the date of Lincoln's emancipation proclamation, as emancipation day, but a majority thought their actual emancipation had come on 3 April, the day Richmond surrendered to Union forces. The city press reacted angrily to the idea of mounting celebrations on that date and Mayor Mayo, city councilmen, Governor Pierpont and General Terry called on African-American church leaders to drop their plans.[23]

Despite official opposition and threats of economic retaliation, thousands of African Americans nevertheless gathered at the Old Fair Grounds on 3 April 1866 and returned annually thereafter. Led by a marching band, participants wore colourful uniforms and carried banners calling for peace, liberty and goodwill. The parade ended on Capitol Square, an area forbidden to African Americans by antebellum black and slave codes, which in consequence became 'crowded with negro men, women, and children'.[24] These celebrations took on an explicit political flavour when one speaker cautioned African-American celebrants to 'never consult a rebel on politics'.[25] Mass parades hailed the recent death of Virginia's Black Codes. Marchers 'pronounced their rights to civic space, and seized the power to define public memory, insisting that their version of the day's history become public history'.[26] The open defiance of Mayo, Pierpont, Terry and city councilmen resolutely announced African Americans' unwillingness to defer to former rebels or to depend solely on the Federal government to lend meaning to their freedom.

A series of street skirmishes aimed at freeing police prisoners further sharpened these emerging political divisions. A certain degree of spontaneity characterized many rescue attempts, and, as in Sally Anderson's case, some efforts failed. If we believe newspaper accounts, however, attacks on city police were deliberate and purposeful. Neighbourhood associations and professional or middle class African Americans organized rescues. Shouts of 'fall-in!' preceded some rescue attempts, and police officers noted that neighbourhood women often became the nucleus of crowd activity.[27] These rescue efforts, which placed participants in danger of arrest themselves, had a communal component and aimed to thwart the city police by overwhelming them with numbers. This can be seen by examining an incident that occurred in May 1867.

The May riot began over a vantage place at a firefighters' competition. Police Captain Charters pushed an African-American man from a spot reserved for firefighters. One white firefighter shoved him again for good measure. Fisticuffs followed. Police Officer Snook arrested the unnamed man, as the white firefighter melted into the crowd, undetected and unarrested. A crowd, led by an African-American barber, quickly formed and 'insist[ed] that he should not be arrested unless the white man was also arrested'. The barber egged the crowd on. Waving his barber's pole he exclaimed 'Come on freedmen! Now's the time to save your nation.' Another speaker told men and women gathered around him to assert their rights: 'Time done come now for us to talk up, and stand up for our rights.'

Protecting community and collective rights in this case meant securing equal treatment before the law by mass mobilization rather than faith in the local justice system. This became explicit after Mayor Mayo arrived. He hurried to the scene, mounted a cart and ordered 'this crowd, in the name of the Commonwealth, to disperse. Go to your homes, every one of you, white and black.' Undeterred, participants taunted Mayo and continued to threaten the police. Throughout this affair, the crowd's displeasure remained focused and purposeful. The *Dispatch* found the mob was 'not very dangerous' for white men 'could walk quietly among them without being disturbed'. The crowd, estimated to contain upwards of 3,000, twice freed the prisoner and ultimately thwarted his incarceration. A company of the US infantry cleared the street once it became clear Mayo and his police force could not.[28]

Risking arrest to free a prisoner seems perhaps foolhardy, especially since rescues had a limited effect on local law enforcement. But this behaviour was merely one part of the contest to reconstruct political and social norms as African Americans looked to the Federal government and communal mobilization to block attempts by local white authorities and civilians to reimpose the deference and arbitrary authority associated with slavery. Rescuers not only sought to wipe away slavery's heritage by preventing an arrest for claiming a portion of the sidewalk but to supplant it with new, slowly forming ideas of equality and political authority. From the bench of the Mayor's Court, Mayo pleaded with 'the colored people to have confidence in him, to believe that [he] would do them justice'. The responding jeers made the broader political context and purpose of the rescues explicit.[29]

Along with the June protest and emancipation day parades, rescues underscored the dynamic nature of urban Reconstruction. They addressed immediate grievances and attacked the local political process. When seen together, however, these events formed one part of what Eric Foner has called a triangular struggle waged by Northerners, Southern whites and African Americans as they adjusted to emancipation and built new political relationships. Former Confederates' efforts to recreate old forms of submission and loyalty lent parades and the rescue of prisoners powerful political overtones.[30] Richmond African Americans, through mass confrontations and petitions to Washington, served notice that citizenship meant more than working without compulsion.

Citizenship, Race and Party Politics

Changes in Federal and State laws further transformed how localized struggles over police, the courts and rights would be settled, and raised the stakes of local electoral competition. The May riot and violence elsewhere in the South angered Northern Republicans, who had come to regard President Johnson's Reconstruction programme as a failure. On 2 March 1867 Congress, led by Northern Republicans, passed the Military Reconstruction Act over Johnson's veto. The act turned Virginia into a military district under General John Schofield's command and mandated the passage of a new state constitution that ratified the Fourteenth Amendment. African Americans accordingly gained voting rights and office-holding privileges while thousands of ex-Confederates found themselves disenfranchised. A subsequent act authorized the military district commander to oversee elections for a constitutional convention and to submit the finished product to voters for ratification.[31]

Changes in Federal law enfranchised more than 6,000 Richmond African Americans, sending political shockwaves through city politics.[32] Military officials and Congress scheduled elections in October to select delegates to the state constitutional convention. Two new state parties, the Republicans and the Conservatives, scrambled to perfect their organizations and to win the loyalties of voters. Conservatives knew from their street and courtroom battles in 1865 and 1866 that African Americans opposed Mayo and other former Confederates and most likely would vote Republican. They made initial overtures to them, however, knowing the number of potential black voters roughly equalled the number of white ones and being unclear how former Whigs would vote. Responding to a call from 13 self-described 'respectable and well-bred colored citizens', the leading Conservatives R.T. Daniel, William Macfarland, Marmaduke Johnson and N.A. Sturdivant addressed an April mass meeting of African-American men and women at the Richmond Theater. They denied any partisan intentions, claiming only to want to set 'before the black man the true aspect of his new relations to Southern society'.[33]

So, on a warm April night, two ex-delegates to the secession convention and a Confederate Army colonel appealed for the votes of former slaves. They talked wistfully of old times while reluctantly acknowledging abolition, but nevertheless wanted to pattern Richmond politics around the mutual duties and habits of command characteristic of the master–slave relationship. Macfarland, a former slaveholder, assured freedmen and freedwomen that 'the rupture of ancient relations' need not spawn feelings of 'unkindness' or party rancour. Emancipation, Macfarland thought, 'has not been a blessing'. The Republican Party had pushed African Americans to the ballot box before educating and uplifting them. Unprepared for the responsibilities of independent citizenship, African Americans ought to follow the lead of their former masters, 'the whites you have known so long and who are your best friends'. In return, white Conservatives promised full employment and decent wages. Employers, another speaker asserted, 'need your labor, and you need no less to be compensated and employed by them, and it is to the advantage of each to be in the interchange of reciprocal kindness'. The speakers saw African Americans as a deferential labouring class whose economic relationship to their potential employers ought to guide them as voters. Only a proper regard for the 'mutual relation' between employers and workers, Sturdivant reminded listeners, would allow the African American to 'eat his own bread' and secure political and 'personal independence'.[34]

Cat-calls greeted these messages. When speakers slandered the Republican Party, anonymous voices defended it and expressed gratitude for Bureau rations. Others asserted African Americans' preparedness for full political participation. 'That's not so!' was heard in response to charges of Union League and Republican Party manipulation of a dependent constituency. Much more was at stake than the merits of Republican Reconstruction. Shouts from the crowd expressed dissatisfaction with a system of political mutualism modelled on slavery and built on the presumption that African Americans would remain labourers forever.

Vocal crowd members expressed notions of citizenship rights that transcended the ballot box and required the reconfiguration of the criminal justice system, public conveyances and accommodation. Voices spoke of a new Richmond with multiracial juries and integrated streetcars. So many questions 'about equality' peppered Sturdivant that one reporter mocked the 'many assailants' for their naiveté.[35] Like race, these different worldviews, forged in slavery and emancipation, separated the speakers from the crowd and Conservatives from Republicans.

Conservative efforts to reach new African-American voters worried local and state Republicans. John Oliver, an African-American carpenter, organized a counter-demonstration on Capitol Square. James Hunnicutt, a Southern-born white minister, attacked former rebels who had given up their political rights. Only fools, he claimed, heeded their advice. The Union League organizer Thomas Conway congratulated Richmond's African Americans who 'had proved themselves too sharp for the speakers [at the Theater]. They always said no when they were expected to say yes, and they said yes when they were expected to say no...' Conway also attacked the slanderers of the Republican Party. Rights and full freedom awaited supporters of the party of Lincoln, for 'you are not "colored" people, but loyal citizens'.[36] Oliver and Conway wanted to create a local Republican Party by uniting newly enfranchised freedmen with uncommitted former Whigs on the basis of principles that crossed racial lines and united Republicans.

Political meetings lent greater precision to local social divisions. Conservatives envisioned a local, non-partisan political system that rested upon notions of reciprocal rights and deference learned under slavery. Republicans used different conceptions of citizenship and rights, slowly forming out of local efforts to rebuild urban political and social structures, to distinguish themselves from Conservatives. This gave political substance to what African-American people already had done in city streets and courts. It also reflected a shrewd attempt to place ideas other than race at the centre of the still-fluid local party identities.

In preparation for the October election, Republicans formed ward committees and sponsored mass rallies. These quickly exposed intellectual and doctrinal divisions. The moderate wing of the city Republican Party rested primarily on former Union Whigs who opposed Johnsonian Reconstruction but denied that Congress held the power to reduce 'a state to the condition of a territory'. Its aim was to build a biracial party with white leadership and a preponderantly African-American electorate.

Local radicals, led by Hunnicutt and the African-American bandleader Lewis Lindsay, supported the right of African Americans to hold political office and backed Confederate disenfranchisement. They further adhered to an expansive understanding of rights, citizenship and political participation that included the freeing of prisoners and the desegregating of streetcars. Though careful not to advocate social equality, they linked civil and political rights and called on municipal government to protect both. They also relied on 'direct participation', which used the mass mobilization of men and women to overwhelm opponents.

The showdown for control among state and city activists occurred simultaneously. In early August 1867 state party officials met in Richmond to heal their differences. As the reconciliation convention neared, the *Dispatch* noted a 'good deal of hard swearing and bitter threatening about the streets'. Hunnicutt and the moderate John Minor Botts sharpened the two groups' doctrinal differences by employing strikingly different tactics to mobilize their followers. The St. Charles Hotel housed Botts and his supporters, from where they floated a caucus platform and a declaration of principles that denounced treason, recognized African-American freedom and promoted free public education, payment of the national debt, internal improvements and an appreciation of labour.

While Botts toiled at the Hotel, Hunnicutt worked on direct participation. Radicals, Hunnicutt in particular, enjoyed a strong following in Richmond. On the eve of the reconciliation convention, Hunnicutt urged his followers to attend *en masse*. A committee representing city radicals circulated a broadside among tobacco workers inviting them to stop work, don their Sunday clothes and attend. Two hours before the convention's scheduled start, thousands of Hunnicutt's followers, city partisans as well as state delegates, packed the African Church. To fill the convention, radicals seated not only tobacco workers but women and children. By so doing, they blurred distinctions between the delegates and spectators and between men and women. African-American women broke precedents by speaking and voting from the floor. By the sheer physical power of their numbers, the radicals prevented most moderates from attending, leaving them to mill around in adjoining streets.[37]

Denied a venue, the moderates gravitated to Capitol Square. Gentlemen 'of various colors, shades, and classes' and a larger group of 'colored women and children' heard Mr Chippley of Montgomery plead for party unity and cooperation. According to Chippley, love of office and power, not ideological disagreements, rent Virginia Republicans. Adherence to Republican principles promised to heal this fissure and enhance the party's strength. As he concluded, radicals, who had adjourned from the African Church, joined their moderate colleagues on the Square. Amid a general degree of confusion, this newly expanded outdoor convention created a committee of business. After a brief recess, the committee returned and endorsed the radical programme. The outdoor convention concurred and adjourned as rain started to fall.

Direct participation angered moderates. Most believed Botts had been muzzled by the mass mobilization of non-delegates, and, as one noted, 'even the women and children had a say in it'.[38] The next day, city and state Republicans reassembled on Capitol Square, hoping to salve wounded feelings. To avoid blurring lines of legitimacy, the party faithful, men and women, declared by voice vote that these proceedings constituted a mass meeting, not an official convention. Hunnicutt invited Botts to speak, declaring the party open to all views. Botts assented. He traced his long, personal opposition to Virginia Democrats and his recent conversion to African-American suffrage. A large part of his speech was aimed at rebuilding the party's foundation around loyalty to the Union rather than radicalism. Any other principle threatened to polarize politics along racial lines and condemn the party to perpetual minority status. He concluded by reading his St. Charles Hotel platform. Others followed but the assembly adjourned without addressing his proposals.[39]

The August Convention proved a seminal moment in the development of the Virginia Republican Party. The subsequent meeting missed an opportunity to expand the party's appeal.[40] Embittered, white moderates fell away. Hunnicutt had secured the triumph of the radical wing among Virginia Republicans primarily upon the strength of his oratory and the power of Richmond's black citizenry. Direct participation suggests some of the truly radical potential in local reconstruction. Women participated alongside men and their voices silenced moderates. In response, the Botts wing condemned radical opponents for encouraging African-American women's activism. Some city African Americans disapproved of this 'mob action'[41] but most looked to Hunnicutt's radicalism as a way to continue their opposition to former Confederates and any hint of a paternal partnership with former masters.

City Republicans next turned their attention to the convention, slated for 14 October, at which they would select Republican nominees to the State Constitutional Convention. The Republican ticket would be placed before the general electorate on 21 October. Shut out of state party leadership, moderates resorted to trying to influence this process by organizing city Republicans in Jefferson, Madison and Monroe wards. City radicals, including Hunnicutt, responded by again using direct participation to retain control. A disheartened *Dispatch* reporter noted that the ward meetings had been 'called by the conservative wing of the Republican party, and if their counsels had prevailed it would have been an orderly assemblage, but the result was another triumph of the Hunnicutt mob.'[42]

Moderates made one further attempt to wrest control of the October convention away from radicals. On 4 October they attended a mass meeting to determine how candidates to the constitutional convention would be nominated. More than 200 men and women attended. They heard radicals and moderates clash not so much on substantive issues as over the proper relationship between citizens and government. Moderates proposed that each ward should send one representative for every 500 registered voters to a nominating committee that would choose the candidates. In this case, voters selected their representatives only indirectly. This procedure carried the endorsement of the party's white congressional leaders.

Irate radicals mockingly referred to it as 'virtual representation'. Burnham Wardwell, an ice merchant and former Unionist, did 'not want a few men with white faces and black hearts to meet and make nominations. Our party in this city has started, and to attempt to stop it would be as useless as to try to dam up the James River or to stop a command of God.' An orderly selection process was unacceptable to Hunnicutt if it forced radicals to 'bend the knee to anyone but my God...' In one sense the radicals' arguments served their own best interests. They knew their control over city and state affairs rested on the power of mass mobilization. The August Convention and the Jefferson ward meeting had confirmed this, and, according to one, they did 'not intend to be gagged by a resolution gotten up by a small dinner and table party...' But the principle of direct participation appealed to a broad constituency because it fitted well with what African Americans already had accomplished on the streets and in mass meetings. In short, direct participation not only gave radicals a tactical advantage over moderates but represented the approach favoured by the radicals' most likely supporters.

After long debate, the assembly agreed that '[e]very citizen shall have a direct participation in the affairs of State and in the determination of all measures and questions calculated to affect the public weal as may be compatible with their practical execution.' Pursuant to these sentiments, it charged ward canvassers to poll Republican voters and to compile a list of potential delegates to place before the 14 October city convention.[43]

Less than one week before this event, the ward canvassers reported their findings. Each of the three wards sent at least two moderates to the convention, but the overwhelming majority of the delegates supported Hunnicutt. Thanks to direct participation, African-American women voted in at least two wards and so helped to secure the election of at least one Hunnicutt candidate. The criteria used to select delegates remain obscure but it would seem that Republicans looked to literate men of mixed racial heritage who had been free before the war.[44] Among the city leaders were those who connected radical Republicanism with local efforts to promote civil and political equality. Delegate John Fitchett, a white grocer, supported the confiscation of rebel estates and preferred to 'eat at the black man's table than at a rebel's...' Moses Taylor, an African-American wagon driver from Jefferson ward, attributed his support of radical Republicanism to his arrest 'for nothing' but standin' on the streets'. He vowed in his acceptance speech that he would not 'be saddled and bridled and rode in the Convention by no man'.[45]

The October 1867 convention, held in the city's African Church, opened in a festive air. Tobacco factories had shut down since 'employees have notified their employers that they will not work'. Inside the convention hall, Radical ward representatives presented their candidates and voting proceeded without further discussion. Moderates protested strenuously to no avail. Dr Sterling of Jefferson ward bellowed above the din '[t]he gagging has commenced. I solemnly protest against this.' Over Sterling's objections, city Republicans chose the well-known radicals Hunnicutt, Judge John Underwood, James Morrissey, Joseph Cox and Lewis Lindsay.[46] The Republicans staked their appeal firmly on the city's Radical contingent. Celebrations by Hunnicutt's supporters lasted until midnight.

By the 21 October election, Richmond's Republican Party had established ward-level branches, taken on a radical bent and created locally-based networks of communications and mobilization. The ascendancy of local radicals carried important implications for the party's ability to create a broadly-based, biracial coalition. It also led Conservative leaders to view the 1867 election with complacency.

By comparison, the Republicans' opponents lacked anything approaching a party organization. Belief in white racial supremacy and a hatred of African-American suffrage and Federal Reconstruction had united this loose band of self-proclaimed Conservatives.[47] Instead of taking steps to match the Republicans' organizational drive, they fell back upon the informal political style of antebellum local politics to select nominees. They avoided rallies and ward-level canvassing, for 'there was not time to hold a public meeting'. Instead they held an informal 'conference and consultation with a number of the citizens of Richmond' that produced a Conservative slate which included Marmaduke Johnson and N.A. Sturdivant, who had been among those who had spoken to African-American voters in April.[48]

Growing Racial Polarization

A new era in Richmond's electoral politics dawned on 22 October 1867. Local police and 1,500 Federal soldiers watched as African Americans cast their first ballots for political office. Ninety-six per cent of registered whites and 86 per cent of registered African Americans turned out at the polls. Both whites and blacks exhibited a marked degree of racial and political solidarity. Radicals carried the city by 406 votes but counted few white supporters. Republicans won the ballots of 99 per cent of African-American voters and 1 per cent of white ones. All but 11 (0.3 per cent) African Americans favoured calling a constitutional convention, while 97 per cent of whites opposed it. Conservatives immediately challenged the returns but the results stood. Five Republicans, including two African Americans, would represent the former capital of the Confederacy when the constitutional convention opened.[49]

As delegates gathered for the Constitutional Convention, Conservative political organizers made plans for another convention slated for 11 December. Without 'a general and thorough organization of the Conservatives of the State', one feared, 'Conservatives will be as badly beaten in their next contest with Radicalism as they were in the last.' Richmond ought to spearhead the movement since 'here two weeks ago was fought a gallant, though unequal, contest between civilization and barbarism – between white people and HUNNICUTT negroes…' Cognizant of anti-party sentiments, organizers assured Virginians that Conservatives gathered 'without any intention to dictate to them'. The election had established that white racial consciousness had bridged older political divisions among whites. Richmond Conservatives saw no reason to let it lapse. Those 'in favor of a white man's party' needed to register to vote and support the Conservative convention. Otherwise, wrote one, Virginia might become the next 'Hayti'.[50]

Local notables, including many former councilmen and city officers, scurried about the city. Patriotic addresses given to 'the most respectable citizens' were delivered in each ward. On 15 November former Democrats and Whigs joined in carefully orchestrated ward meetings to select delegates to the Conservative convention. According to the local press, order and unity prevailed. Except for denunciations of radicalism, speakers carefully avoided substantive issues in case they opened up old political wounds. Nomination committees chose men with political experience. This included William Macfarland, N.A. Sturdivant, Marmaduke Johnson and R.T. Daniel, whose efforts to create a partnership between white politicians and African-American voters had been rejected in April. Now they turned to partisanship rather than paternalism to preserve local white political supremacy.[51]

The Conservatives' December Convention closely resembled earlier gatherings in city wards. Delegates worked feverishly to perfect the party's 'completeness and efficiency' and hammered out a rudimentary platform to clarify the relevance of the new Conservative creed. The party formally acknowledged the abolition of slavery and accepted military defeat. This admission meant Reconstruction had worked successfully in Virginia, that the state ought to be restored to the Union and that 'the people of Virginia' ought to receive 'all the rights of freedom'. The platform silently accepted African-American voting rights but firmly opposed African-American office holding, which endangered 'civilization...[and] the fundamental ideas of Government and of civil liberty'. Enslavement, Conservatives believed, had not prepared blacks for governance. Governments 'were formed by white men to be subject to their control; and the suffrage should still be so regulated by the States, as to continue the Federal and State systems under the control and direction of the white race.' Conservatives left the convention pledged to reconstruct the Union and to defend white racial supremacy.[52]

Conservatives in Richmond longed for the full restoration of the state in order to gain control over the local political process. As long as Virginia remained under Federal control, military authorities appointed councilmen and elections for city council were suspended. Under this system, Republicans held a majority of the council seats between 1868 and 1870. Popular support for radical Reconstruction began to sag among some Northerners, and Congress increasingly turned the running of local affairs over to Southern voters. In Virginia, Conservatives gained control over the state government in 1869 and scheduled elections in Richmond, the first since 1866, for May 1870.

Conservatives and Republicans looked to the May elections as referenda on their platforms and a test for future urban supremacy. Since fewer than 200 votes separated Republicans and Conservatives, neither wanted the contests for city officers and council to slip back into the antebellum style of unorganized mobilization. Each relied on elaborate organizational networks rather than informal appeals and the pressure of civic duty to mobilize their respective followers. By doing so they made partisan politics an integral part of elections for not only for state offices but local ones too. Richmond Republicans faced the 1870 elections internally divided over strategy. Moderates wanted to isolate well-known radicals in order to lure back white voters. In Richmond this strategy produced significant changes. Hunnicutt moderated his policies in an unsuccessful effort to curry favour among state leaders. City radicals angrily called Hunnicutt a traitor and turned against him. Indeed, after 1869 Hunnicutt had few Republican supporters and soon left Virginia altogether. The moderate local party chairman, James Humphreys, instituted new party rules that further weakened the control of radicals within the city. In 1869 and 1870 he attacked direct participation, the radicals' primary source of power, by counting only those decisions reached by secret ballot, thus rejecting votes cast by 'rising and sitting'. This effectively limited the radicals' power. Delegates to the city's convention tended to be moderates who pushed for the nomination of an all-white slate. Outraged, radical African Americans assailed the tacit endorsement of Conservatives that only white men ought to hold political power, but to no avail. After a long debate, the convention nominated an all white ticket.[53] Candidates pledged themselves to the immediate enforcement of the Fourteenth and the Fifteenth Amendment, a system of free public education, universal amnesty for Confederate veterans subject to congressional approval, state-financed internal improvements and the 'honest and full enforcement of our new State Constitution in letter and in spirit'.[54] Though moderate in tone, the city platform asked voters to support a distinct image of good government and specific public policies. Republican nominees advocated an activist government, the promotion of education and economic development and the protection of citizenship and voting rights. These proposals generally fell under the purview of state and national governments, but they established an important tone in an era when city government controlled local police, markets and taxes, and when local courts played a seminal role in establishing racial boundaries and defining civil and political rights.

Conservative organizers faced challenges similar to those of Republicans. Ward-based council elections, the first since 1866, promised to be close and hotly contested. Conservatives assumed white voters' support at great hazard. A campaign waged by the Conservative press and ward leaders linked Conservative Party membership to a transethnic, white racial identity and a defence of patriarchal privilege, ultimately fusing the Conservative coalition together.

In rhetoric and substance, Conservative candidates presented Richmond with a clear alternative to Republicans and the city contest in 1870 confirmed the clarity and relevance of Conservative and Republican affiliations for the mass of voters. Republicans who defended African-

American political rights battled Conservatives who advanced white racial supremacy. Both Republicans and Conservatives envisioned an activist government. But Republicans looked to state and national governments as agents of social reform, rights protection and economic development, while Conservatives wanted lawmakers to concentrate solely on urban industrial and commercial progress. In short, Conservatives and Republicans offered city voters two fairly distinct visions of civil society, rights, the urban social structure and the proper roles of city government and courts.

On election day, 26 May 1870, 86 per cent of registered voters went to the polls. Conservatives swept every city office. Most won by between 122 and 172 votes, though two races were decided by fewer than 35 votes. Conservative candidate for Mayor Henry Ellyson squeaked by Republican George Chahoon by 39 votes, and Conservative T. Boldemann became Commissioner of Revenue by a margin of only 33. Council contests were even closer. Led by Horace Kent, Republicans claimed all five council seats in Monroe ward and W.A. Boswell of Marshall ward won the only other Republican seat. Conservative candidates won the remaining 19 council positions, securing a three-to-one majority in city hall. The elections signalled a significant shift in urban political culture. To win local offices, Republican and Conservative political organizers had persuaded city voters to transfer their personal attitudes about race, emancipation and Reconstruction to abstract party institutions.

Substantial evidence suggests that violence and fraud tainted the Conservative victory. City police looked on as an unknown assailant stole ballots which voters in a Jefferson ward precinct had cast for Republicans. The *Dispatch* scoffed at charges of fraud. Ellyson, its editor, welcomed an investigation which would assuredly 'prove the most astonishing frauds on the part of the Radicals', thereby increasing Conservatives' victory margins.

Local and state courts, however, robbed Ellyson of quick vindication. On 20 July 1870 Judge Guigon of the Hustings Court declared all city offices, excepting council, vacant. Temporary appointees filled in until voters elected their replacements on 8 November. The Virginia State Supreme Court validated Guigon's actions. Honour prevented Ellyson from seeking the mayoralty under what looked like dubious circumstances. The city Conservative committee selected A.M. Keiley, Ellyson's opponent in the spring primary, to head its ticket. On election day, Keiley defeated George W. Smith, his Republican challenger, winning 51 per cent of the vote and thereby insuring Conservative dominance over future police and judicial appointments.[55]

Conservatives cheered their victories. But the tallies had been closer than expected. Margins of victory for Conservatives varied greatly by ward, ranging from a majority of six in Marshall ward to 251 in Jefferson. As the party now in power, Conservatives faced the difficult task of governing and holding their diverse coalition together. Decisions concerning taxation, market square regulation, railroads' usage of city streets, poor relief and the city debt awaited Conservative lawmakers. Not all white voters stood to benefit equally from the outcomes. Well-informed political organizers recognized the danger this presented to urban Conservatives. The party was in its infancy and partisan loyalties and identities remained fluid despite the powerful allure of white racial supremacy.

To stabilize their grip on city council, Conservative councilmen redrew the city's ward boundaries. They gerrymandered the great majority of African Americans and Republican voters into one ward. Jackson ward, created on 21 April 1871, contained approximately four times as many African-American voters as any other. This further undercut radical Republicans' chief electoral strategy, which had been the use of mass numbers of men and women to gain control over ward-level meetings. Gerrymandering made that tactic both difficult and impracticable to employ. It also disrupted moderate Republicans' nascent party networks, confining their strength to one ward. Twenty-seven per cent of all Republican voters lived in Jackson ward in 1874, and by 1876 the proportion had increased to 31 per cent. By using new partisan organizations built around racial consciousness and a distinct vision of government Conservatives had secured control over the city council and the Mayor's office, positions they would continue to dominate until the late 1880s.[56]

Conclusions

The emergence of partisan, electoral politics thus resulted from a truly remarkable series of events peculiar to an urban polity but which involved cultural adjustments common to the region. The military defeat of the Confederacy forced Southerners to undertake the previously unimaginable and reconstruct their society and polity without slavery. The abolition of old forms of submission and loyalty touched off a wide-ranging debate over what, if any, changes freedom would bring. Ex-slaves wanted a new political system cleansed of racial and class inequality, while their former masters desired a public sphere patterned closely upon older traditions of deference and hierarchy. Conflicting expectations concerning rights and citizenship first surfaced on city streets and in local courts, as Sally Anderson's case attests. Suffrage reform in 1867 intensified these struggles by removing race restrictions on male voting rights. When African-American voters rejected paternalism as the foundation of urban politics, partisanship and race became the central tools of political mobilization and organization.[57]

Political unrest in Richmond was part of a complex process involving the expansion of free labour. As productive relations changed throughout the Atlantic world, struggles over authority and labour discipline became serious political issues. Freed people in America and the British Caribbean reasserted customary rights, first established under slavery, to provision grounds, housing and medical care. Whatever else freedom meant, it disavowed 'a diminution of either the privileges or level of income [freedmen] had enjoyed as slaves'. This contest involved processes that unfolded differently in the American South and the British Caribbean. The United States was the only place in the whole of the Americas where former slaves demanded and won formal political rights that turned the polity at once into a battleground over the meaning of freedom. But although African Americans possessed unique political powers, they fared little better economically than their Caribbean counterparts. Former masters throughout the Atlantic world used vagrancy statutes, lien laws and tax policies that effectively chained dependent work forces to the land.[58]

Despite similar answers to the labour question in the United States and the British Caribbean, historians have emphasized the unique political experiences of American freed people.[59] But some telling similarities arise once post-emancipation unrest in the British Caribbean is compared to that occurring in the American South between 1865 and 1867, when African Americans struggled without formal rights. Riots in Dominica (1844), Guyana (1856), Saint Vincent (1862), Jamaica (1865), Barbados (1876) and Tobago (1876) involved issues of work and power rooted in slavery and long-simmering dissatisfaction with the local economy.[60] These disturbances erupted as well from the intimate connection between economic and political power and a desire to break from the heritage of slavery. In Richmond, Saint Vincent, Morant Bay and Guyana ex-slaves rescued prisoners whose alleged crimes violated official but not communal norms. The immediate goal of thwarting local constables assumed deeper meaning in a post-emancipation context. Such anti-authoritarian militancy challenged, at least in part, the violence and arbitrary discipline that had been at the heart of slavery. Rescuers attempted to subvert power relations associated with slavery by asserting a collective claim to equal treatment at the hands of criminal justice systems dominated locally by landlords and employers. Post-emancipation militancy by ex-slaves clearly defended customary economic privileges but expressed equally important longings for rights that broke with ideas forged in slavery.

Throughout the Atlantic world, ex-slaves without voting rights acted as if they possessed citizenship rights that had been earned collectively by years of unfree labour. Of course, the substance of these rights varied across time and space and reflected the specific political culture in which freed people lived. Despite some fundamental differences, ex-slaves used public spaces rather than electoral politics as their forums to assert their freedom. Freed people who rescued alleged criminals from the police, marched in communal celebration or in protest of judicial decisions, called for equality before the law, or demanded better wages, benefits and work conditions in ways that they thought their newly-won freedom entitled them to do.

NOTES

1. Mayor's Court, *Dispatch*, 12, 15, 25, 31 December 1868.
2. Proslavery ideas linked diverse communities and social groups in a common cause and gave the region the appearance of consensus despite deep fissures over the economy and government. Quotation from Stephanie McCurry, 'The Two Faces of Republicanism: Gender and Proslavery Politics in Antebellum South Carolina', *Journal of American History*, 78 (March 1992), pp.1245–64. See also James Oakes, *Slavery and Freedom* (New York, NY: Knopf, 1990) and Oakes, *The Ruling Race* (New York, NY: Knopf, 1982), William Stanton, *The Leopard's Spots: Scientific Attitudes toward Race in America, 1815–59* (Chicago, IL: University of Chicago Press, 1960), David Roediger, *The Wages of Whiteness* (New York, NY: Verso, 1991). My intellectual debt to Barbara Jeanne Fields is tremendous. See especially *Slavery and Freedom on the Middle Ground* (New Haven, CT: Yale University Press, 1985), Ch.6 and 7.
3. On this point see C.V. Woodward, *Origins of the New South, 1877–1913* (Baton Rogue, LA: Louisiana State University Press, 1951); James Tice Moore, 'Redeemers reconsidered: Change and continuity in the Democratic South, 1870–1900', *Journal of Southern History*, 44 (Aug.1978), pp.357–78. Efforts across the South to recreate Jacksonian political alliances and forms collapsed under the weight of Reconstruction. Race, finances and Congressional reforms split Southern voters. The Republican Party of Lincoln competed with Conservative-Democrats, vying for the allegiance of former slaves and secessionists. Michael Perman and Daniel Crofts have shown how each faction relied on sophisticated local and state party mechanisms to mobilize support and present their messages. Michael Perman, *The Road to Redemption: Southern Politics, 1869–1879* (Chapel Hill, NC: University of North Carolina Press, 1984); Daniel Crofts, *Old Southampton: Politics and Society in a Virginia County, 1834–1869* (Charlottesville, VA: University Press of Virginia, 1992); James Tice Moore, *Two Paths to the New South: The Virginia Debt Controversy, 1870–1883* (Lexington, KY: The University Press of Kentucky, 1974); J. Mills Thornton, 'Fiscal policy and the failure of Radical Reconstruction in the lower South', in J. Morgan Kousser and James McPherson (eds.), *Region, Race, and Reconstruction* (New York, NY: Oxford University Press, 1982), pp.349–94.
4. Daniel Crofts, *Reluctant Confederates: Upper South Unionists in the Secession Crisis* (Chapel Hill, NC: University of North Carolina Press, 1989), pp.47–8. Most antebellum localities, according to Daniel Crofts, 'were not politically competitive', for 'southerners voted more as members of a community than as individuals'. Aspirants for local office, usually prominent merchants, industrialists and financiers, organized informal, non-partisan campaigns and used familiar, uncontroversial themes. See Lacy K. Ford, *Origins of Southern Radicalism: The South Carolina Upcountry, 1800–1860* (Oxford, NY: Oxford University Press, 1988); J. Mills Thornton, *Politics and Power in a Slave Society: Alabama, 1800–1860* (Baton Rogue, LA: Louisiana State University Press, 1978); George Rable, *The Confederate Republic: A Revolution against Politics* (Chapel Hill, NC: University of North Carolina Press, 1994). Ronald Formisano, *The Transformation of Political Culture: Massachusetts Parties, 1790s–1840s* (New York, NY: Oxford University Press, 1983).
5. Michael Chesson, *Richmond after the War* (Richmond, VA: Virginia State Library, 1981), p.88; Richard Lowe, *Republicans and Reconstruction in Virginia, 1856–1870*

(Charlottesville, VA: University Press of Virginia, 1991), Ch.1–2, pp.17–25 especially.

6. George Waring, *Report on the Social Statistics of Cities* (Washington, DC: Government Printing Office, 1867), p.79. *A Compendium of the Ninth Census* (Washington, DC, 1872), pp.472–3; Chesson, *Richmond after the War*, pp.117–21.

7. Chesson, *Richmond after the War*, quotation from p.138; see also pp.133–8. To chart the development of class tensions in Richmond see Peter Rachleff, *Black Labor in Richmond, 1865–1890* (Urbana, IL: University of Illinois Press, 1989).

8. Lowe, *Republicans and Reconstruction in Virginia*, p.33; Chesson, *Richmond after the War*, pp.90–1; John O'Brien, 'From Bondage to Citizenship: The Richmond Black Community, 1865–1867', (PhD dissertation, University of Rochester, 1975), pp.154–60, *City Council Minutes*, 7 June, 27 July 1865 [hereafter *CCM*]. Army officials required all African Americans to carry employment passes endorsed by 'respectable whites', imposed a 9:00 pm curfew on African Americans and excluded them from receiving Army rations lest they fall into vagrancy and sloth. Attempts to overawe and intimidate freedmen and freedwomen in Richmond epitomized much broader, often violent, efforts across the South by the former master class as it struggled to come to grips with emancipation.

9. *New York Tribune*, 12 June 1865; Elsa Barkley Brown, 'Negotiating and transforming the public sphere: African-American political life in the transition from slavery to freedom', *Public Culture* (Fall 1994), pp.6–8; O'Brien, 'From Bondage to Citizenship', pp.172–85.

10. Letter from Chase, 11 June 1865; Records of the Assistant Commissioner for the State of Virginia, Bureau of refugees, Freedmen, and Abandoned Lands, 1865–1869, Record Group 105, M 1048, Reel 40, National Archives, Washington, DC [hereafter Records of the Assistant Commissioner].

11. Letter from J.S. Fullerton, 15 June 1865; Records of the Assistant Commissioner, Reel 36; Chesson, *Richmond after the War*, pp.90–3; O'Brien, 'From Bondage to Citizenship', pp.180–2.

12. Lowe, *Republicans and Reconstruction in Virginia*, Ch.3.

13. *CCM*, 13 Feb. 1865, Library of Virginia (hereafter LV).

14. Ibid., 27 July 1865; Chesson, *Richmond after the War*, pp.92–3; O'Brien, 'From Bondage to Citizenship', pp.283–90.

15. O'Brien, 'From Bondage to Citizenship', p.288.

16. Special Order No. 12 in *CCM*, 29 July 1865. The victors, according to General Terry, the military commander of the city, embodied 'the feelings of disloyalty that prevail here'. See O'Brien, 'From Bondage to Citizenship', p.287.

17. *CCM*, 23 Aug.1865.

18. Turner secured the resignation of Sturdivant and the Superintendent of the Poor, C.P. Bigger.

19. *Dispatch*, 13, 16 Feb.; 1, 12, 15, 17, 22, 26, 27, 28 March 1866; *CCM*, 31 Oct.; 8 Nov. 1866; 8 Dec. 1866; 29 Jan.; 12, 19, 26 Feb.; 29 March; 7 April 1866.

20. Enslaved African Americans had been excluded from parks and public squares and had to carry signed passes while on public streets and yield city sidewalks to oncoming whites. Executions carried out on Capitol Square and the whipping post used civic space and public punishments to frighten and control African Americans. To be sure, hidden transcripts often bubbled beneath the intended purposes. None the less, antebellum white Richmonders spent tremendous amounts of time and money trying to limit and control the use of public space.

21. O'Brien, 'From Bondage to Citizenship', pp.323–8.

22. My thinking here has been influenced by Mona Ozouf, *Festivals and the French Revolution* (Cambridge, MA: Harvard University Press, 1988); John Bodnar, *Remaking America: Public Memory, Commemoration, and Patriotism in the Twentieth Century* (Princeton, NJ: Princeton University Press, 1992); Susan G. Davis, *Parades and Power: Street Theater in Nineteenth Century Philadelphia* (Philadelphia, PA: Temple University Press, 1986); Clifford Geertz, *The Interpretation of Cultures* (New York, NY: Basic Books, 1973); Anthony Giddens, *The Constitution of Society* (Berkeley, CA: University of California Press, 1987).

23. *Dispatch*, 30 March 1866; *Dispatch*, 26 March 1866; O'Brien, 'From Bondage to Citizenship', pp.334–7. On 3 April the *Dispatch* wrote, 'is indeed no time for rejoicing of anybody here. It was a day of gloom and calamity to be remembered with a shudder....[T]he emancipation of

the negroes is not a matter of rejoicing to their late masters.' The *Whig* and the *Examiner* darkly warned African Americans that economic reprisals surely awaited the celebrants.

24. *Dispatch*, 9 April 1866.
25. Ibid., 9 April 1866, 4 April 1867. Quotation from the Revd Randolph.
26. See Elsa Barkley Brown and Gregg Kimball, 'Mapping the terrain of black Richmond', *Journal of Urban History*, 21, 3 (March 1995), pp.296–346. Quotation on p.309.
27. On this point see especially, *Dispatch*, 23 Oct.1867.
28. *Dispatch*, 10 May 1867; Letter from Benjamin Cook to Paul Hambrick, 29 May 1867; Records of the Assistant Commissioner, Reel 47; Chesson, *Richmond after the War*, pp.61–2.
29. *Dispatch*, 16 May 1867; 31 July 1866. City police remained under the Mayor's control, an office held by Joseph Mayo until May 1868 and they continued to arrest African Americans in disproportionate numbers and on charges from which white men and women were exempted, such as being 'suspicious characters'.
30. On this point see Brown, 'Negotiating and transforming'. Eric Foner, *Reconstruction: America's Unfinished Revolution, 1863–1877* (New York, NY: Harper and Row, 1988).
31. Lowe, *Republicans and Reconstruction in Virginia*, pp.73–4; Perman, *The Road to Redemption*.
32. *Dispatch*, 26 Jan.; 3, 16 Feb.; 10 Oct.; 29 Nov. 1866; 7 Jan.; 1, 18 March 1867.
33. Ibid., 15 April 1867.
34. Ibid., 16 April 1867.
35. Ibid.
36. Ibid., 18–19 April 1867.
37. Ibid., 31 July; 1, 2, 3 Aug. 1867; see also Brown, 'Negotiating and transforming', pp.1–40; Rachleff, *Black Labor in Richmond*.
38. *Dispatch*, 2 Aug.1867.
39. Ibid., 3 Aug. 1867.
40. Lowe, *Republicans and Reconstruction in Virginia*, p.95.
41. See for example Fields Cook's lament in the *Dispatch*, 3 Aug. 1867.
42. Ibid., 1 Oct. 1867.
43. Ibid., 5 Oct. 1867. Chesson *Richmond after the* War, pp.110–11. Wardwell, who became increasingly moderate throughout the 1860s, served a brief stint as superintendent of the Virginia penitentiary. In 1870 he left Richmond amid charges of corruption and settled in New Jersey.
44. Richard Lowe, 'The Freedmen's Bureau and Local Black Leadership', *Journal of American History*, 80, 3 (Dec. 1993), pp.993–5.
45. *Dispatch,* 9 Oct. 1867.
46. Ibid., 14, 15, 18 Oct.1867; see also Richard Hume, 'The membership of the Virginia Constitutional Convention of 1867–1868: A study of the beginnings of Congressional reconstruction in the upper South', *Virginia Magazine of History and Biography*, 86 (Oct. 1978), pp.461–84.
47. See G.A. Myers to Conway Robinson, 23 Aug. 1867; Conway Robinson papers, Virginia Historical Society [VHS]; Wyndham Robertson to Conway Robinson, 7 March 1868; Conway Robinson papers, VHS; R. [?]olmond to John Woolfolk, 7 Nov. 1867; Woolfolk family papers, VHS.
48. *Dispatch*, 16 Oct. 1867.
49. Ibid., 22–27 Oct. 1867; see also William Kennedy papers, VHS.
50. *Dispatch*, 3, 6, 8, 15 Nov.; 7 Dec.1867.
51. Ibid., 16, 22, 26 Nov.; 2, 12, 12–13 Dec.1867.
52. See ibid., 12–13 Dec. 1867.
53. Ibid., 23 May 1870; Rachleff, *Black Labor in Richmond*, pp.50–1; Chesson, *Richmond after the* War, pp.110–11.
54. *Dispatch*, 23 April; 23, 24 May 1870.
55. *Dispatch*, 31 May; 21 July; 3 Aug.; 8, 10 Nov. 1870; *Chahoon v. The Commonwealth*, Virginia Reports, Annotated, Grattan 21, 1871, pp.1036–44; *The Richmond Mayoralty Case*, Virginia Reports, Annotated, Grattan 19, 1870, pp.245–60.
56. *CCM*, 21 April 1871; Michael Chesson, 'Richmond's Black Councilmen, 1871–1896', in

Howard Rabinowitz (ed.), *Southern Black Leaders of the Reconstruction Era* (Chicago, IL: University of Illinois Press, 1982), pp.198–200. On the challenges of the 1880s see Rachleff, *Black Labor in Richmond*, Ch. 9 and 10.

57. These patterns of change touch some of the core historiographic themes concerning nineteenth-century politics and Reconstruction. The 1840s witnessed the emergence of what Silbey termed a new 'American political nation' marked by disciplined political parties, professional politicians and mass participation. This system of mass politics showcased significant ideological, ethnoculutral and economic differences among voters. Local Southern politics remained curiously immune to this trend until emancipation and Congressional Reconstruction jolted and ultimately destroyed the traditional, consensual, elite-dominated political order. In short, local Southern politics became part of the American political nation along regionally distinct routes. This analysis, however, explicitly challenges Silbey's much broader argument that continuity characterized politics from 1838 to 1893. Mass two-party conflicts over local offices in Richmond broke sharply with established patterns and expectations. Descriptions of a distinct 'party period' simply cannot account for the different campaign styles, political ideas and institutions that developed between 1865 and 1870. McCormick, in a highly influential article, described a distinct 'party period' in which 'parties dominated political participation an channeled the flow of government policies'. This coherent 'era in American political history' lasted from the 1830s to the early 1900s and was defined by the distributive economic policies that wedded voters to the major parties. This characterization of both politics and government breaks down at the local level, where government activism occurred most frequently in the nineteenth century. See Joel Silbey, *The American Political Nation* (Stanford, CA: University of California Press, 1991); and Richard McCormick, 'The party period and public policy: an exploratory hypothesis', *Journal of American History*, 66 (Sept. 1979), pp.279–98. The themes of continuity and discontinuity loom large in Southern history, and debates among scholars grind on inconclusively. My own preference sidesteps this debate by tracing the transformation of Southern lives during the emancipation era. More than a semantic shellgame, emphasis upon transformation places equal emphasis upon continuity and discontinuity by asking what changed, for whom, and in what direction? This line of inquiry promises to yield sharper images of social and political developments over time. For a succinct overview of this debate in Southern historiography see Moore, 'Redeemers reconsidered', pp.357–78.

58. Eric Foner, *Nothing but Freedom: Emancipation and Its Legacy* (Baton Rouge, LA: Louisiana State University Press, 1983), pp.46–73; quotation p.57. See as well Dale Tomich, 'Contested terrains: houses, provision grounds, and the reconstitution of labour in post-emancipation Martinique', in *From Chattel Slaves to Wage Slaves: The Dynamics of Labour Bargaining in the Americas*, ed. Mary Turner (Bloomington, IN: Indiana University Press, 1995), pp.241–57. Gad Heuman, 'Post-emancipation protest in Jamaica: the Morant Bay rebellion, 1865', in Turner (ed.), *From Chattel Slaves to Wage Slaves*, pp.258–74. O. Nigel Bolland, 'The Politics of Freedom in the British Caribbean', in Seymour Drescher and Frank McGlynn (eds.), *The Meaning of Freedom: Economics, Politics, and Culture After Slavery* (Pittsburgh, PA: University of Pittsburgh Press, 1992), pp.113–46.

59. Foner, *Nothing but Freedom*, pp.45–6.

60. Russell E. Chace, 'Protest in post-emancipation Dominica: the "Guerre Negre" of 1844', *Journal of Caribbean History*, 23, 2 (1989), pp.118–41; Woodville Marshall, '"Vox populi": the St. Vincent riots and disturbances of 1862', in Barry W. Higman '(ed.), *Trade, Government and Society in Caribbean History: Essays Presented to Douglas Hall* (Kingston, Heinemann, 1983), pp.85–115; Michael Craton, 'Continuity and change: the incidence of unrest among ex-slaves in the British West Indies, 1838–1876', *Slavery and Abolition*, 9, 2 (1988), pp.144–70; Heuman, 'Post-emancipation protest in Jamaica', in Turner (ed.), *From Chattel Slaves to Wage Slaves*; Bridget Brereton, 'Post-emancipation protest in the Caribbean: the "Belmana Riots" in Tobago, 1876', *Caribbean Quarterly*, 5, 30 (1984); Foner, *Nothing but Freedom*; Peter Rachleff, *Black Labor in the South: Richmond, Virginia, 1865–1890* (Urbana: University of Illinois Press, 1989); Eric Arnesen, *Waterfront Workers of New Orleans: Race, Class, and Politics, 1863–1923* (New York, NY: Oxford University Press, 1991).

Fifty Years of Freedom:
The Memory of Emancipation at the
Civil War Semicentennial, 1911–15

DAVID W. BLIGHT

Everyone who now studies the relationship between history and memory in a serious, critical way does so, I suspect, because of the *politics* of memory. Social history, it might also be said, has led us to social memory. But we are also drawn because the study of memory allows us a new kind of access to that old problem of 'presentism' (to revive one of David Hackett Fischer's 'fallacies'). Suppress it as we will, somebody's 'present' hovers over every problem in the study of memory. How cultures and groups use, construct or try to own the past in order to win power or place in the present is why memory studies matter. The process by which societies decide how and when to remember and forget is 'always dangerous', as Friedrich Nietzsche reminds us in 'The Use and Abuse of History'. 'The same life that needs forgetfulness', wrote Nietzsche, 'needs sometimes its destruction; for should the injustice of something ever become obvious ... the thing deserves to fall. Its past is critically examined, the knife put to its roots, and all the "pieties" are grimly trodden under foot'.[1] What Nietzsche describes is the inherently political character of conflicts over the uses of the past, whether they result from the critical, interpretive work of historians or the public controversies we have been experiencing in museums. Serious confrontations with the past – facing down the pieties – is 'always dangerous'. Precisely because of this political danger we need studies of memory that are rooted in good research, sensitive to deep contexts and to the varieties of memory at play in any given situation. We need studies that search for the ways collective memories have evolved into the forms they take in any context. Certainly, fiftieth anniversaries of major events, as we have recently learned in our own time (with all the commemorations related to World War II and the Holocaust), provide good laboratories for investigation.

The process of how societies or nations remember collectively itself has a history. Popular versions of the past which truly take hold as deep myths or, as Eric Hobsbawm has effectively termed them, 'invented traditions', exist in all societies. The most lasting and tenacious of those traditions, as

Hobsbawm has argued, tend to become ritualized practices and interpretations 'which clearly meet a felt – not necessarily a clearly understood – need among particular bodies of people'. Invented traditions are eminently manipulable from one context to another. 'They have to be discovered before being exploited and shaped', argues Hobsbawm. 'It is the historian's business to discover them retrospectively – but also to try to understand why, in terms of changing societies in changing historical situations, such needs came to be felt.'[2]

In America, in western Europe, in much of Africa and elsewhere, we seem to be living in a time when public struggles over the content and meaning of the past have important political stakes. It is as though we are living, once again, through one of those eras when old certainties have dissolved and many of the institutions, empires or ideologies that had defined much of the geopolitics of the world have collapsed into a new order/disorder, the outlines of which we only dimly see or control. The growing American pluralism (which we have renamed multiculturalism) inspires many of us, and frightens others into retreats or attacks. At the end of this century, and the millennium, the question of what stories are welcome in the national narrative is a deeply contested one, as is the question of whether there is a national, master narrative at all. Melancholia and anxiety are, and perhaps always have been, the underside of great and exciting change. The end of the Cold War and all that has flowed from this epochal shift have tended to take our mass culture on what seems a rudderless journey into nostalgia, a search for lost crises, lost civic unity, lost causes, lost heroes, lost apologies, cultural introspection and retrospection. In the United States we have been debating whether the President should 'apologize' to African Americans for slavery, as if in this age of instant communication and internet knowledge we can set the past right by an announcement. Well-meaning in some quarters, the discussion of the apology for slavery has tended to be facile retrospection without having to engage any real history.[3] The discussion is full of 'felt needs', in Hobsbawm's terms, but the only invented tradition that may emerge from this particular public process may be the old American tendency to deny or avoid serious confrontations with the past. Many Americans, frankly, would simply like to see an end to the discussion of slavery and its legacies.

Commemorating the Civil War

This essay is an exploratory look at the semicentennial of the Civil War and emancipation in the period 1911–15. It has three primary aims: one, to suggest the varieties of memory of the Civil War and emancipation at play in the fiftieth anniversary period, among whites and blacks; two, to demonstrate how the American reunion was by 1913 the result of a segregated American memory, how the two commemorations – the war and emancipation – overlapped and did not overlap, how they were happening in the same time, but did not fit the same spaces; and three, to show how slavery, the Civil War and emancipation were by 1913, and perhaps still are, America's unmastered past. Elsewhere I have written about the fiftieth anniversary reunion of the Battle of Gettysburg and about the forging of a national consensus of reconciliation through the mutual valour of Union and Confederate veterans.[4] Here I address the memory of emancipation, of race as well as reunion at the semicentennial.

In 1961 John Hope Franklin delivered an address to the Association for the Study of Negro Life and History on the varieties of Civil War commemoration. Disturbed by the racism practised in the national centennial just under way – what he called a 'national circus' – Franklin reflected on the persistent American tendency to drum the Civil War into a 'common unifying experience'. Franklin analysed the fiftieth anniversary as a time when the nation collectively found it 'convenient' to acknowledge the death of slavery, but forget the rise of white supremacy. Franklin observed the irony that a magazine editor in 1911 could rejoice that President William Howard Taft and Robert Lincoln (the President's son) could play a round of golf at Augusta, Georgia without any hostility in the heart of the old Confederacy, yet express not the slightest concern for how black Georgians were treated by white Georgians in that same commemorative year.[5] Such irony, silence or disregard for the meaning of black freedom abounded in white America during the semicentennial. This may seem a truism, but it needs to be uncovered and explained.

For Americans generally the Civil War has been a defining event upon which we have often imposed unity and continuity in order to blunt its ideological legacies. By the early twentieth century, as today, Americans increasingly came to remember the war in its music and pathos, not its enduring challenges, through the theme of reconciled sectional conflict, rather than resurgent, unresolved racial conflict. As a culture we have sometimes lifted ourselves out of historical time, above the details, and rendered the Civil War safe in a kind of Passover offering as we watch the Blue and the Gray veterans shake hands across the little stone walls at Gettysburg – in a photograph or in Ken Burns's documentary film. The Civil War remains difficult to extract from its shell of sentimentalism; it serves as a mother lode of nostalgia for antimodernists and military history specialists. The historian Nina Silber has demonstrated how sentimentalism took hold of the reunion process during the decades after the war, how gender (conceptions of manliness and femininity, and the popular literary ritual of intersectional marriage) provided a principal source of metaphor and imagery through which sectional reconciliation was achieved. Americans have a great penchant for 'tragedy', William Dean Howells once wrote, as long as it has a 'happy ending'. Or, as W.E.B. Du Bois put it even more directly in 1912: 'this country has had its appetite for facts about the Negro problem spoiled by sweets'.[6]

Through scholarship and schooling much has changed in recent decades regarding the Civil War era and the age of emancipation. But in the half-century after the conflict, as the sections reconciled the races increasingly divided. The intersectional wedding that became such a staple of popular culture had no interracial counterpart in the white popular imagination. Quite the opposite was the case.[7] 'Race' was so powerful a source of division in American social psychology that it served as the antithesis of a culture of reconciliation. The memory of slavery, emancipation, the Thirteenth, Fourteenth and Fifteenth Amendment, or black soldiers who fought for their own freedom and became voters and legislators never fitted well with a culture in which the Old and the New South were romanticized and welcomed back to a 'new nationalism'. If Du Bois was at all correct that 'the problem of the twentieth century is the problem of the color line', then we can begin to see the calculus by which the problem of 'reunion' and the problem of 'race' were trapped in a tragic, mutual dependence. As Americans took stock of who they were in relation to their Civil War at its fiftieth anniversary, they were playing out the important retrospective chapter in Jim Crow's 'strange career'.[8]

The stark distance between the ways blacks and whites tended to remember the Civil War by the turn of the century is reflected in two speeches delivered in Augusta, Georgia, the one by a Confederate veteran in 1903 and the other by a black minister in 1909. Together they illuminate the problem of the colour line in historical memory. At a United Confederate Veterans reunion on Memorial Day, 1903 Major J.C.C. Black spoke to a large gathering of his comrades who stood on the tops of chairs and tables, waved hats and canes, 'shouting ... in delirium'. 'We did not fight to perpetuate African slavery,' declared Black, 'but we fought to preserve and perpetuate for our posterity the God-given right of the freedom of the white man'. A journalist covering the occasion picked up the same theme in his account. 'It was indeed for the freedom of the white man that the people of the South went to war a third of a century ago', reported the *Atlanta News*, and it was 'for the supremacy of the white man that the war of moral suasion, the campaign of enlightened discussion is going on today'. In a statement of a dominant, white, Southern point of view, the reporter described the 'bondage' of the South to Northern interests and the cause which the old veterans now embodied as that of 'Anglo-Saxon emancipation'.[9]

On emancipation day 1 January 1909 a black Baptist minister, Silas X. Floyd, delivered an address entitled 'Abraham Lincoln: Sent of God' to a large celebration sponsored by black churches, fraternal orders and the local Lincoln League. Floyd admonished those blacks who believed that they should forget that 'our race was once enslaved in this country'. 'Did you ever see ... a Confederate veteran who desired to forget that he once wore the gray', asked Floyd, 'or who was unwilling to teach his children that he once proudly marched in battle behind Lee and Gordon, Jackson and Johnston? Did you ever see a Union soldier who was ashamed of the part which he took in the Great War ...?' Floyd waxed biblical, and reminded his people that they too had a great story to tell and preserve:

> And don't you remember that, when the children of Israel under the ... leadership of Moses were on the march from Egypt ... to Canaan ... don't you remember that, after they had safely crossed the Red Sea, the Lord commanded them to set up memorial stones by which the event should be remembered? And yet some old Negroes wish to forget all about slavery – all about the past – and stoutly maintain that we have no right to be celebrating each year the day that brought freedom to our race ... May God forget my people when they forget this day.[10]

Floyd's speech reflects many dilemmas that Southern blacks faced. He was young and charismatic, a member of the post-freedom generation challenging the slavery generation. He raised the central question blacks faced in contemplating their past in America: the meaning of more than two centuries of slavery, and the meaning of emancipation in the Civil War. How to look back, and then forward, with pride and inspiration? Indeed, how to understand and declare their history in the Jim Crow South?

A quick and poignant way to begin to see the varieties of Civil War memory at play in the semicentennial is provided in a scene in James Weldon Johnson's classic *The Autobiography of an Ex-Colored Man*, published anonymously in 1912. The protagonist has just left Fisk University in Nashville, Tennessee, where he has heard the Fisk Jubilee Singers perform, and is riding the train to Macon, Georgia. Since he is passing, he is in a Pullman car. A robust conversation ensues between four characters: a northern, 'Jewish-looking man', who is a cigar manufacturer experimenting with Havana tobacco in Florida; a 'slender bespectacled young man' from Ohio, who teaches at a state college in Alabama; a 'white-moustached, well-dressed' man, an old Union soldier who 'fought through the Civil War' and has numerous investments to attend to in the South; and a loud, 'tall, raw-boned, red-faced man' who is a Texas cotton planter. The discussion moves from mundane matters of the present – the weather, crops and business – to politics, and then rather quickly to the 'Negro question'. The Jew is portrayed as the diplomat, taking all sides at once, opposing no one. The young Northern professor had believed in black rights and opportunity, but a year in the deep South had given him a version of compassion fatigue; he now confessed that he thought the race question should be left to white Southerners to handle as they would. A contentious debate ensued, however, between the veteran of the Grand Army of the Republic and the Texas planter. The debate is one between generations, sections and different conceptions of the meaning of the Civil War. The young Texan argued that the 'Civil War was a criminal mistake on the part of the North and that the humiliation which the South had suffered during Reconstruction could never be forgotten'. The old Union soldier retorts that the 'South was responsible for the war and that the spirit of unforgetfulness on its part was the greatest cause of present friction ...'. At issue was the meaning of black freedom. The Texan assures his listeners that the Anglo-Saxon race will always rule the world, while the noble veteran gives a Lincolnesque commentary on the 'moral responsibility' to help to uplift blacks socially and to guarantee their 'essential rights of men'. The Union veteran bests the New South planter in education and eloquence. After a long exchange about the meaning of what a 'race' is and the requisite query from the Texan to the Old Yankee of whether he would allow his daughter to 'marry a nigger', this discussion among white men ends in laughter, with almost everyone taking a drink from the Texan's flask. Johnson's protagonist watches with a 'chill ... sick at heart' over what he heard from the planter, but admits to an odd sense of admiration for the steadfastness with which Southerners 'defend everything belonging to' them.[11]

Johnson captured many elements of Civil War memory in this single scene: worn-out Yankee liberalism, noble neo-abolitionism on the part of an old soldier, white ethnic indifference to Southern and racial issues and, of course, white Southern hostility to any element of the emancipationist legacy of the Civil War. All of them are busy making money, except the gaunt Ohio professor; and he did not drink from the flask either. That Johnson's passing protagonist, black but not black, observes this conversation is a fitting metaphor for one of the ways many African-Americans would have to watch the semicentennial of *their* Civil War – deeply interested and implicated, but segregated and, to most whites, invisible.

Other ways of understanding the variety of Civil War memory would include adopting some version of Joel Williamson's three-part analysis of white Southern mentalities on race relations – liberal, conservative and radical. Southern 'liberals', according to Williamson, were the smallest group by the turn of the century, but they carried over a conspicuous, articulate faith in black capacities and the progress of race relations from the experience of Reconstruction. 'Conservatives', the core of the Southern white mind, never relinquished the cardinal belief in Negro inferiority and sought in myriad ways to fix the subordinate place (Jim Crow) of black folk in American life, North as well as South. And, the 'Radicals', led in the early twentieth century by the Ben Tillmans, James Vardamans and Thomas Dixons, advanced a racial vision of America where blacks had no place in society, where they would vanish, or be forced to vanish. All three of these mentalities, says Williamson, 'evoked the past to meet the present' with agility and ever-pliant Northern as well as Southern audiences.[12] There are many representative examples one may point to here (from Myrta Lockett Avery to John Spencer Bassett to Tillman's ubiquitous lecture campaigns), but a single illustration from a 1914 Congressional debate will have to suffice.

The Fiftieth Anniversary of Emancipation

Several states and the federal government either funded, or contemplated funding, celebrations and expositions for the fiftieth anniversary. Du Bois in the *Crisis*, as well as other black newspapers, charted and debated these expositions with great interest. In the summer of 1914 a black group in Richmond, Virginia, led by a lawyer, Giles B. Jackson, requested $55,000 from the US Congress for an emancipation celebration in the former Confederate capital. Senator Thomas Martin of Virginia represented a liberal outlook of a sort, declaring himself a close observer of Southern blacks and arguing that they had 'made a progress that is almost astounding, considering the opportunities which they have had'. He was all for a celebration of 'fifty years of their freedom'. Senator James Vardaman of Mississippi held firm to the white supremacist banner. Whites had 'assisted' blacks in every way, said Vardaman, but making 'citizens and voters of them' ought 'never be done'. Hence he opposed any such appropriation. A third Southern Senator, Frank White, of Alabama, held up a version of the conservative racialist tradition, reaching deep into the Lost Cause mythology. White supported the appropriation as a way of honouring the 'loyalty' of former slaves during the war, 'more', he said, 'for what they did for us during the struggle in which their freedom was the issue than for what they did for us in other times'. White said Southern blacks deserved white gratitude because they 'camped with us ... marched with us ... supplied our every want ... guarded our homes and protected our women and children ...', and 'carried their dead masters back to their wives ...'.[13] In this romantic, familial imagery blacks were made into *Confederate veterans* of a sort; they were to be allowed their celebration as gratitude for wartime service. An emancipation commemoration on such terms as these would not in the least transgress the Jim Crow social and political structure that these very senators had helped to construct by 1914. The idea of the loyal slave – an article of faith in white, Southern memory – became a central, necessary element of America's Jim Crow reunion.

Moreover, such discussions on the floor of Congress may demonstrate the ways in which white, Southern attitudes about race and reunion had all but overwhelmed Northern neo-abolitionist thought. Or, as Williamson puts it, 'Conservatives had opened the beachheads that allowed the Radicals to land. Both were shock troops in this latter-day Battle of Gettysburg in which the Northern line was broken and the North invaded. The fruit of the racial campaign was not so much to conquer the North, as it was to free the South'. When Du Bois reported this debate about the emancipation celebrations in the *Crisis,* he did so with disgust and irony, and he placed it right before a verbatim recording of the rules of the recently enacted North Carolina white primary.[14]

That 'beachhead' among Northern whites was not gained, of course, without resistance. For nearly two decades by the time of the semicentennial, neo-abolitionists and reformers of various kinds had trumpeted the 'progress' of blacks in all walks of life. This stemmed from many sources: it was the natural subject of black middle-class intellectual and social circles; it countered the increasingly racist public culture of the country at large; it was a central function of the primarily white founders of the NAACP in its formative years; and it became a major part of the increasingly bitter struggle between the leadership of Booker T. Washington and that of W.E.B. Du Bois in black America. All discussions of black progress since emancipation were, at least tacitly, commentaries on the meaning and memory of the Civil War as the great divide in African-American history.

The fiftieth anniversary season brought this entire idea of black *progress* to a crescendo, coming as it did in the wake of the elections of 1910 and 1912, when the terms 'progressivism' and 'progressive movement' had become part of public, political language. Oswald Garrison Villard, grandson of William Lloyd Garrison, may have spoken for two generations of white neo-abolitionists in 1913, when, in a fiftieth anniversary article about black economic progress, he declared the rise in property ownership 'an astounding showing which by itself gives the lie to those who declare that the negro cannot be compared in efficiency with the white man'. By 1913, three years after 'scientific management' (Taylorism) had gone public, and trumpeting the third of Daniel Rodgers's helpful categories of progressive 'social languages' – the quest for *efficiency* – neo-abolitionist reformers countered theories of black retrogression, as well as the claims of permanency for Jim Crow, with article after article about social scientific progress.[15]

Many magazines and journals ran special issues commemorating emancipation and the progress of the race. In September 1913 *The Annals of the American Academy of Political and Social Science* published a special issue devoted entirely to 'The Negro's Progress in Fifty Years'. Some 24 essays, by 11 blacks and six Northern and seven Southern whites, including social scientists, writers and educators, covered subjects such as business and labour conditions, population growth, sharecropping, public health, statistics on criminality and debt, urban migration and the growth of literacy. The collection ended with pieces by Booker Washington on 'Industrial Education and the Public Schools' and by Du Bois on 'The Negro in Literature and Art'. This collection is an example of what Rodgers calls the 'new breed' sociology and the 'antiphilosophical scientism' of the late progressive era. Many of these works accentuate the role of the social scientific expert, as well as celebrate achievement through the compilation of 'facts'. Du Bois was clearly not comfortable appearing in this volume; his own piece was a token nod to the arts and not his best work. He admired the contributions by Kelly Miller, R.R. Wright, Monroe Work and other black contributors, as well as articles by some whites, such as J.P. Lichtenberger, the editor, which cast the growth of black literacy as a 'phenomenal race achievement'. But a segregationist, white supremacist purpose motivated several of the articles, such as Howard Odum on the need for separate Negro schools, Ray Stannard Baker on confidence in the white South when it came to black voting rights and Thomas Edwards's rosy picture of tenant farming.[16] However cast in data, each essay is a marker about the relationship of past and present; some are social science in the service of an optimistic, interracial memory of emancipation, and others justify the segregated society forged by national reunion. The volume can be read as a microcosm of the nation's dilemma with how to remember emancipation and its legacies.

White neo-abolitionist memory took many forms. A strong dose of nostalgia characterized much neo-abolitionist consciousness. Worried that they had lost the long battle over black rights – that they had lost the struggle over the memory of the Civil War – former abolitionists, or their sons and daughters, seized the occasion of the semicentennial to remember the glory days and make demands on the present. In February 1913 Fanny Garrison Villard (daughter of William Lloyd Garrison) wrote a remarkable recollection of emancipation day, 1 January 1863, in Boston, where she had stood by her father's side at the Music Hall and Tremont Temple celebrations. Waxing mystic, she described the 'Watch Night', waiting for the news of Lincoln's signing of the Proclamation, as 'indescribably thrilling'. Her recollection conforms in some ways to Frederick Douglass's description of the same scenes in his *Life and Times* (1881). She remembers singing 'Blow Ye the Trumpet Blow', hearing an orchestra play Händel,

Mendelssohn and Beethoven, and Ralph Waldo Emerson deliver his 'Boston Hymn'. She remembered a gathering the following evening, surrounded by Emerson, George Luther Stearns, Franklin Sanborn, Wendell Phillips, Julia Ward Howe and her father, when a bust of John Brown was unveiled. Fanny Villard declared herself fortunate to have such an 'antislavery heritage', and then in her final paragraph of this nostalgic *tour de force*, she returned to the reality of the present, declaring that what 'concerns us today is ... whether our duty to the liberated bondmen has been fulfilled. The answer is alas! No'. Whether neo-abolitionist expressions of nostalgia – on a personal or a public level – may fit what Michael Kammen has called the 'creative' or the 'destructive' function of nostalgia requires more research.[17] But it is, I think, a fruitful path to take in uncovering the Progressive era's preoccupation with the backward glance.

African-American Commemorations of Emancipation

The varieties of black memory of emancipation and the war are as diverse as region, education, generation, experience and political and social outlook would shape them. One is reminded here of Du Bois's frequent lament that 'the Negro' was so commonly referred to as a single entity and that blacks were 'Southerners' too.[18] Space allows the development of only a few examples. In 1910 Mary White Ovington, a white social worker and important NAACP operative, recorded the recollections of several ex-slaves in southern Alabama. Anticipating the WPA narratives to follow in the 1930s, these reminiscences provide an interesting picture of ordinary freed people in old age, given their opportunity to reflect on their past at the semicentennial. Ovington found an interesting range of old folks who told of personal pain, hardship, family breakups, labour conditions, progress toward property ownership and insights, as well as tall tales about the war and the coming of freedom. Perhaps a woman identified only as 'Granny' left a story with the most scope and impact. Very old, with features of 'an African', she told of being sold away from her four children in North Carolina, sent in the domestic slave trade westward to Alabama, forced to give birth to a fifth child fathered by her new, cruel master. She remembered crying when the master's son died in the Confederate Army, because he was a 'kind chile'. She related tales of being whipped, of her desperate fears of running away and of how she survived only on her faith in 'Master Jesus'. As Ovington was about to leave, she asked Granny about the photograph of Lincoln on the mantel in her cabin. 'I love dat face, Miss', Granny answered. 'I love it so dat der lady down here, she done gib me der picture. Dose eyes, dey follow me, dey's so kind. I don' know how ter tell you how much I lub dat man dat made us free – *an' all der oders, too dat helped.*'

Granny and Ovington are both reminded of a lyric from a plantation song as they 'looked out on the fields where men guided the mules in the plowing', and the ex-slave concludes: 'I's seen a heap o' sorrow an' trouble, but it's ober for me. I t'ank de Lord dat I' free; dat us all, chillen, an' women, an' men, is free.' Is this a collaborative work of nostalgia in the reminiscence industry, or a revealing window into freedmen's memory? Is it neo-abolitionist pathos or the place to start in any consideration of black social memory in the fiftieth anniversary season? It is probably a mixture of all these elements, and a continuation of the kind of writing Du Bois had begun in the *Souls of Black Folk,* especially the chapter called 'Of the Black Belt', works that sought to counter the tremendous growth industry of the plantation school of popular literature (spread most widely by Thomas Nelson Page) that fashioned an enduring picture of the Old South and slavery full of contented and loyal black folk.[19] There were no happy darkies in Du Bois's Black Belt of 1903, and the only element of comedy in Ovington's recording of Granny in 1910 is deeply embedded in the old woman's tragic sensibility.

A rough categorization of black memory might include (and these are only preliminary, suggested labels): one, black antiquarianism; two, the genuinely patriotic mode, characterized by a fierce claim that the black experience ought to be at the centre of America's national memory; three, a progressive-celebratory mode manifested in numerous emancipation expositions, in pageantry, and sometimes in public and educational avoidance of the slave past; four, a conservative-assimilationist form of black nationalism that asserted self-improvement more than, or in place of, historical consciousness (a Civil War memory in conformity to the social philosophy of Booker T. Washington); five, a combination of pan-Africanism and Ethiopianism, the cluster of ideas (more a teleological theory of history than a political movement before Marcus Garvey, and rooted in Psalm 68) that viewed black destiny as the creation of an exemplary civilization, perhaps in Africa or elsewhere, and which saw the American emancipation as only a part of a long continuity of Christian development; and finally, six, what we might call a black jeremiadic memory, the use of commemorative moments as occasions for bitter appeals against injustice, past and present. Virtually all of these categories overlap, or flow into one another.

Numerous local emancipation commemorations may fit the category of antiquarian through their collecting of objects and their exhibition of crafts and wares. Most certainly the Frederick Douglass Shoe Company, Inc., of Lynn, Massachusetts does. The company sold a Fred Douglass brand for men and a Phillis Wheatley brand for women by mail order. The National Afro-Art Company of Washington, DC offered 11-inch busts of Richard Allen,

Douglass and Washington for $1.25 each. The *New York Age* offered 20x24 inch photogravures of several black historical figures for $3.00 each.[20] Such collecting, as well as the consumer appeal now attached to black history, fits its age of mass-market culture. But it may also have represented for many black families a form of empowerment, class aspirations and a way of declaring and exhibiting a heroic past. These objects may also have been icons through which the dialectic of 'double consciousness' (being black and American) played out in a segregated society.

The Tuskegee Institute President, Booker T. Washington, the most influential black leader in America, laboured both quietly and publicly to gain Congressional approval for emancipation exhibitions. But a Bookerite memory of slavery, emancipation and the war did emerge full-blown, especially in Washington's speeches, as well as those of his legions of followers. In a typical address at Auburn, New York in June 1914, dedicating a memorial to the recently deceased Harriet Tubman, Washington eulogized the liberator of fugitive slaves as an example of 'the law-abiding Negro' who 'brought the two races nearer together and made it possible for the white race to know the black race ...'. The Wizard of Tuskegee turned his tribute to this underground revolutionary into an exaltation about the 'progress' of 50 years. He declared Tubman's work 'not in vain' after ticking off the acreage of black land ownership and the numbers of black-owned grocery stores, drygood stores, shoe stores, drug stores and banks. Business enterprise was the legacy of the Underground Railroad in the age of capital. He ended the speech, as he did most of his commemorative-progress orations, with the argument that the 'antislavery heroes' had freed two races in the South, the white and the black.[21]

The patriotic mode of black memory may be best illustrated by James Weldon Johnson's poem, 'Fifty Years', published on 1 January 1913 in the *New York Times*, and reprinted in black newspapers and delivered as a reading at some commemorations to follow. Anticipating Langston Hughes and Woody Guthrie, Johnson's poem is a striking statement about African-American birthright. Seven verses into the poem, Johnson strikes his central theme:

> Then let us here erect a stone,
> To mark the place, to mark the time;
> A witness to God's mercies shown,
> A pledge to hold this day sublime.
>
> And let that stone an altar be,
> Whereon thanksgivings we may lay,
> Where we in deep humility,
> For faith and strength renewed may pray.

With open hearts ask from above
New zeal, new courage and new pow'rs,
That we may grow more worthy of
This country and this land of ours.

For never let the thought arise
That we are here on sufferance bare;
Outcasts, asylumed 'neath these skies,
And aliens without part or share.

This land is ours by right of birth,
This land is ours by right of toil;
We helped to turn its virgin earth,
Our sweat is in its fruitful soil.

Johnson claims the centre of America's historical memory by right of immigration and by right of labour. In the poem's middle he claims it by right of soldiering, of 'blood' and devotion to the 'flag': 'We've bought a rightful sonship here,/ And we have more than paid the price'. As the poem reaches its hopeful ending, Johnson celebrates the abolitionist tradition as America's national destiny.[22]

Such a poetic sense provided the tone for the many local meetings and public expositions celebrating emancipation that occurred in the semicentennial season. The states of New York, New Jersey, Pennsylvania and Illinois gave appropriations of varying amounts for expositions ($20,000 in Pennsylvania and approximately $25,000 in New York). Cities as large as Washington, DC, Chicago, Philadelphia, New Orleans and Atlanta, and as small as Richmond, Indiana, Savin Rock, Connecticut, Corpus Christi, Texas and Quincy, Illinois had their own celebrations. Some expositions, modelled on world fairs, were elaborate celebrations of black progress on every front, and others were essentially speeches, readings or musical events. Organizations of all kinds, such as the National Baptist Convention, the Freedmen's Relief Committee of Philadelphia and the National Association of Colored Nurses held their own celebrations.[23] Research into as many of these local commemorations as possible will reveal regional, and perhaps even class and political patterns of remembrance. A clear theme of each was the celebration of *black progress* and achievement in the professions, business, education, inventions, women's status and the arts. In New Jersey the organizing committee worked on and off for more than a year, dividing themselves into some 37 'leagues', each devoted to sending out questionnaires and gathering facts and statistics on everything from needlework and dressmaking to real estate and music. Some even did 'house -to-house canvasses' to gather such data, leading the editor of the Topeka, Kansas *Capital* to rejoice in all the commemoration, especially 'these cheering statistics'.[24]

By far the most elaborate exposition was organized in New York City by Du Bois and others, and staged at the 12th Regiment Armory, 62nd Street near Broadway between 22 and 31 October 1913. It was called the 'National Emancipation Exposition', and Du Bois declared that he and the other commissioners were 'determined to make this ... a complete picture of Negro progress and attainment in America'. Du Bois's own social scientific and Victorian earnestness were in full force. 'With detailed charts, models, moving pictures, maps and a few typical exhibits,' he said, 'a complete picture of present conditions will be presented, while a magnificent pageant ... with music and costume, will give the historic setting.' He promised 'no endless repetition and country-fair effect ...', only 'one fine and dignified presentation of *great facts* in simple form, with a frame of beauty and music ...'[25] (italics added).

Here we have the progressive-celebratory mode of black remembrance in full flower – the 'great facts' about the present put into 'historic setting', past and present achievement displayed as arguments about current oppression, and grand appeals to public memory as reform. This exposition had some 15 divisions of Negro life and labour, all represented by booths, photographs and other displays, and an extraordinary Temple of Beauty in the Great Court of Freedom, complete with Egyptian wall paintings and obelisks. But it was 'The Star of Ethiopia' pageant, written and directed by Du Bois (with the assistance of Charles Burroughs), that provided the most remarkable element of the New York exposition. By the early twentieth century, pageantry had become a popular form of public history and theatre, as well as a mirror of social and community tensions during the Progressive era and beyond. Space does not allow me a detailed analysis of the content of 'The Star of Ethiopia'. With a cast of 350, the pageant depicted five epochs in six episodes of African and American history from the 'gift of iron' from prehistoric African societies, to the 'gift of the Nile' from ancient Egyptian civilization, to the 'gift' of the 'faith of Mohammed', on to America where blacks experience slavery and the 'gift of Humiliation', complete with the singing of spirituals and a 'Dance of Death and Pain', to the age of the 'gift of Struggle Toward Freedom' led by 'brave maroons and valiant Haytians', Crispus Attucks and Nat Turner. The final episode brings the age of emancipation and its aftermath, the 'gift of Freedom', with William Lloyd Garrison, John Brown, Abraham Lincoln, David Walker, Frederick Douglass and Sojourner Truth all playing roles amid marching black Union soldiers, and a chorus of 'O Freedom'. The pageant was performed four times during the New York celebration, playing to large crowds; about 30,000 people (almost all black) in all attended the Exhibition.[26]

Du Bois staged 'The Star of Ethiopia' twice more, in Washington, DC in 1915 and in Philadelphia in 1916. He experienced considerable hostility – outright refusal of support – within the NAACP leadership over his work on the pageant and the exposition. 'What a task that was!' Du Bois declared, reflecting back in December 1915. 'I have been through a good many laborious jobs and had to bear on many occasions accusations difficult to rest under, but without doubt the New York Emancipation Exposition was the worst of all my experiences. Such an avalanche of altogether unmerited and absurd attacks it had never been my fortune to experience.' Much criticism seems to have been directed at the epic level of pomp and romanticization evident in the pageant. Some upright reformers and aesthetes saw pageantry as a vulgar art form, and no doubt some blacks themselves may have seen a pandering to or an uncomfortable backward glance at slavery, as a hundred bondsmen danced their mournful steps. This may also have been an early precursor of some of our current disputes over just how public history and memory should become, of what ought to be the substance of historical commemoration and who ought to have authority to do it. To Du Bois the pageant in 1913 was 'this one new thing in the dead level of uninteresting exhibitions'. 'We had our ups and downs ...', he wrote, 'it was difficult to get hold of the people ... more difficult to keep them'. But, as though he were a participant in the great debate over Disney's Virginia Theme Park, Du Bois concluded: 'This is what the people want ... this is the gown and paraphernalia in which the message of education and reasonable race pride can deck itself.'[27] In those words he aptly captured the dilemma and the inspiration of the scholar and activist-journalist turned public historian during the fiftieth anniversary season. He mixed the patriotic, progressive-celebratory and Ethiopian voices with remarkable results.

But those were not the only voices Du Bois and other black leaders used during the semicentennial. Sometimes with angry editorials, and sometimes with satire, parable or poetry Du Bois forged the jeremiadic mode of black memory as well as anyone. His poetry and short fiction in these years are replete with images of death and rebirth, of Christ figures and resurrections. In April 1913 he published a poem in the *Crisis* called 'Easter-Emancipation, 1863–1913'. The 'I' pronoun of this long, enigmatic poem is the slave woman as Christ figure, who is repeatedly crucified and enveloped in 'the folding and unfolding of Almighty wings' (the 'wings of Ethiopia'?). Through her many agonies and deaths come life and freedom. These apocalyptic, death-rebirth images were tough medicine for the semicentennial. They were warnings about the evil and sorrow in the past and the persistent betrayals of the present. In his January 1913 editorial on 'Emancipation', Du Bois reminded his readers that the American people had not freed the slaves 'deliberately and with lofty purpose', but in a war to 'destroy the power of the South'. Bringing full civil and political rights to the freedmen was a 'task of awful proportions'. Facing the challenge of black equality, Du Bois said, 'the nation faltered, quibbled and finally is trying an actual *volte-face*'. Turning away from historical responsibility in such an about-face, Americans had built 'barriers to decent human intercourse and understanding between the races that today few white men dare call a Negro friend'. Far too many, North and South, Du Bois despaired, 'would greet the death of every black man in the world with a sigh of relief'. On the cover of that special Emancipation issue of the *Crisis* was an extraordinary drawing by Laura Wheeler of an elderly black man with eyes and head slightly bowed with dignity.[28]

A year earlier, in the January 1912 *Crisis* Du Bois wrote perhaps his most striking fiftieth anniversary piece. Modelled on Jonathan Swift's famous essay 'A Modest Proposal', Du Bois called his satire 'A Mild Suggestion'. Similar to Johnson's parable on the Pullman car, Du Bois places five characters on the deck of ship: a Little Old Lady, the Westerner, the Southerner, the New Yorker and the Colored Man. The Southerner is recovering from severe seasickness, but, as the sun comes out, all resume a conversation about the Negro Problem within hearing of the Colored Man. The usual solutions of education, work, emigration and so forth are discussed. Finally they ask the black man for his opinion. He sits down and lays out his 'perfect solution'. He urges rejection of education because it will lead only to 'ambition, dissatisfaction and revolt', scorns work because it can bring only job competition and the disruption of social circles, and refuses emigration because it is impracticable and inhumane. Instead, the Colored Man proposes that on 1 January 1913, 'for historical reasons', each white American who has a black friend should invite him to dinner. This, he thought, would encompass 'black mammies and faithful old servants of the South'. Those blacks without such an invitation would be urged to come to white churches and YM or YWCAs. There they would be seated in a fully integrated manner at dinner. All remaining blacks in the country should be 'induced to assemble among themselves at their own churches or at little parties and house warmings'. Stragglers and vagrants should also be rounded up and watched. Then, he suggested, at the ringing of a bell, or the 'singing of the national hymn', blacks at the dinners were to be given potassium cyanide pills, those at the large meetings were to be dispatched with stilettos and all others would be shot with Winchester rifles. With the Southerner staring and forgetting 'to pose', the Westerner staring in 'admiration', the New Yorker 'smiling' and the Little Old Lady in 'tears', the Colored Man concludes: 'The next morning there would be ten million funerals, and therefore no Negro problem.' No celebratory voice here, no cant about progress, and no nostalgia. Only a prophetic altar call to a national conscience, the bitterest of appeals against everything from lynching (the NAACP counted more than 70 in 1913) to the meaning of segregation. In a time of celebration Du Bois would not let black folk think about Emancipation Day, past or present, without a reminder, however bleakly it would be taken, from his Colored Man in this story who, while admitting that his solution 'may seem a little cruel', asks is it 'more cruel than present conditions'.[29]

Like James Weldon Johnson and others, Du Bois employed many modes of remembrance in 1913. Satire has always been a literary or journalistic form that works best in worlds of absurdity; so much of segregated America and the semicentennial of emancipation and the Civil War was just such a world. George Bernard Shaw once claimed, perhaps with a little hyperbole, that on the satirist depended 'the salvation of the world'. And Swift himself said in 1728 that satire is motivated not merely by ridicule, but by 'a public spirit, prompting men of genius and virtue to mend the world so far as they are able'.[30]

NOTES

1. Friedrich Nietzsche, 'The Use and Abuse of History', in *The Use and Abuse of History*, translated by Adrian Collins, introduction by Julius Kraft (New York, 1949), p.29; David Hackett Fischer, *Historians' Fallacies: Toward a Logic of Historical Thought* (New York, 1970), pp.135–42. On the need for studies of memory in their contexts and the idea of varieties of memory, see Michael Kammen's review essay in *History and Theory: Studies in the Philosophy of History*, 34 (1995), pp.246–61.
2. Eric Hobsbawm, 'Mass-Producing Traditions: Europe, 1870–1914', in Eric Hobsbawm and Terence Ranger (eds.), *The Invention of Tradition* (Cambridge: Cambridge University Press, 1983), p.307.
3. For two of the more interesting reflections on the idea of an apology for slavery see Ira Berlin, 'Before We Apologize, We Should Learn What Slavery Means', *Washington Post*, 29 June 1997; and Patricia Williams, 'Apologia Qua Amnesia', *Nation*, 14 July 1997. On the role of melancholy in this age of memory-consciousness see Charles S. Maier, 'A Surfeit of Memory? Reflections on History, Melancholy and Denial', *History and Memory: Studies in the Representation of the Past*, 5 (Fall/Winter 1993), pp.136–52.
4. See David W. Blight, 'Quarrel Forgotten or a Revolution Remembered? Reunion and Race in the Memory of the Civil War, 1875–1913', in David W. Blight and Brooks D. Simpson (eds.), *Union and Emancipation: Essays on Race and Politics in the Civil War Era* (Kent, OH: Kent State University Press, 1997), pp.151–79.
5. John Hope Franklin, 'A Century of Civil War Observances', *Journal of Negro History* (April 1962), pp.98–9, 106.
6. Nina Silber, *The Romance of Reunion: Northerners and the South, 1865–1900* (Chapel Hill, NC: University of North Carolina Press, 1993), p.3; Howells is quoted in Allan Gurganus, *The Oldest Confederate Widow Tells All* (New York, NY: 1984), epigraph; Du Bois, *Crisis*, 3 (Feb. 1912), p.153.
7. The important exception here might be the fiction of black writers such as Charles Chesnutt, Pauline Hopkins and perhaps Sutton Griggs, who wrote novels where interracial mixture was a central theme. On these writers see Dickson J. Bruce, *Black American Writing from the Nadir: The Evolution of a Literary Tradition* (Baton Rouge, LA: Louisiana State University Press, 1989), pp.136–89.
8. W.E.B. Du Bois, *The Souls of Black Folk*, David W. Blight and Robert Gooding-Williams (eds.) (1903; reprinted, Boston, MA: Bedford Books, 1997), p.45. C. Vann Woodward, *The*

Strange Career of Jim Crow (1955; reprinted, New York, NY: Oxford University Press, 1974), pp.7–10.

9. *Atlanta News,* 31 May 1903.

10. *Atlanta Constitution,* 2 Jan. 1909.

11. James Weldon Johnson, *The Autobiography of an Ex-Colored Ma* (1912; reprinted, New York, NY: 1960), pp.156–66.

12. Joel Williamson, *The Crucible of Race: Black-White Relations in the American South Since Emancipation* (New York, NY: Oxford University Press, 1984), pp.4–7, 36–9. On the longevity and persistence of white supremacist thought see John David Smith, *An Old Creed for the New South: Proslavery Ideology and Historiography, 1865–1918* (Westport, CT: Greenwood Press, 1985) and George Fredrickson, *The Black Image in the White Mind: The Debate on Afro-American Character and Destiny, 1817–1914* (New York, NY: Harper & Row, 1917).

13. *Congressional Record,* 63rd Congress, 2nd Session, vol. 51, 8 July 1914, pp.11797–8.

14. *Crisis,* 8 (Sept. 1914), pp.227–28; Williamson, *Crucible,* 335.

15. Oswald Garrison Villard, *New York Evening Post,* 4 Jan. 1913; Daniel T. Rodgers, 'In Search of Progressivism', *Reviews in American History* (Dec. 1982), pp.123, 125–7. On neo-abolitionists see James McPherson, *The Abolitionist Legacy: From Reconstruction to the NAACP* (Princeton, NJ: 1975).

16. 'The Negro's Progress in Fifty Years', *Annals of the American Academy of Political and Social Science,* 49 (Sept. 1913), pp.1–237; 184. For Du Bois's critique of this issue see *Crisis,* 7 (Feb. 1914), p.202.

17. Fanny Garrison Villard, 'How Boston Received the Emancipation Proclamation', *American Review of Reviews,* 47 (Feb. 1913), pp.177–8. On nostalgia see Michael Kammen, *Mystic Chords of Memory: The Transformation of Tradition in American Culture* (New York, NY: Knopf, 1991), pp.275–92.

18. *Crisis,* 3 (Feb. 1912), p.153.

19. Mary White Ovington, 'Slaves' Reminiscences of Slavery', *The Independent,* 68 (26 May 1910), pp.1131–6; Du Bois, *Souls of Black Folk,* Ch.7.

20. Mail order advertisement, *Crisis* (10 May 1915), p.47; *New York Age,* 5 Oct. 1911.

21. 'Extracts from an Address at the Unveiling of the Harriet Tubman Memorial', Auburn, NY, 12 June 1914, in Louis Harlan (ed.), *Booker T. Washington Papers* (Urbana, IL: University of Illinois Press, 1981), Vol.13, pp.58–61. On Washington's support for emancipation exhibitions and lobbying of Congress, see *Washington Bee,* 6 Aug. 1910.

22. James Weldon Johnson, *Fifty Years and Other Poems* (Boston, MA: Cornhill, 1917), pp.1–5.

23. Du Bois monitored, promoted and criticized these celebrations. See *Crisis* (Feb.–Nov. 1913); ibid., 10 (May 1915), pp.31–2.

24. *Crisis,* 6 (Oct. 1913), p.297. Du Bois declared that the New Jersey exposition had 'many disappointments' in its scope and execution. See *Crisis,* 6 (Aug. 1913), p.183; *Topeka Capital* (KS), 7 Aug. 1910.

25. *Crisis,* 6 (Aug. 1913), p.183.

26. For photographs of the exhibits as well as the pageant see *Crisis,* 7 (Dec. 1913), centrefold; and ibid., 11 (Dec. 1915), pp., 89–93. On the 15 divisions or categories of exhibit see ibid., 6 (Oct. 1913), p.297. The script of the 'Star of Ethiopia' is reprinted in ibid., 7 (Nov. 1913), pp.339–41. Attendance figures are in ibid., 7 (Dec. 1913), p.84. On pageantry, see David Glassberg, *America Historical Pageantry, The Uses of Tradition in the Early Twentieth Century* (Chapel Hill, NC: 1990), pp.131–4; and Glassberg, 'History and the Public: Legacies of the Progressive Era', *Journal of American History,* 73 (March 1987), pp.957–80.

27. *Crisis,* 11 (Dec. 1915), p.89. On the hostility and criticism see Du Bois's report to the Board of Directors of the NAACP, 'The Pageant', 1915, in Du Bois Papers, University of Massachusetts Library, reel 5; and Du Bois to Joel Spingarn, 3 Nov. 1915, Du Bois Papers, reel 5.

28. *Crisis,* 5 (Jan. 1913), pp.128–9. The cover is by L. Wheeler.

29. 'A Mild Suggestion', *Crisis,* 3 (Jan. 1912), pp.115–16.

30. Shaw and Swift quoted in Jonathan Swift, *A Modest Proposal and Other Stories,* introduction by George R. Levine (Amherst, NY: Prometheus Books, 1955), p.14.

Riots and Resistance in the Caribbean at the Moment of Freedom

GAD HEUMAN

Slavery did not come to an end in the Anglophone Caribbean in 1834. Although slaves were declared legally free on 1 August, they were obliged to serve a period of apprenticeship to their former masters. From the point of view of the ex-slaves, apprenticeship had a number of conditions; the most important was that they were legally obligated to work without compensation for their former masters for up to 45 hours per week. Their term of continued compulsory labour depended on their status; former field slaves were to be apprenticed for six years while skilled apprentices and domestics were to be fully free after four years.[1]

Thomas Holt has called the apprenticeship 'a half-way covenant', since the relationship between the planter and the worker was much the same as slavery during part of the week while the remaining time was negotiable. In the case of Jamaica, where the Assembly stipulated that the apprentice should work 40½ hours, the planters were required to supply the customary rations and allowances that they had provided during slavery. Beyond the time required by law for the apprentices to serve their former masters, ex-slaves were free to negotiate conditions of work and wages with their former masters or with another employer. They could also choose not to work at all.[2]

Apprenticeship offered the planters significant advantages. It provided them with the time to develop appropriate methods of labour management as well as to introduce new equipment in the light of the ending of slavery. For the planters, the system of apprenticeship was an additional form of compensation. In England and at the Colonial Office, apprenticeship was also regarded as essential. New banking and legal structures were needed for a free system as well as time to prepare the ex-slaves for freedom. Missionaries would have additional time 'to mould the thinking of the apprentices, to encourage habits of industry, to build churches, and to establish stable social patterns that would induce freedmen to remain in settled estate villages when the system ended'. As the Governor of Jamaica in 1834, Lord Sligo, put it in an address to the apprentices, 'you will be APPRENTICED to your former owners for a few years, in order to fit you all for freedom'.[3]

An additional mechanism was instituted to safeguard the apprentices. Special magistrates were appointed, largely from England, to adjudicate disputes between masters and their former slaves. The role of these magistrates was crucial, as planters and former slave owners were no longer empowered to punish their ex-slaves. In a further proclamation to the apprentices of Jamaica, Sligo advised them that 'neither your master, your overseer, your book-keeper, your driver, nor any other person can strike you, or put you into the stocks, nor can you be punished at all, except by the order of a Special Magistrate'.[4]

The intent of those responsible for the establishment of the apprenticeship system was clear. Above all, they sought to create the conditions which would 'perpetuate the established order' while at the same time protecting the ex-slaves. Historians have discussed the institutional apparatus of apprenticeship and, in particular, the role of the special magistrates. What is less obvious is the perspective of the apprentices themselves. While it is difficult to reconstruct their views, it is apparent from the actions of many apprentices that they strongly opposed apprenticeship. In discussing their hostility to the system it may be possible to suggest how the apprentices saw freedom rather than how others saw it for them.[5]

Resistance to Apprenticeship

On at least one island in the Caribbean, St. Kitts, there were early signs of trouble even before the introduction of apprenticeship. There the slaves indicated that they would resist apprenticeship and would strike on 1 August. As they explained to the Lieutenant-Governor of the island, J. Lyons Nixon, they would 'only work for wages, and that they will dictate terms, being convinced from the King's Proclamation that they are to have unrestricted freedom on the 1st August next'.[6]

Faced with this outburst, Nixon toured the island, speaking in each of the nine parishes to blacks from every estate. The Lieutenant-Governor sought to clarify the basic provisions of the system and also warned the slaves about the importance of continuing to work. However, his addresses to the blacks failed to calm them; on the contrary, they were hostile and in at least one instance threatened an overseer with violence. As Nixon reported it, the people in two parishes near the capital Basseterre were

> highly insubordinate and disgraceful. They *una voce* protested against the apprenticeship system, declaring their resolution to resist it, and not to work after the 1st of August without wages, saying that on that day they were to be free, as announced by the King's proclamation,

and that their masters could not take their houses or provision-grounds from them, having so long occupied them ...[7]

The apprentices had developed a compelling justification for their behaviour. Since the slaves of nearby Antigua were to be freed without the apprenticeship, the St. Kitts' apprentices could not understand why they should not be treated in the same manner. Indeed, the apprentices on St. Kitts were correct: Antigua was one of the two colonies in the region to reject apprenticeship and to opt for full freedom in 1834. Moreover, blacks in St. Kitts complained to Nixon that he was sent there by the whites to deceive them; Nixon was only the Lieutenant-Governor and it was the Governor of Antigua who had freed them as well as the people of Antigua. For the slaves on St. Kitts, Nixon had been brought there by the planters to cheat them out of their freedom. As he tried to explain the apprenticeship to them, the people 'hooted, and in some instances threw banana husks at or towards me, and walked off shouting, and could not be brought back by their owners or overseers'.[8]

It was not just that Antigua had dispensed with apprenticeship. According to a missionary in Basseterre, slaves in St. Kitts expected that the Act of Abolition would grant them unrestricted freedom; he noted that they often said, 'Now we shall soon get our freedom.' They also maintained that the King had granted them their freedom and that it was the planters who wanted them to be apprentices. In their view, one of the special magistrates had gone to see the King and would bring back the papers which would free them. This belief in the Crown or the Imperial authority was familiar. In the 1831 rebellion in Jamaica slaves maintained that the Crown had already freed them and that it was the whites who were withholding their freedom. Furthermore, since they were free, the slaves maintained that they would not meet any resistance from the King's troops during a rebellion.[9]

The slaves on St. Kitts also complained that some planters had suggested that apprenticeship would be harsher than slavery. In addition, there was a lack of consistency among the planters about the treatment of the apprentices. At least one absentee owner, Lord Romney, had decided to free his slaves unconditionally on 1 August.[10] Since some planters had chosen to dispense with apprenticeship, the blacks concluded that those proprietors were complying with the 'King's law' while the others who adopted the system were violating it. In the end, it was the contradictory nature of apprenticeship which made it hard to accept. As a Wesleyan missionary described it:

> it was difficult to make them understand how they could be 'discharged of and from all manner of slavery, and absolutely and fore ever manumitted', and yet to be compelled to work the greater part of

their time for the same masters without adequate wages. Freedom and compulsory labour, without payment, and for no crime, appeared to them incongruous.[11]

Given the reactions of the slaves, the authorities on St. Kitts had no choice but to prepare for the worst. The House of Assembly and the Council on the island not only stepped up security but also sent an urgent request to the Governor of the Leeward Islands, E.J. Murray MacGregor, for Imperial troops. Many plantation families moved to Basseterre for greater security as 1 August approached. Although initially reluctant to send troops to St. Kitts because of similar demands from other parts of the Caribbean, MacGregor relented in the face of continued pressure from the St. Kitts' authorities. On 21 July he sent arms and ammunition to the island as well as a company of the 36th regiment on board a British warship.[12]

The show of force did little good. Initially, apprentices on about a dozen estates in the eastern part of the island went on strike. By 4 August the strike had become widespread and affected most of the island's 156 estates. Although there was no violence as proprietors sought to arrest leaders of the strike, the apprentices refused to work without pay. Many fled to the hilly central section of St. Kitts; in some cases this included all the apprentices on a plantation. Once in the interior they joined a band of runaway slaves under the command of an African named Markus. It was clear to the authorities that 'no order may be expected in the country unless he is taken'. MacGregor arrived on the island from Antigua and declared martial law.[13]

Relying on the Army as well as the militia, the whites moved against the apprentices and the runaways. In a combined operation begun in the middle of August, the forces captured most of the runaways and the apprentices, many of whom were publicly flogged after being brought before the military courts. Within a few days, the apprentices returned to their plantations and MacGregor proclaimed an end to martial law. In the trials which followed the strike, 15 apprentices were tried for sedition, five of whom were banished for life. From the evidence at the trials, it became apparent that the strike had been planned for some weeks before August. Although there was no further open resistance on the island, the Lieutenant-Governor attributed this 'to the severe and numerous punishments inflicted during the existence of martial law'.[14]

The speedy suppression of the apprentices' strike in St. Kitts had significant ramifications for neighbouring islands as well. The Lieutenant-Governor of Dominica, Sir Charles Schomberg, reported that there were close connections between the apprentices in Dominica and those in St. Kitts. Schomberg had heard that Dominican apprentices were proclaiming,

'We free; no bind; no work, as in St. Christopher's'. His view was that if the strike in St. Kitts had not been put down quickly, there would have been 'a dire situation in Dominica'.[15]

As it was, there were disturbances on the island. In at least two districts of Dominica apprentices refused to work; in the parish of St. Peter, for example, apprentices declared themselves as free as the magistrates, and one apprentice 'became so outrageous as to offer his breast to be shot rather than obey the law'. Elsewhere, in Colihaut, it required a detachment of the 76th Regiment to put down the resistance of the apprentices. As in St. Kitts, apprentices in Dominica claimed that the King had freed them. Again, it was the local authorities who were responsible for the apprenticeship and for 'endeavouring to keep them in bondage'.[16]

Further afield in the Caribbean, there were also serious difficulties among the apprentices. In Trinidad the apprentices vowed to strike and repeated some of the same themes as the apprentices in St. Kitts and Dominica. According to one report, the Trinidad apprentices believed that the King had freed them outright and that apprenticeship was a plan hatched by their masters and the Governor. For the apprentices, the planters were 'dam tief' and the Governor 'an old rogue'; after all, the King had enough money to buy them fully out of slavery and was not such a fool as to make them only half free.[17]

Again, there was a problem with the logic of apprenticeship. The apprentices could not understand how the King could call them 'free' and yet force them to work for their former owners. Parodying the concept of apprenticeship, the apprentices also claimed that they already knew their work sufficiently and did not need an 'apprenticeship' of any kind. As in St. Kitts, the apprentices also complained about the slaves who were freed unconditionally; in the case of Trinidad, it was a group of Government slaves who became fully free on 1 August. This made it difficult for the apprentices to understand why they were being treated differently.[18]

Unlike the apprentices in St. Kitts who fled to the mountains, the Trinidad apprentices left their estates and marched to Government House in Port of Spain to inform the Governor that they had resolved to strike. In a dispatch to the Colonial Office the Governor reported that entire gangs of labourers on 25 of the principal estates had struck work and were intent on marching to the capital. Confronted with a mob of at least 400 people, the Governor and the Special Magistrates sought to explain the terms of the apprenticeship. But the crowd would not listen and reportedly became more turbulent. The authorities 'were not only utterly disregarded but grossly insulted, and openly set at defiance; explanation was drowned by vociferations; persuasion was attributed to fear and treated with disdain, while threats met with contempt'.

The crowd dispersed at night but returned in the same mood the next day. Despite the mustering of the militia and the arrest and punishment of 17 of the most prominent ringleaders, the crowd vowed to resist and even to suffer death rather than return to work. When the militia and the Army eventually cleared the streets, many women collected in small groups and still continued to resist. This continued for several days, despite the arrests of at least 60 more people, many of whom were flogged while others were sent to prison.[19]

The hostility towards apprenticeship was equally strong in British Guiana. Although the Governor there reported that the churches and chapels were crowded on 1 August, he had subsequently learned that the apprentices were determined to do no more than half the work they had done as slaves. Moreover, the apprentices understood that this was the King's orders. In one of the provinces of British Guiana, Essequibo, apprentices took things much further. There they occupied a church and a churchyard for three days from 9 August, flew flags and generally sought to encourage apprentices in the area to resist apprenticeship. It eventually required soldiers and the police to clear the rioters; they arrested the ringleaders, who were subsequently tried for riotous and seditious behaviour. The Supreme Court took a harsh view of the activities of the apprentices: the court sentenced one apprentice to death, four to be transported and 32 to be flogged.[20]

During the court proceedings the apprentices provided further justifications for their actions. As with apprentices elsewhere, they did not believe the local authorities about the nature of apprenticeship. The rector of Trinity parish, John Halloway Duke, provided evidence of this: he reported that he had read out the new conditions to the apprentices. But, in response, they claimed that he was reading from the wrong 'paper', that he was reading the 'paper' which a planter had given him rather than one from the Crown.[21]

A senior magistrate in the same parish gave evidence about the views of the apprentices in his district. Some of the more intelligent men on an estate had told him that they were free and, furthermore, that the Governor had told them that they would be as free as any white man on 1 August. Accordingly, they would not work unless they were paid. When the magistrate explained the nature of apprenticeship, the apprentices decided that they would work two hours a day to pay their former master for their houses and grounds; for them, that was more than sufficient. Although the disturbances eventually subsided, it was clear that apprentices in British Guiana shared many of the same views as ex-slaves in St. Kitts, Dominica and Trinidad.[22]

In Jamaica the transition from slavery to apprenticeship went relatively smoothly. Lord Sligo, the Governor, reported that 1 August was celebrated across the island in churches and chapels; in addition, proprietors on many estates had celebratory dinners for their apprentices. The markets on the following day were unusually large and, by Monday, 4 August, most of the apprentices had returned to work. The one exception to this picture of calm was the parish of St. Ann.[23]

There the situation was difficult. Across the parish apprentices struck, vowing not to work except for wages. One report claimed that the apprentices swore that 'they will have their heads cut off, or shot, before they will be bound apprentices'. As elsewhere in the Caribbean, apprentices questioned whether the King could be responsible for the legislation or whether, instead, it emanated from Jamaica. They asked the authorities a series of rather telling questions: '1st. Is it the King's law? 2d. Would you swear that the King make it? 3d. Did not the Jamaica House make it? 4th. Did not Lord Sligo put him name to it because him have slaves? 5th. Could you swear it is the Law of Jesus Christ?'

Sligo provided additional explanations for the strike in St. Ann. One involved the previous Governor, Lord Mulgrave, who had toured the island before he left in 1834. Mulgrave had promised that slavery would come to an end on 1 August and that there would be no slaves in the island after that date. Calling this Mulgrave's Law, the apprentices claimed that they did not wish to make Mulgrave ashamed of them by going to work and 'again be bound to their masters'.[24]

Sligo maintained that the whites in St. Ann were also partly responsible for the behaviour of the apprentices. During Mulgrave's administration the planters in the parish had adopted a policy of passive resistance to the Governor's attempts to improve the condition of the slaves. The apprentices had now turned this policy on its head; they were passively resisting their masters' attempts to make them work. In fact, Sligo reported that the apprentices were not simply refusing to work; they were also encouraging each other to accept their punishments. As Sligo put it, 'they have committed no overt act whatever, but doggedly refuse to work, submitting with the appearance of pleasure, to their punishment, their comrades exhorting them to bear it for the sake of freedom'.[25]

There was an additional reason why the apprentices in St. Ann may have decided to strike. As in the case of St. Kitts, where one planter had decided to free his slaves unconditionally, a proprietor in St. Ann, Price Watkis, had chosen to pay his apprentices full wages for their work. When the apprentices on surrounding estates learned of Watkis's actions they immediately ceased working.[26]

Sligo soon realized that St. Ann was not the only problem he faced. In St. Thomas-in-the-Vale apprentices on the Ginger Hall estate vowed not to work unless they were paid. Although the stipendiary magistrate threatened that the apprentices would be punished if they did not obey the law, the apprentices continued in their vow to resist. Fearing the potential impact of this resistance, Sligo sent troops and police to arrest the ringleaders on the estate. The soldiers successfully rounded up the leaders of the disturbances on the early morning of 3 August; by 4 August, the first day of work under the new system, these men had been tried and publicly flogged on the estate. As Swithin Wilmot has concluded, 'the lightning strike of the security forces in the early morning of 3 August 1834, aborted whatever plans the workers on Ginger Hall had had to strike on the following day.'[27]

There were also difficulties elsewhere on the island for the authorities. In particular, Sligo complained bitterly about the planters in St. James and their withdrawal of privileges formerly given to the slaves and now withheld from the apprentices. These included the forcing of women who had formerly been excused from field labour because of old age or because they had produced six children, back into the gangs; not allowing mothers to suckle their children in the fields; and taking away all field cooks and nurses to watch the children in the fields. For Sligo, it was 'strange that St. James should be the place where this conduct is now most exhibited and was the place where the Rebellion broke out in 1831'. As in the case of St. Ann, Sligo was disturbed about the behaviour of the whites: he saw it as 'outrageous and oppressive' and believed that it was producing very negative effects among the apprentices.[28]

Eventually, the apprentices reacted against this policy, although the most violent reaction occurred in St. Thomas in the East rather than in St. James. There, on Belvidere Estate, a prominent planter and President of the Legislative Council, a Mr Cuthbert, had withdrawn the usual allowances from the apprentices. They had become discontented, turned out late for work and were sentenced to be punished for their actions. But, as the police were marching several of the apprentices to the workhouse,

> an old woman, Christian Mowatt, 70 years of age and the estates midwife…called upon them in the most excited manner, not to allow her three children to be sent to the workhouse, that this was the third time they had been sent there since Christmas. She used the most violent language and impassioned features, the only apparent effect of which was, that nearly all the Negroes followed the Police with the prisoners…

Their attempt to rescue the prisoners failed, but later that day the apprentices set fire to at least two of the trash houses on the estate and refused to help to put the fires out. Two of the prisoners were subsequently sentenced to death for arson, although the island's chief justice later commuted this to banishment for life.[29]

In addition to the problem of allowances, there were also disputes about the hours of work. An overseer on Gibraltar Estate in the parish of St. George's had orders to divide the apprentice workforce into two shifts beginning at 4.00 a.m. and ending at midnight. Since this was reminiscent of the practices during slavery, the apprentices refused to accept it. They would not work 'a moment before sun-rise or after sun-set for anybody, they were as well aware of the law as I was myself'. When the overseer called in a special magistrate to adjudicate the dispute the apprentices ran away. The following night there was a fire on the plantation, but most of the plantation apprentices refused to help to put it out. Another fire broke out on the estate at 3.00 a.m. the next morning; again the apprentices refused to assist those attempting to control the blaze.[30]

The apprentices on Golden Grove Estate in St. Thomas in the East were also concerned about the number of hours they were meant to work. When the special magistrate informed the apprentices that they could be obliged to work their hours at any time within the 24-hour cycle, they shouted and refused to be quiet. The special magistrate then 'ordered a woman who was most noisy to be put into confinement; on which the people declared they would all go in the dark room, and followed her towards the place of confinement; when near it, they rescued her, and took her away; when they came to the gate near the house, they gave three cheers in triumph'. In response, the magistrate called up the police and the Army and the ringleaders were punished: nine men were whipped, two of whom were sent to the house of correction along with six women.[31]

There was another level of protest which was more generalized and more difficult to control. James Scott has described this behaviour of peasants in terms of 'hidden transcripts', using 'foot-dragging' or 'poaching' as part of an everyday form of resistance. Apprentices in Jamaica employed such tactics. Sligo commented on the reaction of many apprentices who were unhappy with the new system: they resorted to 'turning out late, irregularity to work, and idling of time'. To some degree, these 'delinquencies' were dealt with by the special magistrates; but there was the additional problem of what planters perceived as 'insolence and insubordination'. The use of language was significant in this context; a special magistrate E.D. Baynes, reported that the apprentice was 'daily becoming more heedless of and more disrespectful to his manager'. According to Baynes, apprentices were no longer willing to accept the language of their former owners without an appropriate retort.[32]

Although this pattern of day-to-day resistance was not easy to manage, the more overt acts of resistance were suppressed quickly. In the most significant of the outbreaks, the problems in St. Ann, Sligo dispatched a steamship with 160 soldiers who were deployed throughout the parish. At first, the apprentices believed that the troops had come to protect them, but they soon realized that this was not the case. As one observer noted, the troops quelled 'that spirit of passive resistance' which the apprentices had adopted. Even then, the forces had to punish 'a vast number of the Negroes' by whipping and by putting them in the workhouse. In the face of this considerable show of force the apprentices had little choice: 'finding the soldiers so close upon them in every direction', they returned to work.[33]

The Apprentices' Vision of Freedom

The reaction of the apprentices to their first year in this status was highly revealing. It was clear that their image of freedom differed substantially from that of the policymakers in the Colonial Office as well as of their former masters. For those in authority, it was critical to maintain the established order and the existing hierarchies in the Caribbean. Certainly, there was a recognized need to protect the apprentices, but it was also important to ensure the continuity of the plantation system and the production of sugar.

For the apprentices, and especially those who resisted the establishment of apprenticeship, it was difficult to comprehend the new system. Like the apprentices in Trinidad, they felt that they needed no 'apprenticeship'; they needed no training for freedom or for their work on the plantations. In fact, the nature of the slaves' own economy in the Caribbean, with its extensive provision-ground system and highly developed markets, meant that slaves were probably better prepared for freedom than their former masters.[34] At the onset of apprenticeship, ex-slaves wanted to be fully free; they sought 'unrestricted freedom' and not a system of forced labour, even for part of the week. Apprentices were prepared to work for wages, but many also believed that their houses and their provision grounds belonged to them and not to the planters.

Apprentices also believed that the Crown would not impose a system of half-freedom on them. In their view, apprenticeship was a creation of the local authorities; it was either the planters or the local legislature which was seeking to deny them full freedom. This was not a new idea. Slaves had claimed that their freedom was being withheld from them earlier in the century. In every major Caribbean slave rebellion in the nineteenth century slaves claimed that the Crown had already freed them. Writing about a similar phenomenon elsewhere, Eric Hobsbawm has described this view as 'populist legitism'; for him, the distant ruler represents justice and symbolizes the aspirations of the people. This was equally the case of peasant movements in Tsarist Russia as for slave rebellions in the Caribbean.[35]

Apprentices were concerned about any aspect of the system which could be perceived as a continuation of slavery. Under the apprenticeship, all children under the age of six were freed; however, it was possible for parents to apprentice their free children and make their former masters responsible for the material welfare of the children. Yet apprentices universally refused to consider the apprenticing of their children. As Woodville Marshall suggests, 'they [apprentices] set such store by the free children's new status that they were not prepared to participate in any scheme for their maintenance by planters which would imperil it'.[36]

Similarly, apprentices were often reluctant to accept work on the plantations outside the time they were obliged to labour. In Marshall's terms, they were asserting 'control over the labour time at their disposal'. Some of the apprentices feared that working in their free time would mean a further period of slavery. A Jamaican planter reported his apprentices as telling him that they could not do extra work; 'if they did so, they would be kept in slavery seven years longer'. For the special magistrate Frederic White, it was the Baptists who were responsible for spreading this idea, making the apprentices afraid of 'eternal damnation in the next world and perpetual slavery in this', if they worked for wages in their own time. Although apprentices subsequently did labour in their own time on the plantations, they also withheld their labour, sometimes as a protest and at other times to use it more productively in the provision-ground system or elsewhere in the informal economy.[37]

One of the most noticeable aspects of the apprentices' resistance to the system was the role of women. They were prominent in the march on Government House in Trinidad and in several of the disturbances in Jamaica. The authorities repeatedly complained about the women apprentices; for example, Governor Sligo wrote home that 'it is notorious that they [the women] are all over the Island the most troublesome'. Nor did their activities cease in 1834.[38]

There are repeated cases of trouble among women apprentices during the later period of apprenticeship. More than a year after the system had been established, one of the special magistrates in British Guiana, A.M. Lyons, reported on the 'insubordination' of women apprentices. According to Lyons, on plantation 'Kitty', 'about twenty-five women, apprenticed labourers, conducted themselves in a most unruly manner, in attempting to rescue four men convicted by me of conspiring not to perform their work, and sentenced to be punished by whipping'. And asked whether this was part of a conspiracy or combination, Lyons reported that 'on plantation "Kitty" the women have attempted to set all authority at defiance; the whole have combined together not to perform their work'.[39]

Later in the same year there were complaints elsewhere in British

Guiana about 'idle and disorderly apprentices', most of whom were women. In early 1836 Lyons again reported on the behaviour of women on two plantations: on one the women were very rude to those in authority and on the second some of the pregnant women pretended to be ill and would do no work. In another case, the whole women's gang refused to work 'in consequence of some women having been required to go to their work after having been discharged by the medical attendant'.[40]

Similar cases were also reported in Jamaica. Two observers who were sent by the Society of Friends to assess the apprenticeship, John Sturge and Thomas Harvey, reported on a series of abuses of women apprentices. In one incident, on an estate near Falmouth, police were called to quell a disturbance among the nursing mothers. The women had refused to come to work before breakfast, 'as it was very wet, and they were obliged to carry their children into the fields with them'. Brought before the special magistrate, the apprentices were sentenced to work six extra Saturdays. They explained the difficulties this would cause, as the women devoted Saturdays to tending their provision grounds and 'without their Saturdays, they had no means of obtaining subsistence. For their contumacy, they were sent to the workhouse for three days, and will still have to work the six Saturdays'.[41]

As Mimi Sheller suggests, Sturge and Harvey used such cases to demonstrate how planters exploited apprentices generally and women in particular. The British visitors were particularly sympathetic to the plight of these female apprentices, in part because some of their own support came from metropolitan middle-class women, many of whom who had been involved in anti-slavery campaigns. As Sheller concludes:

> The incident demonstrates the women's concerted efforts to resist the plantation labour regime by stopping work, presenting justifications in terms of their need to protect and feed their children, and protesting their lack of subsistence and free time, both of which they had formerly depended on to support their families.[42]

There were good reasons, then, why women were so prominent in the resistance to apprenticeship. As Holt has pointed out, female apprentices formed the majority of the field labouring force on the plantations, just as they had during slavery. Regulations about hours and working practices would therefore have affected women more directly than men. When Golden Grove estate in Jamaica employed workers on nine-hour shifts, for example, it was women who were the leaders in protesting about these arrangements. The special magistrate for the district reported that 'the women always foremost protested against such mode of labour the ringleader of whom I felt obliged to punish by sentence of one month's hard labour'. In this particular case the magistrate released the woman on the promise of good behaviour by the other workers on the estate.[43]

However, the explanation for the role of women as ringleaders against apprenticeship is more complicated than simple numerical predominance. In her article Sheller discusses women's role in Jamaica during this period as both workers and mothers; as she suggests, 'unlike their male counterparts, female field labourers could make claims for improved working conditions not simply as free workers, but specifically as mothers who were struggling to support their families'. The planters' withdrawal of privileges during apprenticeship and, specifically, those affecting pregnant women, women with children and the role of elderly matriarchs, impinged directly on women. 'Female apprentices were punished in large numbers for trying to assert and protect the limited rights they had won as mothers of the slave labour force...' In the end, the harsh treatment of women rebounded against the planters and helped to discredit the whole apprenticeship scheme and led to its premature abolition in 1838.[44]

Towards the end of the apprenticeship one of the special magistrates in Jamaica described the system as 'a mere mockery of Freedom'.[45] Yet it was also true that, in opposing apprenticeship, apprentices throughout the Caribbean had expressed their own vision of freedom. It was very different from the planters' perception of the aftermath of slavery and, when full freedom did come in 1838, blacks were well prepared to contest further the nature of that emancipation.

NOTES

I am grateful to Bridget Brereton and Arnold Sio for their comments on an earlier draft of this chapter.

1. The most comprehensive treatment of apprenticeship remains W.L. Burn, *Emancipation and Apprenticeship in the British West Indies* (London: Cape, 1937). See also William A. Green, *British Slave Emancipation: The Sugar Colonies and the Great Experiment, 1830–1865* (Oxford: Clarendon Press, 1976); idem, 'The apprenticeship in British Guiana, 1834–1838', *Caribbean Studies*, 9 (1969), pp.44–66; Thomas C. Holt, *The Problem of Freedom: Race, Labor, and Politics in Jamaica and Britain, 1832–1938* (Baltimore, MD: Johns Hopkins University Press, 1992); Douglas Hall, 'The apprenticeship period in Jamaica, 1834–1838', *Caribbean Quarterly*, 3 (Dec. 1953), pp.142–66; and Swithin Wilmot, 'Not "full free: the ex-slaves and the apprenticeship system in Jamaica, 1834–1838', *Jamaica Journal*, 17 (Aug.–Oct. 1984), pp.2–10.
2. Holt, *The Problem of Freedom*, pp.56–7.
3. Green, *British Slave Emancipation*, p.130; CO 137/192, Sligo to Stanley, private, 27 May 1834, no. 19.
4. *Supplement to The Royal Gazette*, 16–23 Aug. 1834, Proclamation: Sligo to the Newly Made Apprentices of Jamaica.
5. Green, *British Slave Emancipation*, p.130. A useful starting point to examine blacks' expectations of freedom is Woodville K. Marshall, '"We be wise to many more tings": blacks' hopes and expectations of emancipation', in Hilary Beckles and Verene Shepherd

(eds.), *Caribbean Freedom: Society and Economy from Emancipation to the Present* (Kingston: Ian Randle, 1993), pp.12–20.

6. *British Parliamentary Papers* (Irish University Press edn), [hereafter *PP*], 1835 (278–2), 50, Nixon to Stanley, 10 July 1834, no.198.

7. Ibid., MacGregor to Spring Rice, 21 July 1834, no. 200.

8. Ibid.

9. Ibid., MacGregor to Spring Rice, 19 Aug. 1834, no. 207, encl: Bigler to MacGregor, no. 7, 17 Aug., p.614; Richard Frucht, 'From slavery to unfreedom in the plantation society of St. Kitts, W.I.', in *Comparative Perspectives on Slavery in New World Plantation Societies*, ed. Vera Rubin and Arthur Tuden (New York, NY: New York Academy of Sciences, 1977), p.383; Gad Heuman, *'The Killing Time': The Morant Bay Rebellion in Jamaica* (London: Macmillan Caribbean, 1994), p.36.

10. *PP*, 1835 (278–2), 50, MacGregor to Spring Rice, 19 Aug. 1834, no. 207, encl. no. 6, Davis to MacGregor, 13 Aug. 1834, pp.79–80.

11. Ibid., Cox to MacGregor, encl. no. 8, 18 Aug. 1834, p.616.

12. Robert S. Shelton, 'A modified crime: the apprenticeship System in St. Kitts', *Slavery and Abolition*, 16 (Dec. 1995), p.333.

13. Ibid., pp.333–4; *PP*, 1835 (278–2), 50, MacGregor to Spring Rice, 19 Aug. 1834, no. 207, encl: Pogson to Bedingfeld, 11 Aug. 1834, p.613.

14. Shelton, 'A modified crime', p.334; CO 239/37: MacGregor to Spring Rice, 15 Aug. 1834, no. 166, encl: *The Saint Christopher Advertiser*, 12 Aug. 1834; Nixon to Spring Rice, 29 Aug. 1834. xx

15. *PP*, 1835 (278–2), 50, MacGregor to Spring Rice, 1 Jan. 1835, no. 216, encl: Schomberg to MacGregor, 2 Dec. 1834, no. 4, p.635.

16. *The Royal Gazette of British Guiana*, 11 Sept. 1834, citing *The Observer*, 6 Aug. 1834 and *The Colonist*, 9 Aug. 1834.

17. *Supplement to The Royal Gazette*, 13–20 Sept. 1834.

18. *PP*, 1835 (278–2), 50, Hill to Spring Rice, 7 Aug.1834, no. 301, p.736.

19. *PP*, 1835 (278–1), 50, Hill to Smith, 3 Aug. 1834, encl. no. 1; *Supplement to the Royal Gazette*, 13–20 Sept. 1834.

20. *PP*, 1835 (278–1), 50: Smyth to Spring Rice, 9 Aug. 1834, no. 113; Smyth to Spring Rice, 12 Oct. 1834, no. 3.

21. Ibid., extract from the Criminal Note Book of the Chief Justice of the Supreme Court of Demerara and Essequibo, 11th Criminal Session, p.323.

22. Ibid., evidence of Thomas Coleman, senior special magistrate in Trinity Parish, p.329.

23. CO 137/192, Sligo to Spring Rice, 13 Aug. 1834, no.16.

24. *Postscript to The Royal Gazette*, 2–9 Aug. 1834.

25. CO 137/192, Sligo to Spring Rice, 13 Aug. 1834, no.16.

26. National Library of Jamaica, Ms 228, Letters of Lord Sligo, vol. 5, Sligo to Cockburn, 31 Aug. 1834, p.150.

27. Wilmot, 'Not "full free"', pp.3–4.

28. Letters of Lord Sligo, vol. 5: Sligo to Cockburn, 31 Aug. 1834, p.151; Sligo to Bishop of Jamaica, 2 Sept. 1834, p.156.

29. CO 137/193, Sligo to Spring Rice, 4 Oct.1834, no.36; *Postscript to The Royal Gazette*, 13–20 Sept. 1834; Holt, *The Problem of Freedom*, p.61.

30. CO 137/194, Sligo to Spring Rice, 29 December 1834, no. 121.

31. Ibid., Thomas McCornock, 11 Nov. 1834, before the House of Assembly.

32. James Scott, *Domination and the Arts of Resistance: Hidden Transcripts* (New Haven, CT: Yale University Press, 1990), p.xiii; CO 137/215, Sligo to Glenelg, 5 March 1836, no. 362, encl: Murchison to Nunes, 1 March 1835; *PP*, 1836 (166–I), 48, Sligo to Glenelg, 2 April 1836, encl: Report of E.D. Baynes, 28 March 1836, p.343.

33. *Supplement to The Royal Gazette*, 9–16 Aug. 1834; *Postscript to The Royal Gazette*, 9–16 Aug. 1834; CO 137/192, Sligo to Spring Rice, 13 Aug. 1834, no. 16.

34. For an important collection on this theme see Ira Berlin and Philip D. Morgan (eds.), *The Slaves' Economy: Independent Production by Slaves in the Americas* (London: Frank Cass, 1991).

35. E.J. Hobsbawm, *Primitive Rebels: Studies in Archaic Forms of Social Movement in the 19th and 20th Centuries* (New York, NY: Norton, 1965), pp.119–20.
36. Marshall, '"We be wise to many more tings"', p.15.
37. Ibid.; CO 137/194, Sligo to Spring Rice, 29 Dec. 1834, no. 121: Examination of William Stanford Grignon before the House of Assembly; Examination of Frederic White, SM, before the House of Assembly.
38. CO 137/194, Sligo to Spring Rice, 9 Dec. 1834, no. 91.
39. *PP*, 1836 (166-II), Pt III, 49, Smyth to Glenelg, 12 Nov. 1835, no. 249, encl: Epitome of the monthly reports from special magistrates in British Guiana for October 1835.
40. Ibid., Smyth to Glenelg, 13 Dec. 1835, no. 255, encl: Epitome of the monthly reports from special magistrates in British Guiana for November 1835; Smyth to Glenelg, 28 Jan. 1836, no. 257, encl: Epitome of the monthly reports from special magistrates in British Guiana for December 1835.
41. John Sturge and Thomas Harvey, *The West Indies in 1837* (London: Hamilton, Adams, 1838), pp.217–18.
42. Mimi Sheller, 'Quasheba, mother, queen: black women's public leadership and protest in postemancipation Jamaica, 1834–1865', *Slavery and Abolition*, 19 (Dec. 1998), p.95.
43. Holt, *The Problem of Freedom*, p.64; CO 137/194, Sligo to Spring Rice, 9 Dec. 1834, no. 91.
44. Sheller, 'Quasheba', pp.93, 94. See also the important discussion of this issue in Bridget Brereton, 'Family strategies, gender, and the shift to wage labour in the British Caribbean', Paper presented at the Association of Caribbean Historians' Conference, Martinique, 1997, p.3.
45. CO 137/222, Smith to Glenelg, 21 Feb. 1838, no. 28, encl: Report of S. Pryce, Trelawny, 30 Sept. 1837.

'A Spirit of Independence' or Lack of Education for the Market? Freedmen and Asian Indentured Labourers in the Post-Emancipation Caribbean, 1834–1917

PIETER EMMER

In principle, the ending of the terrible and inefficient system of slavery should have produced progress, optimism and gratitude on all fronts. To many, however, the end of slavery in the Caribbean was a big disappointment. On average, the ex-slaves did not become yeomen farmers nor did they improve their income and status as free plantation workers as many had hoped. The abolitionists in Europe and North America, who had fought so gallantly to get slavery abolished, were dismayed. The pessimistic predictions of their adversaries about a dramatic decline in plantation output had proved all too realistic.[1] Most abolitionists had not expected that so many of the freedmen would leave the plantations nor that so many failed to become the hard-working, God-fearing peasantry they had envisioned. Unwilling to admit that the fault lay with the unrealistic assessment on their own part, they attributed the blame to the planters as well as the colonial and the home government. Obstinacy or obstruction on the part of the planters and the colonial civil servants could only result in the freedmen's having experienced stagnation, or even decline, in their living and working conditions. Yet, the planters were also disappointed. They realized that their slaves had not been emancipated in order to improve the profitability of their plantations, but only a few planters had expected that their supply of permanent plantation labour would be reduced so dramatically. In order to fill the gap they were forced to search for reliable labourers in such far away places as India and China. In sum, the abolition of slavery seemed to have produced nothing but disappointment all around.[2]

In the existing historiography the traditional *bêtes noires* are the planters. They are accused of clinging to an old-fashioned and wasteful production system. This system, it is claimed, had already adversely affected profits during the last decades of slavery and it continued to do so after slavery had ceased. These continuities between the pre- and the post-emancipation period have constituted the traditional explanation for the fact that the effects of slave emancipation did not come up to expectation.[3]

Over the past 30 years, however, the role of the planters in the Caribbean plantation economy has been reinterpreted. The view of the planters as 'uneconomic', wasteful and backward-looking autocratic rulers of a crumbling empire has been turned almost upside down. Recent studies of the nineteenth-century slave economies in the Americas now portray the planters as highly efficient managers in the most prosperous sections of the world economy at the time. New interpretations based on plantation records confirm that the planters carefully tuned the purchase of slaves to their needs and avoided creating a wasteful mix of labour and capital. On the contrary, recent studies stress the fact that sugar planters were keen to introduce new machinery in the boiling houses of their plantations as well as to experiment with new crops (cotton) and new varieties of sugar cane. With slave prices rising, the planters also attempted to influence the natality and mortality of their slave populations by spending more of their income on providing better food, housing and medical care.[4]

Strangely, these new views regarding the management of Caribbean plantations and of the slave economies in general have so far influenced the historiography regarding planters and freedmen in the post-emancipation era scarcely at all. Studies of the emancipation experience continue to stress the decline of the plantations, the dominance of the planters and the relatively weak position of the ex-slaves. Even the arrival of a new influx of 'workers in the cane' was incorporated into the existing, negative interpretation of the post-slavery era. The title of the first survey of labour migration from India to the Caribbean is telling: *A New System of Slavery.*[5]

Thus the prevailing view has been that the freedmen were underdogs, who could not be accused of making mistakes, or, if they did, could be excused on the grounds of the high level of compulsion in the post-emancipation society. Similarly, it is claimed, indentured labourers from Asia were so badly treated that they could not possibly succeed in building a new and successful existence in the West Indies. The Caribbean plantation world always had been and had remained a 'bad' region and anyone going there must have been forced, misinformed or otherwise duped by crooks and profiteers.[6]

However, the surprisingly optimistic findings derived from the recent research regarding Caribbean plantation slavery have found their corollary in the new interpretation of the labour migration from Asia during the nineteenth century. New research obliges us to re-evaluate the view that indentured labour migration was simply the slave trade and slavery in another guise. Rather than harming themselves, it has now been established, Indians on average increased their living standard considerably by moving to the Caribbean. Their well- being also improved. Overseas Indian women had fewer children than those in India but the death rate in the Caribbean –

except in the early years when the first immigrants arrived – was also considerably lower, resulting in a demographic growth rate higher than in India itself. Suicide, marital violence and return migration decreased over time, but possession of land, savings and even physical stature increased. New research has also destroyed the (no doubt racially biased) assumption of the abolitionists that more than a million Asian migrants were of such limited intellectual capacity as to be misled for almost a century into inadvertently degrading themselves. In reality, the attraction of the earning potential of the Caribbean can be deduced from the massive influx of Asian migrants. After all, they could have opted to go to many destinations in Africa and Asia, or, for that matter, elsewhere in India itself.[7]

These findings put the traditional interpretation of the post-slavery period into question. Unfortunately, it is not as yet possible to arrive at definitive conclusions as the relevant data regarding demography, income levels and other aspects of the lives of ex-slaves in the Caribbean have not been fully unearthed. To arrive at a body of statistical evidence regarding the ex-slaves will not be easy since those who could have provided the data, such as colonial civil servants and the planters, have left much less information about the freedmen than about the slaves. Once the freedmen moved away from the plantations, they removed themselves from quantitative history. We have no mortality and natality rates, no records of diseases and their treatment, and no information on incomes and expenditure.

In view of this dearth of data we have to rely on circumstantial evidence. Thus it is of the utmost importance to use our new insights into the nature of the plantation economy and of indentured migration from Asia to test the existing interpretations regarding the post-emancipation societies. While we might be approaching the 'end of history' in the historiography of slavery, we certainly have not reached this point in analysing the relevant information about the subsequent period.[8]

In this essay the economic behaviour of the ex-slaves and that of the indentured labourers from Asia will be compared. In contrast to the freedmen, the Asians continued to profit from Caribbean agriculture, be it as plantation workers or as small-scale farmers. Why did the freedmen opt to reduce their employment on the plantations and why were the indentured labourers from Asia willing to do the opposite? And why were – later in Caribbean history – the ex-indentured Asians more reluctant to leave small-scale farming than the freedmen?[9]

To throw light on the dynamics of Caribbean plantation agriculture the second section of this study summarizes some of the new research findings regarding the last decades of slavery, indicating that Caribbean plantations had the potential of being able to finance an important increase in slave incomes. The third section analyses the labour market in the post-emancipation Caribbean, indicating that psychological rather than economic reasons explain the decline of ex-slave labour. The fourth section surveys the sources of Asian migratory labour and its choice of destinations, indicating that Asian labour migration entailed only a minute section of the Asian population and that most of the migrants had economic motives for deciding to travel to the Caribbean. The final section examines the different attitudes of the freedmen and the Indians towards agricultural labour and, in conclusion, suggests that the ex-slaves and the ex-indentured Asians had had a different education for the market and that it is this dissimilarity more than anything else which explains why these two groups opted for different economic lives.

The Slaves and the Second Plantation Revolution: The Policy of Amelioration

Detailed historical research over the past 20 years, drawing upon the many surviving plantation archives, provides us with a remarkably new picture of the New World plantations. These studies make the point that we should strongly distinguish between the first, pioneer phase of the capitalist plantations in the Caribbean – roughly between 1650 and 1750 – and the second phase, which is to say between 1750 and 1850 during which the mature plantation system developed. The differences between the two periods are striking.

- The plantations, both in the American South as well as in the Caribbean, showed a sustained and high rate of economic growth during the second phase of plantation agriculture. For the sugar plantations the cultivation of a new, high-yield cane variety increased productivity as well as the mechanization of extracting and refining the cane juice. A sharp rise in demand for cotton products greatly increased the profit rates of cotton plantations.[10]

- The increase in plantation incomes that resulted from the increased growth was distributed more evenly among the factors of production than during the first period of plantation agriculture. Investors, owners, management and slaves all profited from this development. A recent study of the major sugar areas of the British Caribbean shows that the rise in slave incomes was as high as 35 per cent during the period from 1760 to 1832. Similar observations have been made about the income of slaves on the cotton plantations in the American South.[11] These increases contrast sharply with the downward changes in income of the proletariat in Britain during the first phase of the Industrial Revolution, which took place during the same period.[12]

- The increase in the expenditure on slaves was forced upon the planters by the market. It is true that the Atlantic slave trade continued to supply almost any number of slaves, but after 1750 it did so at constantly rising prices. The continuous rise of prices stimulated the planters to try to improve the demographic growth of their slaves in an attempt to overcome the main drawbacks of the Caribbean plantation economy, which had always prevented autochthonous demographic growth among both European migrants and African slaves, at least in the British, French and Dutch Caribbean.[13] The Caribbean planters embarked upon a policy of 'amelioration', which entailed a package of improvements in working and living conditions, unique at the time. Amelioration provided the slaves with better housing, a maximum number of working hours per week, pregnancy leave for female slaves, minimum food rations and constant availability of medical care. It should be added that this policy was not based on economic motives alone. Some of it was forced upon the planters by the colonial governments, which in turn were under pressure from the powerful abolitionist lobbies in western Europe and in the United States.[14]

- In addition to these points, there is one 'growth' factor in the plantation world that has received only intermittent attention from researchers: the production of foodstuff by slaves during their free time. It has always been known that slaves used small plots of land, allotted to them by the planters, on which they grew many types of crop and where they also raised chickens, goats and even cows. Some of this produce was consumed in order to supplement the rations distributed by the plantation management, and some was sold on the market.[15] There are no figures indicating exactly how much growth this sector experienced. It has been pointed out that towards the end of the eighteenth century most, if not all, of the food for sale in Jamaica had been produced by slaves during their free time. Unfortunately, that does not say very much since most of the food consumed in Jamaica was not offered on a local market. Some have claimed the growth of this production as a 'breach' in the 'slave mode of production', a 'contradiction and inconsistency of the slave regime' and as a sure sign of the decline of the plantation system.[16] Yet, rather than showing the decline of the plantation system, the growth of garden-plot production indicates an increased efficiency of plantation production. Because of the amelioration policies, the slaves had more time on their hands and perhaps more physical energy left than before. Similarly, there is no reason to assume that the dramatic reduction of the working week in western Europe and North America, the gigantic growth in incomes and the increase in free time and subsequently of 'domestic' activities after World War II in any way signalled a decline in the efficiency still less the end of the 'capitalist mode of production'. It should be stressed, however, that the agricultural pursuits of the slaves and their marketing skills did not constitute a preparation for the life of an independent farmer after emancipation. Until the end of slavery, owners were obliged to spend increasing amounts of their money on the distribution of food, household items, medical care and housing. Whatever the slaves produced and sold themselves was extra, perhaps best described as a vent for surplus.[17]

The changes on Caribbean plantations after 1760 were as fundamental as those during the period after 1640. In view of that it is possible to speak of a *second* plantation revolution. Rather than being dying, blood-sucking leeches at the periphery of world capitalism, modern archival research has shown that after 1760 plantations in most parts of the New World became rather successful economic enterprises, with a strong potential for economic growth as well as for improvement of the working and living conditions of their labourers. In the British Caribbean most of these improvements were already in place before 1800, while in other parts of the area the second plantation revolution occurred during the first half of the nineteenth century.[18]

It was during this period of rapid growth that slavery was abolished. In theory, abolition might have been to the advantage of all concerned. It would have allowed the freedmen to select those employers paying the highest wages and it would have allowed the planters to dispense with payments for costs not directly related to productive labour on the plantation, such as housing, plantation hospitals and medical care and rations for those too young or too old to work.[19]

In some of the smaller islands in the Caribbean, especially those with a high population density, plantations did prosper after emancipation without the arrival of additional labour, their operations being based on modern, capitalist labour relations. In most parts of the Caribbean, however, rising wages were unable to attract enough ex-slaves to work on the plantations. The law of supply and demand simply did not function in those parts of the Caribbean where freedmen had the opportunity to obtain land of their own. In spite of the fact that there was usually a decline in personal incomes as soon as the ex-slaves opted to become peasants, rising wages did not reverse the 'flight from the plantations'. In fact, higher wages further stimulated the freedmen's move away from the plantation, as their need for a regular money income was limited. That explained their 'backward bending' supply of labour.[20]

The Demand for Labour in the Caribbean after Slave Emancipation: Compulsion or Choice?

Very rapidly after emancipation the labour costs of Caribbean plantations reached a level at which it became attractive for the planters to hire labourers from Europe and Asia. Planters were, in addition, willing to pay high prices for former slaves and migrant labourers brought in from elsewhere in the region as well as for illegally imported slaves. They tapped a wide variety of sources. Traditionally, they had turned to Africa, but the supply of Africans was minimal. Paradoxically, the Africans stopped migrating across the Atlantic at the very moment in which the African migrants themselves could finally have negotiated a price for their participation in international migration.[21]

Therefore planters recruited labour in Europe (mainly Spain and Portugal but also Germany) and in India and China. After a transitional period extending roughly from 1830 to 1870, most migrant labour to the Caribbean came from British India and Spain.[22] Why were the planters in the Caribbean so desperate to attract labour bonded to work for a certain period on their plantations? It has been suggested that the reason for the world-wide search for labour was of a political nature and not economic in origin. The planters in the Caribbean, it is said, had been used to working with unfree labour. Emancipation had created a free labour market that the planters wanted to avoid and, in order to achieve this, they imported indentured labour from outside the region.[23]

New research on the plantocracy in the Caribbean sheds doubt on this supposition. Planters had been innovating in their work methods both before and after the abolition of slavery. Unfortunately, it turned out to be technically impossible to save on labour in the fields, whether it be to plant or to harvest sugar cane, cotton or coffee beans. In view of that, most plantations needed a sizeable labour force that lived on the plantations and could perform daily tasks in the field. In order to produce competitively, the plantations thus required a special type of labour. The only way to ensure its regular availability in sparsely populated areas without a market-driven supply of labour was to conclude contracts. The ex-slaves did enter into such contracts but increasingly withdrew from permanent positions as resident field labourers. A decreasing number of freedmen did remain available to work on the plantations on a seasonal basis as members of so-called 'jobbing gangs' whose arrival on the plantation could not be planned with absolute certainty.[24]

There has been some debate among historians about the 'flight from the plantations'. Did the ex-slaves go of their own volition or did the planters push them? The answer is that a combination of the two occurred but that the decisions of the freedmen were the decisive factor. In principle, the situation was clear: many freedmen wanted to continue living in the ex-slave quarters where they always had lived even when they preferred not to work on the plantation. Planters, on the other hand, wanted only those freedmen to live on their estates who intended to provide more than an occasional day's work. Others should leave or pay rent. Those, who provided neither labour nor rent, were accordingly evicted.[25]

Thus stated the options looked clear-cut. In practice, however, decisions to evict former slaves from the estates were not so easy to carry out. By evicting a non-working family member the danger was that all the ex-slaves of that family would leave, some of whom might be valued workers. That is the reason why there were only 'one or two' evictions in Guiana and the same seems to have been the case with Trinidad. The planters and the government did evict ex-slaves in Jamaica from estate or Crown lands, but evicted squatters could move elsewhere or they could buy land, especially when the government had instituted a land grant scheme for the East Indian immigrants. The availability of land was the crucial factor. This explains why the eviction scheme failed to produce a new body of landless freedmen with no choice but to work on plantations.[26]

The replacement of slaves and freedmen by indentured immigrants took time. In the British Caribbean the first indentured labourers arrived after the end of the period of apprenticeship (1834–38), which had artificially prevented the large-scale withdrawal of labour from the plantations. In the French and the Dutch Caribbean slavery had not been ended when the British planters were already experimenting with indentured immigrant labour. In the Spanish Caribbean the use of indentured immigrant labour came to an end even before the slaves had been emancipated. In addition to the different timings of slave emancipation, the ability of the planters to choose among the several possibilities varied widely. The British planters – mainly in Guyana – had been able to attract indentured labourers from the poor regions of Portugal, especially from Madeira, which was economically depressed at the time. In similar fashion, the Cuban planters could recruit from the poor regions of continental Spain as well as from the Canary Islands. Planters in the French and the Dutch Caribbean did not have these options. The British government did not allow the Cuban, Peruvian or Brazilian planters to recruit labour in British India, while this opportunity was granted to British, French, Danish and Dutch planters.[27]

In sum it seems that the planters continued their pre-emancipation drive to increase the productivity of their plantations in order to combat rising labour costs and international competition. They continued to apply their traditional, successful formula by improving the milling and refining procedures. On the labour market, however, slave emancipation had made the Caribbean planter one of the most vulnerable employers in the Atlantic world, at least in the more sparsely populated areas of the region. There the planters had no choice but to adjust their demand for labour to the preferences of the freedmen. There is no reason to assume that by replacing freedmen by Asian immigrants they showed a penchant for creating a loyal rather than an economical workforce, in spite of the fact that in hiring indentured labour from Asia they seemed willing to engage many more labourers than were required as a nuclear workforce. The extra labour must have been economically advantageous as the planters obviously wanted to move away from the system of the 'jobbing gangs' composed of freedmen, who arrived irregularly and on short notice and were willing to perform only certain types of work. Generally speaking, the planters were unable to rely on additional labour from the ex-slaves and could expect little help from the colonial government in disciplining the freedmen. Lack of personnel, abolitionist pressures from the metropolis and the relatively easy access to land all made it impossible for the planters and the West Indian government to imitate the governments of western Europe in their attempts to create a labour force responsive to monetary incentives. Draconian vagrancy laws did not work, as their implementation required the creation of a colonial police state that – among other reasons – could not be financed.[28]

There remained a strong demand for labour on the Caribbean plantations despite the application of labour-saving methods on account of the fact that – at least until the 1930s – the technology of harvesting sugar cane remained extremely labour-intensive. In addition to this labour scarcity, there was the problem that planters had little economic room for manoeuvre as protection for their products was progressively removed. The constantly diminishing number of plantations in the Caribbean is proof of the fact that the West Indian planter could, indeed, go bankrupt by offering higher wages, by providing for the ineffective family members, by allowing labourers more time to tend their private plots and by providing better housing and more social services in general.[29]

The Supply of Asian Labour: Push or Pull?

As the elasticity of the supply varied widely, it took some time before it became clear which region or area could best provide migrant labour at competitive prices. The migration of Portuguese labourers came to a sudden halt when economic conditions improved in Portugal and when more promising destinations such as Brazil opened up. Similarly, the supply of 'free Africans' dried up when the number of those freed from slave ships by the Royal Navy declined. The Atlantic slave trade had been the main supplier of indentured Africans recruited from among former slaves landed in Sierra Leone from slave ships. In contrast to the supply of Europeans and Africans for work in the Caribbean, the supply of Asian labour remained elastic throughout the entire period.[30]

The emigration of Chinese and Indian contract labourers to overseas destinations was part of a long-term push-movement, which seems to have increased dramatically during the course of the nineteenth century, albeit for different reasons.

In the case of China, a rapid demographic increase seems to have been a dominant factor: between the years 1650 and 1850 the population trebled. During most of these years an increased efficiency in agriculture helped to feed the growing population, assisted by a continuous emigration to the overseas Chinese communities around the Indian Ocean littoral. From the earliest stages, the Chinese became important minorities in the Asian empires of the British, the Dutch and the Portuguese. During the nineteenth century Chinese emigration to destinations within Asia itself increased rapidly. It has been estimated that between 1847 and 1874 approximately 1.5 million Chinese, out of 430 million, left for foreign shores. This amounted to 0.3 per cent of the Chinese population. Of these 1.5 million emigrants only around 160,000 went to the Caribbean, amounting to little more than 10 per cent of the total.[31]

The push to emigrate from India had not been caused by a corresponding increase in population, as had been the case in China. The stimuli for migration are usually described as economic, rather than demographic. Indian emigration was of a much more recent date than the Chinese one and was clearly linked to the penetration of the expanding world market, in part a consequence of India's incorporation into the British Empire. This penetration favoured an increase in the size of landholdings, and the consequent 'enclosure movement' pushed considerable numbers of small farmers into a state of landlessness. Meanwhile, Indian urban growth was rapid, for reasons not unlike those operating in parts of Europe at the time.[32]

Emigration from India was closely connected with this internal, long-distance migration. Important destinations for the migration overland were the recruiting offices of the colonial army, the tea gardens of Assam and the textile industries of Bengal. The volume of this long-distance migration within India was much larger than that of the government-regulated migration overseas. It has been estimated that about 20 million Indians, or 6.7 per cent of the native population (estimated at 300 million), participated in long-distance migration during the nineteenth century. Of these 20 million only 1.25 million went overseas under government-supervised schemes, half of whom went to the Caribbean.[33]

In summing up the available evidence on long-distance emigration out of Asia, the following observations may be made:

- the migration of contract labourers to the Caribbean constituted only a minor percentage of the population of China and India;

- the migration of indentured labourers from India and China to the Caribbean never amounted to more than 10 per cent of the Indian and Chinese overseas emigration in general;

- the migration of about 500,000 indentured labourers from India, 30,000 from Java and 150,000 from China to the Caribbean was not halted because of a diminishing demand for migrants. In all three cases migration came to an end because of political decisions.[34]

The emigration of indentured labourers from China was halted in 1874 by the Chinese government after publications in the Western press of horror stories about the conditions aboard the 'coolie ships'. The emigration of Indians was halted in 1916 by the Viceroy under pressure from nationalists, and the emigration of indentured migrants from Java ceased in 1939 due to the outbreak of war.

These data alone are sufficient evidence to suggests that, in general, Asians were not misled into migrating to the Caribbean, which was simply one of many destinations for Asians chosen because its plantations offered comparatively attractive conditions for living and working. By signing a contract of indenture they invested in the opportunity to obtain a better life. As the overwhelming majority of Asian indentured labourers came from India, the following comparison between the freedmen and migrants will be based on the data pertaining to indentured labourers from India.

Freedmen and Indian Indentureds in the Caribbean Market Place

By around 1900 some striking differences had become evident between the position of the freedmen and those of the Asians who had stayed after the termination of their contracts of indenture. After arrival, the Indians had shown remarkable demographic growth, while the Africans had only ceased their centuries-long decline. Secondly, the Asians had almost monopolized jobs in the sugar plantations, even the temporary ones. Thirdly, the Asians had been disproportionally successful as small farmers, whether producing food for the local market or cash crops such as sugar cane and cocoa for export.[35]

How was it possible that the Indians seemed to have profited so much more from the Caribbean economy than the freedmen who had the advantages of being there first and of knowing the opportunities and pitfalls of the region better than any other group? In order to answer this question the economic strategies of the freedmen and the Indian ex-indentureds will be discussed vis-à-vis plantation agriculture, small-scale farming, and family 'resource pooling'.

The differences between the freedmen and the Asian immigrants with regards to plantation agriculture are striking. Time and again researchers have pointed out that the ex-slaves tried to leave the plantations as quickly as possible, while the immigrants left only when they had firm proof that they could earn more outside the plantations than in. In some of the older historical interpretations the 'flight from the plantations' was considered to be economically advantageous for the freedmen. Plantations were a thing of the past, failing undertakings well before the slaves were emancipated. However, as has been pointed out, more recent research has indicated that the Caribbean plantations had a strong potential for growth and that they were able to compete with the producers of tropical cash crops elsewhere. That means that the freedmen were cutting their ties with the most expansive sector of the economy and thus forgoing considerable amounts of income.

In discussing the problem of evictions earlier, it was pointed out that, in general, the freedmen were not compelled to leave the plantations but voluntarily chose to break their ties, thus disconnecting themselves from the most reliable employment sector in the region. It was also pointed out that the break with the plantations was not immediate and never quite complete. That is true; it took several decades before the Asian immigrants became the main source of hired labour; but in view of the centuries-old link between Afro-Caribbeans and the plantations, the dramatic decline in creole labour supply may justly be described as a 'flight' which prevented the freedmen from profiting from the readiness of the planters to pay a market wage.[36]

Asian immigrants, by contrast, displayed a quite different attitude towards plantation labour. First, it should be pointed out that most immigrants were forced to offer their labour to the plantations by the very nature of their indentures. All contracts stipulated that indentured labourers should stay on the plantations to which they had been allotted for a period of five years. In order to qualify for a free return, they were compelled to stay in the colonies to which they had been brought for a period of between five and ten years.[37]

In view of these stipulations it may be safely assumed that virtually all Asian immigrants offered their labour to the plantations during the first five years of their residence. If that behaviour was the result of choice, it was not one based on the economic opportunities within the colony of residence but rather on the difference between working and living on a Caribbean plantation and staying in India. That same choice was available after the expiration of the contracts of indenture.[38]

Virtually the only alternative to plantation labour was small-scale farming. This type of farming could have two objectives: self-sufficiency or production for the market. Usually, small-scale farmers produced crops with both these objectives in mind. Unfortunately, there are no statistics that allow us to compare the performance of the creole and the Asian farmer in the Caribbean. In most of the literature concerning those Caribbean colonies with a sizeable Indian component the formerly indentured labourers are depicted as very successful, whereas the creole farmers are shown to have done less well. This difference would explain why in the present-day Caribbean a much larger percentage of Afro-Caribbeans have moved out of agriculture altogether whereas the Indo-Caribbeans have not. The explanation for this could be found in the fact that in the past the groups had had different educations for small-scale farming. The vast majority of Indians had been small-scale farmers or sharecroppers in India, while the creole farmers had been slaves. Thus the Indians had been used to a market system, while the Creoles had been operating in a non-market, redistributive economic system.

As has also been pointed out, by their very nature the small-scale farming activities could not have prepared the slaves for the post-emancipation market society. Research reveals the fact that the slaves sold at least half of their produce on local markets, which, one might have thought, would have tutored them for a life as farmers after emancipation. As long as the planters were obliged to provide the basic necessities of life, the garden-plot production of the slaves remained something extra. The slaves were not obliged to maximize yields and incomes because they were not dependent upon their garden plots for their survival. In fact, it could be argued that the garden-plot system provided the slaves with a type of education that was a hindrance rather than a help in their post-emancipation lives.[39]

This is demonstrated first by the attitude of the freedmen to land. In spite of the fact that the slaves had the constant use of their own plots of land on the plantations, which they could even transfer to others, the freedmen often left the plantations in order to live together in villages based on the collective ownership of land. The results are clearly visible today:

> The practical outcome of this situation is that land in African villages can become very poorly utilised as control and ownership remain unclear. This is demonstrated very dramatically from the air where, for instance, the one wholly African village in the West Demerara stands out as a tangle of largely uncultivated land in the midst of thousands of acres of sugar estates and rice cultivation in Indian villages.[40]

Secondly, in their haste to leave the plantations, the freedmen seemed to have been more interested in the production items that they could themselves consume. Unlike the Indian farmers, the creoles seemed to have had little interest in producing foodstuffs which they could sell to replace expensive imports from abroad, such as flour, salted meat and fish, which the management of the plantations had traditionally proved for their workers.[41]

A third observation regarding small-scale farming concerns the location of the creole settlements. The majority of the ex-slaves preferred to move away from the plantations, thus reducing the opportunities to obtain medical care and education and to sell their produce. Indians, on the other hand, instead of moving into the hills, usually settled on lands close to the plantations, which allowed them, among other things, to produce sugar cane. In addition, a much larger share of food production by Indians was marketed than that of the creoles, who preferred to grow a variety of crops and only in small quantities. Of course, it should be realized that that Caribbean did not constitute an ideal testing ground for such comparisons. At the time the ex-slaves were setting themselves up as small farmers, the antagonism between the planters and those freedmen not willing to work on the plantations was still considerable. Also, immediately after emancipation most schemes to provide ex-slaves with land of their own were executed by missionaries, whereas most ex-indentureds obtained land in a scheme set up by the government.[42]

Yet that same spirit of antagonism could, at least technically, have also resulted in a more strident, a more organized creole peasantry. True, a small group of creole farmers managed to become successful entrepreneurs, but that elite did not become a model for the poor peasantry in experimenting with new crops and agricultural methods or in introducing new machinery, marketing methods and credit institutions.[43]

The last factor on the list of differences between freedmen and Asian immigrants is the family. Why did the creoles fail to use the post-slavery period to create two-headed households, while the Indians did achieve this once the percentage of women in their community started growing?

The first possible explanation is the difference between the conditions of free peasants and of slaves. By pooling resources and income, Indian men and women were able to get ahead. The two-headed family proved able to produce enough offspring to overcome the relatively high child mortality of the region, allowing the parents to survive in old age with the help of their remaining children. For the slaves, the conditions had been quite different. On the plantations the distribution of food, medical care and housing did not make the two-headed family an appropriate instrument for survival. Each member of the workforce could survive by him or herself, the very young children excepted. Women slaves were not economically dependent upon their male counterparts. Elderly slaves also received food, housing and medical care. Offspring as an insurance against old age were not a necessity. In sum, Indian society made the two-headed family an important instrument of physical survival that the Caribbean slave society had not done. The overseas Indians returned to the two-headed family structure as soon as the number of women allowed for it. The freedmen, on the other hand, preferred to cling to social organizations that had been moulded in response to the individually distributed incomes that came with plantation work rather than adapt themselves to the new demands of post-slavery society.[44]

Conclusion: 'A Spirit of Independence' or the Wrong Education for the Market?

When the American journalist William G. Sewell toured the post-emancipation Caribbean in 1861 he was elated. The abolition of slavery had brought nothing but progress and had greatly improved Caribbean society. The sooner the United States emancipated its slaves the better. However, in some rare moments even Sewell had to admit that emancipation sometimes had worsened their plight:

> The people of Jamaica ware not cared for; they perish miserably in the country districts for want of medical aid; they are not instructed; they have no opportunities to improve themselves in agriculture or mechanics; every effort is made to check a spirit of independence, which in the African is counted as a heinous crime, but in all other people is regarded as a lofty virtue, and the germ of national courage, enterprise, and progress.[45]

As this study has shown, Sewell was mistaken. The 'spirit of independence' among the freedmen resulted in a number of the wrong choices, which cost them dearly. The Asian immigrants made better choices. Their 'spirit of independence' made them leave India and sign a contract of indenture by which they sacrificed some of their independence in order to invest in a better future. The Indians succeeded in reaping some of the profits in exploiting the – admittedly diminishing – geographical advantage of the Caribbean in the production of tropical cash crops. The 'spirit of independence' also made the freedmen move, but their movements usually did not help them to obtain improved living and working conditions. Out in the hinterland of the plantation belts, freedmen tried to eke out a livelihood without education, without improving their primitive agricultural methods and without medical care. The range of products they offered for sale was traditional and did not cut into the range of imports. Those who moved to towns did not succeed in developing an artisan sector that could have substituted for imports from Europe and North America.

In contrast, Indian immigrants on average were able to improve their standard of living considerably. In the beginning, their income and land ownership compared favourably with what they had left behind in India. Towards the end of the nineteenth century the prosperity of the Indians was on a par with if not ahead of, that of the freedmen and their descendants.

Other Asian immigrants were also successful, but not to the same extent. The Chinese could not match the Indian example because there were hardly any women among them and this prevented their becoming a sizeable community. The Javanese indentured labourers, imported into Suriname only between 1890 and 1939 under the same conditions as the Indians, did improve their material and demographic well-being, but never as rapidly and as fully as did the Indians.[46]

The Indian success story was not limited to the Caribbean. Indian immigrants were equally successful in South Africa, Uganda, Mauritius and Fiji. Thus the culture of the country of departure must have been the driving force behind the advancement of Indian migrants rather than the culture of the receiving areas. The three centuries of plantation slavery might have given birth to a 'spirit of independence', but the African, European and Caribbean cultural mix it produced somehow failed to educate its workers for the market society which suddenly came into existence after the end of slavery. The ex-slaves were not prepared to face the ups and downs not only in the market for labour but also in the market for consumer goods. Consequently, riots and rebellions against the vicissitudes of the market economy replaced the rebellions and riots against the pressures within the slavery system. The Asians, on the other hand, never rebelled against the system of indentured labour as such.[47]

So we are back to the question as to why the ex-slaves were so disappointed about their life in freedom, whereas most Indians seemed grateful to have migrated to the post-emancipation Caribbean. The answer must be that their perspectives were different. The Indians had left India behind with its poverty and caste system and found the West Indies a relatively agreeable place to live. The great majority of them showed no inclination to return to India. Most ex-slaves, however, experienced economic decline after emancipation. Moving away from plantation agriculture caused a reduction of their economic well-being as virtually every alternative activity in the Caribbean provided less income.

India taught its inhabitants to like those activities that brought in most money and to maximize their incomes. The Caribbean plantations seem to have done the opposite. The slave plantations produced for the market, even for the world market, but had for centuries shielded their workers from the impact of those market forces which they would have needed to understand and exploit if they were to improve their lives as freedmen.

NOTES

1. On the post-emancipation decline in sugar production and per capita income see Herbert S. Klein and Stanley L. Engerman, 'The transition from slave to free labor: notes on a comparative economic model', in Manuel Moreno Fraginals, Frank Moya Pons and Stanley L. Engerman (eds.), *Between Slavery and Free Labor: The Spanish-Speaking Caribbean in the Nineteenth Century* (Baltimore, MD/London: The Johns Hopkins University Press, 1985), pp.255–69.
2. See Peter Kolchin, 'The tragic era? interpreting Southern reconstruction in comparative perspective', in: Frank McGlynn and Seymour Drescher (eds.), *The Meaning of Freedom, Economics, Politics, and Culture after Slavery* (Pittsburgh, PA/London: University of Pittsburgh Press, 1992), pp.292–311.
3. As 'pars pro toto' I mention only two recent studies: Michael J. Craton, 'Reshuffling the pack: the transition from slavery to other forms of labor in the British Caribbean, ca. 1790–1890', in: *New West Indian Guide*, 68 (1994), pp.23–75 and O. Nigel Bolland, 'The politics of freedom in the British Caribbean', in McGlynn and Drescher (eds.), *The Meaning of Freedom*, pp.113–46.
4. The – by now classic – argument for the viability of the West Indian plantations was put forward by Seymour Drescher, *Econocide: British Slavery in the Era of Abolition* (Pittsburgh, PA: University of Pittsburgh Press, 1977). On the 'policy of amelioration' see J.R. Ward, *British West Indian Slavery, 1750–1834: The Process of Amelioration* (Oxford: Oxford University Press, 1988).
5. H. Tinker, *A New System of Slavery; the Export of Indian Labour Overseas, 1830–1820* (London: Oxford University Press, 1974).
6. '...the plantocracies with the connivance of the imperial government and the British government in India began the steady importation of an alternative labour force of East Indians under terms of indentureship that were little better than "a new system of slavery"', Michael Craton, 'The transition from slavery to free wage labour in the Caribbean, 1780–1890: a survey with particular reference to recent scholarship', *Slavery and Abolition*, 13, 2 (Aug. 1992), p.45.
7. David Northrup, *Indentured Labor in the Age of Imperialism, 1834–1922* (Cambridge: Cambridge University Press, 1995), pp.120–39.
8. Pieter C. Emmer, 'Scholarship or solidarity? The post-emancipation era in the Caribbean reconsidered', *New West Indian Guide*, 69, 3 (1995), pp.277–90 and Michael J. Craton, 'Response to Pieter C. Emmer's "Reconsideration"', ibid., 69, 3 (1995), pp.291–7.
9. A. Lemon and N. Pollock (eds.), *Studies in Overseas Settlements and Population* (London: Longman, 1980), p.228.
10. Robert William Fogel, *Without Consent or Contract: the Rise and Fall of American Slavery* (New York, NY: W.W. Norton, 1989), pp.60–113.
11. Robert William Fogel and Stanley L. Engerman, *Time on the Cross: The Economics of American Negro Slavery* (London: Wildwood House, 1974), pp.144–57, 238–9.
12. Ward, *British West Indian Slavery*, p.192.
13. B.W. Higman, *Slave Populations of the British Caribbean, 1807–1834* (Baltimore, MD/London: The Johns Hopkins University Press, 1976), pp.303–7.
14. Michael Craton, James Walvin and David Wright (eds.), *Slavery, Abolition and Emancipation: Black Slaves and the British Empire* (London: Longman, 1976), pp.310–15.
15. Sidney W. Mintz, 'The origins of reconstituted peasantries' in: Hilary Beckles and Verene Shepherd (eds.), *Caribbean Freedom; Economy and Society from Emancipation to the Present; A Student Reader* (Kingston/London: Randle/Curry, 1993), pp.94–8.
16. Ira Berlin and Philip D. Morgan, 'Introduction', *Slavery and Abolition*, 12, 1 (May 1991), p.1.
17. William A. Green, *British Slave Emancipation: The Sugar Colonies and the Great Experiment, 1830–1865* (Oxford: Oxford University Press, 1976), p.27.
18. Drescher, *Econocide*, pp.65–91.
19. David Eltis, 'Abolitionist perceptions of society after slavery', in J. Walvin (ed.), *Slavery and British Society, 1776–1846* (London: Macmillan, 1982), pp.195–213.

20. Green, *British Slave Emancipation*, pp.196–9; Alan H. Adamson, *Sugar without Slaves: The Political Economy of British Guiana, 1838–1904* (New Haven, CT: Yale University Press, 1972), pp.119–21; Stanley L. Engerman, 'Economic adjustments to emancipation in the United States and British West Indies', *Journal of Interdisciplinary History*, 13 (1982), pp.200–1.

21. Paul E. Lovejoy, *Transformations in Slavery: A History of Slavery in Africa* (Cambridge: Cambridge University Press, 1983), pp.146, 147; W.G. Clarence-Smith, 'Emigration from Western Africa, 1807–1940', in P.C. Emmer and Magnus Mörner (eds.), *European Expansion and Migration: Essays on the Intercontinental Migration from Africa, Asia and Europe* (New York, NY/Oxford: Berg Publishers, 1992), pp.197–210.

22. P.C. Emmer, 'Immigration into the Caribbean: the introduction of Chinese and East Indian indentured labourers between 1839 and 1917', in Emmer and Mörner (eds.), *European Expansion and Migration*, p.251.

23. Eric Foner, *Nothing but Freedom: Emancipation and its Legacy* (Baton Rouge, LA/London: Louisiana State University Press, 1983), p.22.

24. Emmer, 'The price of freedom: the constraints of change in postemancipation America', in McGlynn and Drescher (eds.), *The Meaning of Freedom*, p. 30; Craton, 'The transition from slavery to free wage labour', p.60, suggests that plantation managers forced the system of 'jobbing gangs' upon the freedmen. However, Craton does not provide evidence that the freedmen were willing to offer their labour in any other way.

25. The classic article on evictions from the estates is Douglas Hall, 'The flight from the estates reconsidered: the British West Indies, 1838–1842', in Beckles and Shepherd (eds.), *Caribbean Freedom*, pp.55–64.

26. Green, *British Slave Emancipation*, pp.297–300; Philip J. McLewin, *Power and Economic Change; The Response to Emancipation in Jamaica and British Guiana, 1840–1865* (New York, NY/London: Garland Publishing, 1987), pp.199, 200.

27. Stanley L. Engerman, 'Servants to slaves to servants: contract labour and European expansion', in P.C. Emmer (ed.), *Colonialism and Migration: Indentured Labour before and after Slavery* (Dordrecht: Nÿhoff Publishers, 1986), pp.270–6.

28. I have not been able to find the data allowing me to calculate the percentage of military and police per 1,000 inhabitants in the north Atlantic world. As there must have been a general increase during the nineteenth century my suggestion is that the ratio still remained much smaller in the Caribbean than in western Europe.

29. Roberta M. Delson, 'Sugar production for the nineteenth century British market: rethinking the roles of Brazil and the British West Indies', in Bill Albert and Adrian Graves (eds.), *Crisis and Change in the International Sugar Economy, 1860–1914* (Norwich/Edinburgh: JSC Press, 1984), pp.59–82 The importation of foreign sugar in Britain increased from 0 in 1844 to 42 per cent in 1860.

30. Emmer, 'Immigration into the Caribbean', pp.255–8.

31. Ibid., p.252.

32. Gail Omvedt, 'Migration in colonial India: the articulation of feudalism and capitalism by the colonial state', *Journal of Peasant Studies*, 7 (1980), pp.185–212; Armand A. Yang, 'Peasants on the move: a study of internal migration in India', *Journal of Interdisciplinary History*, 10, 1 (1979), pp.37–58; Walton Look Lai, *Indentured Labour, Caribbean Sugar; Chinese and Indian Migrants to the British West Indies, 1838–1918* (Baltimore, MD/London: The Johns Hopkins University Press, 1993), pp.20–37.

33. Emmer, 'Immigration into the Caribbean', pp.253, 254.

34. Joseph Arnold Meagher, 'The Introduction of Chinese Laborers to Latin America: The "Coolie" Trade, 1847–1874', PhD thesis (Davis: University of California, 1975), pp.307–46; Tinker, *A New System of Slavery*, pp.334–67; Joseph Ismael, *De Immigratie van Indonesiërs in Suriname* (Leiden: Luctor et Emergo, 1949), pp.66–76.

35. Eric Hanley, 'The Guyanese rice industry and development planning. The wrong solution for the wrong problem?', in Jean Besson and Janet Momsen (eds.), *Land and Development in the Caribbean* (London: Macmillan, 1987), pp.172–93.

36. The ups and downs of the estate wages in Jamaica are analysed in Thomas C. Holt, *The Problem of Freedom; Race, Labor, and Politics in Jamaica and Britain, 1832–1938*

(Kingston: Jan Randle, 1992), pp.126–8.

37. K.O. Lawrence, 'The evolution of long-term labour contracts in Trinidad and British Guiana, 1834–1863', in Beckles and Shepherd (eds.), *Caribbean Freedom*, pp.141–51.

38. An interesting account of one return voyage to India and an evaluation of the return voyage system from Trinidad to India: Marianne Soares Ramesar, 'The repatriates', in David Dabydeen and Brinsley Samaroo (eds.), *Across the Dark Waters; Ethnicity and Indian Indentiy in the Caribbean* (London: Macmillan, 1996), pp.175–200.

39. Two authors view the slaves as 'proto peasants': Sidney Mintz, 'The origins of reconstituted peasanties', in Beckles and Shepherd (eds.), *Caribbean Freedom*, pp.94–9 and Woodville Marshall, 'Notes on peasant development in the West Indies since 1838', in ibid., pp.99–107.

40. Hanley, 'The Guyanese rice industry', p.185.

41. Douglas Hall, *Free Jamaica, 1838–1865: An Economic History* (Aylesbury: Caribbean Universities Press/Ginn and Company Ltd., 1978), p.165.

42. D. Wood, *Trinidad in Transition* (London: Oxford University Press, 1968), pp.274–7 and Adamson, *Sugar without Slaves*, pp.94–8.

43. J.R. Ward, *Poverty and Progress in the Caribbean, 1800–1960* (London; Macmillan, 1985), pp.56–60.

44. Sidney Mintz, 'Black women, economic roles and cultural traditions', in Beckles and Shepherd (eds.), *Caribbean Freedom*, pp.238–45.

45. William G. Sewell, *The Ordeal of Free Labour in the British West Indies* (London: Frank Cass, 1968), p.178.

46   P.C. Emmer, 'Asians compared: some observations regarding Indian and Indonesian labourers in Surinam, 1873–1939', *Itinerario*, 11 (1981), pp.149–54.

47. Freedmen and their descendents rebelled against 'white oppression' in general, according to Michael Craton, 'The incidence of unrest among ex-slaves in the British West Indies, 1838–1876', in Beckles and Shephard (eds.), *Caribbean Freedom*, pp.192–206, while Indian indentureds sometimes protested against the working and living condition on their particular plantation: Kusha Haraksingh, 'The worker and the wage in a plantation economy. Trinidad in the late nineteenth century', in Mary Turner (ed.), *From Chattel Slaves to Wage Slaves; The Dynamics of Labour Bargaining in the Americas* (Kingston/London: Ian Randle/James Curry, 1995), pp.224–38.

The Delegalization of Slavery in British India

HOWARD TEMPERLEY

External Pressures on the Government of India

The question of Indian slavery first engaged Parliament's attention in June 1833. The old East India Company Charter was expiring and a new one had to be approved. By a remarkable coincidence this happened to be at the very time Parliament was considering the Emancipation Bill freeing the slaves in the Caribbean, Mauritius and elsewhere in the British Empire. In fact the new East India Charter Bill received its first reading in the Commons on 28 June, exactly a week before the introduction of the Emancipation Bill, so both were passing through the stages necessary for legislative approval at virtually the same time. Of the two, the Charter bill, at least in its original form, was the more radical in its approach to slavery. Whereas the Emancipation bill allowed for a transition period of 12 years (later reduced to six) before the final freeing of the slaves and provided generous compensation of £20 million to their owners, the Charter bill made no provision whatever for compensation and stated categorically that slavery would end by 12 April 1837.[1]

Considering the extent to which West Indian slavery had engrossed public attention over the preceding half century, it may seem surprising that it had taken so long for slavery in the East Indies to come to Parliament's notice. It must be remembered, however, that what happened in India was primarily the concern of the East India Company, a commercial institution operating under royal charter, rather than of Parliament. More importantly, slavery in India was a very different proposition from slavery in the New World in that it was an institution the British had inherited – for the most part only recently – rather than one that they had themselves created. The existence of Indian slavery stirred no sense of national guilt or impulse to remedy past wrongs in the way West Indian slavery did. There was no question, as in the West, of one race exploiting another. So far as race and colour were concerned, apart from minor variations associated with caste, owners and slaves were of similar appearance and origin. But what perhaps more than anything distinguished it was its intimate relationship with the Indian caste system. Slavery in the East was a native growth of great antiquity. Indian society, moreover, was deeply conservative. From top to bottom it was characterized by strongly-held notions of hierarchy and deference, one result of which was that there was no ready way of distinguishing where obligations associated with slavery ended and other types of obligation began. Two things, however, were clear. One was that Western ideas of individual freedom were at odds with the prevailing assumptions governing Indian society. The other was that, with only a tiny army at its disposal, the Company's authority depended on the support of India's slaveholding elite. For these reasons any attempt to do in the East what was being done in the West was bound to have very different repercussions.

Abolitionists had hitherto been so preoccupied with West Indian slavery that the very existence of slavery in the East Indies had largely escaped their notice. How many slaves there were and how they were treated neither they nor anyone else had any clear idea. In any case, divided as they were over apprenticeship, paying compensation to planters and other features of the Emancipation Bill, they were ill-prepared to take up, still less devote serious thought to, a wholly new issue.

The field was thus left open for critics of the Charter bill to warn Parliament of the perils of what was being proposed. As the measure wound its way through the two Houses, one speaker after another bore witness to the fragile nature of British rule, conjuring up alarming visions of the mayhem and bloodshed that would inevitably follow any hasty action. Cutler Fergusson entertained his fellow MPs with the bizarre picture of measures being taken to 'throw open the harems of the Mohammedans and the zenanas of the natives to the inspection of the Company's officers'. Indians, he said, were notoriously protective of their religious and domestic practices and any attempt to interfere with them would 'throw the whole country into a flame'.[2] Speaking in the Lords, the Earl of Ellenborough described slavery in India as a generally mild institution. In fact, to call it slavery at all was a misnomer since the gradations implicit in India's caste system were the essential issue. To interfere with them, as was apparently proposed, was simply 'insanity'. 'What was it,' he demanded, 'but to say ... that there should be insurrection in every part of India?'[3] In similar vein, the Duke of Wellington took it upon himself to remind the peers, on the basis of his own long experience in India, of the need to 'uphold the ancient laws, customs, and religion of the country'. So far as slavery was concerned, if they valued their Indian possessions they should 'deal lightly with the subject'.[4]

Among the most passionate speakers was the recently elected T.B. Macaulay. As he saw it, the Company's rule took the form of 'an enlightened and paternal despotism'. Britain stood for all that was noble and good – in contrast to India's previous rulers, who had been 'miserable tyrants'. In consequence of past misrule the Indian masses had remained sunk in the lowest depths of slavery and superstition. It was Britain's destiny in the fullness of time to confer on them a measure of her own freedom and civilization; but in order to do that she would need to proceed with caution, paying respect to 'feelings generated by differences of religion, of nation, of caste'. As the ruling power, the Company could not shrug off its responsibility for seeing that the rule of law was maintained. The problem was that in practice there was no agreed set of principles to guide those whose task it was to adjudicate such matters. Local advisers, whether Muslim or Hindu, were of little help and often disagreed with one another. That left everything to the discretion of individual judges. What was practised, according to Macaulay, was not law at all but a series of *ad hoc* decisions delivered by baffled colonial functionaries who presided over a people whose minds they could not read and whose customs they did not fully understand.

> I asked a most distinguished Civil Servant of the Company whether, at present, if a dancing girl ran away from her master, the Judge would force her to go back. 'Some Judges', he said, 'send a girl back, others set her at liberty. The whole is a mere matter of chance. Everything depends on the temper of the individual Judge.'[5]

In other words it was all 'a mere lottery'. For the sake of equity, if nothing else, some agreed set of principles was needed. But slavery was a complicated matter so it would be best to refer that question to the Governor General for further consideration. Sir Thomas Fowell Buxton, the leading abolitionist spokesman in the Commons, agreed that, at least for the present, that would be the best course to follow.[6]

Thus, during its successive readings, the bill was progressively emasculated – first by the removal of the date specifying when slavery would be abolished, then by the insertion of provisions giving wide discretionary powers to the Indian authorities, and finally by the addition of a clause delegating virtually all responsibility to the Indian government. In this much-amended form it received the Royal Assent on 28 August 1833.[7]

What was now supposed to happen was that the Company's Court of Directors in London would inform Delhi of Parliament's instructions. The Indian government, consisting of the Governor General and a council of three, would then draw up a draft act indicating how it proposed to deal with the topic, which it would then transmit to London for approval. Once the Court of Directors had given it their attention, a copy together with any required amendments would be sent back to Delhi where steps would be taken to ensure that it was promptly implemented. Meanwhile, the Court of

Directors, through the India Board, whose chairman was a member of the Cabinet, would see that Parliament and the government were kept informed of what was happening and answer any questions put to the Indian authorities regarding the progress being made. In theory nothing could have been more straightforward.

In practice what ensued were nine years of bureaucratic muddle and delay. Mainly this was because the Indian authorities were in no hurry to come to grips with what they plainly regarded as a troublesome question foisted on them by outsiders ignorant of Indian customs and unfamiliar with the actual problems involved in governing a vast continent, ten times larger than Britain itself, with a heterogeneous and volatile population. As also became evident, the opportunities for prevarication were virtually limitless. Given that the only method of communication was by sea, an exchange of letters between London and Delhi could take the better part of a year and might take even longer if it was thought that the provincial administrations in Bombay and Madras should also be consulted. To complicate matters further, the Court of Directors' instructions regarding slavery arrived in Delhi at the same time as news of the impending arrival of the newly-appointed Indian Law Commission with none other than the young Macaulay at its head. Parliament had taken Macaulay's criticisms to heart and given this body the task of looking into Indian legal practices with a view to drafting a single, comprehensive penal code for the whole of the subcontinent. To the Delhi authorities the prospect of being able to call on the advice of so well qualified a group appeared a singular stroke of good fortune. They accordingly informed the Court of Directors that they intended to refer the issue of slavery to the Commission.[8]

Three years now elapsed without further news. Meanwhile, the abolitionists, with the issue of West Indian slavery largely settled, found themselves more at liberty to turn their attention to other areas of endeavour, among them the question of slavery in the East Indies. Like everyone else, they were under the impression that progress of some sort was occurring. Not surprisingly, therefore, they were concerned to discover that the Indian government had signally failed to do as it had promised, namely to draw the attention of the Law Commissioners to the issue. As a result, the Commissioners were under the impression that they were expected to concern themselves with slavery only in so far as was necessary in order to complete their penal code. To make matters worse, the Indian overnment now refused to grant them permission to enquire further on the grounds that Parliament was impatient and a report on the subject was urgently needed. Fortunately the Commissioners had already collected a sizeable body of material, and it was on the basis of this in December 1838 that they began compiling a new report specifically on the subject of slavery.

Presented to Parliament in 1841, their report is the most detailed contemporary account we have of servitude in early nineteenth-century India.[9] Meanwhile, other accounts had been appearing, among them *Slavery in India* (London, 1839) by the Reverend James Peggs, a former missionary. Another was the Reverend William Adam's *The Law and Custom of Slavery in British India* (Boston, 1840). Adam, also a former British missionary and now a professor at Harvard, addressed the 1840 World Anti-Slavery Convention on the subject. In 1841 a new periodical *The British India Advocate* appeared.[10] This was the organ of the British India Society, a body founded, largely by abolitionists, in 1839 with a view to encouraging the development of free-grown East Indian cotton and sugar as substitutes for the slave-grown New World varieties, a possibility that much intrigued American abolitionists.[11] With more attention focusing on India, it was becoming clear that the Indian government could not shrug off the issue of slavery indefinitely. Something would have to be done.

The Character of Indian Slavery

As more was learned about Indian slavery it became increasingly clear that it bore little relation to its New World counterpart. What had given rise to slavery in the West were an abundance of resources and a lack of labour, whereas in the densely populated East the situation was quite the reverse: there was an abundance of labour and a lack of resources. Slavery in the West was the direct consequence of Europe's voracious demand for sugar, cotton and other staples and the want of an indigenous workforce capable of meeting it. Native Americans, it had been discovered, were neither numerous nor resilient enough for the task. Nor would immigrant labour suffice. There simply was not enough of it, partly because Europeans refused to migrate to the Americas to labour on plantations, partly because, with a superfluity of land available for settlement, those who did migrate preferred to become landowners in their own right. Even had free migrants been prepared to devote the greater part of their productive energies to producing export staples they could not have satisfied Europe's demands as cheaply and effectively as slaves did.

That meant developing the Americas with a labour force drawn largely from Africa. In the 300 years before 1820 three times as many Africans as Europeans migrated to the Americas.[12] Where land was so readily available, and without the labour to work it virtually valueless, they became their owners' principal source of wealth. Thus New World slavery was a highly capitalized form of economic endeavour, based on legally sanctioned coercion. Over the years, as Christopher Schmidt-Nowara shows in his contribution to the present collection, this gave rise to some of the largest and most profitable enterprises in the entire West. Looked at in one way it represented a natural response to the absence of the pressures that in societies with less favourable ratios of land to population ensure the availability of labour. Yet, paradoxically, the kind of frontier conditions favouring bondage in the case of Africans allowed European settlers an exceptional degree of liberty thanks to the ready availability of land and other easily exploitable resources. Often, in consequence of living far from the centres of political authority, they were freed also from many of the traditional restraints of government. In a sense, therefore, New World freedom and New World slavery were opposite sides of the same coin. Maintaining two systems based on diametrically opposing principles – an unusual degree of freedom allowed some in contrast to the heavy burden of servitude imposed on others – within the same body politic presented problems. As always, arguments could be found, but they were apt to appear more plausible to the owners of slaves than to the slaves themselves. One of the Indian Law Commissioners, contrasting New World slavery with slavery in the East, described it as 'a system of mere violence and oppression – a system of which the vivifying principle is the dread of the cart whip'.[13] If masters had every reason for wanting to hold on to their slaves, the slaves, who could not but be aware of the benefits they were being denied, had every bit as much reason for wanting to be free.

Slavery in India was quite a different matter.[14] For a start, it was almost totally lacking those capitalistic features that characterized slavery in the West. Mostly slave labour was not associated with primary production or pecuniary profit. Those who held slaves did so mainly because having workers to till their fields, and thereby help to support their retinues of hereditary domestics and retainers, suited their convenience and were a sign of affluence and station. Their primary purpose was to contribute to the comfort of themselves, their families and their dependants and not, as in the West, to accumulate a fortune out of the surplus – for which, it should be added, the country's economic system offered little scope. Most Indian slavery, according to the reports of both the Law Commissioners and the Indian government, was relatively benign. Far from contradicting the basic principles on which the larger society rested, it was rather one form of dependency among many in a culture based on notions of social interdependence. From the point of view of India's new rulers it appeared a natural response to the vicissitudes of life on the subcontinent, held together both by the mutual interests of owners and slaves and by the force of habit. Summing up his impressions, C.H. Cameron, one of the Commissioners, observed:

> Our researches into the subject of Indian slavery have led me to believe that it operates in a great degree in mitigation of the evils that

are incident to the state of society prevailing in the greater part of this country. I believe that it mitigates the evils of poverty, at all times pressing heavily on the lower orders, in times of dearth and famine pressing with intolerable severity. Slavery may be regarded as the Indian poor law and preventive of infanticide.[15]

Slaves could not but be aware of the advantages of their position as compared with that of landless labourers, and, so far as he could tell, there was no conscious desire for freedom on their part. Slavery implied a two-way obligation: slaves were expected to work for their owners and in return owners were expected to find work and supply sustenance for their slaves. At the very least slaves were saved from having to resort to begging for a living. In a society where crops frequently failed and where the population pressed heavily on available resources there were advantages to having a protector in times of need.

In their Report the Commissioners listed 16 ways in which slaves might be acquired. Most slaves, it noted, were born on the estates or into the households to which they belonged, but others might be inherited, bought from dealers, acquired in discharge of debt or as a result of being maintained in times of famine.[16] So-called 'free' labourers, whose custom it was to hire themselves out for long periods, could become slaves if they fell into debt. Employers who advanced money, say for marriage expenses, expected their employees to pay this off by monthly deductions, but in practice this process often extended over so long a period that the borrower and his descendants became effectively bondsmen.[17] The sale or gift of children by their parents was by no means always or even usually the act of gross inhumanity that it might appear to Westerners. During the great Bengal famine of 1833 women offering to sell their children in return for a few handfuls of rice thronged the streets of Calcutta. When the Commissioners looked into this practice in 1840 they concluded that, deplorable though it was, they were unwilling to forbid it as there might well be no other way of ensuring survival. So far as they could see there was no feasible way of setting up machinery to provide public relief. India's problems were simply too great to allow the kinds of solution that might be applicable in the West. As the Governor General Lord Auckland reported in 1841, there were limits to what the Government of India could do.

We must deeply pity and lament whatever there may be of degradation, poverty and helplessness among the lower classes of our Indian subjects, and those under subjection, under any form or designation, to those of better birth, to the powerful and wealthy. It behoves us to watch their condition with a vigilant eye and to do what may be in the power of the Government for its amelioration. But we ought not, through a misuse of names, to form an erroneous idea of things, or seek violently to disturb relations to which in many cases all who share in them are attached, regarding them as a service of mutual advantage, or even an honour and distinction.[18]

In common with most Indian government officials, Auckland regarded slavery as being the least of India's problems. In a society predicated on notions of unfreedom the existence of particular forms of it hardly seemed to matter. In any case, as he saw it anything that could legitimately be called slavery had effectively ceased to exist throughout the territories under Company control. What went on in the native states was not the Company's responsibility.

Given that the Company's policy was not to interfere with India's domestic institutions any more than the maintenance of civil order required, it may be doubted whether slavery was quite as limited in scope or as benign as he and others claimed. The Commissioners spent much time discussing whether owners should be allowed to continue employing ropes and canes as a form of 'moderate chastisement', noting that a 'moderate right of correction' was traditional in India and by no means confined to slaves.[19] Trafficking in women for purposes of prostitution was also apparently a common practice although already technically illegal. In former times slaves had been imported from Africa, black eunuchs being particularly favoured for employment in harems, but that traffic had allegedly been stopped in 1811. So too, at least in theory, had the transportation of slaves between provinces, a practice forbidden by the Indian government in 1832. But, as the Commissioners were continually reminded, it was never easy to distinguish what was supposed to happen from what actually did happen. Much of what occurred never reached the attention of Company officials.

Among the things that made the problem hard to grasp and clearly distinguished Indian slavery from its Western counterpart was its diversity. Under Hindu law, the Commissioners noted, there were five categories of person owing service: pupils, apprentices, hirelings, overseers, and slaves – whose precise duties were not always easy to distinguish. But even in the case of so-called slaves there hardly seemed a form of human servitude, however bizarre, that did not occur somewhere on the Indian subcontinent. There were hill tribes whose members were regarded as the legitimate property of whoever could catch them. There were slave families with quasi-religious functions, such as those who attended the Temple of Juggernaut. There were individuals who were considered free in some situations but servile in others, as was the case with freemen who married slaves. Generally speaking, children assumed the status of their mothers, but in this, as in almost everything else, much depended on local custom and the whims of their owners.[20]

How many slaves there were it was also impossible to say, partly on account of lack of knowledge but also because of the problem of definition. James Peggs put the number at under one million, but William Adam supposed it came to considerably more. At the 1840 World Anti-Slavery Convention the figure of 6–8 million was mooted. The highest estimate was that of Sir Bartle Frere, who supposed that if the British protectorates and princely territories were taken together the total might be 16 million. If true, this was 20 times the number freed in Britain's colonies by the 1833 Emancipation Act and some four times greater than the entire slave population of the New World. On the other hand, it would not have constituted an especially large proportion of India's total population, then estimated at around 150 million.[21]

Much slavery, it appeared, was of a domestic variety and involved cooking, waiting at table, sweeping, working in the stables and other similar functions. It was common practice for well-off families to have retinues of slave servants. As in the West, these might be bought, sold and moved about at will, although on the basis of the information gathered it would appear that that rarely happened. There were also reported to be strong conventions that discouraged the breaking up of families. In the case of agrarian slaves the type of service required and the degree of freedom permitted also varied enormously. Most might more accurately be described as serfs or peons, being attached to the land on which they worked by some form of financial indebtedness or by hereditary loyalties to particular land-owning families, or by some combination of the two. Others were effectively chattels in the full sense. Some spent their entire lives working under close supervision spurred on by the threat of punishment; others, by virtue of having well-established claims to the use of the land that they cultivated, had managed to attain virtual independence. In some cases their servitude was conditional on their owners continuing to provide an agreed measure of subsistence, in others it was not. Virtually all agricultural workers were allowed small plots of land from which they were expected to provide for most of their needs. In parts of southern India such as Malabar, Kanara and the Tamil country, as much as a fifth of the agricultural population consisted of persons belonging to this category. In all probability similar conditions obtained elsewhere. As their entire livelihood depended on their owners' patronage there was little chance of slaves running away. Contemporary accounts contain no evidence pointing to large-scale plantation agriculture of the type practised in the West. So far as can be gleaned, the day-to-day labours of south India's slaves did not differ greatly in kind from those of the surrounding peasantry who, as elsewhere on the subcontinent, constituted the greater part of the agricultural workforce.[22]

What rendered slavery in India most bewildering to Europeans, however, was its relation to – or, more precisely, the way it was super-imposed on – India's caste system. Like their Muslim predecessors, the British had not attempted to change the caste practices of the Hindus. The Law Commissioners laboured long, albeit ineffectually, to make sense of Hindu and Muslim texts on the topic, compiling lists of the groups involved and their relative privileges and disabilities. There being competing schools of thought, however, the authorities seldom agreed, and even when this happened what they said was seldom of much help in adjudicating particular disputes. Like most things in India, decisions were generally based on combinations of law and convention as modified by local practice.[23] In short, the situation was much as Macaulay had described it.

So far as practices relating to caste were concerned, the range of variation was so great that even the best modern authorities provide little guidance. Supposedly all Indians belonged to one of five broad categories: Brahmans (priests), Kshatriyas (warriors), Vaishas (farmers and traders), Sudras (artisans and labourers), and Untouchables (a pariah caste whose task it was to perform functions commonly regarded as degrading). Each of these categories, in turn, was made up of many subcategories. Thus in any particular area there might be as many as 200 distinct caste groupings membership of which determined an individual's social standing, cultural character, mode of attire and choice of spouse. This applied at all levels of society. In Uttar Pradesh, for example, the lowest castes included the Bhangi (sweepers), Chamar (leatherworkers) and Dhobi (clothes washers). These were considered untouchable not only by those of higher rank but, in the case of the Dhobis and Bhangis, by one another. There were, moreover, varying degrees of untouchability. Some castes considered particularly impure were compelled to live in hamlets outside the main villages and to draw their water from separate wells. They were further forbidden to wear shoes and in some instances obliged to announce their approach by crying out warnings. Even contact with their shadows could be regarded as polluting. Yet they were far from being total outcasts. Although regarded as impure, Dhobis performed a cleansing function and so were allowed to enter homes for the purpose of collecting and delivering washing. There were also elaborate rules about who could serve food to whom and what categories of food it was permissible for them to serve.[24]

These practices reflected the deeply held, quasi-religious beliefs on which the entire structure of Indian society rested and so were much more than mere matters of social etiquette. Fundamental to this whole structure was the idea of a largely static hierarchy of hereditary groups and subgroups loosely associated with certain functions and spanning the whole of society from the Brahmins at the top to the Dhobis and other impure castes at the bottom. The notion of society as being an arena within which free and self-sufficient individuals competed for position was thus wholly alien to Indian thinking. So too was the Western concept of society itself as having originated as a voluntary association that individuals freely entered into as if by contract and on the basis of which they obtained rights. This did not mean that Indians did not have rights. On the contrary, the entire structure of Indian society was conceived of as an intricate system of reciprocal rights and obligations. These, however, were divinely sanctified and entered into at birth, not the product of free choice or any sort of contract. In short, Indians subscribed to a holistic view of society, seeing it as a quasi-religious entity within which each individual, by virtue of belonging to a particular group, had his or her preordained place, the interaction of the parts contributing to the well-being of the whole.[25]

This, however, did not prevent individuals from being enslaved. Apart from Brahmins, to whom special provisions applied, anyone might be enslaved for any number of reasons – as, in the event of apostasy, so too could Brahmins. Being a slave, however, did not have the effect of nullifying an individual's caste status. Untouchables remained untouchable; higher caste slaves continued to occupy the same positions as formerly in so far as their religious status and ritualistic functions were concerned. Individuals held in slavery were naturally subject to the particular disabilities deriving from their servile status. On the other hand, they did not suffer the 'social death' which, it has been argued, is the common consequence of enslavement.[26] From this it followed that, unlike slaves in the West, slaves in India did not necessarily belong to the lowest rung of society. In practice, most slaves worked as artisans or on the land and were members of India's lower castes. Others were recruited from India's tribal communities whose members also were regarded as of lowly status. But domestic slaves, particularly those employed in handling foodstuffs and looking after children, had of necessity to belong to castes above whatever so far as their owners were concerned constituted the line of impurity. Hindu law further provided that, in order that enslavement remain consonant with religious prescriptions, owners were forbidden from employing slaves of a caste superior to their own. Religious and social prescriptions limited owners' freedom of action in other ways also. In the case of slave marriages and funerals, for example, owners were obligated to ensure that the same conventions be observed as with marriages and funerals involving non-slaves of the same caste.[27]

Had Indian slavery been based on capitalist principles such prescriptions would, of course, have gone by the board. How effectively they were enforced it is impossible to say. There are accounts of Thugs kidnapping children and offering them for sale. Thuggery was a practice the British were in the process of stamping out. Nevertheless, it is doubtful whether those who acquired such children or bought slaves from other dealers either wished to know or were always correctly informed as to their true caste status. On the other hand, had there been a commonly held perception that religious prescriptions were routinely flouted, the Law Commissioners would presumably have noted the fact. They would hardly have gone to the trouble that they did examining Hindu and Muslim texts had they regarded them as inoperative. Commentators, both at the time and since, have assumed that slavery operated in ways roughly consistent with the holistic assumptions of which the caste system was a reflection.[28]

This would go far towards explaining another common observation, namely the lack of discernible discontent or rebelliousness on the part of India's slave population. As already indicated, slaves enjoyed a measure of security generally unavailable to landless freemen. Over and above that, however, it is reasonable to suppose that they subscribed to the same assumptions as those governing the behaviour of other members of a society based on principles of hierarchy and deference. Although slavery was one thing and caste another, the rights and obligations involved were closely related, both being based on notions of authority and subordination. Violations of caste convention were apt to provoke violent reprisals.[29] To those already burdened with a low caste status, the temptation to contest their servile status was accordingly reduced. Auckland cited a number of cases of slaves positively refusing to be emancipated. He also referred to the experience of an English employer:

> In Malabar, all the influence of the English proprietor of an estate cannot obtain for his labourers a greater degree of respect than the strict usages of caste allow them; they remain, whatever the liberty of action he accords them, as degraded as before, for they cannot raise themselves above the class to which they belong.[29]

There was not, in other words, the same contrast between being a slave and being free in India that there was in the West. Slaves had, of course, every reason to resent brutal treatment or any other form of behaviour on the part of masters that violated accepted notions of reciprocity and might appeal for help on that account. Those who were Hindu might further hope that in some future reincarnation they would enjoy a more favoured position. But that was a very different thing from aspiring to freedom in the Western sense, a concept as far removed from their way of thinking as from that of Indians in general.

Act V of 1843

The Law Commissioners' draft proposals for India's new penal code were submitted to the Company's Court of Directors in London for their approval in the autumn of 1838. These had been composed before the Commissioners were aware of Parliament's instruction to make a particular point of looking into ways of ending Indian slavery. Nevertheless, among their recommendations was one to the effect that 'no act which would be an offence if done against a free person be exempted from punishment because it is done against a slave'. This was just the sort of thing Parliament had been waiting for. The Directors therefore instructed Lord Auckland, the Governor General, to see that the Indian government lost no time in adopting appropriate measures. Thus, for a moment, it looked as if the whole issue were settled. But Auckland was sceptical about what was being proposed, arguing that the Company's officials fully recognized the principle that owners and slaves be placed on an equal footing so far as the law was concerned. The matter was therefore referred back for further advice, first to the Law Commissioners and then to the provincial governments of Madras and Bombay.[31]

Abolitionists by this time were naturally becoming restive. In 1833, in the aftermath of the Emancipation Act, they had proudly boasted to the world that slavery had ended throughout the British Empire only to discover that that was not strictly true. They had since launched campaigns to persuade the United States, France and other powers to follow Britain's example by getting rid of their slave systems. The British and Foreign Anti-Slavery Society's much heralded World Anti-Slavery Convention, held in London in the summer of 1840, was essentially an assertion of Britain's claim to moral leadership in such matters. The United States, France and the other powers targeted, needless to say, remained unimpressed. If only to reaffirm Britain's moral credentials something needed to be done about India.

In April 1841, having taken note of Parliament's desire that they focus their attention specifically on the issue of slavery, the Law Commissioners finally got around to submitting their report on the subject. Their aim, as they admitted, was not to effect sweeping changes of the kind advocated by abolitionists but rather to ameliorate the system by doing away with its harsher features. This, they argued, was not only the safer course but also the one most likely to benefit the slaves themselves. They accordingly came up with 33 recommendations dealing with issues that they regarded as peculiarly objectionable, such as the breaking up of families and the buying and selling of women for use as prostitutes. The result of their additional labours was thus considerably more cautious in its approach than the document they had submitted three years earlier.[32] To add to the abolitionists' frustration the Melbourne Whigs, finding themselves outvoted, dissolved Parliament without the report's having even been debated.

The British and Foreign Anti-slavery Society responded by throwing its full weight into arousing the public's awareness of the need for action. In May it published a 72-page pamphlet, *Slavery and the Slave Trade in British India*. This was too costly for free distribution, but when the government announced a June election it rushed out 4,000 copies of an abridged version which it sent to Members and candidates. It also urged its many auxiliary organizations up and down the country to mobilize popular opinion by convening public meetings. 'Your voice has been once heard saying "Africa be free"', declared the *British and Foreign Anti-Slavery Reporter*, 'Let it once more be heard by the oppressed children of the East'.[33] As on earlier occasions, electors were urged to question candidates as to their intentions and where possible obtain pledges regarding their future voting intentions.

What effect, if any, this had on the election results it is impossible to say. Nevertheless, it soon became clear that the new government, led by Peel and the Tories, was less complacent than its predecessors. The abolitionists, for their part, lost no time in presenting a petition to Parliament and sending delegations to wait on the Prime Minister and Lord Ellenborough, the new President of the India Board, making plain their view that the time had come for the issue to be laid to rest. This would seem to have had the required effect for on 19 September Ellenborough sent a secret dispatch to the Governor General explaining that the country was growing impatient, adding 'There will be an attempt on the part of the Anti-Slavery Society to get up agitation during the next three months. I have vainly cautioned them against the dangers of getting up agitation in India, which would be fatal to the success of their own object.'[34] Very likely what he had in mind was what had happened ten years earlier during the run-up to the introduction of the Emancipation Bill when rumours of events in Britain had sparked uprisings in the West Indies. Writing in a similar vein, the Court of Directors expressed its 'apprehension that any delay in complying with the intention of Parliament and the people of this country might lead to some act of hurried and imperfect legislation, which ... might have injurious consequences ... '[35] It would be far better for the Government of India, with its access to local knowledge, to draft the necessary measures than to have less well considered ones imposed on it in response to popular excitement whipped up by abolitionists in Britain. The Directors had cause for unease. Getting Parliament to pass a second Emancipation Bill, it emerged, was precisely what the abolitionists had in mind. Nevertheless, the Indian government continued to prevaricate, principally over the issue of whether owners should be allowed to administer so-called 'moderate' physical correction.

What finally broke the deadlock was Ellenborough's arrival in Delhi as Auckland's successor. Brushing aside both the issue of physical punishment and the Commissioners' 33 recommendations, he reverted to the proposal contained in the original 1838 Commissioners' Report. On 11 February he gave his official consent to Act V of 1843 according to which: (i) public officers were forbidden to sell persons on account of non-payment of taxes or in execution of court decrees; (ii) courts were forbidden to recognize slavery; (iii) no one was to deprive persons of their rightfully acquired property on the grounds of their being slaves; and (iv) acts that would be penal offences if done to free persons would be equally an offence if done to so-called slaves.[36] According to Lord Fitzgerald, Ellenborough's replacement at the India Board, these measures amounted to the 'virtual extinction' of slavery throughout the East India Company's possessions.[37]

Slavery Delegalized

As the contributions by Suzanne Miers and David Seddon show, Act V reflected the approach to indigenous forms of servitude favoured by British and other European colonial administrators throughout the next century. Its great advantage from their point of view was that, being essentially negative, it required no enforcement. They were not obliged to inform slaves of their new legal status. They need not fear offending local elites. They were even relieved of some of their more troublesome former responsibilities such as returning runaways. Owners were henceforward less likely to appeal to the judgment of the courts. Slaves, to be sure, had now acquired such a privilege, but in view of their economic dependency, illiteracy and low caste status that was something they were generally reluctant and ill-equipped to do. From everyone's point of view, except possibly that of the slaves, it was an approach that had everything to commend it.

The fact was that Indian slavery, unlike slavery in the West, had never depended to any significant extent on legal sanctions or judicial decrees, being largely the product of customs associated with caste and existing systems of land tenure. British officials had seldom bothered to concern themselves with the intricate arrangements governing relationships between landlords and tenants, most of which rested on unwritten agreements anyway. Had they attempted to do so they would have found the variety of practices involved baffling. In spite of the high moral tone they adopted in public discourse, they had always been more interested in collecting taxes than promoting social reform or enquiring into such arcane questions.

There was, however, one thing that, in their capacity as tax gatherers British officials understood well and that was the importance of financial obligations. What, then, was to be done in the case of contract workers who were paid for labour which they subsequently failed to provide? Supposing such arrangements to have been freely entered into, employers had a plausible case for claiming recompense. In practice, the economic destitution of a large segment of the population placed them at the mercy of landlords and other employers. It was thus a relatively simple matter to turn precapitalist forms of servitude into capitalist ones by representing slaves as defaulting debtors. Debt bondage was no new phenomenon. It had existed in India since the earliest times. Long before slavery was delegalized it was already common practice for landlords to lure workers into debt by offering them employment conditional on their accepting loans, often at extortionate rates of interest, knowing well that they could never be repaid and in all probability would be passed on to the borrowers' descendants. As the Indian economy became more commercialized, however, and as a result of the impoverishment of the peasantry, such practices became more widespread. The British meanwhile reinforced employers' powers by introducing new legislation, such as the Workman's Breach of Contract Act of 1859, which allowed workers who obtained advances of money and refused to work to be arraigned before a magistrate and ordered to work. If they still refused they would then be offered the choice between repaying the money or being sentenced to up to three months of hard labour. To what extent such legislation promoted the spread of debt bondage the records do not reveal. More likely than not, as in the past, economic pressures and the coercive powers traditionally exercised by landlords sufficed without the need to appeal to higher authority.[38]

More important was the increasing pauperization of India's rural population attributable to population growth, increasing pressures on land use and the progressive breakdown of traditional notions of social interdependence. When Europe experienced similar changes a century or more earlier, workers driven from the land gravitated to the cities where they found alternative employment in factories and service industries. What exacerbated the problem in India was that the displacement of workers from the land coincided with the importing of cheap factory-produced goods from abroad, thereby reducing the number of jobs available in traditional, urban, handicraft industries. The result was an even larger growth than otherwise in the number of vulnerable workers prepared to accept whatever terms of contract employers cared to offer.[39]

Nevertheless, the 1843 Act, combined with the gradual loosening of social constraints, did offer routes of escape. One was by means of emigration. Between 1846 and 1932 some 28 million Indians emigrated to Ceylon, Mauritius, East Africa and the West Indies. Abolitionists, failing to note how many of them were actually fleeing bondage, often condemned this as a new form of slave trade. Undoubtedly it involved hardships of a kind few European workers would have been willing to accept. It was also commonly the case that many who embarked were not made fully aware of what was expected of them. On the other hand, both the British and the Indian government made genuine efforts to mitigate the hardships of the voyage by regulating the numbers carried and ensuring that the vessels involved were appropriately equipped and carried the required number of ships' doctors and other personnel. As indentured labourers, those who volunteered were guaranteed a passage home at the expiration of their indentures. It is significant that many chose not to avail themselves of this option. As Pieter Emmer shows, those who went to the West Indies commonly acquired land and became independent farmers. So, too, in many instances, did those who acquired savings and returned to India.[40]

Much larger in scale, however, were the migrations that occurred within India itself. Although economic progress was slow, opportunities opened up in many new areas such as railway building, canal digging and the construction of public works. Sometimes, as with road construction in remote areas, the authorities relied on requisitioning the services of local labourers to whom it paid less than the going market rates; but elsewhere opportunities occurred for the growth of a free labour force. One common route of escape was by becoming a sepoy. With increasing labour mobility, caste distinctions, although far from disappearing, also became less rigid. Set against this have been the pressures resulting from the six-fold increase in India's population over the last 150 years and the corresponding worsening of the man–land ratio. The results more often than not have been a curious amalgam of the modern and the archaic. In rural areas landlords exploit their power as employers to create forms of dependency that, strictly speaking, are neither capitalist nor feudal but combine elements of both.[41]

Since the achievement of independence in 1947 the Indian government has made strenuous efforts to modernize the country by encouraging economic growth and by attempting to do away with servile and caste distinctions. On the other hand, India has opposed attempts by the International Labour Organization, the World Trade Organization and other outside bodies to make improved labour and human rights practices a condition of allowing Indian textiles and agricultural products access to world markets. American trade union organizations have also demanded action to stamp out child labour, sweatshops and anything else savouring of unfair labour competition. In response, India, along with other developing countries, has argued that restrictions on Third World trade are merely a thinly disguised form of protectionism. By withholding opportunities for employment, it is claimed, they perpetuate poverty and thus actually stand in the way of social reform.[42]

Whatever the justice of these arguments, the fact remains that many practices deemed unacceptable in the West continue to flourish in India. According to conservative estimates, there are at least 10 million bonded labourers in the country, the great majority of them employed by agricultural landlords. Most belong to tribal or low-caste groups and are employed in hard manual labour in fields or at brick kilns. To enforce their authority employers rely on corrupt police, spineless magistrates and physical violence that on occasion amounts to torture. As a result, families toil all their lives to pay off ever-accumulating burdens of debt that they are too ignorant and terrified to question. When such cases are examined it commonly turns out that far from those in bondage owing their landlords money, it is the landlords who owe money to them.[43]

As few things ever entirely disappear in India, many practices deemed contrary to modern notions of freedom have continued to exist in spite of legislative measures by the government and provincial authorities to eradicate them. They include the use of child labour, the buying and selling of women for purposes of prostitution, and forced marriages.[44] In a country where unemployment is high and state welfare unavailable such practices are hard to eradicate. Although they do not amount to slavery in the traditional sense, they involve forms of exploitation no less contrary to the social, moral and intellectual autonomy of the individuals concerned. Often the effect of legislation has been merely to drive them underground. No doubt more could be done by means of better legislation and more effective law enforcement. But in the present, as in the past, the principal task facing those seeking solutions to India's problems is finding ways of eliminating the conditions of poverty, ignorance and squalor that encourage such practices to develop.

NOTES

1. Howard Temperley, *British Antislavery, 1833-1870* (London: Longman, 1972), pp.98–9. For a general account of the way abolitionist pressures were applied, see pp.93–110.
2. *Hansard's Parliamentary Debates, Third Series* (henceforward referred to as *Hansard*), 19 (7 July 1833), col.799.
3. Ibid. (7 July 1833), col.190.
4. Ibid., 20 (5, 9 Aug. 1833), cols. 323, 446.
5. Ibid., 19 (10 July 1833), col.532.
6. Ibid. (17 July 1833), col.799.
7. Temperley, *British Antislavery*, p.99.
8. *Correspondence on the Slave Trade*, Parliamentary Papers (henceforward PP), 1838, 51 (697), p.22.
9. PP, 1841, 38 (238), *Slavery: Correspondence in Continuation of H. of C. Paper 697 of Slavery: Correspondence in Continuation of H. of C. Paper 697 of 1837–38*.
10. *British India Advocate* (London: 1841–42). See also John Hyslop Bell, *British Folks and British India* (London: John Heywood, 1891).
11. British and Foreign Anti-Slavery Society, *Proceedings of the General Anti-Slavery*

Convention of 1840 (London: 1841), p.424. For Adam's account and the Convention's discussion of the Indian slavery issue see pp.77–90.

12. David Eltis, *Economic Growth and the Ending of the Slave Trade* (New York, NY: Oxford University Press, 1987), p.68.
13. PP, 1841, 28 (228), p.38.
14. For general accounts of Indian slavery see: D.R. Banaji, *Slavery in British India* (Bombay: 1933); Dharma Kumar, *Land and Caste in South India* (Cambridge: Cambridge University Press, 1965); and 'Colonialism, bondage and caste in British India', in Martin A. Klein (ed.), *Breaking the Chains: Slavery, Bondage and Emancipation in Modern Africa and Asia* (Madison, WI: University of Wisconsin Press, 1993); Lionial Caplan, 'Power and status in south Asian slavery', in James L. Watson (ed.), *Asian and African Systems of Slavery* (Oxford: Blackwell, 1980); and Utsa Patnaik and Manjari Dingwaney (eds.), *Chains of Servitude: Bondage and Slavery in India* (Madras and London: Sangam Books, 1985).
15. PP, 1841, 28 (328), p.28.
16. Ibid., p.31.
17. Kumar, *Land and Caste*, p.45.
18. *Letter from Governor General in Council*, PP, 1841, Session 2, 3 (54), p.110.
19. PP, 1841, 28 (328), pp.40–7.
20. Kumar, 'Colonialism, bondage and caste', pp.115–19.
21. Temperley, *British Antislavery*, p.94; Caplan, 'Power and status', p.18; Lawrence James, *Raj: The Making and Unmaking of British India* (London: Little, Brown, 1997), p.119.
22. Caplan, 'Power and status', pp.180–6; Kumar, *Land and Caste*, pp.34–48.
23. PP, 1841, 38 (238), p.31.
24. Kumar, 'Colonialism, bondage and caste', p.124; G.S. Ghurye, *Caste and Race in India* (London: Kegan Paul, 1932), pp.1–27; Louis Dumont, *Homo Hierarchicus: The Caste and Its Implications* (London: Weidenfeld & Nicolson, 1966), pp.130–43.
25. Dumont, *Homo Hierarchicus*, pp.33–64.
26. Orlando Patterson, *Slavery and Social Death* (Cambridge, MA: Harvard University Press, 1982); Caplan, 'Power and status', pp.193–4; Kumar, 'Colonialism, bondage and caste', p.127.
27. Caplan, 'Power and status', p.184.
28. PP, 1841, 28 (238), p.31.
29. Kumar, 'Colonialism, bondage and caste', p.124.
30. PP, 1841, Session 2, 3 (54), p.110.
31. Temperley, *British Antislavery*, p.101.
32. PP, 1841, 28 (238), pp.188–222.
33. *British and Foreign Anti-Slavery Reporter*, 30 June 1841.
34. Ellenborough to Auckland, 19 Sept. 1841, in Sir Algernon Law (ed.), *India under Lord Ellenborough* (London: J. Murray, 1926), p.18.
35. Quoted in Banaji, *Slavery in British India*, p.355.
36. *Slavery (East India)*, PP, 1843, 58 (525), p.13.
37. Temperley, *British Antislavery*, p.107.
38. Kumar, 'Colonialism, bondage and caste', pp.122–3.
39. Patnaik and Dingwaney, *Chains of Servitude*, deal with contemporary as well as past forms of servitude.
40. Kumar, 'Colonialism, bondage and caste', p.125; Hugh Tinker, *A New System of Slavery: The Export of Indian Labour Overseas, 1830-1920* (Oxford: Oxford University Press, 1974).
41. Patnaik and Dingwaney, *Chains of Servitude*, pp.1–34.
42. See the accounts of India's role in the 1999 World Trade Organization meeting in Seattle as reported in, for example, *The Independent*, 2 Dec. 1999 and *The Economist*, 11 Dec. 1999.
43. Anti-Slavery International, *Anti-Slavery Reporter* (Oct. 1999), p.9.
44. Ibid. Roger Sawyer, *Slavery in the Twentieth Century* (London: Routledge and Kegan Paul, 1986); Alan Whittaker (ed.), *A Pattern of Slavery: India's Carpet Boys* (London: The Anti-Slavery Society, 1988); Kevin Bales, *Disposable People: New Slavery in the Global Economy* (Berkeley and London: University of California Press, 1998).

The End of Slavery and the End of Empire: Slave Emancipation in Cuba and Puerto Rico

CHRISTOPHER SCHMIDT-NOWARA

In the midst of revolutionary political crisis in Spain and Cuba, the abolitionist and parliamentarian Rafael María de Labra published an open letter to his constituents in the Spanish region of Asturias. Labra explained that his advocacy of immediate slave emancipation in Cuba and Puerto Rico was not only an act of justice but also politically prudent. Given the support for the anti-colonial insurrection in eastern Cuba by unfree labourers, Spanish action against slavery and other forms of servitude was crucial: 'Today the nerve of the insurrection is fed by the coloured race, by escaped slaves and runaway Chinese, by men who, with weapons in hand, carry out abolitionist propaganda ... at the edge of the great sugar mills and within reach of the huge throngs of slaves.' By abolishing slavery and the indentured servitude of Chinese workers imported into Cuba since the 1840s, Labra and the Spanish Abolitionist Society proposed to undermine the legitimacy of the Cuban insurrection and restore hegemony in Spain's most important colony.[1]

Labra's comments capture one of the most striking features of slave emancipation in the Antilles: the confluence of anti-colonial and anti-slavery movements, not unlike the interplay between slave rebellions and political revolution in the French colony of St. Domingue.[2] The struggle to end slavery always involved conflict over the legitimacy of the colonial regime, a convergence that has received increased scholarly attention in recent years. Two interrelated lines of inquiry have shaped this approach to Antillean slave emancipation. On the one hand, studies of the construction of slave regimes have shown that, far from being an archaic labour system as classic accounts held,[3] slavery was flexible and productive. Slaves, it has been demonstrated, were able to carry out the most advanced tasks in an increasingly industrial form of sugar processing (sugar being the main sector of the Antillean economies and the main user of slave labour).[4] Thus, slavery did not wither of its own accord, but finally collapsed under the pressure of specific political challenges to its existence. On the other hand, historians have demonstrated that slaves were not passive recipients of their fate but active players in resisting slavery and in finally subverting it, in part by participating in the struggle against the Spanish colonial state.[5] Moreover, after slavery, while planters successfully reconstituted sugar production in Cuba (but not in Puerto Rico), the deregulation of society and politics inaugurated by emancipation, and by changes in the nature of the late colonial state, allowed the development of a vibrant, indeed explosive, political culture in which former slaves and other groups aggressively agitated for citizenship.[6] This essay will discuss both historiographical trends, beginning with a discussion of the political economy of slavery and emancipation before turning to consider the political effects of slavery's demise.

The Rise and Fall of Antillean Slavery

Many histories of Cuban slavery and sugar depict the British occupation of Havana in 1762–63 as a decisive turning point in the island's history. Spain had always regulated the slave trade to its American colonies and slavery had never reached the scale in Spanish America that it had in Brazil and some of the French, British or Dutch colonies. The British, however, opened Havana to a free trade in slaves and gave Cuban planters a glimpse of the fortunes to be made through the trade and the use of slave labour. After the Spanish retook Havana, they restructured the imperial defence system in such a way that Cuba took on increasing strategic importance. To ensure the loyalty of Cuba's creole elite, the Spanish monarchy conceded important political and economic liberties that allowed planters to liberalize the slave trade and gain some control over local political and military affairs. Thus the British occupation and the Spanish response set the stage for the dramatic growth of Cuban slavery.[7]

Puerto Rican slavery took off slightly later. Whereas Cuba was already importing almost 70,000 slaves in the 1790s,[8] Puerto Rican planters did not turn to slave labour in significant numbers until the early nineteenth century. Scarano has attributed the later rise of Puerto Rican sugar and slavery to the lesser capital endowments of the Puerto Rican economy of the late eighteenth century which was still dominated by peasant production. None the less, the openings in the world sugar market created by the revolution of St. Domingue, the liberalization of Spanish political and economic control, and the growth of demand in the United States, created opportunities for Puerto Rican planters to turn to plantation production. Until its abolition, slavery formed the core of the plantation labour force.[9]

Recently, historians have looked at the decade of the 1830s as another benchmark in the history of Antillean slavery. Again, the political and the economic strands interwine in important ways. In that decade the Spanish government, in its transition from an absolutist monarchy to a liberal parliamentary regime, not only consolidated the slave trade and slavery but also began to take back many of the liberties conceded in the late eighteenth century to the Antillean elite. Moreover, after the loss of the greater part of the American empire in the 1820s Spanish planters and merchants moved into the Caribbean in aggressive fashion and helped to lay the foundations for a second expansion of the Cuban slave and sugar complex as it moved westward from Havana into the hitherto largely undeveloped province of Matanzas. The period between the 1830s and the revolutionary year 1868 saw the increased marginalization of creoles from political and military affairs and the ascendance of Spanish merchants in the island's economic life under a strict protectionist regime. Futhermore, over the course of the century Cuba in particular moved increasingly into the economic orbit of the United States, finding its main sugar market there, the Spanish market becoming largely irrelevant. Metropolitan protectionism, tightened in the 1830s, intensified the friction between Spain and the Antilles. None the less, Spain was the sole European power to defend both slavery and the slave trade until the late nineteenth century, and the centrality of these institutions to the Antillean economies insured the loyalty of the colonial elite.[10]

Soon after the consolidation of the colonial order, there occurred important divergences in the character of Cuban and Puerto Rican slavery. One difference that shaped slavery in both islands was the level of capital investment in technological improvement. Cuban planters were at the forefront of modernization, investing in railways to carry sugar cane more rapidly to grinding mills and finished sugar to port, and in the latest processing technology that enabled them to drive down costs in an increasingly competitive world sugar market. Puerto Rican planters, in contrast, were constrained by the scarcity of credit from investing in new technology and were less able to modify production in response to changing markets. By mid-century the long-term trend in Puerto Rican sugar production was towards stagnation and decline, a process keenly perceived by contemporaries. As one critic of the Puerto Rican economy put it: 'If the island continues along the same road it follows today regarding sugar production, it will suffer a profound crisis that will be its ruin'.[11]

Despite the differences in technological investment, both plantation sectors continued to be labour intensive. Again, however, the tremendous wealth of Cuban planters and the relative penury of their Puerto Rican counterparts produced important differences. In Puerto Rico the largely intra-Caribbean slave trade which had fed the growth of plantation labour came to a virtual halt in the 1840s. The slave population there reached its peak of approximately 50,000 in the mid 1840s and fell to around 40,000 by 1860, less than 10 per cent of the total population, maintaining that level until the emancipation process began. Though planters clamoured for a revival of the slave trade or for a new traffic in indentured African and Chinese labourers, it was hard for them to afford such a costly form of labour. Instead, they turned inwards, compelling, with the help of the colonial state, landless labourers and smallholders to work on the plantations through the institution known as the *libreta* (workbook) by which workers had to demonstrate that they were gainfully employed. Though a constant source of discontent on all sides, the *libreta* remained from the 1840s through to its abolition in 1873 a crucial supplement to slave labour in the plantation economy.[12]

In contrast, the slave trade to Cuba continued to be the primary source of new labour for the plantation economy, despite British efforts, and Spanish treaties, to suppress it. Between 1790 and the trade's suppression in 1867, Cuba imported 780,200 slaves. In 1846 the island's slave population numbered 323,759 out of a total of 898,752. By 1862 those figures had grown to 368,550 out of 1,359,238.[13] However, planters employed other types of labour as well. Not only was the demand for plantation labour constant, but the vulnerability of slavery as a source of labour was also a matter of concern. Planters feared both the British efforts against the slave trade and doubted the reliability of the slave population itself, especially in the aftermath of the aborted rebellion known as the Conspiracy of La Escalera (1843–44). The most important alternative was the traffic in indentured Chinese labourers between the 1840s and the 1870s. This was carried out primarily from the Portuguese port of Macao and involved more than 100,000 Chinese labourers. Though nominally protected by contracts that spelled out their rights, the lack of legal recourse reduced most of the Chinese to a condition of *de facto* slavery on the Cuban plantations. Planters also briefly started a trade of indigenous labourers from Yucatan in the 1860s.[14]

The 1860s were a time of real crisis for slave economies founded in the late eighteenth and the early nineteenth century and consolidated in the 1830s. The American Civil War, slave emancipation in the US and new Anglo-American efforts against the Cuban slave trade forced the colonial planter class and the Spanish government to introduce and contemplate important changes. The slave trade finally ended in 1867 once an effective Anglo-American initiative forced the Spanish to comply with its numerous treaties banning the trade. Throughout the decade Spanish and Antillean elites debated political reforms and talked vaguely of measures for the eventual abolition of slavery. The Spanish Abolitionist Society, composed primarily of Puerto Rican and Spanish liberals and republicans, was founded in Madrid in 1865. Puerto Rican planters, faced with a static slave population and a relatively small one in the island as a whole, were willing to consider an indemnified emancipation. But Cuban planters were not prepared to discuss emancipation, given that they continued to rely heavily on slave labour, while the island's total slave population of 368,550 (1862) put indemnification far beyond the reach of the penurious Spanish government. Moreover, many creole elites believed that slave emancipation in Cuba would lead inevitably to violent racial conflict.[15]

The outbreak of rebellions in Spain, Cuba and Puerto Rico in the autumn of 1868 gave new urgency to the mild reformism of the 1860s. In Cuba disgruntled planters in the eastern end of the island rose up against Spanish rule after years of political inertia. Though initially committed to the rights of property, the rebel leadership ultimately turned abolitionist in recognition that the uprising had mobilized people across class and racial lines in the eastern provinces and had weakend labour discipline there. Despite a separatist and abolitionist force active in Cuba, the planters of the western provinces, where the vast majority of the slaves worked, held out defiantly and successfully against immediate abolition. Indeed, major planters such as the Spaniard Julián Zulueta continued to open new plantations with massive slave labour forces well into the 1870s.[16]

The Cuban conflict was to last for ten years. The Puerto Rican uprising of October 1868 was shorter-lived. The Grito de Lares took place in the interior province of Utuado, a coffee-growing region dominated by Spanish merchants. Though part of an island-wide conspiracy, the uprising took hold in the town of Lares. Marginalized creole planters, smallholders, rural proletarians and slaves joined together against the Spanish state and the local merchant class. After a week of fighting the government regained control of Lares and the surrounding area and began a harsh repression of suspected conspirators.[17]

The colonial rebellions forced the hand of the Spanish goverment, itself subjected to change by the civilian–military uprising of September 1868. The new regime came to power with a significant will to carry out colonial reforms. Prominent figures in the revolution's leadership, such as the Generals Francisco Serrano, Domingo Dulce and Juan Prim, had served as Captain Generals in the Antilles, and the first two had reputations as reformers. Moreover, the liberal and republican parties that supported the revolution were advocates of political and economic liberalization in the colonies. Finally, using the quite broad freedoms of the new constitution (1869), the Spanish Abolitionist Society began to agitate for the immediate abolition of colonial slavery. Though initially a fairly narrow association of political and intellectual elites gathered in Madrid, the Society successfully harnessed its campaign to the political agendas of the major revolutionary parties and for the duration of the revolution (1868–74) transformed metropolitan abolitionism into a broadly based movement with considerable popular support.[18]

In 1870 the new goverment passed an emancipation law that did indeed engender discontent among most parties. The Moret Law, named after the Minister of Ultramar, Segismundo Moret y Prendergast, initiated a gradual emancipation process that deferred to the interests of Cuban planters. Children born to slaves were freed but had to work for their mother's owner. The law also freed slaves who reached the age of 60 and the *emancipados*, approximately 10,000 men and women captured by the government in its sporadic efforts to suppress the slave trade. Though nominally free, the *emancipados* had generally been forced to work for planters who treated them as slaves. The law also called for a definitive emancipation act once the Cuban insurgency had ended.[19]

The Moret Law met with immediate resistance. Planters in Cuba and Puerto Rico refused to allow government officials on to their plantations to take the censuses needed to carry out the law's measures. Cuban planters successfully delayed publication of the law in Cuba and loaded the oversight committees with individuals from their own class. In both islands, planters and merchants, especially Spaniards, had organized irregular military forces known as Volunteers, giving them considerable firepower in their defiance of the government and the protection of plantations against insurgent forces. However, some slaves did gain their freedom under the Moret Law in both Cuba and Puerto Rico. The slave population declined in both islands, though less so in the major sugar regions where planters successfully retained slavery as the core of their labour force, supplementing it with both coerced and free labour. For instance, in Cuba's Matanzas province the population of working-age slaves had declined only from 78,800 in 1862 to 70,850 in 1877, whereas the total Cuban slave population had declined from 368,550 to 199,094 between those years. Thus one of the Moret Law's effects was to concentrate slavery in the key economic sector, sugar.[20]

Discontent was also manifest in the Peninsula. Pressure groups organized by the Spanish bourgeoisie sought to defend slavery so as to ensure Antillean social stability and prosperity. Given their dominance of the Antillean markets through a strict protectionist regime, shippers, growers and manufacturers jealously guarded the Antillean status quo in the name of the 'national' economy. Criticism also came from the revolutionary left. The Spanish Abolitionist Society and left-wing parties such as the Federal Republicans and the Radicals argued that only immediate emancipation would bring the rebellion in eastern Cuba to a halt by winning the loyalty of the slave population. As a first step in this strategy the Abolitionist Society and its allies in the Spanish Cortes acted first against Puerto Rican slavery. Puerto Rican reformers had helped to found the Society in 1865 and abolition enjoyed some support among the planter class. In December 1872 the Radical party introduced a bill for immediate abolition in Puerto Rico. The bill was passed into law on 22 March 1873, now under the auspices of Spain's First Republic, which had been declared in February 1873. The new law called for indemnification (which was ultimately slow in coming) and for slaves to sign three-year contracts with their former owners or with the government. The Republic was inclined to enforce the contracts lightly, but its overthrow in 1874 and the eventual restoration of the Bourbon monarchy in 1875 produced a notable tightening of the contracts and also impeded the Abolitionist Society's efforts to carry out a similar plan in Cuba.[21]

Though the restored monarchy could not undo Puerto Rican abolition, it did assist planters in continuing to coerce the now free population for several years. Not only did the colonial state enforce the three-year contracts, it also created stricter vagrancy laws and policing powers. None the less, the imminent defeat of the Cuban insurgency led the Spanish government to back away from its control of the labour market. With a new plan for Cuban slave emancipation and the reintroduction of constitutional rights into both islands in the offing, the government refused to force *libertos* (freed slaves) to sign new contracts or to institute a new *libreta* system, despite the constant pleas of Puerto Rican planters. Moreover, the new Spanish penal code, also introduced into the colonies, decriminalized vagrancy. By the time of the Pact of Zanjón (1878), which brought the war in Cuba to an end, the Spanish state had decided to leave Puerto Rican planters and labourers to their own devices. Though the colonial state was not completely passive in post-emancipation Antillean society, it never contemplated as massive a project as Reconstruction in the United States.[22]

The gradual end of coerced labour led to a severe decline in the Puerto Rican sugar industry. Though Puerto Rico's considerable population density hindered the option of flight and squatting for freed slaves, they nevertheless had the right to choose their work and many moved from plantation to plantation. Given the mobility of the labour force and the reluctance of the colonial state to coerce free labourers on to the plantations, planters had to devise new means of recruiting a workforce. These included grants of cultivation grounds and houses, and the payment of wages in tokens redeemable only at company stores. Though there were attempts to invest in new processing technology, the scarcity of credit and the competitiveness of the world sugar market made modernization difficult. By the end of the century coffee, a sector that developed with the use of free labour, had replaced sugar as the island's main export.[23]

In Cuba the economic effects of emancipation were quite different. In 1880 the Spanish Cortes legislated a new emancipation law called the *patronato*, which in name abolished slavery but in fact maintained the traditional prerogatives of slave-owners through eight-year apprenticeships and the continued use of corporal punishment. The war in the east had freed many slaves, as did the Moret Law and the Pact of Zanjón which liberated those slaves who had fought for both the rebel forces and for the Spanish side. But in 1877 there were still just under 200,000 slaves remaining in Cuba, with most concentrated on the western sugar estates. The *patronato* freed a certain number of slaves per year by quota and by lottery and it also gave slaves (now referred to as *patrocinados*) greater recourse to purchase their own freedom or that of family members. Though the new law mandated an eight-year apprenticeship, the response to the law by the *patrocinados* and free family members produced a dramatic drop in the population of forced labourers. In 1886 the number of *patrocinados* had plunged to 25,381 and the Spanish government acted to abolish the *patronato* two years early. Slavery had finally come to an end in the Spanish Caribbean.

Ex-slaves in the agrarian sector responded to freedom in a variety of ways. Some remained on the plantations of their former owners or moved to other plantations to work as wage labourers. Many, however, were able to balance wage labour with some economic autonomy. Given the difficulty that planters had in immediately switching to a wage relationship, they often had to concede certain rights to workers, such as the right to provision ground, or the leasing of land. Some ex-slaves chose flight from the plantation zone altogether, moving to the cities or to less developed regions of the island in the eastern provinces.[24]

While many ex-slaves found ways to avoid proletarianization, the Cuban planter class was generally successful in maintaining an extensive labour force, though there is some disagreement about the impact of emancipation in Cuba on the sugar industry. Rebecca Scott has shown how planters reconstituted production and a labour force through several methods, including the division between the cultivation and processing of sugar cane, investment in sugar mills (*centrales*) with huge grinding capacities, and the recruitment of a now free labour force through large-scale immigration, mostly from Spain, and the use of a variety of arrangements to guarantee both workers and access to cane. By the end of the 1880s the most competitive segment of the sugar industry was dominated by the owners of *centrales* who grew some of their own cane and bought more from *colonos*, farmers who grew cane and sold it direct to the *centrales*. This latter class of cultivator varied considerably in size and autonomy, from plantation owners to former slaves leasing a small plot of land. The industry thus came to rely on diverse types of labour. Mills could retain a core labour force and recruit additional workers from nearby towns or farms during the peak grinding period. Moreover, *colonos* who sold cane to the mills were now responsible for recruiting their own labour forces. In other words, by decentralizing the production process the leaders of the Cuban sugar industry came to rely on labour forces that were recruited and controlled in a number of ways.[25]

Another study of emancipation's impact concurs with the main lines of Scott's description of post-emancipation sugar production. However, Bergad takes a much more catastrophist view of the process. The transition to free labour was not a time of successful adaptation but of profound crisis for the planter class. While agreeing that sugar emerged triumphant from the emancipation process, Bergad shows that the planter class of one of the richest regions, Matanzas, did not. The reorganization of production, including the introduction of *centrales*, the *colonos* and a growing cash nexus between planters and workers, together spelled the 'coup de grace to the old planter class'.[26] Increasingly, immigrants from Spain with better access to capital replaced the creole planters who had built the Matanzas sugar economy. Emancipation for that class, if not for the Matanzas economy as a whole, was a cataclysmic event.[27] Nevertheless, despite accentuating the changes in the composition of the dominant class, Bergad concurs with Scott that planters and mill-owners successfully reorganized production and recruited a free labour force. Cuban sugar producers, unlike their counterparts in Puerto Rico and other post-emancipation societies, weathered the economic storm of emancipation and emerged in the 1880s and the 1890s with a greater productive capacity than before.

Politics after Emancipation

But the effects of slave emancipation were not strictly economic. It profoundly affected Antillean (and Spanish) politics. The Pact of Zanjón set the stage for the *patronato* while also transforming the nature of the colonial state. After Zanjón, Cuba and Puerto Rico enjoyed constitutional government with evolving political and civil rights. For Cuba this period was the first experiment with constitutional rule since the Spanish Cortes had expelled the colonial deputies in 1837 and subjected the colonies to exceptional rule. For Puerto Rico the new regime was an approximation of the broad constitutional protection it had enjoyed between 1868 and 1874 under Spain's September revolution (the Spanish government had not extended the constitution to Cuba during the Ten Years' War). Taken together, slave emancipation and political reform radicalized colonial society, a confluence that has received increased scholarly attention.

In Cuban historiography recent work has emphasized the diversity of claims for citizenship stemming from the new political and social conditions. Where once historians had seen a clear line from 1868 to the defeat of the Spanish empire in 1898, during which a coherent and unified Cuban nation emerged, they now see a tortuous maze composed of multiple nationalist projects that sometimes converged but often did not.[28] Studies of Puerto Rican politics after emancipation tend now to explore the vibrancy of autonomist politics. These recent studies have emerged from attempts to explain why Cuba produced a mass separatist movement and Puerto Rico did not. Rather than seeing autonomism as a failure of nationalist sentiment, historians now see it as a successful vehicle for nationalist and democratic politics.[29]

The post-Zanjón order gave rise to a remarkably diverse and contentious imperial polity. Autonomist parties, separatist movements, organized labour, civil rights movements in the Antilles and republican parties in Spain, often in cooperation with one another, sometimes in competition, vied with conservative parties and the colonial state for greater civil and political rights for all male members of colonial society. The question of the rights of ex-slaves was paramount. A quick glance at the networks of one of the most committed reformers of the time will give some sense of the political energies released as Cuba and Puerto Rico made the transition from slave to market societies ruled by constitutional government. As we shall see, emancipation not only ended the direct bondage of a large part of the Antillean population, it also brought with it a lessening of the intense social control, racial segregation and political repression that had characterized Cuban and Puerto Rican slave society hitherto.

Rafael María de Labra was a leading member of the Spanish Abolitionist Society and one of the heads of both the Cuban and the Puerto Rican Autonomist parties. He represented the latter in the Spanish Cortes and was also one of the major republican politicians in late nineteenth- and early twentieth-century Spain. Though born in Cuba of a creole mother from the dominant class, he spent most of his life in Spain and resolutely identified himself as a Spaniard, though with obvious connections to the Antilles. During Spain's September Revolution, Labra, as a director of the Spanish Abolitionist Society and determined supporter of the short-lived First Republic, had been one of the major strategists in favour of immediate slave emancipation in both Puerto Rico and Cuba. Aside from the inherent justice of the action, Labra argued that in Puerto Rico immediate emancipation was feasible given the relatively small size of the slave population, while in Cuba it was a political imperative given the need to defeat the Cuban insurgency. Emancipation and citizenship for ex-slaves would win for Spain a loyal population and undermine the appeal of an independent Cuba. Moreover, despite the gloom of emancipators in Great Britain and the United States by the 1870s and the catastrophic predictions of Spanish and Antillean conservatives, Labra and other abolitionists viewed slave emancipation in the Americas as successful and satisfying for all concerned parties. Labra was especially impressed by the government activism in the radical phase of Reconstruction in the United States.[30]

The overthrow of the September Revolution and the First Republic in 1874 temporarily ended that strategy. None the less, Labra and other republicans and abolitionists continued to advocate a reformed imperial order based on universal rights and political participation until the outbreak of the Cuban war for independence in 1895. This goal brought him into contact with a broad array of political actors. For instance, one of his closest colleagues from this period was one of the leading Afro-Cuban intellectuals of the time, Juan Gualberto Gomez. Together, Labra and Gomez had brought a successful case before the Spanish Supreme Court to lift the ban on Cuban periodicals and on other publications from discussing the separatist movement.[31] Labra also supported Gomez in his work as the head of the Directorio Central de las Sociedades de la Raza de Color. Founded in 1887 when Gomez returned to Cuba from political exile in Spain, the Directorio's goal was to organize Afro-Cuban claims for greater political and civil rights after slavery. These included the right to the honorific title of 'don', free entry into public establishments and full political rights. This latter cause particularly moved Gomez and Labra once Spain reintroduced universal manhood suffrage in 1890. Though Cuba and Puerto Rico were supposed to enjoy the same political and civil rights as the metropolis, the new measure merely extended the franchise in the colonies and maintained an income provision that excluded many ex-slaves.[32]

Both Labra and Gomez were also close political associates of the noted creole reformer Nicolás Azcárate. Though born into the creole slave-owning class, Azcárate had been a life-long critic of slavery, albeit only a timid abolitionist until the 1880s. After Zanjón, he helped to found the Democratic Party as an alternative to the major political parties, the Cuban Liberal Party (better known as the Autonomist Party) and the Constitutional Union, which represented the Cuban and the Spanish elite, respectively. Azcárate had established the party with Saturnino Martínez, a tobacco worker and one of the leaders of the rising Havana labour movement.[33]

Indeed, the end of slavery had opened up new horizons for collective action by workers in both the city and the country. Unlike in most Caribbean slave societies, slaves were never the majority of the population in Cuba and Puerto Rico; there was always a larger free population of diverse racial backgrounds. Yet under the slave regime all labour was subject to close political scrutiny and social control. Even far from the sugar plantations workers saw their freedom of movement, to associate, or to strike sharply curtailed. The *libreta* in Puerto Rico was one such example of the coercion of free labour. Clerks in Havana shops were subject to the authority of the owner who closely monitored their movements and controlled their time, often forbidding them from leaving the shop more than once a week. Not only did the end of slavery lighten the intense social control, but the introduction of constitutional government expanded the rights of all labourers. Workers could more easily form unions, join political parties such as Azcárate's Democratic Party or Labra's Autonomist Party, and go out on strike for improved wages and working conditions. By the 1890s organized urban labour had become a major player in colonial politics.[34]

Moreover, transformations in the sugar sector of Cuba had created a diverse workforce. Blacks and whites worked together in greater numbers than before, a shared experience that facilitated the formation of common class interests that often overcame racial differences. The decentralization of the sugar complex had also created new opportunities for political action. During the Ten Years' War sugar plantations in the western provinces were as tightly controlled as fortresses. Slavery enabled planters to monitor and discipline their workforce closely. Some planters continued to expand the plantation belt with impunity during the war. With the transformation of the sugar economy that accompanied emancipation, however, they gained greater flexibility in their workforce though at the cost of physical control. The greater mobility within the countryside made it almost impossible for planters and mill-owners to safeguard their properties from the rebel forces when war broke out again in 1895 or to restrict the movement of the rural population. As a result, the separatist forces successfully invaded the western provinces for the first time and wrought wide-scale destruction. They also recruited heavily among western workers. Indeed, one reason why the most notorious Spanish commander of the war, Valeriano Weyler, chose to force the rural population into concentration camps was because of the inability of the landed elite and the colonial state to control the countryside as they had done between 1868 and 1878.[35]

Labra was also deeply involved with the Cuban and the Puerto Rican Autonomist parties. The Puerto Rican party made the most ground in the post-Zanjón era. In Cuba the autonomists had major political rivals to their left in the separatist movement. In Puerto Rico separatists never achieved the same political or military successes, largely because of the more effective integration of the Puerto Rican economy into the Spanish imperial system. Where Cuba was constantly rocked by fluctuations in the sugar trade with the United States, a market which absorbed more than 90 per cent of Cuban sugar by the 1890s, Puerto Rican coffee, the leading export crop of the 1880s and the 1890s, found its principal market in Spain and Cuba.[36] Working largely within the confines of the imperial polity, Puerto Rican autonomists constructed a broadly-based political movement that aspired to a democratic order with considerable control over local affairs. Though the

Spanish state was generally intransigent, successive political crises gave the autonomists the political leverage they needed to achieve their goals. Once the Cuban war for independence broke out in 1895 the Autonomist Party was able to press Spain into making major concessions. The Carta Autonómica of 1897, which established the autonomous regime, conceded universal male suffrage and extensive political and economic self-rule, broad liberties that the United States overturned once it invaded and annexed Puerto Rico in 1898.[37]

As one can see from these examples, the ending of slavery – slavery being regarded not only as a form of labour but also as a system of social domination and racial segregation that legitimized a repressive political regime – gave rise to novel forms of collective action: a democratic autonomist party in Puerto Rico, vibrant labour and civil rights movements in Cuba, Spanish republicans working closely with Antillean activists of various stripes. Ex-slaves joined in many of these movements, while the struggle against slavery by free and unfree people alike had altered the nature of political action in the late nineteenth-century empire

The contest for expanded rights and freedoms, while fought on many fronts, was probably most dynamic within the Cuban separatist movement. The struggle for freedom and citizenship began in Cuba with the outbreak of the Ten Years' War in 1868. As was mentioned earlier, Carlos Manuel de Céspedes and other leaders of the separatist movement were themselves slave-owners. Céspedes made one of the most famous gestures of the insurgency by freeing his own slaves. However, he saw this action as the prerogative of a property owner and did not question the rights of property or the institution of slavery. Only the broad support for the insurgency by people across class and colour lines, the flight of slaves to the rebel camp and the weakening of labour discipline on plantations in the war zones forced Céspedes and the leadership to become openly abolitionist in late 1870, more than two years after the war began.[38]

Recent studies have shown that the biases and sense of difference and hierarchy that marked the early stage of the rebellion persisted throughout the 30 years of intermittent war against Spain (1868–78, 1879–80 and 1895–98), but that they were always accompanied by broad conceptions of citizenship and the nation. For instance, Ada Ferrer has captured the janus-faced nature of post-emancipation politics by demonstrating how veterans of the Ten Years' War and the Guerra Chiquita (1879–80) struggled over the interpretation and the representation of those conflicts with Spain. Many white combatants sought to downplay the participation and accomplishments of black and mulatto veterans. Ferrer argues that in doing so they were seeking to assuage the fears of white Cubans that the rebellion was a race war waged by ex-slaves against their former masters, a fear of the Cuban elite since the Revolution of St. Domingue, by convincing their public that Cubans of colour played little active role in the insurgency. The implicit message was that should a new war with Spain break out, there would be no danger of violent racial conflict. Black and mulatto veterans, however, did not passively accept this view. They responded with their own memoirs and interpretations that stressed the multiracial nature of the insurgency and argued that the ultimate goal of an independent Cuba should be the creation of a society based on racial equality. The upward mobility of many Cubans of colour into the ranks of the insurgency's officer corps, epitomized by the military leader of the war for independence in 1895 Antonio Maceo, represented to them the possibilities of a free Cuba. Moreover, shared work experiences between blacks and whites after slavery provided further examples of solidarity and a foundation for a multiracial democracy.[39]

These debates over the rights and roles of Cubans continued through the wars against Spain and into the Cuban republic founded in 1902, following the withdrawal of the United States. The extensive participation of Cubans across colour lines in the insurgency had given many Afro-Cubans opportunities to rise through the military and to gain important political offices, especially at the local level, after the war. Furthermore, the new regime was based on universal manhood suffrage. Many veterans and politicians held the view that the war of independence had once and for all purged racism from Cuban society. The political leader of the war, José Martí, had formed an explicitly anti-racist ideology and an ecumenical vision of the Cuban nation that held out the promise of citizenship to all regardless of colour, class or origin. In one of his most famous essays, Martí asked: 'Will we fear the Negro – the noble black man, our black brother … ?' His response was unequivocal: 'Others may fear him; I love him. Anyone who speaks ill of him I disown, and I say to him openly: "You lie!".'[40]

Historians have interpreted Martí's nationalism as an expression of an egalitarian society that had overcome racism through the common struggle against Spain. Indeed, several studies of Cuban social and political history have suggested that Martí's inclusive vision of the Cuban nation resulted from a keen understanding of the new interracial bonds forged in the post-emancipation labour process, as well as through the camaraderie of the anti-colonial insurgency.[41]

Accompanying this perspective has been a closer attention to the heterogeneity of the nationalist movement and nationalist discourse. From this vantage point, it appears that the emphasis on unity and transcendence sometimes served to silence frank discussion of bias and prejudice. For many of Martí's followers after his death (1895), any expression of difference and peculiarity represented a betrayal of the unified nation.

Therefore, in practice, nationalist discourse sometimes had the effect of obscuring the persistence of real racial discrimination felt by many Cubans of colour in terms of income, schooling, access to public space or office, and in other areas of political and social life. In the early years of the republic Cubans of colour mobilized to demand broader political and civil rights, ultimately forming the Independent Party of Colour (Partido Independiente de Color). In doing so, they also drew upon the anti-racism equally explicit in Cuban nationalism as it emerged from the anti-colonial wars. They represented Martí and other nationalist leaders not only as defenders of unity, but also as active opponents of racial oppression.[42]

The rejoinder from the dominant Cuban parties was swift and negative. As under the colonial regime, politicians denounced the formation of a separate black party as racist and as a betrayal of the universal notion of the Cuban nation. For the political mainstream, there were no Cubans of colour, only Cubans. In 1910, the legislature passed into law a bill written by the mulatto intellectual and politician Manuel Morúa Delgado that forbade the formation of political parties along racial lines.[43] The Independent Party of Colour did not back down from this challenge. Instead, in 1912 it launched an uprising in eastern Cuba to force the government to accept its claims. The government's response was unexpected and brutally violent. It carried out a repression aimed broadly at men of colour in the eastern provinces of the island. Many of the killings were extremely cruel and included decapitation and other spectacular methods that terrorized the local population. One important interpretation of the so-called Race War of 1912 has seen it as conclusive evidence of the overwhelming racism implicit in the Cuban nationalist project. One consequence of the repression of the Independent Party of Colour was the marginalization of ex-slaves and other people of colour from the mainstream of political life, making them second-class citizens under the Cuban republic. In contrast, another scholar views the violence of 1912 as a manifestation of the unresolved tensions within Cuban nationalism, a broad political discourse that vacillated between claims of homogeneity and heterogeneity contested by groups from all sectors of Cuban society. That interpretation also holds that the disappearance of an all-black party from Cuban political life should not be interpreted as a decisive marginalization of Afro-Cubans because multiracial forms of political, cultural and social solidarity, whose origins lay in the nineteenth-century struggle against slavery and colonialism, have persisted throughout the twentieth century.[44]

Conclusion

Though old colonial societies, Cuba and Puerto Rico were latecomers to the boom and bust cycle of Caribbean sugar and slavery. Responding to major economic and geopolitical transformations of the late eighteenth and the early nineteenth century, Cuban, Puerto Rican and Spanish planters constructed robust plantation economies based on slave labour. Cuba, in particular, became one of the major examples of the Atlantic world's 'second slavery', while Puerto Rican sugar planters relied throughout on slavery and other forms of coerced labour. Rather than seeing slavery in the nineteenth century as a sign of archaic or stagnant economies, historians tend now to see it as the cornerstone of the Antilles' dramatic growth and dynamism.[45]

This reappraisal of the slave economies has also led to revisions in the political and social history of Cuba and Puerto Rico. Multiple forms of collective action on both sides of the Atlantic ultimately led to the destruction of Antillean slavery: slaves joining the rebellion in eastern Cuba, freed slaves purchasing the freedom of loved ones after the passage of the Moret Law and the *patronato*, Spanish and Puerto Rican abolitionists seeking the immediate abolition of slavery were among the many acts that transformed and vanquished a highly successful and well-defended labour system.

In Puerto Rico the end of slavery and the *libreta* led to a profound crisis in the sugar sector and a decline in production as planters scrambled to recruit a free labour force among the now mobile ex-slave and rural proletarian populations. In Cuba sugar emerged triumphant, though it was now grown and harvested with new methods, while the Cuban planter class found itself increasingly hard-pressed by immigrant capitalists from Spain. Moreover, while the decentralization of production through the *colonos* and the system of *centrales* resuscitated Cuban sugar production and effectively restructured the post-emancipation labour force, it also undermined the ability of both the planter class and the colonial state to control effectively the agrarian population. Whereas during the Ten Years' War western planters and the Spanish military had generally succeeded in keeping workers on their plantations and rebels at bay, the fluidity of the new system made that level of control impossible. During the War of Independence Cuban rebels successfully invaded the western zone, destroyed numerous plantations and *centrales* and heavily recruited support among the multiracial agrarian workforce.[46]

Recent work in the field has thus tended to concentrate on the intense politicization of Antillean society during and after the process of emancipation. The abolition of slavery and coerced labour along with the advent of constituional government represented a major transformation of late colonial society. The last two decades of Spanish rule saw unprecedented levels of political activity as the mobilizations begun in the struggle over slavery extended into the new era and as diverse groups sought greater political and civil rights, whether within the imperial framework, as in the case of Puerto Rican autonomism, or independent of it, as in the case of the Cuban separatist movement. Democratic and nationalist movements did not, however, make a complete break from the earlier decades of Antillean slave society. If one of the legacies of slave society was the multiracial struggle against slavery, another was the preoccupation with racial and class difference that continued to shape Antillean political and cultural life far beyond 1898.

NOTES

1. R.M.de Labra, *Carta que a varios electores del distrito de Infiesto (Oviedo) dirige su ex-diputado a Cortes* (Madrid: Imprenta de José Noguera, 1872), pp.15–16.
2. On St. Domingue, see C.L.R. James, *The Black Jacobins* (New York: Vintage, 2nd edn, 1963) and R. Blackburn, *The Overthrow of Colonial Slavery, 1776–1848* (London: Verso, 1988).
3. The major study of Cuban slavery and sugar is M. Moreno Fraginals, *El Ingenio*, 3 vols (Havana: Editorial de Ciencias Sociales, 1978), in which the author argues that slave labour was unable to carry out the sophisticated jobs required by changing technology and that the capital investment in labour held back modernization. On Puerto Rican slavery see L.M. Díaz Soler, *Historia de la esclavitud negra en Puerto Rico* (Río Piedras: Editorial Universitaria, 3rd edn, 1981). The author argues that slavery was a marginal institution in Puerto Rican economic life. The views of both authors have been challenged in recent years (see below).
4. F. Scarano, *Sugar and Slavery in Puerto Rico: The Plantation Economy of Ponce, 1800–1850* (Madison, WI: University of Wisconsin Press, 1984); R. Scott, *Slave Emancipation in Cuba: The Transition to Free Labor, 1865–1899* (Princeton, NJ: Princeton University Press, 1985); and L. Bergad, *Cuban Rural Society in the Nineteenth Century: The Social and Economic History of Monoculture in Matanzas* (Princeton, NJ: Princeton University Press, 1990).
5. Rebecca Scott's work has been fundamental in this field. See *Slave Emancipation, passim*. See also G. Baralt, *Esclavos rebeldes: conspiraciónes y sublevaciónes de esclavos en Puerto Rico (1795–1873)* (Río Piedras: Ediciones Huracán, 3rd edn, 1989); R. Paquette, *Sugar Is Made with Blood: The Conspiracy of La Escalera and the Conflict between Empires over Slavery in Cuba* (Middletown, CT: Wesleyan University Press, 1988); L. Figueroa, 'Facing Freedom: The Transition from Slavery to Free Labor in Guayama, Puerto Rico, 1860–1898' PhD thesis (University of Wisconsin, 1991); and A. Ferrer, 'To Make a Free Nation: Race and the Struggle for Independence in Cuba, 1868–1898', PhD thesis (University of Michigan, 1995). This last work was to be published as *Insurgent Cuba: Race, Nation, and Revolution, 1868–1898* (Chapel Hill, NC: University of North Carolina Press, 1999).
6. Ferrer, *Insurgent Cuba*; J. Ibarra, *Ideología mambisa* (Havana: Instituto Cubano del Libro, 1972); A. Helg, *Our Rightful Share: The Afro-Cuban Struggle for Equality, 1886–1912* (Chapel Hill, NC: University of North Carolina Press, 1994); J. Casanovas, *Bread, or Bullets!: Urban Labor and Spanish Colonialism in Cuba, 1850–1898* (Pittsburgh, PA: University of Pittsburgh Press, 1998); A. Cubano-Iguina, 'Political Culture and Male Mass-Party Formation in Late-Nineteenth-Century Puerto Rico', and R. Scott 'Race, Labor, and Citzenship in Cuba: A View from the Sugar District of Cienfuegos, 1886–1909', *Hispanic American Historical Review*, 78 (1998), pp.631–62 and pp.687–728; A. de la Fuente, 'Race, National Discourse, and Politics in Cuba: An Overview', *Latin American Perspectives*, 25 (1998), pp.43–69 and C. Schmidt-Nowara, 'From Slaves to Spaniards: The Failure of

Revolutionary Emancipationism in Spain and Cuba, 1868–1895', *Illes i imperis*, 2 (1999), pp.177–90.

7. See Moreno Fraginals, *El Ingenio*; F.Knight, *Slave Society in Cuba during the Nineteenth Century* (Madison, WI: University of Wisconsin Press, 1970); D. Tomich, 'World Slavery and Caribbean Capitalism: The Cuban Sugar Industry, 1760–1868', *Theory and Society*, 20 (1991), pp.297–319; A. Kuethe, *Cuba, 1753–1815: Crown, Military, and Society* (Knoxville, TN: University of Tennessee Press, 1986); and J.M. Fradera, *Gobernar colonias* (Madrid: Peninsula, 1999).

8. See David Eltis, *Economic Growth and the Ending of the Transatlantic Slave Trade* (New York, NY: Oxford University Press, 1987), p.249.

9. See Scarano, *Sugar and Slavery*, pp.3–34 and J. Curet, 'From Slave to "Liberto": A Study on Slavery and Its Abolition in Puerto Rico, 1840–1880', PhD thesis (Columbia University, 1980).

10. On the new political order see Fradera, *Gobernar colonias* and J.R. Navarro García, *Entre esclavos y constituciónes* (Sevilla: CSIC, 1991). On slavery and the slave trade see Bergad, *Cuban Rural Society* and D. Murray, *Odious Commerce: Britain, Spain and the Abolition of the Cuban Slave Trade* (Cambridge: Cambridge University Press, 1980).

11. J.J. Acosta y Calbo, 'Artículo segundo', *Colección de artículos publicados* (Puerto Rico: Imprenta de Acosta, 1869), p.32. The classic discussion of the Cuban sugar industry is Moreno Fraginals, *El Ingenio*. See also Bergad, *Cuban Rural Society* and O. Zanetti and A. García, *Caminos para el azúcar* (Havana: Editorial de Ciencias Sociales, 1987). On Puerto Rico see Curet, 'From Slave to "Liberto"'; Scarano, *Sugar and Slavery* and A. Ramos Mattei, , *La hacienda azucarera: su crecimiento y crisis en Puerto Rico (siglo XIX)* (San Juan: CEREP, 1981).

12. See F. Picó, *Libertad y servidumbre en el Puerto Rico del siglo XIX* (Río Piedras: Ediciones Huracán, 1979); L. Bergad, *Coffee and the Growth of Agrarian Capitalism in Nineteenth-century Puerto Rico* (Princeton, NJ: Princeton University Press, 1983). For debates over slavery and the *libreta* in this period see C. Schmidt-Nowara, *Empire and Antislavery: Spain, Cuba, and Puerto Rico, 1833–1874* (Pittsburgh, PA: University of Pittsburgh Press, 1999), pp.37–50.

13. See Eltis, *Economic Growth*, p.249 and Scott, *Slave Emancipation*, p.7.

14. See Scott, *Slave Emancipation*, pp.3–41; Bergad, *Cuban Rural Society*; D. Helly, 'Introduction', in *The Cuba Commission Report: A Hidden History of the Chinese in Cuba*, trans. S. Mintz (Baltimore, MD: Johns Hopkins University Press, 1993); P. Estrade, 'Los colonos yucatecos como sustitutos de los esclavos negros', in *Cuba, la perla de las Antillas*, C. Naranjo Orovio and T. Mallo Gutiérrez (eds.) (Madrid: Doce Calles, 1992), pp.93–107; and L. Bergad, F. Iglesias García and M. Barcia, *The Cuban Slave Market, 1790–1880* (Cambridge:Cambridge University Press, 1995).

15. On the general crisis of the 1860s see R. Cepero Bonilla, *Azúcar y abolición* (Havana: Editorial Cénit, 1948); Murray, *Odious Commerce*, pp.298–326; Casanovas, *Bread, or Bullets!*, pp.71–96; Schmidt-Nowara, *Empire and Antislavery*, pp.100–25 and A. Corwin, *Spain and the Abolition of Cuban Slavery, 1817–1886* (Austin, TX: University of Texas Press, 1967). On Puerto Rican planters see Curet, 'From Slave to "Liberto"', pp.226–60. On Cuba see Scott, *Slave Emancipation*, pp.3–45 and Bergad, *Cuban Rural Society*, pp.89–182.

16. On the insurrection and slavery see Scott, *Slave Emancipation*, pp.45–62; Ferrer, *Insurgent Cuba*. On the western planters see Bergad, *Cuban Rural Society*, pp.183–259. For an overview of the conflict see R. Guerra y Sánchez, *La guerra de los diez años, 1868–1878*, 2 vols (Havana: Editorial de Ciencias Sociales, 2nd edn, 1972).

17. On Utuado see Picó, *Libertad y servidumbre* and Bergad, *Coffee*. On the Grito de Lares see O. Jiménez de Wagenheim, *Puerto Rico's Revolt for Independence: El Grito de Lares* (Princeton, NJ: Markus Wiener Publishing, 1993).

18. On Spain's September Revolution and the colonies see Schmidt-Nowara, *Empire and Antislavery*, pp.126–76; Casanovas, *Bread, or Bullets!*, pp.97–126; J. Maluquer de Motes, 'El problema de la esclavitud y la revolución de 1868', *Hispania*, 31 (1971), pp.56–76 and J.A. Piqueras, *La revolución democrática (1868–1874)* (Madrid: Ministerio de Trabajo y Seguridad Social, 1992).

19. See Scott, *Slave Emancipation*, pp.63–83.
20. On the response of planters and the effects of the Moret Law see ibid., pp.84–110; Figueroa, 'Facing Freedom', pp.169–80; and A. Cubano Iguina, *El hilo en el laberinto: claves de la lucha política en Puerto Rico (siglo XIX)* (Río Piedras: Ediciones Huracán, 1990).
21. See Díaz Soler, *Historia de la esclavitud negra*, pp.315–48; Casanovas, *Bread, or Bullets!*, pp.97–126; Schmidt-Nowara, *Empire and Antislavery*, pp.139–60.
22. See Ramos Mattei, *La hacienda azucarera*; Curet, 'From Slave to "Liberto"', pp. 261–80; Figueroa, 'Facing Freedom', pp.169–243; Schmidt-Nowara, *Empire and Antislavery*, pp.161–76.
23. See the two articles by A. Ramos Mattei, 'Technical Innovations and Social Change in the Sugar Industry of Puerto Rico, 1870–1880', in M. Moreno Fraginals, F. Moya Pons and S. Engerman (eds.), *Between Slavery and Free Labor: The Spanish-Speaking Caribbean in the Nineteenth Century* (Baltimore, MD: Johns Hopkins University Press, 1985), pp.158–78; and 'La importación de trabajadores contratados para la industria azucarera puertorriqueña: 1860–1880', in F. Scarano (ed.), *Inmigración y clases sociales en el Puerto Rico del siglo XIX* (Río Piedras: Ediciones Huracán, 1989), pp.125–41.
24. See Scott, *Slave Emancipation*, pp.227–54.
25. Ibid., pp.201–78.
26. Bergad, *Cuban Rural Society*, p.264.
27. Ibid., pp.263–302.
28. For clear summaries see Ferrer, *Insurgent Cuba* and de la Fuente, 'Race, National Discourse'. Other works will be cited below.
29. See Cubano-Iguina, 'Political Culture'.
30. On Labra see L.M. García Mora, 'Rafael María de Labra y la utopía colonial (esbozo biográfico)', *Tzintzun*, 24 (1996), pp.91–102. On Labra's strategy and views of other emancipations see Schmidt-Nowara, *Empire and Antislavery*, pp.100–76. For an example of his writings on the matter see his *La abolición de la esclavitud en el órden económico* (Madrid: Imprenta de J. Norguera, 1873). On the quite different opinions on slave emancipation in Great Britain by the 1870s see T.C. Holt, *The Problem of Freedom: Race, Labor, and Politics in Jamaica and Britain, 1832–1938* (Baltimore, MD: Johns Hopkins University Press, 1992).
31. Ferrer, 'To Make a Free Nation', p.216.
32. See Helg, *Our Rightful Share*, pp. 23–54.
33. On Azcárate see R. Azcárate Rosell, *Nicolás Azcárate el reformista* (Havana: Editorial Trópico, 1939).
34. See Casanovas, *Bread, or Bullets!*, *passim*.
35. See Scott, 'Race, Labor, and Citizenship'. On the war see L.A. Pérez, *Cuba between Empires, 1878–1902* (Pittsburgh, PA: University of Pittsburgh Press, 1983) and A. Elorza and E. Hernández Sandöica, *La Guerra de Cuba (1895–1898)* (Madrid: Alianza, 1998).
36. See the comparison in Cubano Iguina, *El hilo en el laberinto*, pp.120–44.
37. On Puerto Rican autonomism see Cubano-Iguina, 'Political Culture'; L. Náter Vázquez, 'Los autonomismos: de la semilla al proyecto (1809–1887)', Master's thesis (University of Puerto Rico, Río Piedras, 1991); E. Findlay, 'Domination, Decency, and Desire: The Politics of Sexuality in Puerto Rico, 1870–1920', PhD thesis (University of Wisconsin, 1995) and A. Cubano Iguina, 'Las identidades cambiantes del 98 puertorriqueño: Nación, patria y ciudadanía, 1887–1904', *Illes i imperis*, 2 (1999), pp.77–88.
38. See Scott, *Slave Emancipation*, pp.45–62; Ferrer, *Insurgent Cuba* and K. Robert, 'Slavery and Freedom in the Ten Years' War, Cuba, 1868–1878', *Slavery and Abolition*, 13 (1992), pp.181–200.
39. See Ferrer, *Insurgent Cuba*, *passim*.
40. J. Martí, 'With All, and for the Good of All', [1891], in *Our America*, trans. E. Randall with J. de Onís and R. Held Foner, ed. P.S. Foner (New York, NY: Monthly Review Press, 1977), p.259.
41. On Martí and Cuban nationalism see Ibarra, *Ideología mambisa*. On the social foundation of nationalist ideology see Scott, 'Race, Labor, and Citizenship'; Casanovas, *Bread, or Bullets!*; Ferrer, *Insurgent Cuba* and G. Poyo, *'With All, and for the Good of All': The Emergence of*

Popular Nationalism in the Cuban Communities of the United States, 1848–1898 (Durham, NC: Duke University Press, 1989).

42. See de la Fuente, 'Race, National Discourse' and Ferrer, *Insurgent Cuba* for discussions of the multivalence of Cuban nationalist discourse in the late nineteenth and the early twentieth century.

43. See Helg, *Our Rightful Share*, pp.161–91.

44. Ibid., pp.193–226 and de la Fuente, 'Race, National Discourse', pp.54–60; and by the same author, 'Negros y electores: desigualdad y políticas raciales en Cuba, 1900–1930', in C. Naranjo, M.A. Puig-Samper and L.M. García Mora (eds.), *La nación soñada: Cuba, Puerto Rico y Filipinas ante el 98* (Madrid: Editorial Doce Calles, 1996), pp.163–77. Also on the transition from the colony to the early republic see Scott, 'Race, Labor, and Citizenship' and M. Zeuske, 'Clientelas regionales, alianzas interraciales y poder nacional en torno a la "Guerrita de Agosto"', *Illes i imperis*, 2 (1999), pp.127–58.

45. See D. Tomich, 'The "Second Slavery": Bonded Labor and the Transformation of the Nineteenth-century World Economy', in F.O. Ramírez (ed.), *Rethinking the Nineteenth Century* (Stanford, CA: Stanford University Press, 1988), pp.103–17.

46. See the discussion in Scott, *Slave Emancipation* and by the same author, 'Reclamando la mula de Gregoria Quesada: El significado de la libertad en los valles del Arimao y del Caunao, Cienfuegos, Cuba', *Illes i Imperis*, 2 (1999), pp.89–110.

Unfinished Business:
Slavery in Saharan Africa

DAVID SEDDON

Slavery in the Sahara: An Introduction

Saharan Africa is a vast arid region, divided today between ten states – and one disputed territory – whose boundaries were largely determined during the colonial period.[1] Before then, it was virtually defined by its role in the overland trade between the Sahelian savannah zone (which divides the Sahara from the tropics) and north Africa. For more than a thousand years the societies of the desert and desert fringe were involved in this trade, which crossed the Sahara by well-travelled, if arduous, routes (see Map 1).[2]

From 1830 to the 1930s the region experienced the progressive expansion and consolidation of European rule. The suppression of the slave trade and the abolition of slavery were official policy for the two major European powers in the region, England and France, from 1833 and 1848, respectively. The immediate effect, however, was limited; in the mid nineteenth century slaves still provided about half the total value of all items traded across the Sahara, with the number exported annually to the Maghreb amounting to around 10,000.[3] In the early, expansionist period European colonial officers and officials charged with the pacification, control and administration of the Saharan territories were often prepared to condone slavery. Indeed, throughout the colonial period (and well into the second half of the twentieth century) there was a marked reluctance among those responsible for the administration of local populations to implement the official anti-slavery policy too rigorously for fear of disturbing the social and political status quo; this was particularly the case in the remoter desert regions, where resistance to colonial authority was greatest and forms of indirect rule the norm.

Even after political independence slavery continued to exist in countries south of the Sahara, despite the stated abolitionist concerns of their new governments, either (as in Mauritania) because the ruling elite was itself deeply committed to maintaining specific aspects of the 'traditional' hierarchy or (as in Mali and Niger) because they were incapable of transforming or integrating into the new political system the old social orders of marginal groups which maintained slavery as essential to their

MAP 1

MODERN STATES OF THE SAHARA REGION

continuing survival and identity or (as in Chad) both of these at different times. Of all the new states in which slavery continued to exist at independence only Algeria (where a protracted war of independence had generated a widespread commitment to radical social transformation) was able to abolish it within a few years. A similar commitment by the POLISARIO (the Saharawi liberation movement) to a radical social transformation ensured that, in the refugee camps from which after 1976 they waged their own war of independence against Mauritania and Morocco, slavery was effectively abolished.

In Mali, Niger, Chad and Sudan, by contrast, where the state remained weak and unable to deal effectively with deep social and political divisions, forms of slavery and what might be termed 'the heritage of slavery' continued for many years to permeate contemporary politics and everyday economic and social relations. In Mauritania, unique among post-colonial Saharan states in being ruled by elites deeply rooted in the traditions of desert economy and society, slavery still survives.

European Intervention in the Late Nineteenth Century

The Maghreb

Between 1830 and 1870 the French in Algeria were able, despite resistance, to control the coastal regions and the mountains of the Aures and Kabylia; it took them longer to pacify the Saharan interior where slavery was common. The Wargla and Laghouat oases were occupied in 1844 and 1852, respectively, eroding local slave-ownership and diverting much of Algeria's trans-Saharan trade westwards to Morocco, or eastwards to Tunisia and Libya; but it was not until the end of the century that the far south was pacified. In 1881, for example, a French expeditionary force was wiped out by the Tuareg who inhabited some 300,000 square kilometres of desert and mountain massifs (Ajjer and Ahaggar) in southern Algeria.

Historically, many of the material needs of the Kel Ajjer and Kel Ahaggar Tuareg were obtained by raiding, which, together with pastoralism and the control of caravan routes, was the mainstay of their economy. Some gardening had been attempted as early as 1840 in the Ahaggar using slaves, but they proved unsatisfactory cultivators and, during the second half of the nineteenth century, freedmen were brought from oases in the north to augment the numbers of those already working for the Tuareg. While slavery was integral to Tuareg economy and society, the Tuareg were only purchasers and owners of slaves. Even before the French occupation it was rare for Tuareg slave-owners to sell their slaves. It seems that they were generally well-treated; slaves were 'part of the family'.[4] Increasing French control of the surrounding regions in the 1880s limited Tuareg raiding and led to the organization of salt caravans south into Niger where the indigenous Tuareg remained largely beyond the French colonial pale. These caravans, together with livestock production and the continuing use of slave and bonded labour, formed the basis of the Algerian Tuareg economy long after the heavily armed Foureau-Lamy mission, which reached the Ajjer and Ahaggar in 1898–99, enabled the French to establish an effective local presence.

Further east, a treaty signed in 1881 with the Bey of Tunis authorized France to occupy Tunisia as a 'protectorate', and in 1883 a further convention placed the territory entirely under French administration. The traditional hierarchy of local authorities was preserved, but placed under French *controleurs civils*; Islamic courts were retained, with competence in matters concerning Muslims' personal status. Slavery was, however, progressively abolished. Tunisia was the first of the Saharan states to have brought slavery effectively to an end, and the only one to have done so before the twentieth century.

To the west, Morocco – itself a slave-owning society until well into the early twentieth century – had always played a major part in the trans-

Saharan trade. The Moroccan central government rarely achieved enduring political control beyond the Atlas mountains; but the far south was not entirely beyond the authority of the Sultan, who maintained a resident governor in Tafilalt throughout much of the nineteenth century. The largest centre of sedentary cultivators in a region where pastoralism predominated, and principal entrepôt for both trans-Saharan and local regional trade, Tafilalt consisted of seven clusters of oases and fortified villages.

Dunn[5] identified six major social groups in late nineteenth century Tafilalt society: i. those claiming descent from the prophet, ii. holy men and their descendants, iii. freeborn cultivators, iv. freedmen (*harratin*), v. slaves, and vi. Jews. Most *harratin* were dark-skinned with 'black' features. In the eyes of the freeborn they were menials. They were not slaves but share-croppers, working for the sedentary groups of higher status and for the pastoral elite who owned the palm trees. They represented a substantial proportion of the total sedentary population, a majority in some places.

Local men of wealth bought a few slaves every year – about two dozen was the upper limit. But Tafilalt was only a temporary resting place for most of the slaves brought across the Sahara, who were sent on to Marrakesh, Fes and other Moroccan cities.[6] Females predominated as they were in great demand as domestics and concubines: Harris observed in 1895 that 'the girls of the Hausa country fetch the best prices, being considered more cheerful and neater than those from further west'.[7]

Miege[8] considered that the slave trade into Morocco reached its zenith betwen 1840 and 1855, when between 3,500 and 4,000 slaves arrived annually; after that, numbers fell. By the end of the nineteenth century 'the number of slaves living in the [far south] had probably dwindled to a few hundred, owing to the decline of the trans-Saharan slave trade from West Africa'.[9] But, if French intervention in West Africa towards the end of the nineteenth century reduced the flow of slaves from the south, a more direct threat was posed by French incursions from Algeria.

In 1899–1900 the French seized Touat, the oasis complex in the north-central Sahara that also served as an entrepôt for the trans-Saharan trade. They abandoned their declared policy of peaceful penetration in favour of military intervention, and the end of Morocco's long involvement in the trans-Saharan slave trade was in sight.

French West Africa

South of the Sahara, the French reached the Niger river in 1883, built a post at Bamako in 1884, took Timbuktu (the historic centre of the western Saharan slave trade) in 1894 and Gao in 1899. The British and the French initially agreed that the whole sub-Saharan region from the Niger to Lake Chad should be regarded as a French sphere of influence; and then in 1898, following Kitchener's reconquest of the Sudan, agreed to include Wadai and Borku, Ennedi and Tibesti (BET) in Chad.

Early efforts by the French colonial authorities to end the slave trade in west Africa were half-hearted and proved unsuccessful. As Bamako declined as a trading centre after its occupation, Nioro – linked to Segou by a route passing through Banamba – developed as a northern crossroads, attracting trade from the desert and the Upper Senegal. Banamba became a thriving commercial centre, its trade consisting mainly of salt from the desert and kola, cloth and slaves from the south: in 1898 it was described as 'one of the most important salt entrepôts in the French Soudan',[10] on occasion drawing caravans of up to two or three thousand camels. At the turn of the century, slavery and the slave trade was still alive and flourishing in the French territories south of the Sahara.

The Western Sahara

As France extended its control in the Maghreb and west Africa, Spain established a foothold on the Atlantic coast. In 1883–84 the *Sociedad de Africanistas y Colonistas* claimed possession of a strip of territory nearly 500 km long, contracting treaties with chiefs of the Wadi Noun region; posts were established along the coast and Spain announced its protectorate over Rio de Oro and the adjacent regions. In April 1887 a royal decree placed the strip between Cape Bojador and Cape Blanc extending 150 km into the interior, under the authority of the governor general of the Canary Islands.

Resistance to Spanish intervention from the local tribes was organized by Sheikh Ma El Ainin. The Moroccan Sultan sent a military expedition to his aid; and, as French troops advanced north into Mauritania from Senegal at the beginning of the twentieth century, Ma El Ainin received support from tribal groups across the western Sahara, Mauritania and southern Morocco. Resistance proved vain, however, and he eventually withdrew to Tiznit in Morocco, where he died in 1910. The French subsequently extended their control over Mauritania, and the Spanish over the coastal regions of the western Sahara between southern Morocco and Mauritania.[11]

The Central Sahara

According to Bovill,[12] of an estimated 10,000 slaves being traded annually across the Sahara until the mid-nineteenth century, around half entered the Regency of Tripoli (with about 2,500 going to Morocco and the rest to Algeria and Tunisia). But in the 1850s the Ottoman authorities effectively stopped the trade through Tripoli; other towns in the province were also adversely affected,[13] and the main route from the areas around Lake Chad northwards across the Sahara through central Fezzan and Tripolitania to the coast went into decline.

Such measures, however, barely affected remote Cyrenaica; merchants increasingly traded through Benghazi and made use of the route through the Kufra oases. Of critical importance in the development of this route was the rise of the Sanussi Order – an Islamic *sufi* brotherhood, which constructed its first African lodge in the Jebel Akhdar in 1843. In 1856, using *harratin* (freed slaves) to build a 'home' for the Order in the Jughbub oasis, the Sanussi moved south into the terrritory of the Zuwaya.

The Zuwaya nobility of the Kufra region themselves owned slaves; many of the most powerful families participated in the trans-Saharan trade – although often as much was gained from raiding and pillaging the caravans as managing and participating in them. As long as the Kufra oasis was dominated simply by the Zuwaya there was little security; but the Sanussi established lodges and wells at suitable resting points along the route, and both travelling conditions and security were much improved. As the trade in slaves along other routes was increasingly restricted by the French and the Ottoman authorities, the Wadai–Kufra–Benghazi route flourished. The Kufra oases became the hub of a regional trading network connecting slaving routes from the Air massif in Niger to Darfur province in Sudan, and taking in most of Chad. Sanussi intervention ensured the development of the Wadai–Kufra–Benghazi route as the most important of all the trans-Saharan trade links in the late nineteenth century.

Gustav Nachtigal, who visited Wadai in the early 1870s, estimated its export of slaves at 15,000 a year.[14] This route offered the landlocked Sultanate of Wadai in Chad a more direct outlet to the Mediterranean than the roundabout route through Fezzan or the alternative eastern trail through Darfur to Egypt. The Sanussi connection also helped the Sultanate of Wadai to increase its firepower and its capacity to raid and subordinate other groups, and thus provide slaves for the slave trade.[15]

The demand in the north for slaves was considerable. The British consul reported from Benghazi in 1879 that 'almost every Arab notable… residing in this town is a slave owner, and… the sale and purchase of negroes is freely though quietly carried on among the natives. Even the local government actually permits all its functionaries, to the utter disregard of all Firmans and vizieral orders, to possess as many slaves as their circumstances will enable them to maintain'.[16] But about half of the slaves crossing the central Sahara were re-exported annually to Constantinople, Mytilene and Izmir in Turkey, to Cyprus, and even as far north as Albania.

In 1881 travel between Tripoli and Benghazi was facilitated by the opening of a steamship service; Benghazi now became the most important outlet for the Saharan slave trade, which, passing through some of the remotest and most inhospitable parts of the eastern Sahara, was well beyond the observation and diplomatic interference of any European power. The

Sanussi's independence from Ottoman control increased when, in 1895, at the invitation of the Zuwaya, their headquarters moved to Kufra itself. The Wadai–Kufra–Benghazi route also benefited when the Mahdist movement in the Nilotic Sudan cut all eastern outlets for the slave trade through the upper Nile Valley to Egypt and the Red Sea, and the British began after 1882 to curb the slave trade on the upper Nile.

Egypt and Sudan

There had been a considerable trade in slaves between Egypt and Constantinople in the eighteenth century;[17] two caravans a year brought slaves, ivory, hides, skins, gum, ostrich feathers, gold dust and natron from Darfur and Sennar in the Sudan to Asiut in Upper Egypt, from where they were carried north. This trade continued into the first half of the nineteenth century and increased significantly as Muhammad Ali Pasha, under the nominal sovereignty of the Ottoman Sultan, brought the Sudan under the control of the Turco-Egyptian state. He then extended his southern domain until by 1860 it controlled all of the Sudan. It has been suggested that Muhammad Ali Pasha had two main objectives in the Sudan – gold and slaves, particularly the latter.[18] Trading rights in the Sudan were sold to armed adventurers and slaving was carried to extremes. This undoubtedly created some of the preconditions for the later Mahdist revolt; it also resulted in a massive expansion of the slave trade between the Sudan and Egypt.

Slavery was widely practised in mid nineteenth century Egypt: out of a population of some 275,000, there were an estimated 10,000 to 15,000 slaves in Cairo alone; about 5,000 newly acquired slaves used to enter the country every year. Most were women who served mainly as domestics in urban households; a small number of male slaves worked as attendants in better off families or as assistants to artisans, shopkeepers and merchants. Male slave labour was often used on large cash-crop estates – and during times of increased agricultural activity, such as the cotton boom of the 1860s, the use of slave labour rose significantly[19] – although slaves never rivalled the Egyptian free cultivators as a workforce.

In 1863, 14 years after Muhammad Ali's death, his grandson Ismail came to power. Determined to abolish slavery and the slave trade in his own lifetime, he appointed British officials to implement this policy in both Egypt and the Sudan. It is unclear, however, to what extent official proclamations abolishing slavery reflected the reality of the situation. Certainly the reports of Sir Samuel Baker (Governor of Equatoria in 1870) and of his successor, General Gordon, suggest that slavery and the trade in slaves persisted at least until the 1880s. Slavery was, in fact, part of the traditional social system throughout the Nile Valley and continued to provide the basis for the trade with Egypt and Ottoman Turkey throughout the latter part of the century. Even in the north there were indigenous groups – the Nuba of Kordofan and the Fur of Darfur – from whom slaves were taken. South of Juba were the Nilotic groups, and beyond them, in the far southern regions of Equatoria, Bahr el-Ghazal and Upper Nile, other groups, many of whom were greatly reduced in numbers by the slave raids.

In Egypt a military revolt against foreign interference led to a British occupation in 1882. The new 'supervisory' regime was committed to suppress slavery and the slave trade; it was also concerned about the situation further south where the Mahdist revolt, provoked among other things by the attack on slaving, led to the fall of Khartoum in January 1885. The reconquest of the Sudan was initiated to suppress the revolt and ensure control. In the southern Sudan the French had already occupied the Bahar al Ghazal, and in 1896 an expedition was sent to the White Nile to extend French influence. In 1898, two days after the battle of Omdurman brought an end to Sudanese resistance, British and Turkish flags were hoisted on the ruins of Gordon's palace in Khartoum; negotiations with the French led to the withdrawal of their expedition and the first of several protocols defining French and British 'spheres of influence' in Africa south of the Sahara was agreed. In January 1899 an Anglo-Egyptian convention was concluded establishing the Sudan as a joint condominium. It would be several decades, however, before its peoples were brought effectively under control, and even longer than that before slavery and the slave trade were abolished.

Slavery in the Early Twentieth Century

During the first three decades of the twentieth century the pace of European intervention in the Saharan region quickened and more direct forms of political control were introduced. But, despite the formal abolition of slavery and the slave trade in all the colonial territories, both continued to exist in many areas up until the mid 1930s and even thereafter. The combination of reluctance on the part of the European colonial authorities to confront direct the vested interests of the local notables on whom they depended for the effective administration of the vast desert territories and the integral nature of slavery in the economies and societies indigenous to those regions explains slavery's persistence in the deep Sahara.

Egypt and the Sudan

Egypt, under British supervision since 1882, was, following the Anglo-French *entente* of 1904, brought fully under British control. The formal abolition of slavery was duly proclaimed and its gradual elimination in most of Egypt begun. In Sudan, however (and possibly in parts of upper Egypt too), both slave ownership and a trade in slaves continued well into the twentieth century.

In 1901 the British in the Sudan introduced a specific anti-slavery decree, supplemented by the new Sudan Penal Code, and in 1902 the government's first ordinance on slavery was published. These measures provoked angry responses from slave-holders and there were several pro-slavery revolts, among them the Tawlawdi uprising in 1904 and the Blue Nile insurrection in 1906. In 1908 it was officially acknowledged that no swift suppression of slavery was feasible without a liberal scheme of financial compensation to slave-holders, and a pragmatic policy of 'leaving the slaves quietly in the possession of their masters until they either disappear through death or are set free by manumission' was considered the most prudent course.[20]

When the First World War broke out Egypt was declared a British protectorate. There was intense agitation against this and for the restoration of the Sudan to Egypt. Egyptian demands were partly met by the Declaration of 1922, which recognized Egypt as an independent sovereign state – the first one in the Saharan region to gain its formal political independence and the second to have effectively abolished slavery. In the Sudan, however, 'twenty years of vacillating action had neither altered the servile base of Sudanese society nor reconciled the chasm between stated objectives and actual practice'.[21]

In 1924 Egyptian officials and military personnel were withdrawn from the Sudan and the territory came under British rule. The government introduced measures for the suppression of slavery, culminating in a new slavery law in 1925; when the League of Nations introduced a convention in 1926 designed to suppress slavery world-wide, the Sudan swiftly ratified it. But while the government publicly professed to be uprooting slavery, in practice the liberation of slaves in more distant regions such as Darfur and Kordofan did not take place until the 1930s.

In 1936 Britain and Egypt signed a treaty of friendship and alliance; Egypt and Sudan were once again to be administered jointly, under British supervision. In the same year, the government of Sudan produced a report which declared that anti-slavery legislation had reduced slave trafficking to negligible levels. But two years later it was obliged to confess that 'sporadic and rare cases of slave acquisition would occur for a few years yet'.[22]

Libya

To the west, the Italians began the military occupation of Libya in 1911, a few days after having declared war on Turkey. A peace treaty signed in 1912 gave Italy nominal control over Libya; but, in 1914, despite a brief occupation of Fezzan, it still held only the major coastal towns and a few villages. Tripolitania was not occupied until 1925; and the interior, which remained very much the domain of the Sanussi and the Zuwaya,[23] was not brought under control for another six years. Until the Italian occupation of the interior, 'men might travel only with Zuwaya consent, and Zuwaya took fees to guide travellers from water-hole to water-hole on the routes to Kufra and beyond. They had an exclusive licence as desert guides from the Turkish authorities in Benghazi, and they taxed merchants who passed through Kufra... No Christian had visited Kufra before the 1920s.'[24] When they did, they discovered that slavery and the slave trade were still very much in existence.

Rosita Forbes, for example, learned on her visit to Kufra in 1920–21 that caravans were still travelling along the Wadai–Kufra–Benghazi route with smuggled boys and girls.[25] The total population of the Kufra oases was 3,800 in the early 1920s: 1,650 Zuwaya, 1,000 'Sudanese' slaves and freedmen, 400 Sanussi and 250 or so others.[26] But the population of the oases fluctuated considerably as caravans and traders came and went; so too did the price of slaves: the Egyptian traveller Hassanein Bey learned at Kufra in 1923 that the price of a slave girl varied between £30 and £40 – and noted that the price had risen significantly since 1916 when he had been offered a girl for the equivalent of £5 sterling. He attributed the higher prices to a shortage of slaves coming up from Wadai since the French occupation.[27]

To the north, between 1925 and 1929, the Italians gradually occupied the oases of the interior. Knud Holmboe, the Danish Muslim traveller, however, found that slavery was still endemic in Kufra in 1930 and a large slave market was held there every Thursday. A good slave cost up to 1,000 lira (the equivalent of £15 sterling), substantially less than a decade previously,[28] suggesting an ample supply. The Italians eventually occupied the Sanussi headquarters at Kufra and eliminated the last resistance in 1931. Thereafter the trade in slaves was substantially reduced, although there was still much movement between Libya and Chad; but although slavery was formally abolished, the condition of the former slaves changed relatively little in practice in the oases of the Libyan deep south until after the Second World War.

French Sub-Saharan Africa

Further south still, the French had conquered Kanem west of Lake Chad in 1902 and gradually expanded eastwards. In the meanwhile, however, the slave trade from Wadai continued. Guns were used to acquire slaves and slaves were also used to acquire guns – providing the most acceptable 'currency' for imported weapons: in 1907 one slave from Wadai was the price of an 1874 model French rifle in good condition, with 40 cartridges included. However, as one French colonial official observed in 1912, 'it was evident that the occupation of Wadai threatened to ruin the Sanusiyya by suppressing their two great resources: the trade in slaves and the smuggling of arms'.[29]

The French began their occupation of Wadai in 1909 and by 1911 had effectively annexed most of the territory. The Sanussi attempted to enlist the support of the Turks against the French drive into Borku, Ennedi and Tibesti (BET) in 1911–12, but the Turkish garrisons (established there between 1906 and 1911 specifically to prevent French incursions) were withdrawn in 1912 under the terms of the peace treaty between the Ottoman Sultan and the Italians. The Italians, in an effort to forestall the continuing French advance, occupied Fezzan briefly in 1914; but by this time both Borku and Tibesti had been taken by the French, despite resistance from the Sanussi (according to Evans-Pritchard[30] there were ten Sanussi lodges in Chad, widely spread in Tibesti, Wajanga, Borkedi and Ennedi).

The French were fully in control of only Borku and Ennedi, however, after the First World War and were able to establish their authority definitively in Tibesti only in 1929, just two years before the Italians occupied Kufra. There was little change in the structure of the local tribes and peoples of northern Chad over the next decades, although colonial policy – both in French Equatorial Africa (Chad included) and in Libya – officially outlawed slavery and had reduced the slave trade across the Sahara to a trickle by the late 1930s.

Further west, the French completed a railway link between Senegal and the Niger in 1906, helping to consolidate their control over the Territory of Haut Senegal et Niger which now formed a vast military province stretching some 2,000 km from the Senegal River to Lake Chad. Despite this, a territory-wide investigation into slavery carried out between 1903 and 1905 revealed that French conquest had changed little, even in areas under direct rule. In the west, Banamba was still a principal market for salt and slaves; and in southern regions such as Bouguni, slaves sold for the price of a bar of salt in 1903.[31] In the desert fringe areas to the north it seems that the trade in slaves had actually increased.

Gradually, French Africa south of the Sahara was divided into distinct territories; civil administration replaced military control and began to have a progressively greater impact on the local economy and society. In the peri-Saharan and Saharan regions of present-day Mauritania, Mali and Niger, however, change was slow. It was not until 1907, for example, that the boundaries between Algeria and the French possessions south of the Sahara were finally agreed and the Tuareg of the border areas effectively divided between Algeria and Haut Senegal and Niger.

The Iwllemeden Tuareg, who once controlled Timbuktu and the surrounding area, and of whom it was said in 1910 that they 'sold men like cattle',[32] formally submitted to French authority in 1903, but revolted in 1908. In 1909 Commandant Betrix (in charge of the Gao region) obtained the submission of the Kel Adrar of the Adrar n Iforas and a general agreement on the part of all of the major local groups – including the Kel Adrar, the Iwllemeden and the Kel Ahaggar in southern Algeria – to keep the peace. A military post was built at Kidal and from 1910 the Kel Adrar were taxed; in 1911 a locally recruited camel corps was established to help to maintain law and order. In 1916, when the Iwellemeden again rebelled against French rule, a small detachment of Kel Adrar fought on the French side.[33]

In 1911 the military territory of Niger was detached to become a separate administrative entity. The Tuareg population of northern Niger during the early colonial period consisted of the Iwllemeden Kel Dinnik, the Kel Gress and the Kel Ayr. Several Tuareg groups continued to resist the French occupation. A revolt in the north-east by the Kel Ayr (under a leader reported to be the son of a slave woman) was crushed only in 1919 and the last dissidents were defeated only in 1920.[34]

At the apex of Tuareg society in Niger were the warrior nobility; beneath them were the groups with religious status and the vassals; beneath these were the freedmen – *ighawellen* (ex-slaves freed 'a long time ago') and *iderfan* (those more recently freed) – and slaves. The next decades saw a progressive decline in the power of the nobility and a relative increase in the influence and economic position of the religious groups and vassals. There was a gradual decline in slavery – in the pre-colonial period slaves may have constituted at least half of the population – but, although slavery was illegal, most remained dependent on their masters until the late 1930s.[35]

When Niger was detached the Territory of Haut Senegal and Niger remained, to include most of present-day Senegal and Mali. Throughout the early years of the twentieth century the traditional social structures of the Tuareg of what is now northern Mali remained little changed. Slaves were kept, mainly by the dominant sections of the nobility, although some vassal groups acquired them during the French period. Slaves were never numerous among the Kel Adrar, but in other Tuareg groups further south and more fully integrated into the French colonial administration they may have constituted up to half of the total population.[36] Clearly, the official proscription on slavery meant little in practice.

In 1920 this territory became the French Soudan. In the Saharan regions of the French Soudan there were now significant changes. With the suppression of raiding, Tuareg noble clans were no longer able to maintain either their political authority or their economic superiority and their power and influence declined. New wells were dug by the administration; there was also more sharing of pastures and mixing of clans. Nomadic movements became more regular and smaller in scale; and there was an increase in caravanning, especially towards the south, although the traditional caravan routes to Touat and Tidikelt in Algeria also thrived (despite the fact that these involved round trips of some 2,000 km and took two to three months).

Certain elements of the traditional social structures, however, remained throughout the 1920s and into the 1930s. Most noble families owned at least one slave and sometimes several; animals belonging to the noble clans were usually looked after by slaves; domestic work was done by slave women. Very few vassal or tributary clans had slaves. During the ensuing years of the French occupation sporadic attempts were made to change the status of the slaves, without conviction or apparent effect, although the growing administrative towns and villages such as Gao, Burem and Kidal attracted a small number of runaways, who were officially protected from reprisals.

To the north-west of the French Soudan in 1903 Mauritania was made a protectorate administered from St. Louis in Senegal. The overwhelming majority of Mauritania's sparse population was concentrated in the semi-arid southern parts of the country, with the densest population in the regions of Trarza and Brakna north of the Senegal River known as the *gebla*. Beyond were the desert regions which extended northwards into the western Sahara. In 1904 the *gebla* was made a 'special civilian territory'; in the semi-desert areas further north military government was retained to protect the pastoral tribes which had accepted French rule from raids by the Reguibat camel herders who roamed through the entire western Sahara.

All the Moorish tribes of Mauritania shared the same hierarchical structure. At the apex were the 'white' tribes, divided into the nobility – the predominantly Arab 'warriors' and the predominantly Berber religious tribes – and the tribute-paying vassal tribes. Distinct from these and of significantly lower status were the freedmen (*harratin*), while at the bottom came the slaves and the 'outcaste' groups (such as minstrels and blacksmiths). Four tribal confederations in the *gebla* – Trarza, Brakna, Tagant and Adrar – were headed by an overall leader or emir.

In 1905 a comprehensive anti-slavery policy was declared for all of French West Africa. But in 1906, Lt-Col. Montane insisted with respect to Mauritania that France had committed itself 'to change nothing in the social situation of the country and its customs, such as that of slaves, who are considered by the Moors as their property and their things'.[37] For slaves living near the Senegal river flight was possible, but further north the Moors were more secure in their control of their slaves.

Socially distinct from the Moors (who all spoke *hassaniya* Arabic) but physically often indistinguishable from the Moorish 'blacks', were the ethnic black groups who had maintained their cultural and linguistic distinctiveness. These groups – which also kept slaves – historically inhabited the areas along the Senegal River, beyond the pale of Moorish society and politics. During the colonial period, however, their numbers within the *gebla* increased significantly.

Mauritania officially became a French colony and a member of the French West African Federation in 1921. Resistance to French colonization continued in the north until the mid 1930s, but progressive incorporation within the French West African empire had a slow but eventually significant effect on indigenous social structures, including a diminution in the number of slaves and an increase in the number of freedmen. But slavery persisted as an integral feature of Mauritanian economy and society throughout the colonial period.

Western Sahara

In the first decade of the twentieth century France recognized Spanish rights over a vast part of the western Sahara, including Rio de Oro and Seguiat el Hamra (the Spanish Sahara) and the region of Tarfaya to the south of Morocco. After 1912, when the French declared a protectorate in Morocco, the Spanish gradually extended their control over the western Sahara. Resistance continued and progress into the interior was slow, with some areas not occupied until the mid 1930s. As a consequence, Saharawi precolonial structures largely remained intact.

As in Mauritania, indigenous society was divided vertically into tribes and tribal confederations. There were also horizontal divisions in which 'Arab' warriors occupied the highest rank together with 'holy' men; these were distinguished from vassals, of supposedly Berber origin, who were obliged to pay tribute to the nobility. Below these were freedmen and black slaves, with other groups marginal to basic tribal structure. Slaves were mainly procured from further south, through trade and warfare or raiding; they were occasionally freed, only to remain dependent on their former masters.

Despite the exploitation of the tribute-paying tribes and of slaves, western Saharan society was more egalitarian than that of Mauritania. The number of 'blacks', and especially of half-castes, was far smaller than among the Mauritanian tribes: Hodges estimates slaves as no more than 5 per cent of the total population.[38] For whereas slaves were a valuable labour force in parts of Mauritania, they were of little practical use and difficult to maintain in the exceptionally arid western Sahara (which had no oases of consequence between the Adrar of Mauritania and the Draa Valley in southern Morocco, although there was some employment of slaves for grain cultivation in rain-collecting depressions.

The Maghreb

Further north, the French occupation of Touat in 1899–1900 put an end to open slave-trading into Morocco. However, as Dunn observes, 'the demand for slaves in Morocco was insatiable until after the turn of the century'.[39] The French Protectorate outlawed slavery, but the ruling could not be enforced in areas not yet subjugated and the French army took several years to effect the full pacification and control of the far south. Slaves continued to enter Morocco until well into the twentieth century. A former native affairs officer who served in Erfoud in 1925 stated that the slave market at Abou Am in Tafilalt was still in operation;[40] and the trade in slaves may well have continued until the final occupation of Tafilelt in 1932. Slave ownership took even longer to eliminate.

In Algeria, in 1902, the Sahara Company Camel Corps smashed the power of the Ahaggar Tuareg in the far south. In the same year, the Organization of the Southern Territories was created. Gradually, over the next two decades, most of the Saharan Tuareg in Algeria submitted uneasily to French rule, initiating the gradual transformation of their traditional institutions, including slavery and the slave trade. The French established a permanent presence in the Ahaggar in 1920, with their base at Fort Tamanrasset; the Camel Corps was concentrated there in 1929 and subsequently the French administration and military were based in the town. The French Sahara was divided into four military territories: Ain Safra, Ghardaia, Touggourt and Oasis; five 'imperial tracks' crossed it from north to south: i. Tindouf to Senegal (through Mauritania); ii. Colomb-Bechar to Gao; iii. El Gholea to Tahoua (in Niger); iv. Warghla to Tahoua – joining iii north of Tamanrasset; and v. Tunis to Fort Saint Bilma. The extreme south-west of Algeria was not, however, occupied until the whole of Morocco south of the Atlas had been pacified; thus it was only in 1934 that French troops entered Tindouf.

Further south still, the territory that was eventually to be divided between Mali and Niger was still barely under European control. Almost certainly the trans-Saharan trade in slaves continued in an attenuated form in this region during the 1920s, and perhaps even later; and slave ownership remained little challenged until the last decades of colonial rule.

Slavery under Colonialism

By the mid-1930s Saharan Africa was largely subject to direct European rule. The colonial authorities were now able to impose their laws and restrictions on indigenous societies. Even so, in practice, however, they did not always do so. In several parts of the region colonial policy towards slavery remained ambivalent and in some instances actually condoned it.

Algeria

For example, although the French military administration in the Ahaggar brought an end to raiding and slave-trading, thereby effectively undermining the relationship that had existed among the Kel Ahaggar between nobles and vassals, there was no serious attempt to alter indigenous political or social structures. Indeed, the authority of the *amenokal* (the supreme chief) was actually reinforced; pastoralism and migrations to the pastures of Tamesna in northern Niger were uninhibited, while cultivation by freedmen on a servile contract system expanded considerably; and slavery was effectively condoned.

The slaves and the freedmen provided the Tuareg with the labour required both for their domestic as well as their productive and commercial needs. As the Tuareg turned increasingly to the caravan trade and to farming, they had even greater need for them. Under French rule, the slaves (and freedmen), while formally liberated, were in effect still controlled by their Tuareg overlords and occupied a position similar to that of serfs, cultivating the gardens of their lords and also serving them in other ways. There is some evidence that the numbers of both slaves and freedmen actually increased during the colonial period: in 1949 some 3,960 Tuareg in the Ahaggar owned 1,552 slaves; and among certain groups there were more slaves than Tuareg.[41]

Morocco

In Morocco, by contrast, once the pacification of the entire territory had been achieved in the mid-1930s, the formal abolition of slavery was followed by its effective elimination as an institution. Nevertheless, the heritage of slavery continues: the majority of 'black' Moroccans live in the south, beyond the Atlas Mountains, where they are often referred to as *harratin* (freedmen); and there is a tendency for the *harratin* to be among the poorer sections of the population, with some still following the traditional 'despised' crafts of tanning leather and working iron. The subordination of ex-slaves was only gradually eliminated in the far south, even after French colonial rule had been effectively established in the mid 1930s.[42]

Further south still, in the Spanish territories of the western Sahara, in Mauritania and in the sub-Saharan French colonies, slavery persisted well into the second half of the twentieth century.

The Spanish Sahara

Although the Spanish had established a presence along the coast of the western Sahara much earlier, their impact in the interior was extremely limited until the late 1950s. In order to secure their pragmatic accommodation with the local population, the Spanish authorities maintained cooperative relations with the leading families and sheikhs of the noble tribes. They had no interest in fostering reforms in Saharawi society and generally turned a blind eye to such practices as the *horma* (tribute) and slavery, though both were formally banned. They made little attempt to suppress slavery; and, although the existence of Spanish settlements and the limited employment opportunities there allowed a few runaway slaves to seek protection or to find work, slavery continued to exist throughout the territory.

After Moroccan independence in 1956 Saharawis who had fought in the Moroccan Army of Liberation also began a struggle for independence. But both the government of Morocco to the north and the indigenous political leadership in Mauritania to the south laid claim to the territory, and each sought to attract the Saharawis to their cause. In July 1957 Mokhtar Ould Daddah, Vice-President of Mauritania's first indigenous Council of Government, appealed to the tribes of the Spanish Sahara to join the 'white' Moors to the south, Arabic-speaking nomads like themselves, to create a new Mauritania 'uniting all the Arabs from the River Draa to the banks of the Senegal River'.[43]

The French, with Spanish support, reacted swiftly with an effective military operation (*Desert Storm*), which crushed the incipient guerrilla movements emerging in the region. Shortly thereafter, in January 1958, the Spanish government declared the Spanish Sahara and Ifni to be Spanish provinces. Spanish Southern Morocco (Tarfaya) was handed over in April 1958 to the Moroccan government, which rapidly brought it under control. Over the next year the Spanish subdued Saharawi resistance within the areas under their authority, and began – at a time when most colonial territories in sub-Saharan Africa were experiencing 'the wind of change' and progressive decolonization – to consolidate their control over the entire Spanish Sahara.[44]

Mauritania

The French presence in Mauritania meant an end to raiding and a greater degree of security for all. In order to free the vassal tribes from their 'overlords', the administration systematically purchased *horma* (tribute) rights from the nobility and increased the number of wells available (thereby reducing the dependency of the subordinate pastoral tribes on key resources). By 1947 the vassals owned the largest number of sheep in the Adrar and of camels in the Mauritanian Sahel. The suppression of the *horma*, completed in 1952, has been described as 'the single most shattering blow to the traditional notables, especially in Trarza, which had always been

Mauritania's most turbulent emirate';[45] in 1958 the emir of Trarza fled to Morocco.

The French also legally proscribed slavery, but both slave-raiding and slave-trading persisted in Mauritania after the Second World War.[46] The categories of freedmen and slaves became so fluid that their status was increasingly difficult to determine; both, however, remained under the control of their former owners and both continued to undertake the same kinds of work: caring for the herds, cultivating the soil, collecting dates and gum, and performing domestic tasks. The basic difference was that the freedmen (supposedly paid for their services) could in theory buy off their obligations with their earnings and were legally free to seek employment elsewhere.

For the French administration even the slaves were freemen. They were protected by the authorities if they brought complaints against their masters, which was rare; and slave-traders were severely punished if they were caught, which was seldom. A few slaves managed to escape to Senegal or to a French military post. But even when they were freed voluntarily, as happened during the Second World War when their masters could no longer feed them, the majority stayed on as freedmen. In practice, the official 'freedoms' were almost meaningless.

During the late 1950s some of the political activists from among the 'white' Moors supported a closer relationship between Mauritania and Morocco. By contrast, the predominantly ethnic black Mauritanian population of the Senegal River valley region was attracted to the idea of union with the proposed Mali–Senegal Federation, less for its 'socialist' principles than the prospect of being united with fellow blacks and of escaping from a government dominated by 'white' Moors. The 'black' Moors, divided from their ethnic black compatriots by language and culture and from their white overlords by their slave heritage, saw little hope for improvement through secession or integration with another state. They reluctantly concluded that their only hope was to seek advancement in an independent Mauritania. By 1960, when Mauritania gained independence, the more militant 'black' Moors had formulated specific demands, including the freedom to marry, recognition of the legality of their marriages, a separate listing in the national census and above all the suppression or drastic modification of their traditional obligations. These, however, took a long time to materialize.

The French Territories South of the Sahara

Across the border in Mali there was a series of slave revolts in the 1940s in areas under Tuareg domination. Despite the gradual erosion of traditional structures, about 50,000 slaves remained under the control of their Tuareg masters in the northern districts of Niafunke, Goundam, Timbuktu and Gao; 'then, in 1946, among the Imajoren Tuareg, there was an explosion. The word liberation spread like wild fire. *Bella* (slaves) arrived at the post to seek the "peace paper". Many took livestock; others left fields unharvested'.[47] Similar struggles, albeit less dramatic, took place elsewhere, and continued throughout the 1950s. Even so, it was still possible in 1958, several months after the referendum that gave France's West African colonies self-government, to buy a slave in Timbuktu. Slaves had the right to freedom and many had taken it; but many had not been able to do so and remained subject to their masters.[48]

In Niger, although slavery was illegal, most 'ex-slaves' remained highly dependent on their masters until the late 1930s. But over the next two decades many either accumulated some livestock or found new opportunities, and the degree of their economic and social dependence on their lords diminished. The gradual emancipation of the slaves and the reduced dependence of the vassal groups on their overlords greatly reduced the capacity of the Tuareg aristocracy to exact tribute and labour and obliged them to rely increasingly on their own pastoral and agro-pastoral production. The decline of the salt trade (centred around Bilma), particularly after the 1950s, adversely affected those Tuareg groups (notably the Kel Gress) which had relied on caravanning as a major source of revenue.[49] Despite these changes, the lives and livelihoods of many slaves still remained highly dependent on their subordination to their Tuareg masters.

Reluctant to abandon their Saharan territories, the French made several attempts during the late 1950s to create new political entities in the Sahara. A short-lived proposal for the formation of a Republic of Lithamie – named after the *litham* (or face veil) worn by adult Tuareg men – grouping the Tuareg-dominated Saharan territories of Mali, Niger and Algeria, was prevented by the arrest of some of the scheme's main promoters among the Mali nomads. An effort to create a Communal Organization of Saharan Regions in 1957 to provide a single economic unit for the exploitation of the resources of French Saharan territories failed similarly. In 1960, after a short-lived experiment with a Mali–Senegal political entity, both Mali and Senegal became independent; so too did Niger. Formerly a province of French Equatorial Africa, Chad became an autonomous state within the French Community in November 1958 and gained independence in August 1960 (although Borku-Ennedi-Tibesti [BET] remained under French military administration until 1964).

All of the French colonies in north-west Africa, with the exception of Algeria, were now independent. Algeria, the first territory in Saharan Africa to be occupied, had to wait until 1962 before it achieved independence after a bloody war. The Italian and the British colonies (Libya, Egypt and the Sudan) all achieved effective independence during the 1950s.

Libya

By the late 1930s the Italians had established control in Libya and slavery was largely abolished. We have little information regarding the persistence or otherwise of slavery in Libya after the 1930s, although ex-slaves undoubtedly remained a distinct social category. In 1942 Cyrenaica and Tripolitania were occupied by the British and the Fezzan by the French. After the war the territory was administered on a limited 'care and maintenance' basis by the European powers until 1951, when Libya achieved independence.

Egypt and Sudan

In the Sudan domestic slavery was reported to be on the verge of extinction by the eve of the Second World War, but in the more isolated regions of the country social forms of extreme exploitation and oppression, based on slave-like relationships, were still in existence up to and even after independence. Hargey remarks that there were reports throughout the 1940s and the early 1950s of a clandestine trade in slaves between Sudan and the Arabian peninsula.[50]

The case for the indivisibility of the Nile valley had been continually restated by the Egyptians; it was submitted to the UN Security Council in 1947, unsuccessfully. In 1951 the Egyptian government abrogated both the 1899 agreement and the 1936 treaty; but neither the British nor the Sudanese government recognized this unilateral action and administration continued as before. In 1953, after a military *coup d'état*, the new Egyptian government recognized the right of the Sudanese to self-government and the exercise of self-determination within three years. The Sudanese National Union Party (NUP) won a parliamentary majority in 1953 and led the Sudan to full independence in 1956. The Democratic Republic of Sudan promptly ratified the international Supplementary Slavery Convention.

Slavery after Independence

By the mid-1960s all the Saharan region was incorporated within one independent north African state or another, with the exception of the western Sahara – which remained even at the end of the 1990s the subject of international dispute. In some cases, the commitment to eliminate slavery was strong. In Algeria, for example, the willingness of the French colonial administration to 'turn a blind eye' to forms of slavery in Tuareg society was rapidly replaced by strong intervention, with dramatic results. In the western Sahara also, the POLISARIO made a commitment to the elimination of all forms of oppression and subordination in Saharawi society. By the end of the 1970s all the countries of Africa north of the Sahara, as well as the newly declared Saharawi Arab Democratic Republic, had effectively abolished slavery and related forms of institutional subservience. The southern Saharan states had not.

Algeria

In Algeria independence in 1962 brought significant change to the Tuareg in the southern Sahara. The new administration was committed to the assimilation of minority groups into the new Algerian nation and to the welding of north and south into a unified state; it was committed to 'popular democracy', to freedom and to equality. Slavery in any form was unacceptable.

The administration scoured the Tuareg camps and took the slaves with their few belongings away to 'freedom' in Tamanrasset. A few found work as labourers, began to mix with the freedmen and established themselves in a quarter of Tamanrasset. But for many there was no work or means of livelihood. They could not establish themselves as herders (although most of them were skilled in this task) as they had no herds, tents or equipment and no money with which to buy these things. They huddled outside Tamanrasset in shacks.[51]

The creation of agricultural cooperatives in the early years of independence helped some to establish themselves in agriculture (several local cooperatives consisted almost entirely of ex-slaves), but many remained impoverished and without the support to which they were traditionally entitled from their owners. Keenan has likened the liberation of the slaves as 'removing the mortar from the brickwork of Tuareg society'.[52]

With independence, the freedmen began to question their subordination to the freeborn Tuareg, although even in the mid 1960s many worked as sharecroppers, giving half of their harvest to their Tuareg masters. Freedmen and ex-slaves became increasingly unwilling to accept the authority of the Tuareg chiefs and, even more importantly, began to lay claim to land as their own. As a result, Tuareg land was taken over by their former freedmen contract cultivators. In the spring of 1964 there was a skirmish between a group of Tuareg and the ex-slaves of Otoul, where they had formed a cooperative. It seems that certain Tuareg, on arriving back from their winter caravan, were led to believe that they could retake their former slaves, had tried to do so and had met with resistance. Five Tuareg were sent to jail as a result.[53]

The second half of the 1960s saw the implementation of a policy of sedentarization in the Ahaggar. This further strengthened the position of the freedmen and former slaves and reduced the scope for pastoral nomadism.

In the small plots and agricultural cooperatives set up after 1965 Kel Ahaggar nobility could be found working alongside freedmen and their former slaves. Frontier controls also became stricter, particularly after 1966, when an agreement between the Algerian and Nigerien authorities restricted the number of caravans which could leave Ahaggar and the Algerians insisted that all caravans should be checked through Tamanrasset. By the 1970s the caravans had all but ceased and the end of the 'traditional' Tuareg society was nigh.

The Western Sahara

Unlike the other Saharan colonial territories, the Western Sahara remained under Spanish rule. Towards the end of the 1960s a group of young Saharawis established an independence movement – the Harakat Tahrir. This advocated wide-ranging social reforms, including the destruction of the tribal structures and the elimination of the relationships of vassalage and slavery, as well as progress towards decolonization. But when, in June 1970, the demands of the movement were presented openly to the Spanish authorities, clashes with the security forces left some ten or eleven Saharawis dead, and the ensuing repression crushed the Harakat Tahrir.[54] Resistance was not destroyed; in May 1973 the Popular Front for the Liberation of the Seguia el Hamra and the Rio de Oro (POLISARIO) was established. The struggle for self-determination and national liberation had begun.

The changes that had taken place in Saharawi economy and society during the preceding decade had been enormous. Droughts in 1959–63 and in 1972–74 resulted in heavy losses of livestock and large-scale sedentarization. The numbers of Saharawis living in the three main towns – El Ayoun, Smara and Villa Cisneros (now Dakhla) – tripled between 1967 and 1974 to reach 55 per cent of the total Saharawi population. About 1,000 Saharawi children had been admitted to Moroccan schools during or immediately after the 1957–58 war and by the early 1970s some 40 of these had gained entry to Moroccan universities, while the others had graduated into a range of jobs, mainly in the towns. By 1974 there were around 8,000 Saharawi wage-earners, the vast majority of them unskilled labourers and many of them ex-slaves.[55]

These changes gave a distinctive character to the POLISARIO, whose leadership was very much of the new generation of Saharawis. In August 1974 the POLISARIO declared itself in favour of full independence for the Western Sahara. It also outlawed, in the name of national unity, all forms of kinship loyalty, including tribal affiliation, and 'every form of exploitation' – which meant the eradication of both slavery and *horma*, the extraction of tribute from vassals. From this time onwards, those who supported the

POLISARIO knew that they were committed to some extent at least to the eradication of slavery, which, despite the claims of the Spanish to have emancipated 2,000 slaves in their territory,[56] continued to exist. In May 1975 a UN mission visiting the territory reported the persistence of slavery and a market in slaves.[57]

On 16 October 1975 the World Court rejected claims by Morocco and Mauritania of sovereignty over the Western Sahara. Three weeks later, in defiance of this ruling, over half a million Moroccans marched into the Western Sahara from Tarfaya; at the same time, the Moroccan army, supported by aerial cover, moved across the border. As the Moroccans invaded from the north, Mauritania (independent since 1960) invaded from the south.[58] The Spanish began to withdraw and the majority of the Saharawi population fled eastwards, to find refuge and a base for military operations near Tindouf (an old trans-Saharan trading entrepôt) in south-west Algeria. In February 1976, as Spain finally abandoned the Western Sahara, the POLISARIO announced the formation of the independent Saharawi Arab Democratic Republic.

Whereas the colonial occupation had, since the late 1950s, begun a process of transformation in Saharawi society, the Moroccan blitzkrieg and subsequent occupation of much of the Western Sahara had even more profound effects. Forced to flee from their homes and establish refugee camps far to the east in Algerian territory, the Saharawis progressively discarded their traditional social structures as the 'war economy' of the camps came to dominate their lives. In 1978 the fourth congress of the POLISARIO approved once again the suppression of all forms of exploitation; this meant, notably, the eradication of the last vestiges of slavery and of such practices as the *horma*.[59] According to article six of the Constitution of the SADR, 'all citizens are equal before the law'; 'slavery, although not widespread at the time of the establishment of the Saharawi state, was also abolished through the same article of the Constitution'.[60] By the 1980s, although 'refugees in the camps recall the days when slaves could be beaten by their master "as a member of the family" with no recourse to the law…the term *abd* (slave) is now only a historical reference'.[61]

The Saharan Regions of Sub-Saharan States

In Sudan, Chad, Niger and Mali, however, the commitment of newly independent governments to 'radical social transformation' was accompanied by the marginalization of Saharan society and the consolidation of many of its more conservative elements. In these states governments generally proved unable or unwilling either to maintain a strong hold on their Saharan and peri-Saharan regions (despite the prevalence of military regimes), or to incorporate them effectively into an integrated, national, political system. Indeed, on the contrary, these regions were identified as backward and inimical to development. This was strikingly evident in Niger and Mali, both of which have experienced during the last three decades a series of revolts involving the Tuareg in the north. In both countries the hierarchical institutions associated with slavery have been progressively eroded rather than dramatically transformed or eliminated, at least by government policy. Arguably, drought – in the early 1970s and the mid 1980s – was a more effective force for the reconstruction of pastoral economy and society than anything else. Even now, however, the heritage of slavery persists in both countries in several forms of economic and political domination of ex-slaves.

After Mali's independence in 1960 the new 'socialist' government urged all slaves (now officially free men) to leave their masters, and many did so, at once or within a year or so. But those who left had great difficulty in finding work and some drifted back to their former masters, often to work as contract herdsmen, although usually on less good terms than free Tuareg.

By the early 1970s the economic differences between noble and vassal Kel Adrar had largely disappeared. A few slaves had made their way as independent herdsmen, but were marginal to the mainstream Tuareg pastoral economy; they also were no longer a significant part of the labour force in Kel Adrar camps. Those that remained were almost all contract herdsmen, although in many cases they received only food and clothing for their work, rather than the full payment of animals usual with Kel Adrar contract herdsmen from other classes.[62]

Further south, the Illabakan Tuareg still had an appreciable number of slaves working at traditional tasks in the early 1970s: they made up 13 per cent of the total Illabakan population, and a quarter of Illabaken families had one or more slaves working for them; families rich in animals had large numbers.[63] The heritage of slavery continued to determine the structure of economic exploitation and social oppression in northern Mali, but the old structures of Tuareg society were gradually dissolving.

Much the same occurred in Niger (which also became independent in 1960), although here the Tuareg were more numerous and more heavily reliant on agro-pastoralism and agriculture; the maintenance of control over menials and labourers was all the more important, and the hierarchical tribal structures were strongly defended by those who benefited from them. Female slaves suffered more oppression and exploitation even than the men, who enjoyed greater mobility.[64] Even after the drought years of the early 1970s large numbers of slaves remained tied to their masters, particularly among the agro-pastoral Kel Dinnik and Kel Gress. In the early 1980s the great majority of dry-season-sedentary Tuareg were Kel Gress and former Kel Dinnik slaves.[65]

Mauritania

Gaining its independence from the French in 1960, Mauritania's sovereignty was eventually acknowledged in 1969 by Morocco (whose territorial claims had extended as far south as the Senegal River) and in 1973 Mauritania was accepted into the Arab League. President Ould Daddah's alignment of his country with the Arab world produced adverse reactions, among ethnic black Mauritanians in particular. But, by a combination of suppression and concession, he quelled active opposition and avoided the secession of the predominantly 'black' south-west and south.

Two years after independence, Barbour noted that 'raiding and the slave trade have been suppressed and the status of slavery officially abolished'.[66] Certainly, slavery had been declared illegal under the constitution promulgated at independence; but it continued to exist in practice: in the mid 1960s around 200,000 'freed' slaves (*harratin*) were still living with their former masters, totally subservient to their demands.[67] In the 1970s a group of educated 'black' Moors (many of them in senior positions in the army, the bureaucracy and trades unions) established an organization, *El Hor* (The Free Man), to express their opposition to continued slavery in the country. Throughout the Ould Daddah regime slaves were theoretically free to leave their masters, but the institution of slavery actually remained little affected.

In 1978 Ould Daddah was overthrown by a military coup. A ceasefire was signed with the POLISARIO in 1979 and in July 1980 the Military Committee for National Salvation (CMSN) formally abolished slavery – thus confirming that earlier laws had been ineffective or not applied. Despite this, numerous militants in the *El Hor* movement, made up of former slaves and descendants of slaves, were arrested and tortured. In December 1980 a civilian prime minister was appointed by the CMSN to head a transitional government and a draft constitution was published, which provided for a multiparty state with a presidential system of government. But three months later the constitution was suspended and army officers returned to key posts after an attempt to overthrow the chairman of the CMSN.[68]

El Hor continued, during the early 1980s, to fight discrimination against *harratin* and former slaves largely by recourse to the law, even though the law (of 1980) abolishing slavery had not been followed by an enforcement order putting it into effect. A UN mission to Mauritania in 1985 was convinced that 'slavery as an institution protected by law has been genuinely abolished in Mauritania', but recognized that *de facto* slavery still existed.[69]

Nearly ten years later – during which time Mauritania experienced a massive human rights crisis, involving terrible human rights violations and abuses directed largely against ethnic black Mauritanians[70] – the International Federation for Human Rights produced a report (January 1994) on Mauritania in which the persistence of slavery was confirmed.[71] This, despite three previous formal attempts at abolition and the fact that officially, according to the Minister of Justice, slavery no longer existed by the mid-1990s.

Opposition politicians, however, recognized that the law still required effective implementation. According to one prominent opposition leader (and brother to former President Ould Daddah), the total eradication of slavery required legal measures to criminalize it and prescribe the penalties to be incurred by offenders, educational measures promoting the social integration of former slaves, and economic measures (for instance, slaves should have priority in the distribution of work). Other parties also underlined the failure to criminalize slavery and to develop legal measures enabling former slaves to acquire land. The Party for Liberty, Equality and Justice, defining itself as 'a black, non-violent party opposed to slavery', recognized that slavery also exists in black society, at least among the Fulani (Peuhl) and Soninke. The Union for Democratic Progress also opposed slavery – which it argued constituted a live issue in Mauritania. Finally, *El Hor* continued to focus its activities on the fight against slavery, which it asserted continued, in a variety of forms, to characterize social organization in Mauritania.[72]

In 1995 a local non-govermental organization, SOS-Esclave, was founded. It was persistently harassed by government officials as well as by groups representing the interests of slave-holders. In 1997 slaves were still being forced to work for masters and often brutally punished, exchanged and separated from their spouses and children;[73] and in February 1998 I received an email message from a Mauritanian friend: 'Greetings from Mauritania. I tried to get some information on slavery in my country for you, but these last weeks the situation has been a little bit complicated as three people were arrested because they talked to the French TV Channel CFI about slavery.'

Sudan

It is not only in Mauritania that forms of slavery continue to exist, even at the end of the twentieth century. Hargey refers to the resurgence of the slave trade and involuntary servitude in Sudan during the 1980s and the 1990s. He notes that the plight of refugees in the Nile basin eventually exposed this resurrection of chattel slavery and prompted the United Nations Working Group on Contemporary Forms of Slavery to appoint a Special Rapporteur in 1993 to investigate the situation. This report corroborated the linkage between drought, displacement, destitution and the deprivation of human rights in the Sudan, despite vehement official denials that 'slavery is not a practice of the government of the Sudan'.[74]

More recently still, in September 1998, the World Confederation of Labour Tripartite Commission on the implementation of labour standards reported violations by Sudan of Convention 29 on forced labour: 'slavery persists in this country and the government does not undertake any action aimed at putting an end to it. The WCL has repeatedly submitted specific reports on slavery in that country to the experts committee'.[75]

At the start of the new millennium the struggle against slavery in Saharan Africa remains unfinished business.

NOTES

1. Morocco, Mauritania, Algeria, Tunisia, Mali, Niger, Chad, Libya, Sudan and Egypt. The Western Sahara is still a disputed territory.
2. Useful maps are to be found in E. W. Bovill, *The Golden Trade of the Moors* (London: Oxford University Press, 1968), pp.74–5, 184–5, 226–7, 238–9 and 250–1; in Ross Dunn, *Resistance in the Desert: Moroccan Responses to French Imperialism, 1881–1912* (London: University of Wisconsin Press; Croom Helm, 1977), p.108; and in Jeremy Keenan, 'Social change among the Tuareg', in Ernest Gellner and Charles Micaud (eds.), *Arabs and Berbers: from Tribe to Nation in North Africa* (London: Duckworth, 1973), p.346.
3. Bovill, *The Golden Trade*, p.248. For an attempt to quantify the trans-Saharan slave trade over a period of several centuries see Ralph A. Austen, 'The Mediterranean Islamic slave trade out of Africa: a tentative census', *Slavery and Abolition* (special issue on 'The Human Commodity'), 13, 1 (April 1992), pp.214–48.
4. On precolonial Tuareg economy and society see Keenan, 'Social change among the Tuareg', pp.345–60.
5. Dunn, *Resistance*, p.111.
6. Daniel J. Schroeter, 'Slave markets and slavery in Moroccan urban society', *Slavery and Abolition* 13,1 (1992), pp.185–213.
7. Walter Harris, *Tafilet* (London, 1895), p.297.
8. Jean-Louis Miege, *Le Maroc et L'Europe (1830–1894)* (Paris: Presses Universitaires de France, 1963).
9. Dunn, *Resistance*, p.44.
10. Emile Baillaud, *Sur les Routes du Soudan* (Toulouse, 1902), cited in E. Anne McDougall, 'Salt, Saharans and the trans-Saharan slave trade: Nineteenth century developments', *Slavery and Abolition* 13,1 (1992), pp.61–88.
11. For details of the early history of Spanish intervention in the western Sahara see Tony Hodges, *Western Sahara: The Roots of a Desert War* (Westport, CT: Lawrence Hill, 1983), Ch. 4 and 5. Also Virginia Thompson and Richard Adloff, *The Western Saharans* (London: Croom Helm, 1980), Pt II.
12. A. Adu Boahen, *Britain, Sahara and the Western Sudan* (Oxford: Clarendon Press, 1964), p.128, cited in Bovill, *The Golden Trade*, p.248.

13. Lisa Anderson, 'Ramadan al-Suwayhli: Hero of the Libyan Resistance', in Edmund Burke (ed.), *Struggle and Survival in the Modern Middle East* (Berkeley and Los Angeles, CA: University of California Press, 1993), pp.116–17.
14. Gustav Nachtingal, *Sahara and Sudan*, Allan G. B. Fisher and Humphrey J. Fisher (trans. and eds.) (London: Hurst, 1971).
15. John Wright, 'The Wadai–Benghazi slave route', *Slavery and Abolition* 13,1 (1992), p.177. While Sultan Muhammad Sharif owned 300 guns, his successor, Sultan Ali (1858–74) had 4,000 good quality flintlocks, imported mainly from Tripoli; and Sultan Dudmurra (1902–09) had 10,000 rifles. See also Wright, 'Chad and Libya: some historical connections', *Maghreb Review*, 8, 3–4 (May–Aug. 1983), pp.91–5.
16. Wright, 'The Wadai–Benghazi slave route', p.181.
17. Roger Owen, *The Middle East in the World Economy, 1800–1914* (London: Methuen, 1981), pp.52–3.
18. Gerard Prunier, 'Military slavery in the Sudan during the Turkiyya, 1820–1885', *Slavery and Abolition* 13,1 (1992), p.129.
19. Ehud R. Toledano, 'Shemsigul: a Circassian slave in mid-nineteenth-century Cairo', in Burke (ed.), *Struggle and Survival*, p.65.
20. Taj Hargey, '*Festina lente*: Slavery policy and practice in the Anglo-Egyptian Sudan', in Suzanne Miers and Martin Klein (eds.), *Slavery and Abolition* 19,2 (1998), p.254.
21. Hargey, 'Festina lente', p.255.
22. Ibid., p.265.
23. John Davis, *Libyan Politics: Tribe and Revolution* (London: I.B. Tauris, 1987).
24. Ibid., p.188.
25. Cited in Wright, 'The Wadai–Benghazi slave route', p.181.
26. According to E. de Agostini, *Le Popolazioni della Cirenaica* (Tripoli: Benghazi, 1922–3), p.48, cited in Davis, *Libyan Politics,* p.208.
27. Wright, 'The Wadai–Benghazi slave route', p.182.
28. Cited in ibid., p.182.
29. Cited in ibid., p.176.
30. Edward Evans Pritchard, *The Sanusi of Cyrenaica* (London, 1963), pp.24–5.
31. McDougall, 'Salt, Saharans and the trans-Saharan slave trade', p.63.
32. Martin A. Klein, 'Slavery and French rule in the Sahara', in *Slavery and Abolition* (special issue on 'Slavery and Colonial Rule in Africa'), 19, 2 (Aug. 1998), p.76.
33. Jeremy Swift, *The Economics of Traditional Nomadic Pastoralism: the Twareg of the Adrar n Iforas (Mali),* PhD thesis (University of Sussex, 1979; University Microfilms International 1981), p.25.
34. Ibid., p.36.
35. IFAD, *Niger: Programme Special National, Rapport d'Evaluation,* Vol.111, Rapport no. 0080-NG (Rome: Inernational Fund for Agricultural Development, Dec. 1987), p.3.
36. J. Clauzel, 'Evolution de la vie economique et des structures sociales de pays nomade du Mali, de la conquete francaise a l'autonomie interne (1893–1958)', *Tiers Monde*, 3 (1962), p.284.
37. Cited in Klein, 'Slavery and French rule', p.77.
38. Hodges, *Western Sahara*, p.13.
39. Dunn, *Resistance*, p.111.
40. Ibid., p.132.
41. Henri Lhote, *Les Touaregs du Hoggar* (Paris: 2nd edn, 1955), p.224, cited in Keenan, 'Social Change among the Tuareg', p.354.
42. Schroeter, 'Slave markets and slavery', pp.205–6.
43. Hodges, *Western Sahara*, Ch. 8 and 9.
44. Ibid., Ch. 12 and 13.
45. Thompson and Adloff, *The Western Saharans*, p.43.
46. Ibid., p.49; Klein, 'Slavery and French rule', p.83.
47. Klein, 'Slavery and French rule', p.81.
48. Ibid., p.83.
49. IFAD, *Niger*, pp.3, 5.

50. Hargey, 'Festina lente', pp.265–6.
51. Keenan, 'Social change among the Tuareg', p.357.
52. Ibid., p.357.
53. Ibid., p.358.
54. Hodges, Western Sahara, pp.154–5.
55. Ibid., Ch. 12.
56. According to John Mercer, Spanish Sahara (London: Allen & Unwin, 1976), p.130, cited in Thompson and Adloff, The Western Saharans, p.116.
57. Hodges, Western Sahara, p.70.
58. David Seddon, 'Morocco at war', in R. Lawless and Leila Monahan (eds.), War and Refugees: The Western Sahara Conflict (London: Pinter, 1987), pp.98–136.
59. Hodges, Western Sahara, p.164.
60. Anne Lippert, 'The Saharawi refugees: origins and organization, 1975–85', in Lawless and Monahan (eds.), War and Refugees, p.151.
61. James Firebrace, 'The Saharawi refugees: Lessons and prospects', in Lawless and Monahan (eds.), War and Refugees, p.184.
62. Swift, The Economics of Traditional Nomadic Pastoralism, p.164.
63. Edmond Bernus, Les Illabakan (Niger): une tribu touaregue sahelienne et son aire de nomadisation (Paris: ORSTOM, 1974), pp.35–8, 69.
64. IFAD, Niger, p.13.
65. Ibid., p.20.
66. Neville Barbour (ed.), A Survey of North West Africa (The Maghrib) (London: Oxford University Press, 1962), p.272.
67. According to reports produced by the Institut National de la Statistique et de la Recherche Economique and the Societe d'Etudes pour le Developpement Economique et Social, cited in Thompson and Adloff, The Western Saharans, p.99.
68. David Seddon, 'The political economy of Mauritania: an introduction', Review of African Political Economy, 68 (1996), pp.197–214.
69. Klein, 'Slavery and French rule', p.89, fn 58.
70. Seddon, 'The political economy of Mauritania', pp.205–7. Also see Amnesty International, Mauritania, 1986–1989: Background to a Crisis – Three Years of Political Imprisonment, Torture and Unfair Trials (London: Amnesty International, Nov. 1989).
71. IFHR, Mauritania: Investigation into Human Rights and Mass Expulsion of Peoples – Report of an International Commission of Enquiry in Senegal and Mauritania, International Federation of Human Rights/Fédération Internationale des Ligues des Droits de l'Homme (Paris: IFHR, 1994), p.18.
72. Ibid., p.19.
73. Elinor Burkett, 'God created me to be a slave', New York Times Magazine, 12 Oct. 1997, pp.56–60, cited in Klein, 'Slavery and French rule', p.90.
74. Hargey, 'Festina lente', p.267.
75. World Confederation of Labour, 'Report from the 1998 International Labour Conference', WCL Labor Magazine, 1998/3 (Sept. 1998), p.11.

Slavery to Freedom in Sub-Saharan Africa: Expectations and Reality

SUZANNE MIERS

Emancipation came late to most of sub-Saharan Africa. It took several different forms and, since some areas have been heavily researched and others virtually ignored, there are serious gaps in our knowledge. While much is known about the expectations of the British abolitionists and something of the expectations of colonial administrators, there is little information about those of African slave-owners and even less about those of the slaves, whose descendants are still often reluctant to talk about it. The immensity of the subject is daunting. Sub-Saharan Africa was divided between six colonial powers and the two independent states of Ethiopia and Liberia, each with its own form of government and abolitionist policy. African societies ranged from trans-humant pastoralists and small kin-based village groupings to large empires. Economic, social and political conditions and religious practices were greatly varied. The realities of abolition were not only different in each society but they had varying effects on the different types of slaves and owner even in the same society.

This study will concentrate on the abolition of slavery as practised by Africans in British possessions south of the Sahara. A few examples will be drawn from the colonies of other powers for purposes of comparison.[1] This is an arbitrary division, but the British had the lion's share of African territories encompassing many different forms of slavery. Since they were also the greatest promoters of abolitionist ideology, they set the pace of abolition, pressing other powers to follow suit. However, as will be seen, there was a considerable gap between what they preached and what they practised, as good intentions and high moral principles usually foundered in the face of African realities.

First Attempts at Abolition in British African Colonies

In 1833 Britain's African territories were limited to the Cape Colony in the extreme south, a tiny freed slave settlement in Sierra Leone and trading forts on the Gambia river and the Gold Coast, which did not finally become colonies until 1843. In the Cape Colony, where the owners were white and slavery took much the same form as in the New World, the Emancipation

Act of 1833, which I shall call for convenience the 'colonial model of abolition', was applied in all its force. Slavery became illegal just as it did in the Caribbean, Mauritius and certain other dependencies, a transition period of apprenticeship was projected, and owners were promised compensation. This had unforeseen results. Britain's newly acquired Afrikaner subjects were heavily dependent on slave labour. They were already disaffected by the abolition of the slave trade and by British attempts to prevent them from reducing neighbouring Africans to serfdom by appropriating their land. The outlawing of slavery further alienated them, particularly as they found it difficult to get compensation. Moreover, the British further eroded their control over labour by prohibiting the apprenticeship of children, by outlawing labour contracts made outside the colony and by failing to pass a vagrancy law. Thoroughly upset with Britain's 'native' policies, which threatened to put Africans on an equal footing with whites and suffering economic pressures, thousands of them left the colony in a series of emigrations known as the 'great trek'.[2] Although abolition was not the only reason for the trek, it was at the time widely believed to have been a major cause, and the lesson was remembered by British statesmen 60 years later, when discussing the suppression of slavery on the islands of Zanzibar and Pemba on the east coast of Africa.[3]

In the British possessions in West Africa the colonial model of abolition was barely applied. These were tiny enclaves in an African world. Existing by courtesy of the surrounding peoples and dependent for their prosperity on trade, they competed with the nearby trading posts of other European powers. Local administrators soon convinced their superiors in London that any interference with African slave-ownership would provoke resistance and drive away the very trade which was their *raison d'être*. The first solution was to free only the slaves of the few European residents, without paying compensation to the owners, who were too few to have any clout in Parliament. However, the law officers of the Crown ruled that colonies were actual British soil and all slaves had to be freed irrespective of who owned them.

To avoid confrontations with African slave-owners, colonies were henceforth kept as small as possible and surrounding areas were incorporated into the Empire as 'protectorates'. In a protectorate African customs were subjected to minimal interference – those deemed most repugnant such as human sacrifice and the export of slaves were attacked, but slavery and internal slave-trading were ignored. Thus the British were able to avoid enforcing anti-slavery laws and were spared the expense of establishing full-blown colonial administrations. They exercised influence, collected customs, warded off rival powers and mounted the occasional punitive expedition, but otherwise Africans ruled themselves. In 1842 a

Select Committee confirmed that Britain had no legal right to interfere with African slavery in the protectorates, although it might try to suppress it by persuasion, negotiation and 'other means' – whatever that meant.

Problems arose when slaves from the protectorates or from independent areas took refuge in the colonies. Theoretically they should have been freed. In practice, anxious not to alienate their owners, often neighbouring rulers, or to drive away trade by harbouring the runaway slave porters of African merchants, administrators pursued pragmatic policies – sometimes freeing fugitives and sometimes returning them, depending on whether they had been physically ill-treated, on whether their owners were friend or foe, powerful or weak, and on whether the anti-slavery lobby in Britain was likely to hear about any returns and raise a storm in Parliament or the press. Thus, from the start, many a slave, taking refuge in a British colony in the expectation of being freed, was actually returned to his or her owner. Moreover, in the colonies themselves slavery was 'winked at' by the authorities and, in some cases, even the slave trade continued on a small scale into this century.

The 'Indian' Model of Abolition

Only in 1874, when Britain annexed the Gold Coast, its first sizeable protectorate in West Africa, did it become necessary to formulate a new policy for protectorates in order to placate the anti-slavery lobby in Britain. By this time, however, the British had devised a model of abolition which suited their African situation better than the 'colonial' one. This had been worked out in British India, hence I have called it the 'Indian' model.[4] In India, as in Africa, slavery took many forms and the ruling East India Company had few officials and vast territories. The administration depended heavily upon the elite, many of whom were slave-owners, and was reluctant to outlaw an institution about which little was known. The solution was ingenious and set the pattern for the rest of the Empire as it expanded. Slavery was not outlawed. It simply lost its legal status. Theoretically, those slaves who wished to do so could remain with their masters, but those who left could not legally be forced to return or to work for their owners. Property could not be taken from them on the grounds that they were slaves, and any action which was an offence against a free person was an offence against them. Enslavement and slave-trading were outlawed. The expectation was that, deprived of new recruits, slavery would simply die out slowly. Meanwhile slaves would not be deprived of a living by sudden emancipation and owners, knowing that slaves could leave and that there was no new source of supply, would treat them well.

For the government this was the ideal solution. It was cheap. No compensation had to be paid to owners. No alternative means of earning a living needed to be provided for the slaves. Since no effort was made to tell them that they were free, many simply remained where they were. This model of emancipation thus did little for the slaves but it gave owners time to adjust and even enabled them to force former slaves to pay for land, tools and houses, which they had had previously provided for them. It was acceptable to the humanitarians, chastened by the disappointing results of complete emancipation in the Caribbean, because Indian slavery was considered to be 'benign' – meaning that it was free from the worst forms of exploitation found in New World slavery. The argument was also accepted that sudden emancipation would cause hardship to slaves.

The Realities of African Slavery

It was no accident that when the British began annexing large areas of Africa this was the model of abolition adopted. In Africa, as in India, the British word 'slavery' was applied to many different forms of servitude, some clearly more oppressive than others.[5] There were the slaves of small farmers, the former being treated much like junior kinsmen and junior wives. There were the often harshly treated slaves of coastal merchants who did not integrate slaves into their households. There were slaves who were trusted trading agents. There were slave miners and slave craftsmen, who often lived away from their owners and merely paid them a share of their proceeds. There were large holdings of slaves living in separate villages, providing their own sustenance and growing cash crops and food for their owners. There were plantations on which slaves were regimented under overseers. There were villages of slaves planted on the frontiers for defence. There were royal slaves – officials and soldiers – valued not so much for their labour but because they swelled the numbers of retainers upon whom the power and prestige of rulers largely depended. There were slave porters and slave canoe men. There were slave concubines. There was also a form of servitude in which children were dedicated by their parents to a shrine to serve the deity under the control of the priests. The majority of the slaves and a small minority of owners were women.

Treatment and life style varied with the type of slavery and the degree of acculturation, as well as the sex of the slave. The most harshly treated were the newly enslaved, although even first-generation slaves might be singled out to hold high office. Most slaves were provided with wives or husbands, but their children were under the control of their owners. Many women slaves were treated as junior wives. Slave concubines in Muslim households held an honoured place. In Muslim society slaves were also protected by

Muslim law. Among matrilineal peoples children by free wives belonged to their mothers' kin group, and men often preferred slave wives whose children belonged to their own lineage, and swelled the number of their dependants, thereby increasing their power and prestige. Few African societies had the organization and power to deal with numbers of discontented slaves, hence treatment was usually tolerable and integration was often possible, at least over time. In many societies second and later generations of slaves were not normally sold. The process of integration was faster in those societies in which slaves were allowed to intermarry with the free. In other societies there were no mechanisms for manumission or intergenerational incorporation and slaves remained a caste apart. In small kin-based societies in which slaves were incorporated as 'fictive' sons, daughters, brothers or sisters, according to their age at acquisition, emancipation was impossible because they were kinsmen. 'How', Africans asked, 'can we free them when they are our brothers and sisters?' Some African peoples used slaves for human sacrifice at funerals or other ceremonies or, in times of trouble, to appease the gods. In some societies slavery was a punishment for crime. Slaves thus served social, political, economic and religious purposes. Apart from their labour, or, in the case of women, their role in procreation as well as production, they were valuable capital assets and a form of currency.

The type of slavery varied with the political and social formation. There were large states, side by side with little chiefdoms. There were small-scale, kin-based sedentary societies, as well as trans-humant pastoral groups and trading corporations. Owners might be Muslim emirs, ruling hundreds of thousands of subjects, or they might be small kin-groups, corporate trading houses, individual entrepreneurs, priests, market women, plantation-owners and even other slaves. Many of these forms of ownership co-existed in the same society. Moreover, slavery was only one form of unfree status in a continuum which included clientship and pawnship. A pawn was a person, usually a girl, given as collateral for debt.[6] Some of the familiar criteria for establishing slave status in the Western world were missing in Africa. For instance, in many societies free people could be sold by their kinsmen just as slaves could be sold by their owners. There was often no correlation between ethnicity and slavery. The life style of slave and free might be indistinguishable to the outsider. Slaves could be as rich as their owners and were often engaged in the same occupations. The one constant was that slaves were outsiders, marginal to society with no kinsmen to protect them. The realities of African slavery were thus quite different from those in the Western world. Moreover, they were constantly changing in response to evolving political and economic conditions. Even in Muslim societies, where relations were broadly regulated by Muslim law, the relations of slaves and masters varied according to personalities and circumstances, and changed over time.

The 'Indian' Model of Abolition on the Gold Coast

In 1874, when Britain annexed the Gold Coast Protectorate, the Colonial Secretary had no desire to do more than disarm humanitarian criticism in Britain. Sir Bartle Frere, a former Governor of Bombay, assured him that the 'protectorate model' as adopted in India had caused 'no disturbance of labour relations, where the slaves were content they went on serving... there was no excitement and no occasion for compensation'.[7] This then was the model adopted. As in India, slavery lost its legal status – neither British nor native courts could entertain claims arising from it. However, there was a departure from the Indian model. All children born in or entering the Protectorate after 1 January 1875 were to be considered free.[8] Although somewhat illogical if slavery were no longer legal, this reflected the fact that existing slaves who did not exercise their right to leave were still slaves. It also set a time limit – the life-time of existing slaves – for the complete end of slavery.

Delegalizing slavery rather than outlawing it was justified, as in India, on the grounds that sudden emancipation would cause hardship to slaves and that African slavery was 'benign'. But there were also pecuniary reasons. British views on the sanctity of property meant that if slaves were suddenly emancipated masters should be compensated, particularly as they were often the only capital an African possessed. Compensation was expensive and opened up the possibility of endless fraudulent claims since the administration had no way of knowing who was a slave and who was not. Schemes for the government to buy slaves and use them on public works were also dismissed. The Governor thought they would probably desert their jobs.[9] This was a symptom of the widespread belief that Africans were lazy by nature and had few wants. At best freed slaves would work only to produce the bare necessities of life for themselves. At worst they would drift into towns, where the men would take to crime and the women to prostitution. Former masters, it was believed, would not stoop to manual labour. Exports and revenues would drop,[10] and chiefs, deprived of slaves, would not be able to provide the necessary labour for public works,[11] or fulfil their role as the lower rank of local administration.

The problem was how to prevent slaves from taking advantage of their new found 'freedom'. In India the impact was delayed by not informing slaves of their rights. On the Gold Coast, although there was no obligation to inform slaves of the ordinances, there is evidence that they soon heard about them. However, there was a built-in catch. Administrators could not interfere in slavery questions unless a slave appealed for legal assistance to a magistrate or district commissioner, or lodged a complaint against his owner. The Governor, anxious to placate the masters, was careful to explain to chiefs and rulers that slaves would not be encouraged to leave. It was hoped that with these precautions most slaves would stay with their owners and that the immediate impact of the loss of the legal status of slavery would be almost imperceptible.[12]

Scholars are divided as to the actual results of these ordinances on the Gold Coast.[13] The onus for demanding their freedom was on the slaves and their options were strictly limited. They were under strong societal pressure to remain and not to bring charges against their owners.[14] In any case, it was almost impossible to get evidence against owners and to secure convictions. Moreover, for many years there were few European officers to complain to and chiefs were often able to block access to them. Few slaves were confident enough to take their case to court and when they did so administrators often failed to help them and some even returned them to their owners. They also failed to issue certificates of freedom or to keep registers of emancipated children, whom they were supposed to apprentice to farmers, merchants or missionaries.

There were cases where large numbers of slaves left their owners, but these are believed to have been the exception rather than the rule. Discontented slaves had to assess their prospects of finding a secure niche elsewhere. Some found jobs in the small wage-labour force. Some became independent traders. Others joined little settlements of freed slaves. A few attached themselves to Christian missions. But such opportunities were limited, and some slaves, having tasted freedom, returned to their owners. The majority of those who left took the safer option of either becoming tenants of their former owners or of establishing themselves near them and entering into share-cropping relationships.

In spite of all the efforts of administrators to retard the impact of their anti-slavery ordinances, two of the expected results were fulfilled. Some slaves inevitably turned to crime, providing support for those officials who saw slavery as a means of social and labour control and wished to maintain it as long as possible. Secondly, some chiefs did use the ordinances as an excuse for failure to produce labour for public works.[15] The results of abolition on the Gold Coast were considered sufficiently undesirable for it to be argued that it had been premature.[16] Much greater difficulties were, however, to be experienced as the conquest of Africa proceeded and the Indian model was widely applied by British governments and to some extent by the French.

Slavery and the 'Scramble for Africa': Creating Expectations

During the 'scramble for Africa', which peaked in the last decade of the nineteenth century, the slave trade within the continent, as against the export traffic, became an international issue. Already all the colonial powers had outlawed the export trade and in the metropoles and most of their older colonies slavery was no longer legal. Thus the French abolished slavery in their colonies after the revolution of 1848 and freed the slaves in their small outposts in Africa. Then, facing the same difficulties as the British, they disannexed some of the surrounding areas, turning them into protectorates where slavery could continue, and they followed the same pragmatic policies towards runaway slaves who claimed their freedom in French colonies. They also allowed slave children to be brought into their colonies and took no action against French subjects who held slaves or even bought them.[17] The Spanish began dismantling slavery on Fernando Po in 1859, many years before they ended it in Cuba. They were desperately short of labour and this measure enabled them to refuse to return slaves who fled to the island from the nearby Portuguese colony of Principe in the Gulf of Guinea. It also allowed them to import freed slaves as contract labour. Finally it warded off the threat of British intervention.[18]

The Portuguese took a different route. In 1854 they began dismantling slavery. Slaves were called *libertos* and forced to work for their owners for 20 years. In 1878 slavery was abolished. All former slaves were free to contract their services in the labour market, but strict vagrancy laws made them liable to forced labour for the government or for private concerns. In practice, little changed at the grass-roots level. *Libertos* and even contract labourers were bought and sold just as slaves had been. Victims were captured in the interior, marched to the coast in shackles, furnished with 'contracts' and sent off to labour for life on the lucrative cocoa plantations on the islands of São Tomé and Principe. In Angola and Mozambique alike Africans continued to capture and sell slaves long after the nominal abolition of slavery.[19]

The new African colonial rulers, the Germans, the Italians and King Leopold II of Belgium, who was building a personal empire in the Congo,[20] were still in the early stages of conquest. They all subscribed to anti-slavery ideology but they had had little time to develop coherent policies.

In the 1880s slavery in African societies had been increasing for some decades. As the Atlantic slave trade died down and slave exports to the Muslim world and the islands of the Indian Ocean declined, so the growth of legitimate trade provided new uses for slaves on the continent itself, and wars and disturbances fuelled the supply. The reports of explorers, notably David Livingstone, had aroused much public interest in the Western world and particularly in Britain. His accounts of the horrors of slave raids and the pathetic caravans of victims driven down the trade routes were received with amazement. His call for missionaries to save Africa from the ravages of the trade by spreading Christianity, civilization and commerce was answered by Protestants, hotly pursued by Roman Catholics. They established missions in eastern and central Africa ahead of the European conquest. As Africans and their Arab/Swahili allies in the interior became conscious of the advancing European political and economic threat, they attacked these missions.

By 1888 the danger was such that Cardinal Lavigerie, the French founder of the missionary order known as the White Fathers, launched a 'crusade'. Preaching in the capitals of Europe with papal blessing, he called for Christians to send armies of volunteers out to Africa to fight the slavers. By painting all Africans who opposed the European intrusion as slavers, he furthered the imperial cause. His 'crusade' moved the British, who prided themselves as leaders of the anti-slavery movement, to invite King Leopold to call a conference of the colonial, maritime and some other powers to devise a common policy for the suppression of the slave trade. The result was the Brussels Act of 1890, which put an anti-slavery complexion on the conquest and exploitation of Africa by the European colonial powers who were staking out vast territorial claims. The treaty did not bind signatories to end slavery itself. No power was ready to tackle this, but it clearly put it under attack by binding them to end the slave trade and slave raids, and to free and repatriate newly captured or runaway slaves.[21]

During the ensuing wars of conquest, the British, in common with their rivals, used the suppression of slave raiding, the slave traffic, and by implication slavery, as an excuse for waging war and sending out punitive expeditions against Africans who resisted imperial rule. They were aided in this subterfuge by the fact that many of those who fought most bitterly against conquest were also renowned slave raiders and traders. By using the suppression of the slave traffic as an excuse for conquest, they raised public expectations that they would indeed suppress slavery once their new territories had been 'pacified'.

They were soon to be hoist with their own petard, particularly the British. Even before the conquests were complete, the anti-slavery lobby began demanding action. The British and Foreign Anti-Slavery Society, bent on ending slavery world-wide, kept careful watch on events, corresponding with explorers, missionaries and administrators, offering advice and criticism to its own government and to those of other nations. Although its membership and budget were minute, it was able to mount effective campaigns in the press and Parliament, where it had supporters across the political spectrum. Cabinet ministers, civil servants and colonial governors had a healthy respect for its ability to mobilize public opinion, and time and again the cause had been shown to have strong public support. The conquerors thus found themselves pressed to live up to the expectations they had created. The anti-slavery lobby expected slave raiding and trading to end with British conquest. As for slavery itself, they were prepared to accept the argument that outlawing the legal status of slavery rather than forcibly emancipating all slaves was the least disruptive method of ending it. Along with colonial administrators, they believed that the institution, once robbed of its worst features, would die a natural death, and, as African economies were brought into production for the world market, slaves would be replaced by mobile wage-labour or peasant producers. They would become free tax-payers working their own lands, or tenants, share croppers and wage earners, while their former owners would be forced to till their own fields. Essential to the process was the imposition of peace, the fostering of a cash-crop economy, the introduction of money currency to pay wages, the development of modern communications to replace porters – often slaves – and the replacement of rulers, with their slave officials and armies, by a competent paid administrative service staffed, or at least supervised, by Europeans. As the economy developed so new forms of wealth were expected to replace slaves as investments and status symbols for the elite. Moreover, it was believed that former slaves would work harder once they worked for themselves and were spurred out of their inherent laziness by the desire to acquire the consumer goods which were the hallmark of 'civilized' man.

African Realities in the Period of Conquest

This then was the expectation of British humanitarians, as well as of the public in all the European colonial powers. It was also the expectation of British and French administrators in Africa and of their counterparts in other colonial administrations. British officials in particular had come to manhood since 1833 and were steeped in anti-slavery ideology. Anti-slavery societies also existed in the other metropoles, but they tended to be fleeting and public interest was on the whole less. However, many administrators were soon forced to compromise their principles in the face of African realities.

The sudden great expansion of their empires put much strain on the resources and manpower of the metropoles. Administrations had to be set up in a hurry, conquered lands had to be made viable as quickly as possible. For at least two decades after 1890, and much longer in some areas, European officials were thin on the ground and their military forces minimal. Wars of conquest were fought piecemeal and often with the help of Africans, many of whom served in the European forces or were recruited as allies or as irregulars. They expected to keep their prisoners and European officers were often in no position to deny them the fruits of victory. On occasion they sold prisoners on the battlefield or gave them to their allies or shared out the women as 'wives' for their own troops.

Moreover, as colonial rule was established there was an increasing demand for labour to produce food and cash crops, to serve as soldiers, porters, canoe men and miners, and to build roads, railways, docks and irrigation dams. Africans were ready enough to offer themselves for hire for short terms, often to earn the money for bride price or to buy livestock or trade goods. They were not prepared to leave their own lands, which were their ultimate security, for long periods or to work far from home for the meagre wages and the terms of service offered by the Europeans; nor did they want to interrupt their own planting cycle. Since land was plentiful in most areas and they were able to provide most of their needs, there was no mobile wage-labour pool upon which the colonial rulers could draw.

In the early days this was often solved in ways which encouraged slaving. Thus Portuguese administrators in Angola simply demanded labour from the Ovimbundu, who supplied it first by sending their own slaves and then by raiding their neighbours.[22] Poorly paid Portuguese officials in the interior accepted slaves in payment of fines or even staged raids themselves.[23] Officials of King Leopold's Congo Independent State recruited prisoners of war into their own armies and gave the surplus as labour to local chiefs.[24] In West Africa the French bought slaves to conscript them into their forces. In Ubangi-Shari they were even driven to attack slave caravans to acquire labour.[25] Christian missionaries bought slaves to form the nucleus of their congregations and to work in their fields.[26] Examples could be multiplied further. If slaves were not bought outright, they were often hired from their owners. The British, for instance, had to resort to hiring slave porters for expeditions setting off from Zanzibar, and even when they paid the wages direct to the slaves their masters found ways of appropriating the bulk of their earnings.

It is small wonder that for years Africans believed that Europeans were freeing slaves simply to acquire them for themselves. Many early administrators reported this misapprehension, which was encouraged by the fact that the French and the Congo Independent State settled large numbers of the slaves they 'freed' along their lines of communication and then used them as forced labour for the administration,[27] while the British turned them over to missionaries or to 'respectable families' often their own employees.[28] African chiefs who intercepted caravans of slaves at the request of the French expected to keep them. So great was their misunderstanding of French policy that officials were afraid of offering rewards for slaves they freed, for fear that they might start capturing others in order to claim the rewards.[29]

Even slave raiding was tolerated until the conquerors mustered sufficient force to end it. In some cases it was part of the process of conquest. Leopold's agents, for instance, struggling to 'pacify' the region between the Congo and the Ubangi river, appointed and armed chiefs who used the weapons to raid their neighbours, capturing hundreds of people whom they either sold or put to work on their own plantations.[30] In the remoter areas and on international frontiers raiders operated beyond colonial control for many years. Thus villages on the borders of Angola, the Congo Independent State and British Northern Rhodesia were raided by their neighbours and by deserters from Leopold's army in the earlier years of the twentieth century.[31] The French in Dar Kuti countenanced raids by the sultan as long as they were not into their own territories – not because they approved of his depredations but because they feared that he and his followers, upon whom they relied to produce the rubber, ivory and wax needed to keep the economy viable, might decamp into the Anglo-Egyptian Sudan if pressed too hard.[32] Neither the Germans nor the French stopped the raids of the emir of Madagali, Hamman Yaji, in the northern region of Cameroon. He continued to enslave his neighbours until the British occupied the area in 1920, and even then his emirate remained a centre for the slave trade until he was finally deposed, for other reasons, in 1927.[33] Until the 1930s the French had little control over the bellicose raiders known as the *grand nomades*, who covered hundreds of miles a year searching for pasture for their livestock crisscrossing the borders of Mauritania, Morocco and Spanish Rio de Oro (Western Sahara).[34] Slave raiding in south-western Ethiopia continued at least until the Italians conquered the country in 1935.[35]

Slave trading also died hard. All the colonial powers passed laws against it but it was often years before they could enforce them. By the First World War large-scale slave trading had ended in most of colonial Africa but small-scale dealing continued right through the colonial period and there is evidence that it continues to this day.[36] In the independent state of Ethiopia slave trading was illegal but continued, often carried on openly by officials, until the Italian occupation, and thereafter on a decreasing scale.[37] Children were, and still are, kidnapped and taken across frontiers or slipped into towns. Some are transferred under the guise of adoption or early marriage. Such small-scale trafficking could only be suppressed with African cooperation and a change in public attitudes and this took time.

There was also a small export traffic to Arabia at least until slavery there was abolished in the 1960s. Some captives were shipped across the Red Sea in small boats. Others travelled openly under cover of the pilgrimage or were victims of trickery. Thus children entrusted to friends to take them to

Arabia for religious education were sold on their arrival. Women married to apparently devout Muslims were taken on pilgrimages never to return. Adults of both sexes were lured to the Middle East by the promise of good jobs only to find themselves enslaved.[38] Captives were also exported under the guise of contract labour, causing scandals in the Portuguese colonies before 1914 and in Liberia, particularly over recruits forcibly sent to the Spanish island of Fernando Po in the late 1920s.[39]

Pragmatic Solutions in the Face of African Realities: Delaying the Impact of Abolition

The goal of each colonial power was to make its colonies viable as soon as possible. The great problem was how to mobilize the necessary cheap labour and at the same time free the slaves. This was particularly difficult in those areas where slaves were a high percentage of the population and did most of the productive work. On the one hand, they had to be freed, or perceived to be freed, to satisfy public opinion in the metropole; on the other, their owners had to be placated to prevent rebellion, flight and economic collapse. Administrators were expected to solve this conundrum, often with little or no guidance from the home government. In the British case, although there was much discussion between the government and the administrators of the rapidly expanding British possessions in the crucial last decade of the nineteenth and the first decade of the twentieth century, there was little agreement on the details of policy. Officials in the Colonial and Foreign Offices, having no solutions themselves, sometimes resisted sending clear instructions to the men on the spot. The result was a veritable hodge-podge of pragmatic solutions worked out by each administration, even by each official, in response to local demands and, initially anyway, with the aim of delaying rather than hastening the end of slavery – an aim that had to be concealed from the humanitarians and sometimes also from the home government .

Even the laws differed widely. In some territories the colonial government simply ignored slavery. Thus in Bechuanaland, where Tswana cattle owners kept Sarwa herders on their posts by force and exercised all the powers of ownership over them, although rarely selling them, successive adminstrators denied that there was any slavery and passed no laws against it.[40] In Sierra Leone the tiny colony was at first surrounded by an area designated a 'sphere of influence'. When the Governor asked the Colonial Office how slavery was to be treated in a 'sphere of influence', he did not get a straight answer. An official complained that only a 'weak' governor would actually bring to official attention the fact that there was slavery in a British possession.[41] In 1895 the 'sphere of influence' became a protectorate but the legal status of slavery was not abolished. Certainly British courts were forbidden to take account of it and slaves could buy their redemption, but British officials in their administrative capacity could, and often did, uphold the rights of masters. Children were born into slavery. Slaves were still transferred from owner to owner and inherited. Fugitives were returned to their owners and freedom was sometimes refused.[42]

Similar differences between theory and practice also continued on the Gold Coast. Here in 1896 when the powerful kingdom of Asante was conquered, its chiefs were told that they could keep their slaves. In 1901, however both Asante and the Gold Coast Protectorate were redesignated colonies and slavery should have been outlawed under the Emancipation Act. But, the British explained to the League of Nations in the 1920s that 'any open announcement of the abolition of the status of slavery' would have led to 'internal disorganization'. Hence a less obvious method was found. In 1902 ordinances made it a punishable offence to 'compel the services of any person'. Only in 1908 was slavery declared to have lost its legal status in Asante – it was thus treated as a protectorate, although legally it was a colony. The Northern Territories were also a protectorate, but, as in Asante, the laws freeing anyone born in or entering them after a certain date were not applied and administrators followed pragmatic policies of their own.[43]

Action was often taken only because of pressure from the humanitarian lobby and then it was inconsistent. Thus in British East Africa three variants of the protectorate model of abolition were imposed. In Zanzibar and Pemba and on a ten-mile deep strip of the Kenya coast the British ruled 'indirectly' through the sultan and his Arab/Swahili aristocracy. These were Muslim landowners who had imported thousands of slaves during the nineteenth century and put them to work in many capacities, but particularly on the lucrative clove and grain plantations. With no desire to disrupt this economy, and fearful of provoking reaction among Muslims in India, Britain abolished the legal status of slavery in 1897, on the islands but not on the coast,[44] and offered owners compensation. The sum was too small to soften the blow, but slaves were discouraged from leaving by having to claim their freedom through courts controlled by owners and by the stipulation that, once freed, they would have to pay rent for their homes and their plots of land and would be treated as vagrants if they had no means of support.

On the coast, where British power was more tenuous, the legal status of slavery was ended only a decade later, when the plantations had already declined because many slaves had decamped after 1897 when the British, under humanitarian pressure, ceased to return runaways. Here slaves did not have to go to court to claim their freedom and owners were compensated only if they left or refused to work as a result of the ordinance. The impact varied. In Lamu nothing happened until 1910 and then many masters collected compensation but did not free their slaves, who colluded in the deception.[45] Elsewhere slaves squatted on the lands of their owners or left the plantations to work in the towns and along the routes into the interior.

Behind the coastal strip social formations were small and slave-owners were not Muslim. Therefore the political and economic repercussions of abolition were less feared and the British simply ignored the institution from the start but did nothing to precipitate its demise. The first intimation that owners had was when the British refused to return runaway slaves. According to the masters, it took a full decade for the news to permeate down to the grass-roots level.[46]

Similarly, different policies were followed in different parts of Nigeria. In the north Frederick (later Lord) Lugard, who was to become a renowned authority on slavery, faced the herculean task of conquering and administering a huge area dominated by the Muslim Caliphate of Sokoto and its tributary emirs. Slave-holding was pervasive and the slave population numbered an estimated 1 to 2½ million. Slaves served an endless variety of purposes from agricultural labour to officials of state. Thousands were paid annually to rulers as tribute. Raiding and trading were rife. Already the previous administration – the Royal Niger Company – had raised the expectations of slaves and the fears of their owners by declaring slavery abolished, but had then created confusion by following contradictory policies. However, slaves, their hopes raised, began a mass exodus which continued as Lugard strove to establish British control. With slender resources and powerful enemies, he sought to rule through the existing structure with its Muslim rulers, officials and law courts. Faced with the spectre of rebellion, an economy in ruins and having to provide for hundreds of thousands of destitute slaves, he resorted to a range of devices to keep slaves in place and at work.

His solutions were ingenious and largely successful. In 1899 he abolished the legal status of slavery without offering compensation to owners, and declared all children born after 31 March 1901 free. Existing slaves, however, if they wished to leave, had to pay their owners for their redemption – a form of manumission recognized by Muslim law. Thus the slaves and not the government nor the owners were to bear the cost of emancipation. If necessary the government was to provide paid work to assist them. Alternatively they could grow cash crops. Once freed they were subject to Vagrancy and Master and Servant laws. Those who tried to leave without paying redemption were denied permission to settle on the land. Homes were established for freed women and children. The women were encouraged to marry men who could pay a sum equivalent to the cost of redemption. Girls were prepared for marriage and boys were sent to a home where hard work was the order of the day.

Fugitive slaves always posed the acid test of good faith, and here Lugard resorted to real subterfuge. In contravention of the Brussels Act, he ordered his subordinates to help only those who had been ill-treated or, if this was likely to arouse resentment, they were to arrange for them to 'escape'. Otherwise they were to refuse to find them land or jobs, and to charge them with vagrancy. Many were handed over to Muslim courts which, unlike British ones, could hear slavery cases and return runaways to their owners.. Lugard's policies put his subordinates in the unenviable position of actually breaking the law if they returned fugitives, but as one of them put it: 'Of course we give them back... it has to be done.. if we freed every slave who bolted, the whole country would be in ruin: the masters would be ruined and the slaves, would in numberless cases, ... roam through the country looting and raiding.' As he said, it was indeed 'lucky that nothing gets into the papers', for Lugard was 'up to all sorts of dodges...for avoiding the slavery proclamations'.[47]

In the Protectorate of Southern Nigeria the legal status of slavery was duly abolished soon after the administration was established, but the economy of the Niger delta region depended on trading corporations known as Houses. These were composed of free dependants, clients and slaves under the control of a House head. To protect these corporations from the effects of the delegalization of slavery, a House Rule Ordinance was issued in 1901.[48] Members of Houses were now called 'apprentices' and were bound by contract to remain in their Houses. The system was extended to areas where there were no Houses. The result was virtually to legalize slavery under another name. The ordinance was repealed only in 1915 after an outcry in Britain. Until then the authorities and the Native Courts upheld the authority of House heads. Among the Yoruba policy was different again. Here officials began by encouraging slave desertions, but as numbers escalated they tried to prevent them and finally fixed a redemption fee which had to be paid before a slave could officially leave.[49]

The French were equally anxious to keep slaves in place as they took over their extensive territories in West Africa, in some of which slaves may have comprised between one-third and half the population.[50] In the early days, facing the same problems as the British, they usually upheld slavery – assuring chiefs and rulers that they could keep their slaves, and returning runaways except in cases of ill-treatment – and even ill-treatment might be defined differently according to whether the owner of the fugitive was a friend or foe. However, between 1903 and 1905, embarrassed by revelations of slaving, they tightened up regulations against slave-trading and the return of fugitives. In 1905 in the Banamba area of Soudan large numbers of slaves began to leave their masters. Many had only recently been enslaved and, spurred by harsh treatment, decided to return to their homelands. Administrators tried to stop the exodus, convinced the economy would be ruined and that both slaves and masters would starve. Troops were sent in. Masters and slaves both took up arms. Officials arrested slaves who left without permission and tried in vain to arrange reconciliations, but desertions increased and spread to other areas.

Unable to stop the exodus, the French came to terms with it, persuading former slaves to renegotiate their terms of service, to become share croppers or to set up on their own as farmers. They soon found that their predictions of doom and gloom were not met. In many cases productivity increased as former owners had to till their own fields and former slaves worked harder for themselves. Many also drifted into the wage-labour market. Between 1905 and 1908 an estimated 200,000 to 500,000 slaves ceased to work for their owners. As a result productivity and prosperity rose in some areas and declined in others.[51] Although large numbers of slaves departed, only certain regions were affected – mainly where slaves had been recently captured and were not well treated and where they had a good chance of returning home or of re-establishing themselves elsewhere. It is believed that in French West Africa, as in British Africa, most slaves stayed with their owners and over time renegotiated their terms of service.

Space precludes further examples, but, in general, the colonial rulers, whether they were British, French, Italian, Portuguese, Belgian, German or Spanish, tried in some areas for many years to soften the impact of their anti-slavery legislation or their declared policies. The laws they passed and the efforts they made varied with the colonial power and the degree of humanitarian pressure exerted in the metropoles, as well as with the economic needs of the colonies themselves. Thus the expectations of the humanitarians and of the general public in the mother countries that slavery would disappear with colonial rule had not been met in some areas as late as the 1930s and sometimes even later. Ironically, too, there were instances in which slavery actually became harsher as masters became more demanding in response either to the new market opportunities opened up by colonial rule[52] or because their wealth and power was being eroded or challenged.[53]

The Expectations of Slave-owners and Slaves versus Reality

Detailed studies of the ending of slavery at the grass-roots level are only now emerging, but there is plenty of evidence that owners immediately recognized abolition as a serious threat to their interests and adopted tactics to counteract it. In some cases it was one of the reasons for prolonged resistance to colonial rule. Thus in south-eastern Nigeria Igbo entrepreneurial groups, who relied heavily on slave labour for crop production and trade, were not conquered until 1911.[54] Almost everywhere as colonial administration was imposed, owners protested forcibly that if they lost their slaves they would be ruined, and in many cases the colonial rulers, needing their support, promised them that they would be able to keep the slaves. Sometimes the conquerors used slavery as a carrot and stick – freeing the slaves of those who resisted them and allowing their allies to retain theirs or to acquire more. Even once colonial rule was established and slavery lost its legal status, ways were found, as has been seen, to delay the impact. Those owners who retained control over access to land or over Native and Muslim courts or, under systems of indirect rule, exerted some political power were able to use their position to maintain their dominant position in society. They even found new ways to exploit former slaves, sending them, for instance, for forced labour on colonial projects and then appropriating a large proportion of their earnings.[55] As time went on, some owners, realizing that the end of slavery was inevitable, encouraged slaves to redeem themselves as a way of salvaging something from a dying institution.[56] But in spite of the collusion between owners and the colonial rulers, in the long run slavery gradually disappeared, and the fate of masters was mixed. In general, they were right in their expectations that the end of slavery would deal a serious blow to their position, but it was only one of a great number of changes resulting from colonial conquest and in many cases they and their descendants managed to retain their dominant position in society and invest in new forms of wealth. Others, particularly those who did not acquire a Western education, lost political and economic power. Even in such cases, however, their descendants have often been able to maintain a social distance between themselves and the descendants of their slaves.[57]

If the fate of the owners as a category at this stage of research defies generalization, too little is also known about the impact of abolition on their households. The wives of owners were often the prime beneficiaries of slave labour, male as well as female, since male slaves often did women's work. Households deprived of slaves often made increased demands on junior kinsmen and junior wives. In the long run, such demands on males probably became less acceptable as the changes resulting from colonial rule gave them new opportunities to set up on their own and hence escape the control of their elders. The full burden of these demands may thus have fallen primarily on junior wives, increasing friction between them and their seniors.[58] More research is needed too on this subject and on the change in marriage patterns resulting from the end of slave concubinage.[59]

As for the slaves, those who left certainly expected to throw off the yoke of their owners and to improve their situation. Their prospects of doing this depended on such variables as their age, sex, location, the degree to which they had been assimilated into their owners' lineages and the policies of particular administrators. Some simply fled, but others appealed to the courts or to administrators for their freedom. They had to assess their chances of finding a secure niche elsewhere. This was easiest for those who had been recently acquired and could return home, as many did during the disorders of conquest. However, slaves were often afraid to make the journey or were uncertain of their reception. Those who had been physically ill-treated could often get a sympathetic reception from officials, who theoretically were bound to repatriate or resettle them, but, as has been seen, many who expected to gain their freedom though the colonial administration or Native or Muslim Courts were forced to return to their owners or to pay them for their redemption. Nevertheless, thousands successfully left. Those who could make their way to the growing urban centres, such as Bamako, Enugu and Mombasa, could expect to find wage labour. In the countryside, if land was plentiful, neighbouring chiefs or European administrators often welcomed them as free cultivators, whose cash cropping would swell their revenues. Thousands settled along the line of the railway in Nigeria, for instance, and supplied both domestic and export markets.[60] A minority found wage labour harder work and less secure than slavery and returned to their former owners. The majority remained in or near their owners and over time renegotiated their terms of service – a process about which little is known.

Recent research has shown that slaves not only played a large part in their own liberation, but once they were free they often redeemed their relations or their prospective brides. Those who established themselves as freemen encouraged others to follow their example. In the Anglo-Egyptian Sudan, for instance, their settlements provided a haven for those who came after them.[61] In some cases colonial soldiers helped their fellow countrymen to gain their freedom. Thus many Yoruba owners found their slaves freed by the actions of Hausa soldiers in the colonial forces, who were often themselves freed slaves.[62]

One category of slaves which deserves separate mention is royal slaves – the officials, soldiers and retainers of rulers, some of whom had many hundreds in their retinues. The power and influence of these slaves depended upon their servile status and they therefore had no desire to be freed. Research on royal slaves has only just begun. Some, as in Kano, managed to retain their position for many years until they were dispersed against their will and replaced by paid officials and professional soldiers.[63] Their expectation that freedom would be against their interests was certainly true.

The greatest difficulties were faced by women.[64] European administrators, like their African subjects, believed that women should be under the control of male 'guardians'. In some areas, southern Nigeria for instance, women could make money trading and in a number of societies a few women owned slaves, but most, even prosperous female traders, were subordinate to men, who controlled land and wealth. In Muslim societies women were perpetual minors unable to give evidence in courts of law. The colonial rulers tended to regard female slaves as women and wives rather than as slaves, although in African eyes the distinction was very clear since no bride wealth had been paid for slaves and they had no kinsmen to protect them. Administrators were unwilling to interfere in African domestic life. They often also feared that, because women's prospects in wage labour were more limited than those of men, freed women might end up as prostitutes. Where possible they pressed them to remain with their owners. Sometimes they returned them by force. Sometimes they tried to make them pay for their redemption. When they did free women it was usually for ill-treatment and they would then try to find them 'reliable' husbands, place them in Christian families or put them under the care of missionaries or of village headmen or other officials, or send them to homes for freed women where husbands would be found for them.

Concubines in Muslim societies faced particular difficulties. They were slaves by definition but they had a privileged position. If they had borne their master a child, they were not normally sold and were usually freed on his death. Unlike free wives, they could not be divorced and there was no legal way they could be freed without their owner's consent. The British, wary of upsetting owners – normally the richer and most influential members of society – simply did not treat them as slaves. Thus in Zanzibar and Pemba they were excluded from the abolition ordinance of 1897 and not allowed to leave their harems. From 1909 they could leave but owners could not claim compensation as they had done for other slaves, and the concubines forfeited their right to material support and could not get custody of their children.[65] In the 1907 ordinance on the Kenya coast concubines were simply equated with free wives – an impossibility under Muslim law. By implication, they were free to leave but again no compensation was offered. The ordinance explicitly stated that nothing in it was to be considered as altering 'their rights and duties' – an ambiguous statement at best. The French faced similar problems in distinguishing slaves from wives, with the result that for many years after slavery had been outlawed in West Africa they ignored the problem and slave concubines continued to be acquired.[66]

The patriarchal attitudes of administrators and the fact that the Native and Muslim courts which dealt with most marital questions were dominated by men, meant that the rights of females were often disregarded. If a woman did obtain her freedom, the best she could usually expect was to become the dependant of a different male; if she was fortunate this was the man of her choice. Female fugitives sometimes took matters into their own hands and ran off with male companions. Some found men ready to pay for their redemption – at best in order to marry them, at worst such payments were a disguised form of slave dealing.

Differing Views of Freedom

This raises the vexed question of what freedom actually meant in Africa.[67] One may generalize by saying that for both sexes it meant achieving equality in all fields, economic, social, political and religious, with the free. This was, and in some cases still is, unobtainable. In Muslim law, for instance, freed slaves and their descendants become clients of their former owners and their descendants in perpetuity. In theory, therefore, even legal manumission by Muslim law does not give them the same rights and status as the free. The discrimination may be minimal in terms of actual exploitation. It may amount simply to the cooking of meals on feast days or the giving or receiving of gifts. It may be willingly performed in order to keep alive the ties of dependency where these are seen to have an advantage. However, it may also include social and religious discrimination such as a prohibition on leading prayers in the mosque or a ban on intermarriage with the free. Even when not economically significant these indicators of inferiority can affect the status and self-esteem of the individual.[68]

In non-Muslim societies perceptions of freedom varied between societies, between kin groups and doubtless between households – depending on ever-changing political, social and economic conditions as well as on personalities. In some, manumission was possible, in others it was not. In some over the generations the descendants of slaves were absorbed into kin groups and became indistinguishable from the freeborn. The process was accelerated if they were allowed to intermarry with the free. In others, the life style of former slaves was the same as that of free junior kinsmen, but their servile origins were, and are, remembered in questions of status, inheritance, marriage and the performance of rituals. Today such 'vestiges of slavery' remain even in cases where the descendants of slaves are more prosperous than those of their former owners.

The European rulers viewed freedom in a more straightforward way. To them the question was primarily an economic one. If slaves could leave their owners, dispose of their labour where they wished and keep and pass to their heirs all the fruits of their efforts, they were free. When they issued ordinances declaring that slaves were free to depart if they wished, they thought they had liberated them. They sometimes issued freedom certificates and were baffled when they found that this did not raise the recipients' standing in their own eyes, those of their owners or in those of society as a whole. In some cases slaves, male and female, freed unconditionally by administrators, insisted on paying for their ransom before they could think of themselves as free. But even this was not enough to give them real equality, particularly in societies where there were no indigenous mechanisms for manumission. The problem was even more complex for women. Even if their lifestyle was like that of other women, they might not think of themselves as really free if bride wealth had not been paid for them or a regular marriage service had not been performed, or even, in some cases, if they were not living among their own people.[69] In Muslim societies, in an ironic twist, defying Western concepts of freedom, slave women when freed sometimes curtailed their actual liberty by moving voluntarily into purdah – previously open only to those of high status.

The ritual, social and even the political dimensions of the problem often escaped Europeans. A graphic illustration of this occurred when violent clashes broke out between slaves, the *Ohu*, and their masters in the Nkanu clan in south-eastern Nigeria in 1922.[70] The British tried to restore order by getting the slaves to pay rent, even suggesting that it might be paid in labour, although labour demands were among the main slave grievances. When this was not acceptable to either side, they proposed that slaves should redeem themselves for a nominal sum – negating their own myth that slavery was no longer legal. This too was rejected by many slaves and owners. To the slaves, the exactions of their masters, which included labour services, a proportion of any earnings and the inheritance of their property, were only part of the story. They could and did accumulate wealth, and some even owned slaves of their own, and they could follow the same occupations as the freeborn; but to be their equals they had to have the same unconditional rights to land – rights ascribed to the free with ritual sanction as 'sons of the soil'. They had to be eligible for the highest ranks in the title societies – the symbols of wealth and status. They had to have the right to make the same animal sacrifices at their funerals, to dance the same dances and beat the same drums. To ensure the reproduction of the slave household and mark the fact that they were people and not property, their masters would have to give up the right to inherit slave women and children, to abduct them at will and to sacrifice them at funeral or title ceremonies. Moreover, slaves had to be allowed to intermarry with the free and pay their own bride price for their wives so that their children would belong to their own lineages. The denial of these rights was the indicator of their perpetual marginality – the factor that was deeply resented because it made them permanent outsiders. It was also, naturally, the factor most cherished by their owners.

The British could outlaw the sacrificing of slave women and children, and they could appoint slaves as chiefs. They could enable slaves to sit in

Native courts. They could ensure they had access to land through the payment of redemption. They could not, however, make a slave the real equal of the freeborn. Eventually the slaves themselves gave up the struggle for complete acceptance as 'sons of the soil' and settled for the right to be called by a new name. It became illegal to call anyone an *Ohu*. Instead they were known as *Ndi Awbia* – those from elsewhere. Some also moved into villages of their own. Conflicts, however, continued throughout the colonial period and even erupted in the 1970s.

This is an extreme case – one end of a continuum. At the other end the pressures of colonial rule led some peoples in central Africa to intensify the process of integrating slaves into their lineages as 'fictive kin'. Whereas in the past slaves who were fictive kin had not been treated as well as natural-born kin, now their slave origins were deliberately forgotten and discrimination ended. As a result, when offered 'freedom' by the Belgians, they refused it, as it would have ended their ability to achieve complete integration – the only real freedom in their eyes.[71]

Further research is also needed on the life histories of different categories of slave before a general picture can be drawn of whether or not their expectations of freedom were met. In cases where the freed were able to set up their own communities or were given their own lands to cultivate, they may have been met in full, although 'vestiges' of slave status may persist and in the Nkanu case their villages are today notably poorer than those of the freeborn. Where their former masters retained the rights to land they became share-croppers, squatters or low-paid labour. In some areas – the Kenya coast, for instance – many deserted the land and sought work in the towns or joined settlements of ex-slaves or entered African kin groups. Thus possibly they, and certainly their descendants, escaped from the stigma of slavery. Some ironically benefited from being among the earliest Africans to receive a Western education which qualified them for jobs in the administration. These were children who were freed and handed over to Christian missions, or they were slave children sent to school by their owners who were unwilling to see their own children educated in the ways of the white man.

The Colonial State and the End of Slavery

Colonial rule itself changed the context in which slavery was practised. Although, as has been shown, colonial governments tried to delay its end, leading to confusion and contradictory policies, in the long run the changes they introduced hastened its demise. The laws, whether they outlawed slavery or merely ended it as a legal status, were only one factor in its gradual decline. More important were the economic and political changes which over time decreased both the need for, and the advantage, of owning slaves. The building of roads and railways and the advent of steamboats ended the call for many thousands of slave porters and canoe men. The imposition of peace ended the demand for slave soldiers and retainers. The gradual usurpation of many of the functions of African rulers and chiefs curtailed the use of 'royal' slaves. The resort to forced labour by the colonial governments was at first filled largely by slaves recruited by their owners, but it became a levelling factor as time went on and the poorer free were conscripted together with the slaves. Where such labour was paid, slaves were able to buy their redemption or set up on their own. As wage labour and cash cropping opened new opportunities for slaves to acquire wealth, they became more aware of their rights and less willing to submit to their masters' exactions. For their part, chiefs and 'big men' became less ready to invest in slaves. Wage labour and share-cropping provided alternatives, and when head taxes were levied slaves became an expense. Numbers of dependants ceased to be the main status symbol as consumer goods became more widely available and a Western education became the route to power and wealth.

By the end of the Second World War, slavery was no longer an important issue in most of Sub-Saharan Africa.[72] Its demise was not achieved without significant resort to unfree labour in various forms by the colonial rulers themselves. Whereas at first they turned slavery to their own advantage by supporting the owners, they slowly supplemented and then supplanted it by such devices as forced labour, contract labour, land alienation, regressive taxation and compulsory crop production – all of which were often more oppressive and exploitative than the indigenous forms of slavery they had attacked. By the 1940s there was also a considerable wage-labour force upon which they could draw.

Today chattel slavery as a legal institution no longer exists in Africa. However, vestiges of it remain. Among some peoples it is remembered as a social status and invoked when it comes to questions of marriage, inheritance and ritual. Cult slavery still continues in parts of West Africa. In Ghana, for instance, girls are still dedicated to shrines. Small-scale trading in children continues across borders. Most disturbing in Sudan, as a byproduct of the long war between north and south, people have been captured in the south and carried north against their will and sold. The government does not recognize slavery and it is not clear what the ultimate fate of these people, mainly women and children, will be.

If the expectations of the abolitionists have been realized as far chattel slavery is concerned, what are called 'contemporary forms of slavery', which include child labour, forced marriage, child marriage, servile marriage, forced prostitution, debt-bondage, forced labour and cult slavery, can still be found, just as they can be, usually to a greater extent, in other areas of the world.[73]

NOTES

1. For examples of the course of abolition in the colonies of other colonial powers see Suzanne Miers and Richard Roberts (eds.), *The End of Slavery in Africa* (Wisconsin: 1988) and Suzanne Miers and Martin A. Klein (eds.), *Slavery and Colonial Rule in Africa* (London/Portland, OR: 1998).

2. For abolition in the Cape see C. Crais, 'Slavery and freedom along a frontier: the Eastern Cape, South Africa 1770–1838', *Slavery and Abolition*, 11, 2 (1990), pp.190–215; J.B. Peires, 'The British and the Cape 1813–1934', in R.Elphick and H.Giliomee (eds.), *The Shaping of South African Society, 1652–1840* (Middletown: 1988), pp.472–518; R.L.Watson, *The Slave Question: Liberty and Property in South Africa* (Hanover/London: 1990); N.Worden and C. Crais (eds.), *Breaking the Chains: Slavery and its Legacy in the Nineteenth Century Cape Colony* (Johannesburg: 1994); Robert Shell, *Children of Bondage: A Social History of Slave Society at the Cape of Good Hope, 1652–1838* (Hanover, 1994); E. Eldridge and Fred Morton (eds.), *Slavery in South Africa: Captive Labor on the Dutch Frontier* (Boulder, CO/San Francisco, CA/Oxford,1994).

3. Memorandum by Salisbury,16 Dec.1895, Foreign Office Confidential Print [FOCP] 6709, cited in G.N. Uzoigwe, *Britain and the Conquest of Africa: the Age of Salisbury* (Ann Arbor, MI: 1974), p.158.

4. For the end of slavery in India see Howard. Temperley, *British Antislavery, 1833–1870* (London:1972); D.R. Banaji, *Slavery in British India* (Bombay: 1933); L. Caplan, 'Power and status in south Asian slavery', in J. L.Watson (ed.), *Asian and African Systems of Slavery* (Oxford: 1980), pp.169–94; A.K. Chattopadhyay, *Slavery in the Bengal Presidency 1772–1843* (London: 1977); B. Hjejle, 'Slavery and agricultural bondage in south India in the nineteenth century', *Scandinavian Economic History Review*, 14, 2 (1966), pp.71–126; D. Kumar, 'Colonialism, bondage, and caste in British India', in Martin A. Klein (ed.), *Breaking the Chains: Slavery, Bondage and Emancipation in Africa and Asia* (Madison:1993), pp.112–30; G. Prakash, 'Terms of servitude: the colonial discourse on slavery and bondage in India' in ibid., pp.131–49.

5. I leave aside here the vexed question of finding a definition for all types of slavery. This has caused much debate and led to no consensus. For the various types of slave in Africa see, *inter alia*, Patrick Manning, *Slavery and African Life: Occidental, Oriental and African Slave Trade* (Cambridge: 1990); John Ralph Willis (ed.), *Slaves and Slavery in Muslim Africa,* 2 vols (London: 1985); Paul E. Lovejoy, *Transformations in Slavery: A History of Slavery in Africa* (Cambridge: 1983), pp.159ff.; Claire Robertson and Martin A. Klein (eds.), *Women and Slavery in Africa* (Madison:1983); Paul E. Lovejoy (ed.), *The Ideology of Slavery in Africa* (London: 1981); Suzanne Miers and Igor Kopytoff (eds.), *Slavery in Africa: Historical and Anthropological Studies* (Madison: 1977); Claude Meillassoux (ed.), *L'esclavage en Afrique précoloniale* (Paris: 1975). There are also numerous studies of separate societies and regions.

6. For pawnship see Toyin Falola and Paul E. Lovejoy (eds.), *Pawnship in Africa: Debt Bondage in Historical Perspective* (Boulder, CO/San Francisco, CA/Oxford: 1994).

7. Quoted in R. Dumett, 'Pressure groups, bureaucracy, and the decision-making process: the case of slavery, abolition and colonial expansion in the Gold Coast, 1874', *Journal of Imperial and Commonwealth History*, 9, 2, pp.193–215.

8. The ordinances are nos.1 and 2 of 1874 and no.1 of 1875, E. Hertslet, *Commercial Treaties,* 15, pp.527ff.

9. G.E. Metcalfe, *Great Britain and Documents of Ghana History 1807–1957* (London: 1964), pp.373, 377.

10. Suzanne Miers, *Britain and the Ending of the Slave Trade* (London and New York:

Longman, 1975), p.158.

11. Metcalfe, *Ghana History*, p.400; R. Dumett and M. Johnson, 'Britain and the suppression of slavery in the Gold Coast Colony, Ashanti, and Northern Territories', in Miers and Roberts, *End of Slavery*, pp.71–116, p.85.

12. Griffiths to Knutsford, confidential, 26 Jan.1891, CO 96/215.

13. Compare for instance Dumett and Johnson (n.11) with G. McSheffrey, 'Slavery, indentured servitude, legitimate trade and the impact of abolition in the Gold Coast: 1874–1901', *Journal of African History*, 34, 3 (1983), pp.349–68. See also Kwabena Opare-Akurang, 'The administration of the abolition laws, african responses, and post-proclamation slavery in the Gold Coast, 1874–1940', in Miers and Klein, *Slavery and Colonial* Rule, pp.149–66; Claire C. Robertson, 'Post-proclamation slavery in Accra: a female affair', in Robertson and Klein, *Women and Slavery*, pp.220–45.

14. Dumett and Johnson, 'Britain and the suppression of slavery', p.85.

15. Metcalfe, *Ghana History*, p.400.

16. F. Wolfson, 'British Relations with the Gold Coast, 1843–1888', PhD thesis, University of London, 1950), p.339; McSheffrey, 'Slavery, indentured servitude', pp.351, 354.

17. For a recent study of French policy see Martin A. Klein, *Slavery and Colonial Rule in French West Africa* (Cambridge: 1998).

18. I. Sundiata, *From Slaving to Neoslavery: The Bight of Biafra and Fernando Po in the Era of Abolition, 1827–1930* (Madison:1996), pp.50–1.

19. For examples see J. Duffy, *A Question of Slavery: Labor Policies in Portuguese Africa and the British Protest* (Cambridge, MA/Oxford: 1957); G. Clarence-Smith, *Slaves, Peasants and Capitalists in Southern Angola, 1840–1926* (Cambridge: 1979) and *The Third Portuguese Empire, 1825–1975: A Study in Economic Imperialism* (Manchester: 1985); Linda Heywood, 'Slavery and forced labor in the changing economy of central Angola', in Miers and Roberts, *End of Slavery*, pp.415–36; A. Isaacman and A. Rosenthal, 'Slaves, soldiers, and police: power and dependency among the Chikunda of Mozambique, ca.1825–1920', in Miers and Roberts, *End of Slavery*, pp.220– 58, L.Vail and L.White, *Capitalism and Colonialism in Mozambique: A Study of Quelimane District* (London/Nairobi/Ibadan: 1980).

20. King Leopold's Congo Independent State (Congo Free State) became a Belgian colony in 1908.

21. For the Cardinal's crusade see *Lavigerie, l'esclavage Africain et l'Europe 1868–1892* (Paris: 1971), vol.2; for the Brussels Act see Miers, *Britain and the Ending of the Slave Trade*, pp.236ff.

22. Heywood, 'Slavery and forced labor', pp.419–22.

23. See extract from Schindler to FO, 29 April 1904, FO2/876; Teixeira-de-Mattos to Beak, 2 Jan. 1909, enclosed in Beak to Thesiger, 11 Jan.1909, FO 367/156; Report on the Condition of Coloured Labour employed on the Cocoa Plantations of S.Thomé and Principe and the Methods of Procuring it in Angola, by Joseph Burtt, 24 Dec. 1906, with a confidential supplement, FO 367/46 28725; Mackie to Grey, confidential no.5, 15 March 1908, FO 367/87; Report by Mr C. Swan on his Recent Journey to Africa, enclosed in Swan to FO, 2 June 1909, FOCP [Foreign Office Confidential Print] 9547 [FO 403/407].

24. D. Northrup, 'The ending of slavery in the eastern Belgian Congo', in Miers and Roberts, *End of Slavery*, pp.467–9.

25. D. Cordell, 'The delicate balance of force and flight: the end of slavery in Ubangi-Shari', in Miers and Roberts, *End of Slavery*, pp.150–71.

26. R. Oliver, *The Missionary Factor in East Africa* (London 2nd edn, 1965), pp.22–3; F. Renault, *Lavigerie*, 1, pp.142, 188ff.

27. D. Bouche, *Les Villages de liberté en Afrique noire française* (Paris: 1968); Andrew Clark, 'Slavery and its demise in the Upper Senegal Valley, West Africa, 1890–1920', *Slavery and Abolition*, 15, 1 (1994), pp.51–71 and 'Freedom villages in the Upper Senegal Valley, 1887–1910: a reassessment', *Slavery and Abolition*, 16, 3 (1995), pp.311–30; Bogumil Jewsiewicki and Mumbanza Mwa Bawele, 'The social context of slavery in equatorial Africa during the 19th and 20th centuries', in Lovejoy, *Ideology of Slavery*, pp.73–98; Northrup, 'Ending of slavery'.

28. Lugard to Chamberlain, no.143, 16 June 1900, CO 446/7.
29. Administrator, Sine Saloum to Directeur des Affaires Politiques, no.262, 27 Sept. 1893, no.313, 21 Dec. 1893, no.348 and 6 Feb.1894; Directeur des Affaires Politiques to Administrator, Sine Saloum, no.1203 confidential, 2 Aug. 1893 and confidential, 21 Sept.1893, AOF/K/13.
30. Jewsiewicki and Mumbanza Mwa Bawele, 'The social context of slavery', pp.92–6.
31. See n.23.
32. Cordell, 'The delicate balance'.
33. Anthony Kirk-Greene and James Vaughan (eds.), *The Diary of Hamman Yaji. Chronicle of a West African Ruler* (Bloomington, IN: 1995).
34. E.Ann McDougall, 'A topsy-turvy world: slaves and freed slaves in the Mauritanian Adrar, 1910–1950', in Miers and Roberts, *End of Slavery*, p.367.
35. Suzanne Miers, 'Britain and the suppression of slavery in Ethiopia', *Slavery and Abolition*, 18, 3 (Dec.1997), pp.257–88.
36. For the colonial period see examples in M. Klein and R. Roberts, 'Pawning in the depression in French West Africa', *African Economic History*, 16, pp.23–37; Miers, *Britain and the Ending of the Slave Trade*, pp.296ff.; D. Ohadike, 'The decline of slavery among the Igbo people', in Miers and Roberts, *End of Slavery*, pp.437–61; Robin Maugham, *The Slaves of Timbuktu* New York , NY: 1961). For modern trafficking see n.73.
37. Miers, 'Suppression of slavery in Ethiopia'.
38. C.W.W. Greenidge, *Slavery* (London: 1958); Miers, *Britain and the Ending of the Slave Trade*, pp.295–6; Suzanne Miers, 'Britain and Consular Manumission in Hijaz 1921–1936', *Slavery and Abolition*, 10, 3 (Dec. 1989). There were numerous press articles on the slave trade to Arabia in the 1960s.
39. Duffy, *A Question of Slavery*; Ibrahim Sundiata, *Black Scandal: the United States and the Liberian Crisis of 1929* (Philadelphia Institute for the Study of Human Issues, 1980).
40. Suzanne. Miers and Michael Crowder, 'The politics of slavery in Bechuanaland: power struggles and the plight of the Basarwa in the Bamangwato Reserve, 1926–40', in Miers and Roberts, *End of Slavery*, pp.172–200.
41. J. Grace, *Domestic Slavery in West Africa: With Particular Reference to the Sierra Leone Protectorate, 1896–1927* (London: 1975), p.84.
42. Ibid.; and Ismail Rashid, 'Do dady nor lef me make dem carry me': slave resistance and emancipation in Sierra Leone 1894–1928', in Miers and Klein, *Slavery and Colonial Rule in Africa*, pp.208–31.
43. See Dumett and Johnson, 'Britain and the suppression of slavery'; enclosures in Governor to Passfield, 23 Nov. 1929, CO 323/1027; British Reply to League of Nations for the Gold Coast, League of Nations A.25 (a) 1924. VI.
44. See F. Cooper, *Slaves to Squatters: Plantation Labor and Agriculture in Zanzibar and Coastal Kenya, 1890–1925* (New Haven, CT/London: 1980).
45. P. Romero, 'Where have all the slaves gone? emancipation and post-emancipation in Lamu, Kenya', *Journal of African History*, 27, 3 (1986), pp.497–512.
46. Interview with Kiponda wa Mwavuo conducted by S. Miers, 3 Nov. 1974.
47. Quoted in P. Lovejoy and J. Hogendorn, *Slow Death for Slavery: The Course of Abolition in Northern Nigeria, 1897–1936* (Cambridge: 1993), p.88.
48. For a discussion of the ordinance and its effects see J.C. Anene, *Southern Nigeria in Transition 1885–1906* (Cambridge: 1966), pp.294, 305–8; P.A. Igbafe, *Benin under British Administration: the Impact of Colonial Rule on an African Kingdom 1897–1938* (New Jersey: 1979), pp.243–6; Ohadike, 'Decline of slavery among the Igbo people'; T.N. Tamuno, *The Evolution of the Nigerian State* (Ibadan: 1972).
49. Toyin Falola, 'The end of slavery among the Yoruba', in Miers and Klein, *Slavery and Colonial Rule in Africa*, pp.232–49.
50. Klein, *Slavery and Colonial Rule in French West Africa*; see also Clark, 'Slavery and its demise in the Upper Senegal Valley' and 'Freedom villages in the Upper Senegal Valley'; M. Klein, 'Slave resistance and slave emancipation in coastal Guinea', in Miers and Roberts, *End of Slavery*, pp.203–19; Richard Roberts, 'The End of Slavery in the French Soudan, 1905–1914', in Miers and Roberts, *End of Slavery* pp.282–307; Richard Roberts and M.

Klein, 'The Banamba slave exodus and the decline of slavery in the western Soudan', *Journal of African History*, 21, 3 (1980), pp.375–94; Richard Roberts, *Warriors, Merchants and Slaves: The State and the Economy in the Middle Niger Valley, 1700–1914* (Stanford, CA: 1987), pp.174ff.

51. Roberts, 'The End of Slavery in the French Soudan'.

52. As in the Banamba case, Roberts, *Warriors, Merchants and Slaves*, pp.188–9.

53. As in the case of Nkanu, see Carolyn A. Brown, 'Testing the boundaries of marginality: twentieth-century slavery and emancipation struggles in Nkanu, northern Igboland, 1920–29', *Journal of African History*, 37, 1 (1996), pp.51–80.

54. D. Ohadike, 'When slaves left, owners wept: entrepreneurs and emancipation among the Igbo people', in Miers and Klein, *Slavery and Colonial Rule in Africa*, pp.189–207.

55. As in Nkanu, see Brown, 'Testing the boundaries'.

56. See for example Jan Georg Deutsch, 'The "freeing" of slaves in German East Africa. The statistical record, 1890–1914', in Miers and Klein, *Slavery and Colonial Rule in Africa*, pp.109–32, p.128.

57. For examples see Miers and Klein, *Slavery and Colonial Rule in Africa*.

58. See for example Barbara M. Cooper, *Marriage in Maradi: Gender and Culture in a Hausa Society in Niger, 1900–1989* (Portsmouth, NH/Oxford: 1997), pp.10–13.

59. Richard Roberts and Suzanne Miers, 'Introduction', in Miers and Roberts, *End of Slavery*, pp.3–68.

60. Lovejoy and Hogendorn, *Slow Death for Slavery*.

61. See, for instance, Taj Hargey, 'Festina lente: slavery policy and practice in the Anglo-Egyptian Sudan', in Miers and Klein, *Slavery and Colonial Rule in Africa*, pp.250–72.

62. See Falola, 'The end of slavery among the Yoruba'.

63. Sean Stilwell, '"Amana" and "Asiri": royal slave culture and the colonial regime in Kano, 1903–1926', in Miers and Klein, *Slavery and Colonial Rule in Africa*, pp.167–82.

64. See, *inter alia*, Lovejoy and Hogendorn, *Slow Death for Slavery*, pp.116–26, pp.234ff.; Robertson, 'Post- proclamation slavery'; Marcia Wright, *Strategies of Women and Slaves: Life Stories from East/Cental Africa* (New York, NY/ London, 1993), pp.168–75.

65. Free women also faced the same disabilities but at least if they left their husbands they could usually return to their natal families from whom they could also expect some protection.

66. Cooper, *Marriage in Maradi*, pp.10–12.

67. For a review of the discussion on this point see J. Glassman, 'The bondsmen's new clothes: the contradictory consciousness of slave resistance on the Swahili coast', *Journal of African History*, 32, 2 (1991), pp.277–312.

68. For examples see Andrew Clark, '"The ties that bind": servility and dependency among the Fulbe Bundu (Senegambia)', in Miers and Klein, *Slavery and Colonial Rule in Africa*, pp.91–108.

69. See for example Marcia Wright, 'Bwanikwa: consciousness and protest among slave women in central Africa, 1886–1911', in Robertson and Klein, *Women and Slavery*, pp.246–67, pp.263–4; and Robertson, 'Post–proclamation slavery', pp.239–42.

70. See Brown, 'Testing the boundaries'.

71. See Jewsiewicki and Mumbanza, 'The social context of slavery', pp.90–6.

72. It persisted in Mauritania and other parts of the Sahara, however.

73. For information on contemporary forms of slavery see the reports of the UN Working Group on Contemporary Forms of Slavery since 1976, reports of the UN Special Rapporteurs, and the reports and publications of Anti-Slavery International, Human Rights Watch, Africa Watch, Sudan Watch, Christian Solidarity International, the Abolitionist Federation and other non-governmental organizations, as well as the press.

The Aborigines Protection Society, 1837–1909

CHARLES SWAISLAND

For many in the abolition movement the Emancipation Act of 1833 seemed the end of a long road. Certainly it was the end of the mass movement,[1] but for the battle-hardened leadership it was no more than a significant milestone in a much longer journey. Slavery was still legal in some countries and their dependencies, and the slave trade still carried on in ships under their flags. Although now illegal in British colonies, had slavery stopped in all of them? In reality not, for slavery-like conditions prevailed in many parts, encouraged by the periods of apprenticeship imposed by the Act.[2]

The campaigners regrouped, the British and Foreign Anti-Slavery Society[3] being formed to combat continuing chattel slavery and, in direct response to the report of the Parliamentary Committee on Aborigines (British Settlement) 1834–37, the Aborigines Protection Society (APS) was established to oppose the exploitation of indigenous peoples in British colonies. For 70 years until they amalgamated in 1909, the two Societies worked together, usually in harmony, but with divergent viewpoints on some issues and occasional acerbity as their secretaries sought to defend from threatened encroachment the interests and territories they considered their own.[4]

One reason for the infrequency of such clashes was the early sharing out of the world. The British and Foreign Anti-Slavery Society (BFASS) concentrated on the continuing slave trade and slavery outside the British Empire, while the APS mainly addressed problems caused by British imperialism. There was some overlap; for historical reasons the BFASS retained the main interest in the West Indies and, in 1890, the APS was active in famine relief on the Red Sea coast of the Sudan, territory over which the sister organization had long campaigned. Both were engaged in the south Pacific, where labour recruitment had started before Britain had any political authority in the region, and where practices were sometimes indistinguishable from slave-raiding. Indian matters were left to the British India Society,[5] until the traffic in indentured labour became a major movement and brought both in.

Organization and methods were similar and the two Societies shared not a few members. Each had a world-wide network of correspondents, some of whom supplied information to both. Members of Parliament were lobbied[6] and representations, often cocooned in sonorous generality,[7] were made to Secretaries of State. The chance was rarely lost of writing long, closely-reasoned letters to newspapers. Most of their activity was reported in the *The Anti-Slavery Reporter* and *The Aborigines Friend* together with, in the latter, the text of correspondence with the Colonial Office.[8]

Who were the people mounting a challenge to the government of Empire by setting up and belonging to a body of ill-defined membership and an annual income of three to four hundred pounds? Some of the anti-slavery bodies and other groups at work before abolition had enjoyed royal and aristocratic patronage. The short-lived African Civilisation Society had the Queen's husband at its head and the BFASS would one day have the King of England as its patron. The APS never had such connections. One or two relatively minor peers associated themselves with it from time to time over particular matters, as did a few bishops, while a sprinkling of baronets and knights of the shires gave more constant service. But beyond them the membership was largely made up of middle-class professionals and others in commerce and industry. In religious affiliation they were mostly Nonconformist or, if Anglican, evangelical. Most voted Liberal in general elections.

A more fruitful question is: who provided and maintained motivation in the work? Two men were of particular importance in the history of the Society. Indeed, the minutes of correspondence in Colonial Office files justly claim that each in turn *was* the Society.[9] The two men were its successive secretaries. Frederick William Chesson (1855–88) had spent some of his adolescent years in New York State where the case of a fugitive slave made him a committed abolitionist. Henry Richard Fox Bourne (1889–1909), who had once been a clerk in the War Office, was the son of a magistrate in the West Indies.

Next in importance in the work was the network of correspondents. Most representation and much of the content of *The Aborigines Friend* was based on the information they supplied. Except where the person was too well known,[10] identities were kept secret even from other correspondents in the territory. That was a help in testing the reliability and independence of the reporting. After one or two unhappy experiences when the Colonial Office, in communicating with governors, had not respected confidential disclosure, identification of sources was firmly refused. Unfortunately, in Whitehall and colonial secretariats that was often used as an excuse for not taking effective action.

Correspondents came from many walks of life. There were traders and clerics, the latter mainly missionaries from Britain. Two prominent clerics, whose integrity was never in question, were Bishop John William Colenso of Natal, whose voluminous correspondence was maintained by members of his family after his death in 1883, and the African Bishop James Johnson of Lagos, whose letters also lack any suggestion of self-interest. Most correspondents were European, but there were some highly educated West Africans and a much smaller number of South Africans. Tengo Jabavu and Kirkland Soga, both newspaper men, sent material from the Eastern Cape, while Dr Abdullah Abdurahman organized and sent petitions from Cape Town calling for votes for non-white citizens when South Africa became a Union. Maori majors of militia, men from St. Helena having problems in Durban finding schools for their children and mixed-race people being harassed by pass laws in Johannesburg were able to handle their own correspondence, as were some Indians in Mauritius, but the quality of the English in letters signed by petitioners of the humbler sort showed that they were written by English-speaking amanuenses.[11]

A particularly interesting class of correspondent consisted of colonial civil servants in touch with the APS; some like Sir Henry Barkly, former Governor of the Cape of Good Hope and High Commissioner in South Africa, and Sir Benson Maxwell, former Chief Justice of Malaya, collaborated only after retirement, but most were in touch while in service. Sir Arthur Gordon[12] and Sir John Pope Hennessy,[13] both sent Chesson copies of their confidential dispatches to Whitehall so that questions inconvenient to the Colonial Secretary could be asked in Parliament.

Despite the spirit of reform affecting the Home Civil Service, patronage still ruled colonial appointments, and most of their colonial service correspondents at some time sought the secretary's help when seeking an advantage in their careers. Some had roots in Scotland and Ireland and may have felt disadvantaged when it came to postings and promotion. There are indications that Chesson could sometimes help.

The Aborigines Protection Society was born out of concern for the welfare of indigenous peoples under pressure from growing emigration from western Europe, carried by power of steam and possessing increasingly powerful weapons. Reaching foreign shores in large numbers, the immigrants were equipped to despoil the inhabitants of land and compel their labour. The Society never resolved the tension between a Darwinian belief in the inevitability of emigration to distant and seemingly more spacious lands[14] and the manifest detriment to the interests and welfare of the indigenous inhabitants. Thus, Sir Thomas Fowell Buxton, grandson of the first president, speaking in 1889, said:

> There is one tendency which we cannot forget and that is, those vast spaces of unoccupied and unused territory in South Africa and other parts of the world cannot remain as they are with the human race

increasing ... the space will be filled up ... [and all that government can do] is to control and direct it, and see that the progress goes on with as little mischief as possible to all concerned.[15]

The following year Fox Bourne, in a paper delivered at the Universal Peace Congress in Westminster Town Hall, went even further:

We are confronted at starting by the great natural law of the 'survival of the fittest' which applies to human beings no less than to the rest of animal creation. ... All we dare hope for and strive after is that the encroachments shall be effected under conditions most equitable, or least inequitable, to the natives....[16]

The Indian Coolies

Because of their involvement in commerce and industry as well as religious persuasion, most members associated personal and social virtue with honest toil backed by responsible capital. When the latter had an overtly humanitarian motive, such as the African Civilisation Society's Niger venture of 1841, the appeal was strong indeed. Belief was never lost in commerce, first as the supplanter of the slave trade and then as a vehicle of civilization, though the activities of chartered companies were to test it.

A small, idealistic settlement up the Niger, a suggestion that American humanitarians should establish a similar settlement to Liberia on the East African coast,[17] and a proposal for a joint Anglo-Irish-Maltese colony in Cyrenaica[18] were not seen at the time as a threat to Africa. What made the idea acceptable was the assumption that the settlers would be using their own muscle power, as had been the case in New England and on the Cape Frontier in 1820. But in tropical countries immigrants soon sought to become landlords needing labour. Former slaves in Mauritius and the West Indian colonies were reluctant to carry on working in conditions differing little from their former state, so a regular and biddable replacement had to be found. Only rarely could local people supply what was wanted, either because they were few in number or had a social organization that did not fit in with regular employment. The answer was indentured labour mainly recruited from India, China and the South Sea Islands.[19] The way in which it was recruited, transported and employed occasioned much abuse.[20] If settlement was not a clear-cut issue for the Society, abuses stemming from it were and the most extensive of these related to harsh conditions of employment. The successors of the abolitionists were back at a business they understood well.

The APS took an interest in the conditions in the West Indies of Indian labour and the Carib remnant, and the welfare of Chinese labourers in Latin

America, whether on Cuban plantations or in Peru, where it was said a thousand had been killed near Santa Rosa by 'a body of Negroes'.[21] Questions were asked about Dutch plantations in Surinam and even more pointed ones about Indian labour conditions in Cayenne, Martinique and Guadeloupe in 1897,[22] as well as about the five-year indenturing to farmers offered by the Cape Government in 1897 to alleged Bechuana rebels as an alternative to their being tried for treason. All these inspired a vigorous but unsuccessful campaign for imperial intervention. Their main labour concerns, however, were Indians in Réunion and Mauritius, traffic in Pacific Islands labour to Queensland, the importation of Chinese on to the Rand and the appalling conditions discovered in the Congo Free State.

There was little the APS could do about the recruitment in India, although one or two representations were made about reducing the length of contract from five to three years for labourers working within India.[23] They were also concerned about conditions in the Assam tea gardens.[24] When Sir Arthur Gordon, in his last governorship, was able to pay to Tamil labourers from public funds wages owed by a bankrupt tea estate in Ceylon, they warmly approved.[25]

The Indian Ocean traffic was on a large scale, with most of the labourers coming from Madras. When Chesson and Sir Charles Wingfield interviewed William Adam, Governor of the province, in London he claimed that 138,535 had left Madras between 1842 and 1870, 110,825 bound for Mauritius. Arrivals on the island in 1879 numbered 1,500 and a like total was expected in 1880.[26]

There were 40,000 Indians in Réunion in 1881,[27] a particularly large number having been recruited the year before because of a threatened suspension of recruitment. That threat, made from time to time and occasionally carried out because of bad conditions on the plantations, had unfortunate consequences.[28] Pre-emptive over-recruitment brought down wages and placed extra strains on medical and other facilities. Entry was denied to one shipload reaching Réunion because there was no market for their labour and the *Marguerite* sailed into Port Louis in the hope of disposing of the men to Mauritian estates. According to the *Mauritian Mercantile Record and Commercial Gazette*, the 400 people aboard had been 'kidnapped' from all over British India and shipped from Pondicherry contrary to the terms of the Anglo-French convention of 1861.[29]

The convention allowing French recruitment from British India was said to be the price paid for the abolition of a revived slave trade from east Africa, principally Mozambique.[30] It required that, before a labourer left India, there had to exist a contract either with a receiving government or a designated owner of the soil to be worked, and there were conditions applying to the accommodation aboard ship. An anomaly in the latter was discovered when Chesson took up with the India Office the plight of some time-expired labourers on their way home from Réunion. They were landed in the Seychelles from the leaking 380-ton barque *Francis*, a ship with a capacity of 200 passengers but with 400 aboard on arrival. When the 400-ton *Jacques* arrived to collect them, even she was not big enough and 67 were left behind when the voyage to Pondicherry was resumed.[31] The convention prescribed conditions on the outward journey, but said nothing about them on the way home.[32]

The Society was handicapped in dealing with the situation in Réunion for want of reliable information. What they had, suggested that conditions were bad, but there was no intention on the part of the French of making it easy for foreigners to investigate. Even Victor Schoelcher, an ardent, French, anti-slavery campaigner with whom the Society enjoyed a co-operative relationship, told Chesson that not only would French planters in Réunion and the West Indies as well as the French government refuse inspection of the plantations by a British consul, but, 'despite my hatred of immigration, I would be the first to oppose our Government if it agreed to it'.[33] Consequently, reliable reports from Réunion were scarce, the India Office being unable to furnish official consular reports for the years 1872–74. In 1871 Colonel Seagrave, the British Consul, had received 771 complaints from or about Indians, of whom a third, he said, were in prison at any one time.

Conditions in Mauritius were not much better, as letters from many correspondents made clear, though the report of the Royal Commission, received in April 1875, surprisingly said that they were rather better on the estates than was commonly supposed.[34] All was far from well, however. There were arrangements for a quarter of every shipload to be made up of women which, even if the requirement were fully met, meant a serious imbalance of population. As Colonel O'Brien, Inspector of Police, remarked, it made polyandry almost an acknowledged system.[35] Medical cover was also inadequate, hospital accommodation on the two d'Arifat estates at Flacq being cited because the mortality rate there had been higher than average.[36] J.J. Daly, a Canadian barrister and magistrate as well as an APS correspondent, conducted three inquiries between 1877 and 1879 into hospital and labour regulations and found that conditions had improved since the report appeared and a new labour ordinance had come into operation.[37]

In Mauritius it was those known as 'Old Immigrants' who were the most disadvantaged. Having completed their indentured time and lacking in many cases the money to get home, they were stranded, for Mauritian planters had managed to get contracts lacking provision for return passages.[38] To survive, many were forced into a further period of indentured labour. Their plight was brought to government and APS notice in 1871 by a pamphlet written by Adolph de Plevitz, a former Prussian Army officer and then a planter in Mauritius, who had helped 9,401 Indians to address a petition to Sir Arthur Gordon.[39] It was a catalogue of their complaints, starting with criticism of the recruiting system in India, of wages paid sometimes six months in arrears and, when their time was done, liability to arrest as vagrants if they were found without a costly ticket bearing a photograph and a pass valid only for one district unless it had been endorsed by a police inspector for wider use. If the fine could not be paid, imprisonment followed.

The punishment of offenders could be harsh. Heavy fines and costs sent many a person to gaol, where punishment for an offence against prison discipline could be caning. Corporal punishment was all too common. W. Kennedy, Superintendent of Prisons, claimed that over a ten-year period there had been more than 500 floggings in what he thought were inappropriate cases. A commission set up to inquire into practice found that caning was administered to unfit persons and that the punishment in Port Louis prison was sanctioned by a disciplinary committee without its hearing the evidence.[40]

Planters may have welcomed a stranded pool of experienced labour harried back into employment by a draconian vagrancy law, but a few perceptive observers saw beyond the present scene. One such was Owen O'Connor of the Immigration Department. Of the estimated Mauritian population of 325,000 in 1872, 225,000 were Indian. O'Connor noted that many of the latter had become small proprietors and within 10 to 15 years they would become influential. Even he could not have imagined that they would one day supplant the plantocracy as the island's rulers.[41]

Boer 'Slavery'

The Great Trek convinced the APS that Boers leaving the Cape Colony were seeking freedom to practise the slavery they had recently been required by the 1833 Emancipation Act to give up. It was a view of the Boers they were to hold tenaciously almost to the end. Writing to Lord Glenelg, the Secretary of State, Thomas Hodgkin was astonished that the colonial government had allowed so large an armed force to trek, even though he agreed that they had suffered grievous provocation at the hands of that government and from the unjust arrangement for paying slave compensation only in London.[42] The Society, having warmly applauded the abandonment, on instructions from London, of the ceded Queen Adelaide territory in 1836, pressed Glenelg to annexe Port Natal temporarily to bar further Boer expansion.[43] Sir Harry Smith's proclamation of the Orange

River State in 1848 passed without comment in *The Aborigines Friend*, but on the abandonment of the territory six years later it was noted that 'this territory ... having been unjustly acquired has been recklessly thrown away'.[44] 'A piece of egregious folly', the editor called it. The annexation of the Transvaal in 1877 was welcomed and the retrocession in 1881 deplored, lest it lead to a resurgence of slavery or, as Lord Shaftesbury put it at the Society's Annual General Meeting in May 1881, the Boers planting 'their tyrannous foot on the necks of the native races'.[45]

Not only did the APS petition the British government but, from time to time, Boer leaders were also addressed. There is no evidence of how Andries Pretorius took it when the Society observed, 'with deep regret, that the inhabitants of the Transvaal Republic have been seriously deficient in their duty to their weaker fellow men...'.[46] The father's generation seemingly persisting in the hardness of their hearts, the Secretary next tried with the son, Marthinus Wessel Pretorius, successively President of the Orange Free State and the Transvaal.[47] He too ignored them. But the Transvaalers bided their time and the chance came. On 26 June 1880 Kruger and Joubert wrote to Leonard Courtney, MP, who had opposed Transvaal annexation in 1877, circulating copies of their letter to newspapers in South Africa: 'Even now calumny gains the ear of the Colonial Secretary who the other day was told by a deputation of the Aborigines Protection Society that slavery still exists in the Transvaal.'[48]

It was a British official who gave the Boer leaders their opening. Melmoth Osborn, Sir Theophilus Shepstone's successor as Administrator of the annexed Transvaal, had apprenticed 800 children orphaned in the renewed attack on Sekhukhuni. A Volksraad Select Committee, in recording the fact, said that this was 'slavery according to Mr Chesson ... carried on by the English Government ... Never under the Republic was a child apprenticed without the consent of the parents...'.[49] As G.W. Steyn, a former landdrost of Potchefstroom, in a letter to *The Friend of the Free State* asked, how many of the 4,000 or more sold in the Transvaal since 1850 had been orphans unless they had been made so 'by the bullet of some ruffian of a Boer'.[50]

In *The Times* of 13 November 1883 the Transvaal delegates then in London to negotiate the London Convention launched another attack in an open letter addressed to the members of both the Anti-Slavery and the Aborigines Protection Society. It was a curious document, quaintly constructed and revealing that, if the APS had failed to understand the outlook of the Boers, the misunderstanding was mutual. The authors claimed to be 'most deeply hurt ... there still prevails the opinion that the Transvaal Christians understand less thoroughly than Christians in this country the duty which they owe to Kaffirs ...' They wrote that they heartily approved of the Society's principles and most desirable objectives and it was not for them to judge whether its influence had always prevented colonial officials in South Africa from interfering with native lives.

> The painful accusation is brought against us that we not only keep the natives in a degraded position but also encroach on their person liberty, ... We cannot refrain from demanding of you, on behalf of the Transvaal, a share of the same human compassion which you devote so largely to our aboriginal neighbours in Africa.[51]

It was nauseating and it was inept. The readership of *The Times* included many critics of the APS and the editor had long deplored the Society's attitude towards settlers, but that tissue of lachrymose self-pity was going to recruit few of them to the Boer cause. It is no wonder that R.N. Fowler, then Lord Mayor of London and treasurer of the Society, four days later administered the almost unprecedented snub to foreign leaders of refusing to receive them at the Mansion House.

Later in the century the Society's correspondence and the pages of *The Aborigines Friend* mellowed. Sir Richard Southey, an occasional correspondent of the Society,[52] when both in and out of office, Saul Solomon, Cape politician and J.H. Froude, Carnarvon's informal emissary on South African federation, all thought Boer attitudes improving as British behaviour in South Africa deteriorated. Even disillusioned African opinion was shifting. Tengo Jabavu, a Mfengu journalist, as early as 1881 told Chesson that the natives were beginning to have confidence in the 'Dutch' section of the community.[53]

Such moderating views received sceptical acceptance in APS circles, but by 1899 Fox Bourne went so far as to admit the APS's failure to be fair to the two republics.[54] It was the performance of foreign capital which forced the grudging admission. The Boers, it was said, were not as harsh as the Uitlanders on the Rand. Two years later he wrote to *The Times*:

> The Boer policy towards natives ... is notoriously degraded in theory and often cruel in practice ... [but they have] dealt more leniently than Cape colonists and newcomers from Europe with the great majority of natives outside their actual purview ... All the special and oppressive legislation introduced into Transvaal since 1884 has been at the behest of Uitlanders.[55]

Chinese Labour in the Transvaal

The employment of Chinese labour was a matter of great controversy in South Africa, with reverberations in the British general election of 1906. It might have been expected that the Boers would have had much to say about it but they were tactically silent, for General Botha hoped that the reaction of others would hasten the return to self-government in the province.

The Aborigines Protection Society was far from silent. When the proposal was first made to meet the labour demands of the 300 mining companies on the Rand after the war, they manned the ramparts. As early as 1872 they had condemned the traffic in Chinese coolie labour as 'an insidious form of slavery'.[56] The campaign they waged showed traces of unusual racial prejudice. Fox Bourne wrote, 'Whatever his merits the Chinaman has habits and methods which render his influence on the "inferior" races of other lands altogether pernicious'.[57]

> Later that year, in a letter to Alfred Lyttleton, the Colonial Secretary, he wrote Grievous and incurable injuries will be inflicted on the natives of South Africa, in addition to the inconveniences and wrongs to which some of the whites in contact with them will be liable, unless they are safeguarded against the bodily disease and social corruption from which the Chinese immigrants for short terms are being brought.[58]

The social and moral aspects of importation concerned the Archbishop of Canterbury and other churchmen, as well as the APS. Sir Frank Swettenham, Governor of Malaya, had been consulted by the Colonial Office and had warned that a labourer could not be held a virtual prisoner in the mining compound during the whole period of his indenture without problems arising. Fox Bourne was more explicit; 50,000 or more Chinese could not be kept in enforced celibacy 'without monstrous abuses growing'.[59] Swettenham had referred to the men's need to find occasional solace in brothels in the compounds,[60] but no Colonial Secretary was able politically to give countenance to licensed prostitution. The problem was never satisfactorily solved. Men did get out of the compounds, some in the hope of making their way back to China. Inevitably there were violent incidents when Chinese associated with African women in kraals.

For once the Society was on the side of the big battalions. Trade unions, churchmen and a host of voluntary societies in the United Kingdom and South Africa and, eventually, the Liberal Party in Britain, united in opposition to the system. Once South African public opinion in general had been mobilized it was brought down. Even though siding with powerful interests, the Society's still managed to be a dissenting voice. Their fear was that if the battle cry of 'Chinese slavery' rang out too clearly, the system might survive if mine owners found the labour so profitable that they purged it of the grossest abuses. That would deny Africans the chance of selling their labour. After all, time-expired, indentured Indians leaving the Natal sugar-cane fields had elbowed Zulus out of many aspects of the local economy. Sir Percy Fitzpatrick and a few others who favoured importation also saw the danger, and at the 1903 Bloemfontein Customs Conference succeeded in obtaining a resolution that there should be terminal repatriation after an indenture period limited to three years.[61] Importation ceased at the end of 1905, but the last labourers sailed homeward past Durban Head only in March 1910.

King Leopold's Estate

If the part played by the Society over the importation of Chinese labour on to the Rand was of limited effect, the same cannot be said of their opposition to King Leopold's Congo fiefdom.

Before they clashed there was more than a decade of harmonious relationship. Early in 1878 the Society wished to acknowledge Leopold's avowed scientific interest in central Africa and invited him to become their patron. The canny monarch was pleased, but declined.[62] As late as January 1890 in the wake of the Brussels Conference on the Slave Trade they congratulated him on his efforts on behalf of the Congo natives. But H.M. Stanley's *In Darkest Africa*[63] appeared in June and on 12 December Dr Grattan Guiness of the Regions Beyond Missionary Union spoke at a meeting the APS had convened at the Westminster Palace Hotel. It was clear that much was amiss in the Congo basin.[64] From then on the Society maintained pressure on the Foreign Office in the hope of stirring the government to exercise their treaty rights under the Berlin General Act of 1885, and eventually to press a reluctant Belgian government to take over the Congo Free State.

Credit is usually given to Edmund Dene Morel, editor of the *West African Mail*, for the success of the campaign. Rightly so, because it was his knowledge of West African trade and ability to marshal the facts, as well as the founding and directing of the Congo Reform Association, which built up the relentless pressure which achieved the objective. But the APS were active forerunners and Fox Bourne's *Civilisation in* Congoland,[65] a seminal work, preceded Morel's *King Leopold's Rule in Africa*[66] by almost two years. Both men wielded powerful pens, though Morel's style, when compared with Fox Bourne's sonorous rotundity of phrase, was a precursor of tabloid journalism. It was no surprise when Roger Casement, whose idea the Congo Reform Association was, invited the two men to join in organizing it, that Fox Bourne refused or rather argued that, if he were do so, it would have to be on his own terms. He thought Liverpool not close enough to the centre of government and that Morel had too many irons in the fire – as though he himself had not! Why, he asked, was a separate body needed? Why not a co-ordinating committee like the many Chesson had set up in his day, working from the APS office with himself as secretary? Eventually Sir Charles Dilke and Casement overcame his opposition and the Congo Reform Association (CRA) was set up in Liverpool with Morel as its executive and Fox Bourne a respected member of the committee. In the APS annual report for 1908 he told members that CRA activity made it unnecessary for the Society to keep up the pressure on His Majesty's Government, especially as he and many of his readers were members of both bodies.[67]

Conclusions

'It surely behoves the British public that the colonial rule of Britain be no longer such as to stain her name with the reproach of cruelty and injustice.'[68]

That was written in 1839 in the report to the Society's second annual general meeting. It was the introduction to what would now be called the 'mission statement' of a pressure group. For 72 years they remonstrated with, cajoled and, when allowed, cooperated with governments, chartered companies and settlers in measures to achieve that goal. How effective were their efforts? They asked themselves that in 1874 and were forced to conclude that:

> Our predecessors vainly hoped that, in successfully fighting against slavery and the slave trade in the British dominions, they had forever put an end to the two greatest evils that had cursed their day and generation. It has been our fate to realise that ... institutions may change their form, and yet be animated by the same principles of oppression.[69]

It is a fair judgement that by the time the Society amalgamated with the Anti-Slavery Society they had achieved far less than they had dared to hope in 1837, but more than in 1909 they dared to believe. There were no great achievements, no landmarks such as the Emancipation Act to point to; just a few cases of individual hardship alleviated and petty wrongs righted. Their work may have seemed successful on those occasions when they were moving with the political current and, at other times, things might have gone harder with their clients if the vigil had not been kept. They never turned the Colonial Office from the pursuit of a British interest and rarely goaded them into action if the Secretary of State and his officials saw no national interest to be served by it. But such a summary does not supply a full answer to the question.

The single-minded pursuit of an objective held to be as valid at the end as at the beginning does not imply that the Society's thinking was static and their outlook unchanged. From a base in evangelical Christianity and a belief in Western civilization as the vehicle to carry its supreme values to the unenlightened of other lands and faiths, they moved towards a more secular view. In earlier years British citizenship with all its rights was seen as a blessing to which everyone in the Empire was entitled. By 1909, while still holding to the right of everyone wanting it to have it, Fox Bourne also believed in the right of others to reject it.[70]

There were shifts in political thinking, too, from Little Englanderism, through two decades of belief in responsible imperialism and then a drift back to the earlier belief. Between 1869 and 1888 Fiji, Basutoland, the Gold Coast and Bechuanaland came under British control with the Society's urging and they campaigned vigorously against the proposed cession of the Gambia to France. Indeed, there were so many calls for intervention and control in those years that it seemed to the Colonial Office and many humanitarians that the Society was a leading exponent of imperial expansion. They certainly made it more acceptable in Noncomformist circles and, to some extent, in constituency Liberal parties. In the last decade of the century, when the settler dominions were self-governing and beyond Colonial Office control and while France and Britain were pressing their interests in West Africa, the APS once again took up a stance against imperial expansion.

The most valuable service rendered by the Society was not its political advocacy, for much of that inevitably consisted of generalities with which many of their critics could agree, but the provision of a second channel of communication from the colonies to the Colonial Office and, if need be, beyond to Parliament. Lord Carnarvon once remarked that the APS called the Department's attention to many points which they might have overlooked if left entirely to themselves.[71] The rules of petition to the Secretary of State were well established, the matter being submitted through every step in the bureaucratic hierarchy, with each official having the right to comment. The petitioner had neither the opportunity nor the right to see comments, and so had no redress against error, or even malice. When it reached Whitehall it faced another hazard. As Mr Justice Gorrie in Mauritius pointed out, the Colonial Office usually backed their men in the field.[72] A problem for the Society was tainted sources of information. So often a complainant had a sense of grievance without it having substance, or it was a matter which had been properly dealt with in the colony, but not to his or her liking. Such cases given forceful support – particularly by Fox Bourne – did the Society's standing no good.

The Colonial Office accepted the APS as a fact of political life, a regrettable one by and large, but certainly one never to be ignored. Dealing with their submissions was an exercise in fine judgement. Say too much in reply and the Secretary came back with further argument; say too little and there could be an awkward question in Parliament.[73]

In his classic work on the Indian Civil Service, Philip Woodruff observed that 'a permanent opposition is bound to display a certain amount of permanent perversity'.[74] It was so with the Society; like trees bent by the prevailing wind, they were set in a posture of opposition, yet, if the Colonial Office or a Governor sought their help, it was willingly, almost eagerly, given. Although the Colonial Office were wary in dealing with them, judgement on the value of their work was expressed by two other members of the Colonial Office in minutes which, because they were not expected to see the light of day, were perhaps more telling than Lord Carnarvon's pronouncement. R. Antrobus, First Class Clerk, wrote: 'Mr Fox Bourne is continually bringing false and unreasonable accusations against the Government, but he and his Society do a certain amount of good in keeping us all up to the mark.'[75]

It was to be expected and not unfitting that, when the Parliamentary Under-Secretary said much the same thing a few years earlier, there was more of an oratorical flourish to it: 'The APS and kindred societies [though] sometimes, perhaps often, weak as to their facts, help by their criticisms to keep Governors and Captains up to the mark of a high level of humanity.'[76]

NOTES

Abbreviations

AF   *The Aborigines Friend*
ASC   APS Correspondence in the Rhodes House Library, Oxford G refers to items in boxes. Where there is no letter before the number, the item is to be found in a bound volume in the C series.
CO   Colonial Office files in the Public Record Office
PP.C 'Blue Books' (Parliamentary Papers)

1. I.N. Crumpston, *Indians Overseas in British Territories 1834–1854* (Oxford: Oxford University Press, 1953), p.169. The author was surprised that the abolitionists could still attract 3,000 people to meetings in the 1840s. The APS never had that sort of support.
2. Six years for field workers, four for domestic servants.
3. Now Anti-Slavery International.
4. One such disagreement spilled over into the letter columns of *The Times*. The Anti-Slavery Society committee thought it would inhibit anti-slavery progress in Africa at the Brussels Conference in 1890 to consider also the arms and liquor trades. As payment for slaves was often made in these commodities it made sense to the APS to deal with them together. C.H. Allen to *The Times*, 20 Jan. 1890, p.10 and subsequent letters.
5. Founded 1839.
6. At one time there were 80 Liberal MPs willing to ask questions in the House of Commons for the APS.
7. 'The Society loves to deal in generality and leave the harder task of getting at and stating the facts'. APS to Chamberlain, 15 February 1901, minute by G. Grindle, C0417/339. That was hardly fair; much detail was sometimes furnished only to have the matter taken less seriously by the Colonial Office for some minor inaccuracy.

8. For a few years *The Aborigines Friend* was called *The Colonial Intelligencer* and occasionally both.

9. In coming to that conclusion they were not alone, William Cadbury, writing on 18 December 1907 to John Harris, Organising Secretary of the Anti-Slavery Society, was 'pretty satisfied that [Fox Bourne] has run the whole business for the last year or two, and [the Committee] has meekly followed in his wake'. ASC G486.

10. The Colenso family in Natal and Bishop James Johnson were examples. Episcopal status was also thought to give warranty to facts alleged.

11. Cetewayo, the Zulu king, learned to sign his name during imprisonment in Cape Town Castle.

12. Gordon held governerships in New Brunswick, Trinidad, Mauritius, Fiji, New Zealand and Ceylon.

13. Pope Hennessy held governerships in Labuan, West Africa, West Indies, Hong Kong and Mauritius. On retirement he (a Roman Catholic) became Nationalist MP for Kilkenny and a member of the APS committee.

14. Dr Thomas Hodgkin, virtual founder of the APS, was co-founder in 1843 of the Ethnological Society.

15. AF, June 1889, p.581.

16. AF, April 1891, p.170 *et seq.*

17. E.D. Parkes to T. Hodgkin, undated, ASC 122/50.

18. T. Hodgkin to G.G.S. Lefevre, undated, ASC 122/72.

19. 'Coolie labour obtained either in India or China, is the chief element in the industrial system of several of our most important colonies, notably of Mauritius and Guiana'. F.W. Chesson at a conference on Colonial Questions, 21 July 1871. Report in AF, Dec. 1871, p.344.

20. 'Experience has shown … in colonies steeped in traditions of slavery [that] immigration under labour contracts, in spite of attempted safeguards, ever led to gross abuse, and tended to reduce the immigrants to a servile condition'. Sir Charles Wingfield speaking when a deputation called on Lord Salisbury at the India Office, 3 Aug. 1875. AF, Nov. 1875, p.233.

21. AF, Aug. 1881, p.379 fn.

22. Chesson and Fox Bourne were both fluent in French, but that did not eliminate an anti-French bias which persisted throughout the Society's history. Except in its anxiety to prevent passage to the north being cut in South Africa by collusion between the Germans and the Boers, there was no obvious feeling against the Germans.

23. Hartington to APS, 19 April 1882, ASC 164/260.

24. Cross to APS, 16 Feb. 1887, ASC 164/262.

25. Gordon – S/S Colonial Office, 3 Oct. 1887, ASC 164/242, enclosed with CO to APS, 11 Nov 1887, ASC 164/241.

26. AF, Jan. 1881, p.315.

27. AF, Aug. 1881.

28. AF, April 1880, p.228.

29. 14 Sept. 1880, APS to Hartington 30 Oct. 1880. Hartington to APS, 23 Nov. 1880, ASC 164/258.

30. Madagascar domestic slaves were angered when their Queen on 30 June 1877 emancipated the Mozambiquan slaves but kept them in slavery. AF, Jan. 1878, p.468. The *Gazety Malagasy* of 12 June 1885 reported that three dhows had landed Mozambiquans at Sakalawa, selling men at £8 and women at £6–12 to Frenchmen, probably to send to Réunion. AF, Nov. 1885, p.228. The AF for Oct.–Dec. 1858 had reported the kidnapping of a number of the islanders from the Kingswill Islands in the Pacific for work in Réunion, p.500.

31. AF, April 1882, p.489.

32. J.F. Kelsey to Chesson, 27 Dec. 1881, ASC 139/138.

33. Schoelcher to Chesson, 17 March 1882, ASC 146/125.

34. The planters were pleased and not least because it was they who had asked for a commission of enquiry to be appointed.

35. Reported in AF, Nov. 1875, p.237.

36. William Seed to Chesson, April 1876, ASC 146/138.

37. The Daly Reports, ASC G35/B2, Items 1–3.

38. In his dispatch No. 26 of 11 March 1875 [C–1188], Carnarvon virtually instructed Sir Arthur Phayre, the Governor of Mauritius, to include in a new labour ordinance contractual provision of return passages. On 19 July, when speaking in the House of Lords, he claimed that every coolie was entitled to a passage back to his country, *Lords Hansard,* XXCCV, col.1639, yet the revised labour law was not introduced for almost another three years.

39. *The Old Immigrants of Mauritius.* On its publication planters demanded that de Plevitz be deported. Gordon refused, but a year later he left Mauritius for good, making his way to Fiji where, after he had failed to make a living, he was eventually helped by Sir Arthur Gordon and William Seed, both of whom had known him in Mauritius, by being made a sergeant of police.

40. Pope-Hennessy to Chesson, 8 June 1884, ASC 137/240 and O'Connor to Chesson, 15 March 1884, ASC 144/7.

41. O'Connor to Chesson, 15 March 1884, ASC 144/7.

42. APS to Glenelg, 7 Aug. 1838, reproduced in APS Extracts, Vol.3, p.74. The Emancipation Act 1833 provided £20 million for compensating owners for the loss of their slaves, but it could only be collected in London. Even then only two-fifths of the assessed value would be paid, part in cash and the rest in government stock. Few Boers were in a position to collect in person and so sold their claims at heavy discount to travelling agents.

43. CO 48/197 and APS Extracts, Vol.3, p.74.

44. APS address to Sir G. Grey, Colonial Secretary, 8 July 1854, AF, July–Dec. 1854, p.341.

45. AF, Aug. 1881, p.388.

46. AF, April–Sept. 1856, p.128. Undated reference. Andreas Pretorius died 23 July 1853!

47. 6 Dec. 1867, AF, March 1868, p.62. Once again the document was reported as addressed to Andreas Pretorius.

48. Copy in the *Cape Argus,* 3 July 1880.

49. South African newspaper cutting, undated. ASC G12/5, Item 6 and AF, Dec. 1881, p.430 and *De Volksstem,* 10 Dec. 1881.

50. 13 March 1866. AF, Feb. 1871, p.301.

51. 12 Nov. 1883. *The Times,* 13 Nov. 1883, p.8.

52. Colonial Secretary, Cape Colony 1864–1872. Lieutenant Governor, Griqualand West 1873–75.

53. Jabavu to Chesson, 18 May 1881, ASC 139/2.

54. H.R. Fox Bourne, *The Aborigines Protection Society – Chapters in its History,* Jan. 1899.

55. 24 Aug. 1901; *The Times,* 26 Aug. 1901, p.9.

56. Report of the AGM 1872, p.9.

57. AF, Feb. 1904, p.15.

58. Fox Bourne to Lyttleton, 15 Dec. 1904, CO 291/78.

59. AF, Oct. 1905, p.415.

60. Swettenham's opinions are to be found in CO 291/79.

61. 10–23 March 1903; AF, Aug. 1903, p.427.

62. A. Couvrier to APS, 18 Feb. 1878, ASC 129/115.

63. *In Darkest Africa* (London: Sampson Low, 1890).

64. For an eminently readable account see Ruth Slade, *King Leopold's Congo* (Oxford: Oxford University Press, 1962).

65. P.S. King and Son, Jan. 1903.

66. Heineman, 1904.

67. Annual Report 1908, p.11.

68. Report on 2nd AGM, 21 May 1839, p.28.

69. Annual Report 1874, p.121.

70. Report of 3rd AGM, 23 June 1840 and AF, Oct. 1908, p.188.

71. Carnarvon was addressing a deputation which called upon him on 6 March 1874. He added that they should be credible cases supported by accurate facts. AF, May 1874, pp.60–70.

72. Gorrie to Chesson, 12 Nov. 1875, ASC 135/127.

73. Fox Bourne to Chamberlain, 24 Dec. 1897. Minute by Graham, CO 48/536.

74. *The Men Who Ruled India,* Vol. 2, *The Guardians* (London: Cape, 1954) p.167.

75. On Fox Bourne to Chamberlain, 2 March 1896, CO 96/284, R. Antrobus.

76. APS to Ripon, 13 Feb. 1893. Minute by Sydney Buxton (Parliamentary Under-Secretary 1892–95), CO 147/92.

Comparative Approaches to the Ending of Slavery

STANLEY ENGERMAN

Introduction

As the first decade of transition in eastern Europe draws to a close, there is a rather pervasive sense of disappointment with the changes that have occurred. While few call for a return to the former conditions, the hopes that such dramatic political changes would soon lead to highly favourable economic, social, and cultural changes have been dashed. Debates about how fast the transitions should have been, whether shock therapy would have been more effective than gradual adjustment, and what constraints political factors should have been allowed to have on economic change, indicate that the early optimism that adjustment could be smooth and rapid has not been realized. Of course, some had argued that this unsatisfactory outcome was only to be expected, but that prediction was generally made by those who had been opposed to change and wished to keep the previous political and economic conditions.

It is, perhaps, not surprising that a similar range of opinion existed about a major nineteenth-century transition in laws concerning controls over labour. The end of slavery in many nations and their colonies began in the late eighteenth century and continued into the twentieth.[1] It was a radical change in the rights of labourers, freeing them from the control of their owners and permitting them, at least legally, to choose places of residence and location. It was, in some ways, also conservative, in that in only one major case was there a dramatic shift in political power or in the pattern of land ownership. Indeed, in many cases the former slave owners were compensated for their loss, while in no case were the former slaves compensated by either cash or land. Debates about policies for transition preceded most emancipations, and then ensuing events were carefully watched.

As with other great reforms, the emancipation of the slaves in most parts of the world aroused high expectations, but ended with a major sense of disappointment about what had been accomplished. Expectations were high as to the expected effects upon not only the ex-slaves but also upon other members of society, who were expected to gain. Disappointment was widely spread among groups in society, since ex-slaves, ex-slave owners and other members of society all believed that emancipation had failed to achieve most of its promised ends, and that considerably more remained to be done if society were ever able to receive the expected benefits. The different expectations and times required to achieve the desired ends meant that different short-term, as well as long-term, policies were desired by the several parties, pointing to a major difficulty in evaluating the response to emancipation. Nevertheless, the fact that few individuals seemed satisfied with the outcome of emancipation suggests that perhaps the outcomes were mixed, with no one getting all he had hoped for, yet each getting some desired benefits.

Arguments for and against Emancipation

There are several types of comparison that have been made in describing the adjustments to emancipation. In particular, outcomes have frequently been compared with those claimed in the rhetoric of the reform movements agitating for emancipation. Some of this may have reflected the actual beliefs of their proponents, but there were probably some points that had been advocated for their political value, in providing for a broader, and more successful, political appeal for a reform that might otherwise have been too narrowly based to succeed. But, whatever goals were accomplished after emancipation, their achievement could not have solved the full range of social problems confronted by the ex-slaves and others. Indeed, any gain may have led to the desire for even greater changes, so that a backward look from today's vantage point, over one century later, could suggest that, at the time of emancipation, the benefits were quite limited, possibly non-existent. While losses for one of the parties to emancipation may on occasion have meant gains for other parties, situations where all the parties lost, albeit at different rates, doubtless occurred also.

Emancipations came with expectations as to what would happen, economically and socially, to various individuals as well as to society as a whole. Such expectations were influenced, and their anticipated prospects constrained, by the views held as to the nature of slavery and its impacts, particularly on the enslaved. Beliefs as to how psychologically 'destructive' the institution was and beliefs as to whether slavery's destructive power was to be attributed to African backgrounds (as argued by the pro-slavery defenders) or to the sociological and psychological aspects of the slave relationship (as argued by anti-slavery groups) were the basis for the advocating of different post-emancipation policies. These beliefs also generated different expectations as to what ex-slaves would be able to achieve and how long a time period would be necessary to reach these goals.

If, for example, it was believed that slavery destroyed the enslaved, then policies with only limited interference with ex-slaves would seem of little use in solving key problems. And, given the belief that the major sin of slavery was the domination of the slaves by others, a change from control of the slaves by private individuals to control of ex-slaves by government agents would pose internal contradictions.

Among the members of society it is about the expectations of slaves that relatively less is known, beyond that of the simple wish for the ending of slavery. Clearly there was a desire for freedom and for the ability to move, if desired, to different geographical areas. Haiti was unique in its changes in political controls, with the replacement of a white political leadership by a black and mulatto elite, but such a change was not to be expected elsewhere, as was to be the case. Haiti, however, also provided more complicated messages and was an often-quoted example in subsequent debates concerning emancipation.

As Carolyn Fick points out, the military confrontation between blacks and whites meant that the initial transition could be accomplished only under rather difficult conditions. The early leadership of a free Haiti tried to maintain a plantation-based, export-production system in order to obtain the means of trading in the world market. Such attempts, tried for over a quarter of a century, did not succeed, and the output of export crops fell sharply – most dramatically for sugar, less so for coffee, but that too continued to fall. At bottom, the desire of the ex-slaves to acquire smallholdings of their own rather than to work on plantations meant that the plantation sector disappeared, with a decline in exports and probably of all agricultural output as well. Haiti moved from probably the richest area in the world in the 1780s to a country whose income position continued to deteriorate until it is now the country with the lowest income in the Americas, with per capita income at sub-Saharan levels. The early date of the freeing of Haiti's slaves and its sharp decline in export-crop output meant that its experience was used elsewhere as a frequent argument for the dangers of emancipation.

Moreover, Haiti's black political rule did not preclude racial conflict and civil war, nor did it guarantee a high standard of living.[2] And the Haitian desire for smallholdings indicated that the acquisition of such landholdings in agriculture was possible, even if at the cost of a reduction in colonial output; but whether the desire was for income needed in order to acquire more land in the future, a higher standard of living or else to permit a withdrawal into self-sufficiency removed from the market still remains unclear. The trade-off between income and leisure or easier working conditions is important to understand, since the choices made at the time of emancipation would have significant long-term impacts.

The general expectations of the anti-slavery movement seem fairly clear, following from the contours of their attack on slavery. At the time, little attention was paid by the anti-slavery movement to the specifying of the detailed expectations of post-emancipation behaviour and in drawing inferences from the outcomes of earlier emancipations. Ending slavery was seen as strictly a moral issue, and there was a fear that to predict what might happen next could only lead in too conservative a direction and thus prove counterproductive.

In the economic sphere it was generally argued that ending slavery and moving to free labour would lead to higher output and more efficient production of those crops previously produced. The superior incentives and discipline of free labour, with labourers working harder when given the opportunities to benefit from their increased production when free, would lead to outcomes that were in sharp contrast with the presumed low productivity under the coercive control of the slave system. As Seymour Drescher points out, the contrast between the productivity of slave and free labour was central to the British attack on slavery. It was widely proclaimed, though probably less widely believed, that the incentives given to free wage workers meant that their productivity would be greater that that of coerced slaves, who were presumably without any such incentives to raise output. Some problems existed in the full advocacy of the argument, given the distinction between production in the tropics and the production of temperate-zone crops, as well as the awareness of the apparent difficulties in Haiti's economic transition. Nevertheless, the comparisons of free and slave labour, however theoretical and not empirical, pointed to expected benefits from economic prosperity, due to a greater and more-highly motivated labour force after emancipation.

Higher labour input would lead to higher land values, so that some of the benefits of freed labour would also go to landowners, as no emancipation resulted in the confiscation of slave-owner land. The fundamentally conservative nature of emancipation may be seen by the fact that slave-owners in many cases were given compensation, with some fraction of the value of the slaves being paid for by the state or by extended labour time, while no slaves (or serfs) were granted compensation.[3] Within the argument of the benefits of free labour there was, however, less discussion of the specific nature of the economic adjustment anticipated. Some expected the basic plantation system to continue, being necessary to take advantage of the economies of scale in production, but now based upon free-labour-paid wages rather than the coercion of slavery. Others denied the importance of scale economies in the production of those commodities grown by slaves and suggested that the loss of the plantation system would mean its replacement by small, productive farms, either with ex-slaves as owner-operators or ex-slaves as farm workers. Export production was expected to be maintained at least at pre-emancipation levels, whether on plantations or on smallholdings. In either case, however, the expectation was that more labour input would be forthcoming after emancipation and that it would be highly effective, with only some minimal coercion, whether by nature (starvation) or by laws, but with legal freedom.[4]

The high expectations from free labour, a major part of the economic argument against the slave system, were based on comparisons with what were considered to be the successful areas of the northern United States and Britain, where free labour was dominant.[5] The expected time-scale of this future adjustment was seldom discussed and only vaguely argued. The expected duration of education, apprenticeship and other forms of control necessary to ease the transition were not often examined, although the setting of the apprenticeship period provides some indication. The importance of evaluating success in terms of the output of specific products permitted the use of widely available data (such as crop outputs and exports). Few, then, were willing to argue that emancipation would be costly to society, and few suggested that there would be a cost to be paid in the interests of morality.

The expectations of the pro-slavery advocates pointed in a rather different direction. The pro-slavery argument was that production necessarily required coercion to obtain plantation labour; this proposition thus reflected the remarks of Sir James Steuart that people would work either because they were slaves to their wants or slaves to others.[6] There was also a belief in the inability of the uncontrolled and unsupervised ex-slaves to become disciplined and productive workers. Any loss in coercive controls, it was claimed, would lead to a decline in the input of plantation labour and in the output per labourer. In the nineteenth century these arguments were buttressed by the example of Haiti, where freedom had meant a loss in export output when the ex-slaves chose to avoid plantation work, desired to work less intensively and wished to enjoy more leisure rather than to expand work effort and increase consumption. Similar declines in export production were seen in the other French Caribbean colonies where the slaves were temporarily freed during the Napoleonic period. Haiti, however, was seen as the principal test case. There were (and still are) debates as to the possible changes in the standard of living in Haiti, with a positive argument based upon the post-slave era increase in population; but such data were more uncertain as well as more disputed than were the output and export data. There was also much information on Haiti's continued political and social instability. Unlike the optimism, however limited it may have been, of the anti-slavery people, a rather dire set of predictions was given by the defenders of slavery, with expectations of economic collapse and social unrest in the aftermath of emancipation in the absence of some appropriate set of government policies regarding labour supply, immigration and land distribution.

In the nineteenth century there were few discussions of the possibility of a racially-integrated society being successfully achieved, even in societies where there had been no previous occurrence of slavery. Clearly, for the British West Indies, with a population about 90 per cent black, integration in its usual meaning could not be achieved; but there were important issues concerning the nature of political rights on the islands and within the Empire. The belief in the difficulty of achieving integration in the USA had, in the earlier part of the century, led to the emergence of the colonization movement, whether its primary motive was to help the ex-slaves who moved or the whites who did not, but 'benefited' from a more racially homogeneous society. Some described an ultimate end of the race problem, forecasting not integration but rather a disappearance of racial distinctions as the result of racial intermixture.

It was not only in racially-divided societies that post-emancipation economic and social difficulties for ex-slaves existed. The British colony of Sierra Leone, settled by ex-slaves and other blacks, was not economically successful nor, as Howard Temperley points out, was the American settlement of ex-slaves and free blacks in Liberia. Returning blacks suffered from high mortality and the economy was not productive. Relatively few blacks were attracted there and, in perhaps an ultimate irony, the movement of the colonists inland led to extensive disputes with native Africans for control of the land. For those hoping for successful economic and social developments in a land removed from whites, the American and the British African colonies were no doubt a source of disappointment.

Claims for racial integration, however, were infrequent and were not well received, as most whites doubted both the possibility and the desirability of this ever happening. Some greater degree of racial accommodation than was to occur in the United States in the first half of the twentieth century had seemed possible in the immediate aftermath of slavery in the US. Richard Naragon's study of post-emancipation Richmond points to the persistence of racial differences, but also to the ability of blacks to vote and to manoeuvre politically in an attempt to achieve their goals. Such relative openness existed for the next decades, only to be ended in the 1890s, with legislation that effectively precluded most blacks from voting in state, local or national elections. There was, moreover, a hardening of racial attitudes late in the 1890s, with the extension of 'Jim Crow' laws and increases in the numbers lynched.[7]

Patterns of Economic Adjustment

There were a number of quite different patterns of economic adjustments to emancipation in the Americas (see Table 1). In the approximately a hundred years from the start of legislated freedom acts in the northern states of the

TABLE 1

AVERAGE ANNUAL SUGAR PRODUCTION BEFORE AND AFTER EMANCIPATION
(000 TONS)

	Date of abolition	Five years before abolition[a]	Five years after end of restrictions[a]	Percentage change	Period in which pre-emancipation level regained
Haiti	1804	71.7	1.2	-98.3	1960s
Martinique	1847	29.1	20.5	-29.6	1857–61
Guadeloupe	1847	31.9	17.7	-44.5	1868–72
St Croix	1848	9.7	7.3	-24.7	c.1890
Louisiana	1865	177.1	44.0	-75.2	1887–91
Surinam	1873	15.7	9.7	-38.2	1927–31
Puerto Rico	1876	94.0	74.4	-20.9	1900–4
Cuba	1886	595.4	745.7	+25.2	–
Brazil	1888	254.0	170.6	-32.8	1905–9

a Either date of abolition or the ending of the period of apprenticeship, except in the the case of Haiti, where the dates are for the five years before 1791 (the start of the uprising) and the next period for which there are reasonable production data, 1818–22.

Source: Noel Deerr, *The History of Sugar* (London: Chapman & Hall, 1949–50), pp.112, 126, 131, 212, 235, 236, 240, 245 and 250. For specifics of the calculations in this table, see Stanley L. Engerman, 'Economic Adjustments to Emancipation in the United States and British West Indies', *Journal of Interdisciplinary History*, 43 (1982), pp.191–220.

United States to the final freeing of slaves in Brazil, patterns of adjustment varied with respect to, among other things, technology, climate, markets, resources available (including the land–labour ratio) and demographic characteristics. The first large-scale emancipation was not based on legal actions, that being the revolutionary military action in Haiti at the end of the eighteenth century. While freedom for black slaves and political rule by blacks (including mulattos) was accomplished, the long-run political and economic impacts of the ending of the plantation system and the near disappearance of export production left Haiti in a weakened condition for at least the next two centuries. Whether due to the failure to obtain needed external support from France or the United States, the costs of compensation paid to France in the 1820s or else to several internal political and social factors, Haiti's overall record is not one that the anti-slavery advocates elsewhere could easily draw upon as a positive example, although, of course, some, recognizing its importance, did try. And, in a rather unexpected and ironic development in the twentieth century, plantation sugar production in the Dominican Republic and in Cuba was to draw upon seasonal labour migrating from Haiti.[8]

The British emancipation in the Caribbean provides a useful example of the range of economic conditions that followed slavery. Barbados was, at the time, regarded as the one example of a successful adjustment to emancipation, with the maintenance of the plantation sector and an increase in sugar exports. Its ex-slave population was regarded as 'civilized', the economy was growing and there was general political stability. Barbados was, however, of all the islands of the British Caribbean, the one with the most dense population and the lowest wages, and was soon to be a major source of out-migration to elsewhere in the Caribbean, and, in future years, to the US and Britain.

The plantation system also returned, with some lag, in the two areas of the British Caribbean that were expanding most rapidly before emancipation – Trinidad and British Guiana. Here the ex-slaves left the plantation sector to produce foodstuffs on small farms, a movement that may have lowered their long-term prospects for improvement in their material standards of living. The plantation sector returned after several decades, but on the basis of indentured labour imported mainly from India, but also from China, the Portuguese Atlantic islands and Africa. Successful as these colonies may have been in achieving high output levels, they were dependent upon a system of labour that many thought was only a new variant of enslavement (see Table 2). As Pieter Emmer points out, indentured labour from afar was probably not the preferred alternative for landowners in the Caribbean. However, given their inability to force ex-slaves back to their plantations, planters believed they had no other choice than to attract indentured labour. This led to the creation of work forces that were racially and ethnically distinct and, in due course, to differences in income, wealth and employment that have continued to agitate Caribbean policies up to the present day.

A third variant was Jamaica, which was not a booming island at the ending of slavery but did have extensive amounts of land relative to its population. Jamaica, however, suffered an inability to introduce sufficient controls to persuade workers to return to a plantation system based on resident labour. Thus it became an island with limited sugar exports, a small plantation sector and relatively low income. Several of the other islands of the British Caribbean replicated this Jamaican outcome.

There have been debates about other aspects of the labour-force adjustment by ex-slaves. While women may have initially withdrawn from the agricultural labour force, it would seem that within some few years they did return, at least part-time, to field labour. Female labour was often

TABLE 2

ESTIMATES OF INTERCONTINENTAL AND RELATED FLOWS OF
CONTRACT LABOUR, GROSS MOVEMENTS, NINETEENTH AND EARLY
TWENTIETH CENTURY

Area of Origin to Receiving Area		Years	Numbers (000)
India to:	British Guiana	1838–1918	238.9
	Trinidad	1838–1918	143.9
	other British Caribbean	1838–1915	46.8
	Mauritius	1834–1910	451.8
	French Caribbean	1853–85	about 79.7
	Réunion	1826–82	86.9
	Surinam	1873–1916	34.0
	St. Croix	1862	0.4
	Fiji	1878–1917	61.0
	Natal	1860–1912	152.4
	Mombasa	1895–1922	39.5
	Malaya	1844–1910	249.8
China to:	British Guiana	1852–79	13.5
	Trinidad	1852–65	2.6
	other British Caribbean	1852–84	1.7
	Peru	1849–74	about 90.0
	Cuba	1848–74	124.8
	Hawaii	1865–99	33.6
	Transvaal	1904–1907	63.7
Japan to:	Hawaii	1868–99	65.0
	Peru	1898–1923	17.8
Java to:	Surinam	1890–1939	33.0
Portuguese Islands to:	Hawaii	1878–99	10.8
	British Guiana	1835–81	32.2
	other British Caribbean	1835–70	8.8
Pacific Islands to:	Australia	1863–1904	61.2
	elsewhere in Pacific	1863–1914	about 40.0
	Peru	1862–63	3.5
Africa to:	British Guiana	1834–67	14.1
	Jamaica	1834–67	11.4
	Trinidad	1834–67	8.9
	other British Caribbean	1834–67	5.0
	French Caribbean	1854–62	18.5
	Réunion	1848–61	34.3
Yucatan to:	Cuba	1849–71	about 2.0
Angola to:	São Tomé and Principe	1876–1915	about 96.5

Sources: See the data used in Stanley L. Engerman, 'Contract Labour, Sugar, and Technology in the Nineteenth Century', *Journal of Economic History*, 43 (1983), pp.635–59.

important in producing for family consumption, and some have argued that female labour was now coerced by male heads of households, who thus gained relatively more from emancipation than did the women.

In the southern US ex-slaves remained within the agricultural sector, generally still growing cotton, but now producing on small, family-operated units or else working as labourers on small farms owned by whites. Aggregate cotton output was maintained in the late nineteenth century by the movement of whites into the production of cotton throughout the South. White families generally worked on owner-operated farms. The lower measured efficiency of smaller farms led to a decline in the total Southern agricultural output for several decades, higher costs and some loss of the near monopoly position of the South with respect to world cotton production.[9]

In Cuba, as Christopher Schmidt-Nowara points out, the freeing of slaves did not mean a decline of sugar production, thanks to a change in technology and an increased number of white Spanish immigrants producing on small farms attached to central mills. There the emancipation process began with the Moret Law of 1870, legally classifying those born after specific dates as free but subject to a period of labour for the owners of their mothers. The *patronato*, a system of controlled labour for slaves, was introduced in 1880, and slavery was finally brought to an end in 1886, two years before emancipation in Brazil ended the legal existence of slavery in the Americas. Between the ending of slavery in the British and French Caribbean and that in Cuba, a new technology and organization of sugar production and milling permitted production on small farms as well as plantations, and this was a key factor in reducing the post-emancipation decline in sugar output in Cuba relative to the earlier declines elsewhere in the Caribbean. In Brazil the adjustment resembled that of Cuba, as the ex-slaves left the coffee-producing regions and were replaced in coffee production by subsidized immigrants from Italy and Spain, working on smaller farms.

Thus, in general, emancipation led to declines in the number and sizes of plantations, with probable reductions in total agricultural output. There were particularly sharp reductions in the production of export crops, with little development of a manufacturing sector or expansion in the production of other export crops. The effects on the material consumption of ex-slaves are not clear, given the changes in the crops grown, the redistribution of the work forces involved and our presently limited information of pre- and post-emancipation consumption patterns. The ending of slavery did, however, often mean a measured deterioration in health conditions and life expectancy.

Measures of economic output were often used in debates as to the success or failure of emancipation. Even the abolitionists accepted this conceptual framework. Few willingly argued that, even with a fall in output, emancipation could be regarded as a success, albeit now on moral, not economic, grounds. When post-emancipation output fell it was argued that the key to the problem of adjustment was the behaviour of labour. Disagreements did persist as to the causes of the 'labour problem', along rather predictable lines. To some it was the failure of the planters to behave properly toward their workers or to pay them adequate wages; to others it was due to the inherent characteristics of the workers, whose lack of desire for material goods and an unwillingness to work led them to avoid plantation labour or production for the market. In addition, as Gad Heuman points out for the British Caribbean, ex-slaves' resistance to apprenticeship and the demand for immediate freedom affected labour input and production even before the ending of the period of apprenticeship in 1838. After that there were occasional disagreements between workers and employers, leading, at times, to short but intense disturbances and riots. While there were costs to this loss of control they were probably small, while other contemporaries pointed to the negative role of government policy, such as failure to adequately protect sugar production by eliminating protective tariffs in the years after emancipation, thus exposing the free-labour producer to competition from producers who still employed slaves and in some cases (Brazil until the 1840s and Cuba until the 1860s) were still importing slaves direct from Africa.

There were several policies that were frequently discussed to offset the problems with labour and to help to make emancipation a success. One was the acquisition of more labour from new sources, via internal movement or immigration from external areas, via free or subsidized immigration or else by contract labour. Another policy was the attempt to drive ex-slaves back on to the plantations, using vagrancy laws, taxation, land restrictions and other measures to restrict labour freedom. Protection of metropolitan markets against foreign staple producers was another possibility, as was the search for new technologies and methods of production to offset the now reduced labour availability. All these were discussed and tried, but each had its limitations in seeking to have the new economic system achieve the desired ends without offending the moral sensibilities that had led to the abolition of slavery.

In discussing the 'labour problem', its causes and consequences, several questions arose that require more systematic answers to help in understanding the sources of disappointment. Did the ex-slaves leave the plantation market sector immediately, as a response to freedom or after several years, possibly in reaction to reduced wages and deteriorating economic conditions? Related to this is the question of whether immigrant and contract labour was used to push out the ex-slaves from employment they would otherwise have been willing to accept or whether the ex-slaves had left these occupations, thus requiring planters to seek out new types of labour? Were the ex-slaves easily and rapidly replaceable by other labourers in producing similar crops, whether or not on the same sized unit? And, if not replaced by other labourers, could new technologies be designed to substitute for ex-slave labour or for land? These alternative scenarios each had differing implications for the ex-slaves' trade-off between income and leisure, and the problems involved in achieving post-emancipation success.

The most frequent pattern of adjustment to emancipation reflected the ability of the ex-slaves to avoid plantation work. Even when it seems that the planters and controlling governments would have preferred to restore the plantation and to control ex-slaves via plantation discipline, this was seldom achieved (even in Haiti). The full police and military power that might have accomplished that aim did not appear to have been utilized, at least not in sufficient force to achieve the desired ends. Nor were laws introduced or successfully implemented to coerce labourers to return to the plantation. Similarly, non-plantation incomes were apparently sufficient to permit ex-slaves to avoid plantation work, low though the level of income may appear to us today, and regardless of whether or not the material incomes of ex-slaves exceeded that which they had received while slaves. The use of stipendiary magistrates by the British and the creation of the Freedmen's Bureau in the United States were attempts to regulate the labour markets, although whether this was in a search for equity or for control over workers depends upon which contemporary or historian one listens to. While the ex-slaves did not get what they wanted from emancipation, the same also held true for the ex-slave owners and the planters.

The 'labour problem' after slavery led to certain policies that were, for that time, not peculiar to ex-slave societies. After the middle of the nineteenth century several parts of the world that previously had neither sugar production nor slavery introduced sugar plantations. These areas – Fiji, Queensland, Natal – drew upon indentured labour, introduced numerous constraints on its freedom and extended few political rights to the labourers, either during or after their contracted periods. While in some areas indentured labour succeeded slavery, in other cases it had preceded it, and in still others it emerged without there having been slavery. To link the post-slavery experience and policies to the prior existence of slavery may, therefore, overlook the similarity of policies of labour control in those areas that formerly had slavery and those other areas that did not.

In regard to social and political changes a variety of adjustments were required. In no case (except Haiti) was political power given exclusively (or even primarily) to ex-slaves. In one of the few cases in which there was an early granting of political rights, the American South, these were soon limited by Southern whites. Few societies became racially integrated and virtually all had strict labour laws and forms of racial discrimination, as well as periodic race riots. And, in some cases, the post-emancipation circumstances generated their own problems, as when contract labour from India led to economic, social and political conflicts with the ex-slave populations of British Guiana and Trinidad. The movement of contract labour from India to several different parts of the world in the aftermath of slave emancipation was itself in part an unexpected and unintended reaction to the British ending of Indian slavery in the early 1840s. Temperley points out that slavery in India was mainly of an agrarian variety and was not as physically harsh as slavery in the Caribbean. The labour situation in India was quite different from that in the New World, as Indian slavery existed under conditions of labour abundance and resource limitations, and slaves in India were a smaller share of the population than in the New World areas. The low income level of India also meant that agrarian and domestic slavery had a role in offsetting the complications of famines and in reducing infanticide. The removal of this safety-net was thus a factor in the subsequent expansion of internal and external immigration, with the freed labour often moving to East Africa, the Caribbean and other distant overseas locations.[10]

Although disappointment with the outcome of emancipation was pervasive, the causes of the disappointments were not the same for everybody, nor were they always based upon the same implicit or explicit comparisons. There were at least three types of comparison made in evaluating the impact of emancipation. First, guaranteed to lead to disappointment, was with the aspirations, however formed and whether reasonable or not, held by people of the time. By this standard, of course, ex-slaves and also non-slaves could find much to be disappointed about. Second, narrowing the possibilities for disappointment, is comparison with the rights and obligations of those already free and their political, economic and social freedoms. At this time, for many free people, incomes were low, working hours were long and intense, the ability to vote often limited, and, in the cases of the lower classes, many forms of overt social and cultural discrimination existed. Colonial Office discussions of post-emancipation policy concerned the importance of the land–labour ratio and its effects on work input, suggesting the same behaviour for West Indian ex-slaves and Lancashire workers in similar circumstances. A frequent response of the British West Indian elite to charges of having introduced harsh labour legislation applying to the ex-slaves was that they had merely adopted the British Master and Servant Acts. That the ex-slaves may not have fared too badly compared with those already free is suggested by the complaints on behalf of British workers that the ex-slaves were being treated more favourably than they were, as earlier it was argued that slaves had been treated better than factory workers. Economic conditions for the whites in the South in the late nineteenth century were extremely difficult. The collapse of the cotton market in the 1890s imposed heavy costs upon white farmers, even those with more than 40 acres and one mule, and the loss in voting rights suffered by the blacks in the 1890s which led to sharp relative declines in black educational expenditures was based on legislation which also limited the franchise of lower-class whites.[11]

The third comparison and most likely to provide a favourable assessment of emancipation, was with the conditions under slavery. But even here the outcomes appear mixed, because some of the legal gains from mobility and freedom might not have been implemented. There was still a need to work and working conditions were still controlled, while the changing means for the provision of foodstuffs and health care may have resulted in some initial reductions in their quantity as well as quality. Except in India, where servitude was sometimes necessary for survival, there were few, if any, attempts by ex-slaves to return to enslavement. This suggests that emancipation, however much desired by those at the time, had outcomes that were mixed. While that meant more future change was desired, however, a reversal of past changes was not. The memories left by the American Civil War and slave emancipation, as described by David Blight, differed by section and by race, with dispersed views even within these groupings. The war and its accompanying freeing of slaves were regarded by all as having been a major historical turning point, and whether regarded as good or bad, their results were not to be gainsaid.

Given different expectations about the effects of emancipation, the nature of the disappointment among parties varied greatly. To the ex-slaves who expected to obtain the rights of the free, as well as to get land on which to grow crops (whether for the market or for self-sufficiency) or else relatively higher wages, to provide for an increased standard of living, the political, social and economic changes that accompanied emancipation could bring only disappointment. Those who obtained land generally were able to do so only for small acreages with infertile soil, and for the most part ex-slaves became cash tenants or sharecroppers rather than owner-operators. Wages were generally low and declining, and often the ex-slaves needed to go into debt to provide for an adequate standard of living. Political rights were often restricted, violence against ex-slaves could be instigated by governments, while governments frequently would not interfere with private violence of the kind initiated to control blacks. Several legal and illegal means were used to limit ex-slave mobility. Thus, in the New World, the accomplishment of independence from white control, and the ability to attain large economic rewards, were seldom achieved in the half-century or so after emancipation, which generated a sense of only limited benefits received compared with what were the initial expectations or hopes of the freed slaves. The next half century was to bring even more adverse conditions.

Anti-slavery advocates were disappointed that the ending of slavery did not lead to impressive social achievements by either ex-slaves or others in society, and the economic predictions of the free labour argument were not achieved even with the changing labour institutions. Ex-slaves did their best to work on small farms not large plantations and preferred declines in labour intensity and increases in leisure, all leading to a decline in the output of the previously slave-grown staples in most places. Whether due to planter behaviour or to ex-slave tastes, the expected response to free labour incentives did not occur, leading to the description of a 'backward bending' supply curve of labour, and discussion of different labour market responses to be expected from white Europeans and black Africans. The British West Indies and the American South remained areas of relatively low per capita incomes, even when one includes the value of non-market production, long after emancipation, not the situation that had been expected at the time slavery was ended. Not only was this outcome puzzling to advocates of emancipation, but it also meant that future reformers who gave such optimistic predictions would find it more difficult to obtain acceptance of their proposals.

To the planters and other pro-slavery advocates the unfavourable economic outcomes of emancipation were not unexpected, since the desire of ex-slaves to avoid plantation work had been predicted. What was not anticipated, however, were the limits placed by governments upon the planters' attempts to force labour back on to the plantations and on planter attempts to prevent ex-slave settlement and ownership of small farms. The attempts, by legal and illegal measures, to restrict ex-slave options, were not as successful as the planters had hoped. This decline in labour input was costly to planters, causing lowered land values and wealth, leading to property transfers to ex-slaves and losses that were not offset by any compensation provided by the government. Significant also was the fact that emancipation had almost always been achieved by political action against the desires of slave owners. This indicated a decline in planter political power, which influenced future actions regarding the colonies, as seen, for example, in the British reductions in the sugar tariffs after the 1830s.

In some cases the sense of disappointment reflected an unwillingness to examine whether the goals desired by different parties were consistent or whether there were trade-offs that needed to be considered. Some trade-offs may have reflected political actions or legal measures which restricted behaviour, some may have been due to natural events, forcing choices to be made, while others were choices made by ex-slaves to satisfy their current needs. Ex-slave choice for more leisure or for self-sufficient work on small units of land may have meant the obtaining of lower incomes, leading to poorer health conditions, a need for increased borrowing and more debt obligations. These outcomes, of course, were no different than for choices confronted by free workers and their employers, but, given the lower initial levels of income and wealth among the ex-slaves, their costs were higher. Obviously other examples of differential responses and differential disappointments can be pointed to. And, since not everybody benefited or lost to the same extent, a generalized focus on difficulties experienced after emancipation, however important, does not do justice to the full range of experiences that occurred.

Indigenous Slavery in Africa

There was yet another sense in which the British and other New World slave emancipations were disappointing to those in the anti-slavery movement. It was believed that once slavery had been ended anywhere and the success of the move to free labour demonstrated the wish to end slavery would spread to those places where it still persisted, and the moral as well as the economic force of abolition would lead to a slavery-free world. While slavery in the Americas ended in Brazil in 1888, some half-century after the British abolition, it remained in place in parts of Asia and Africa into the twentieth century. While African slavery differed in many regards from American slavery, the numbers enslaved were large and an internal trade continued long after the transatlantic slave trade was halted.[12] Slavery in Africa existed before European settlement and domination as well as after, and was only very slowly limited by decrees of the European powers. The existence of slavery and the slowness of its ending were a cause of disappointment to those remaining in the anti-slavery movement in Europe, leading to lobbying and other forms of agitation to accomplish, however belatedly, the ending of African slavery.

David Seddon and Suzanne Miers concentrate on the late period in African slavery. Each points to its continuation into the twentieth century and to the fact that in some areas the share of slaves in the regional population was relatively large. They claim that slavery had long been a part of traditional social systems, so that the Europeans felt constrained in trying to introduce anti-slavery reform. Even when slavery was ended, however, it was often succeeded by forced labour, controls over land, child labour, regressive taxes and compulsory crop rotations, along with measures to minimize the impact of emancipation upon landowners and the labour force.

Thus, while legal slavery may have finally been ended, what came next was to be a major source of agitation, with frequent comparisons of the new systems with slavery.

Great Disappointments

The recent historiography on emancipation has generally tended to emphasize its failures, particularly the disappointments experienced at the time by those newly freed but by others too. While this may represent an appropriate evaluation, given the hopes that had been conjured up, it is useful to remember that there are relatively few reforms in the past that have not generated a similar sense of disappointment, of having achieved only limited success. Comparing predictions of what would happen once the Cold War had ended with recent discussions of what the 1990s transition from socialism in eastern Europe accomplished, indicates that the optimism of a grand future has not yet been realized. Disappointment followed the many forecasts made about the benefits to be expected from communism in the 1910s and the 1920s, and debates about the meaning of the outcome of the French Revolution persist. Discontent with the effect of progress, whether in general or in regard to specific innovations, has been widespread, since there often remains a belief that things seldom live up to expectations and less has been delivered than was hoped for. At times this reflects, not the absence of progress but the belief, based on this progress, that much more could have been accomplished – 'a revolution of rising expectations'. In other cases, for example, rising productivity leads to some increased demand, so that what are labour-saving innovations lead to increases in output, not to more leisure.

Clearly the disappointments that followed the ending of slavery and the expansion of free labour were similar to those of that other major nineteenth-century emancipation of coerced labour, European serfdom. Most of the areas ending serfdom, certainly those east of Prussia, experienced only limited economic growth and structural change, even without the racism that characterized those areas that had had black slavery. Freeing serfs had a large impact in increasing the flows of population outward to the Americas. Free-labour societies have found that the formation of trade unions, which were expected to have dramatic effects on working conditions and wage levels, have not achieved all that was hoped for, just as increased political rights for workers (and later for women) were not able to generate all that was desired. In the late twentieth-century United States extensive civil rights measures could not accomplish all that people had anticipated, leading some scholars to question the wisdom of these policies, even though there were clearly some positive achievements from them.

Thus it is difficult to find major societal changes, including even the American, the French, the Russian and the Chinese revolution, that have not led some to experience a sense of disappointment and a belief that there has been the achievement of only limited benefits relative to what was needed, expected or desired. Even if some benefited, and were satisfied with their progress, other individuals were left behind, making progress incomplete. At times the solution to one set of problems served to create a new set, whether because of the choices made by individuals or else the impact of circumstances that were forced upon them. The study of reform movements, and the successive attempts to solve problems left unresolved (or created) by earlier measures, further demonstrates that the disappointment that came with emancipation was not unique, but rather an example of a more general attitude to policy changes. The limited impact of even the ending of slavery throughout the Americas can be seen in the considerable amount of slavery and other forms of coerced labour in the twentieth century and the continuation of an Anti-Slavery Society long after the legal ending of slavery throughout the world. Human rights organizations continued to draw attention to abuses claimed as analogous to slavery. Earlier, the British and Foreign Anti-Slavery Society had focused on fostering anti-slavery efforts overseas and issues involving the international slave trade. As described by Charles Swaisland, the Aborigines Protection Society, between its founding in 1837 and its merger with the BFASS in 1909, specialized in attacks on British imperialism, mainly in Africa. The joint organization is now concerned with issues such as female and child labour, debt bondage and low wages and poor working conditions more generally, conditions they find in great abundance in the modern world. The continued widespread use of the word 'slavery' today in describing labouring and living conditions in many parts of the world demonstrates the feeling that much more needs to be done.[13]

There was periodic political unrest after emancipation, often in the form of strikes, but with some more dramatic events such as the Morant Bay uprising in Jamaica in 1865. Political disturbances, of course, are not peculiar to former slave societies. To evaluate emancipation, therefore, also necessitates looking at what happened during the time lags between the initial freeing of the slaves and the eventual accomplishment of desirable goals by ex-slaves. If the lags are long, how do we regard the differing importance of the conditions under slavery, the initial stages of emancipation and the long period of freedom? Events in the intervening periods may have had significant impacts, even if they appear independent of the earlier period of enslavement. Thus, for example, in discussing what are regarded as the mid twentieth-century difficulties of the black family in the United States, E. Franklin Frazier did not just point to the effect of slavery but also to the impact of the mobility of the period of Reconstruction, to the role of the northward movement during and after World War I and to the economic difficulties of the Great Depression in the 1930s.[14]

Unlike most other debates about historical changes, however, few now compare the post-emancipation conditions with some variant of the 'good old days' and argue that the changes that have taken place were undesirable. Nevertheless, the occasional claim that there has been an absence of progress raises the comparison with alternative labour forms and the question of whether slavery was unique in its effects upon people. Certain labour forms, such as convict labour, indentured labour and debt peonage, had preceded slavery in many parts of the world, and often they were to succeed it when slavery was abolished. Indentured labour, the most important of these for transoceanic movements, may be regarded either as primarily voluntary, reflecting a choice made at low incomes, or else as coercive, 'a new system of slavery', since working conditions, even after the initial contractual agreement, were harsh, individuals could be bought and sold and labour mobility was limited. Similarly, if low incomes, with or without legal coercion, are believed to be indicative of exploitation and the persistence of 'wage slavery', it is not surprising that disappointment with the outcome of emancipation occurs, a reaction similar to the disappointment felt with those outcomes in a free labour society which yield low incomes and poor working conditions.

Possibly it would only be if ending slavery led to incomes and political power for ex-slaves similar to those of the free, and both the free and ex-slaves acquired even broader rights, that the sense of disappointment with the outcome of emancipation could be avoided. That these did not occur is, of course, what makes the disappointment of contemporaries and of subsequent commentators unsurprising.

NOTES

1. See Stanley L. Engerman, 'Emancipations in Comparative Perspective: A Long and Wide View', in Gert Oostindie (ed.), *Fifty Years Later: Antislavery, Capitalism, and Modernity in the Dutch Orbit* (Pittsburgh, PA: University of Pittsburgh Press, 1996), pp.223–41. See also the essays in Frank McGlynn and Seymour Drescher (eds.), *The Meaning of Freedom: Economics, Politics, and Culture after Slavery* (Pittsburgh, PA: University of Pittsburgh Press, 1992).
2. Still useful for understanding post-emancipation Haiti are Robert I. Rotberg, *Haiti: The Politics of Squalor* (Boston, MA: Houghton Mifflin, 1971) and Simon M. Fass, *Political Economy in Haiti: The Drama of Survival* (New Brunswick: Rutgers University Press, 1988).
3. On the emancipation of European serfs see Jerome Blum, *The End of the Old Order in Rural Europe* (Princeton, NJ: Princeton University Press, 1978).
4. For another discussion of British West Indian emancipation see William Green, *British Slave Emancipation: The Sugar Colonies and the Great Experiment 1830–1865* (Oxford: Clarendon Press, 1976).

5. See Howard Temperley, 'Capitalism, Slavery and Ideology', *Past and Present*, 75 (1977), pp.94–118.

6. Sir James Steuart, *Works*, Vol.I (reprinted: New York, NY: Augustus M. Kelley, 1967), pp.47–53. Later Steuart argues that slavery is advantageous when the need is for physical labour, but where ingenuity and intelligence are required, free labour is to be preferred (pp.254–62).

7. On the social and political adjustment of the post-bellum South see also Joel Williamson, *The Crucible of Race: Black–White Relations in the American South since Emancipation* (Oxford: Oxford University Press, 1984) and Howard N. Rabinowitz, *Race Relations in the Urban South, 1865–1890* (New York, NY: Oxford University Press, 1978).

8. See Fass, *Political Economy*, p.47, for a description of what he calls 'labour export' from Haiti.

9. On the explanation of the decline in per caput output in the South after the Civil War see James R. Irwin, 'Explaining the Decline in Southern per Capita Output after Emancipation', *Explorations in Economic History*, 31 (1994), pp.336–56 and the works cited there.

10. See Walton Look Lai, *Indentured Labour, Caribbean Sugar: Chinese and Indian Migrants to the British West Indies, 1838–1918* (Baltimore, MD: The Johns Hopkins University Press, 1993).

11. See Robert A Margo, *School Finance and the Economics of Segregated Schools in the US South, 1890–1910* (Chicago, IL: University of Chicago Press, 1985), J. Morgan Kousser, *The Shaping of Southern Politics: Suffrage Restriction and the Establishment of the One-Party South, 1880–1910* (New Haven, CT: Yale University Press, 1974) and Orlando Patterson, *Rituals of Blood: Consequences of Slavery in Two American Centuries* (Washington, DC: Civitas/Counterpoint, 1998), pp.169–232.

12. See Paul Lovejoy, *Transformations in Slavery: A History of Slavery in Africa* (Cambridge: Cambridge University Press, 1983) and David Eltis, *The Rise of African Slavery in the Americas* (Cambridge: Cambridge University Press, 2000).

13. For a recent example see Kevin Bales, *Disposable People: New Slavery in the Global Economy* (Berkeley: University of California Press, 1999).

14. E. Franklin Frazier, *The Negro Family in the United States* (Chicago, IL: University of Chicago Press, 1939).

Notes on Contributors

David W. Blight teaches in the Departments of History and Black Studies at Amherst College, Massachusetts. His publications include *Frederick Douglass' Civil War* (1989), an edited edition of *The Life of Frederick Douglass* (1993) and *Race and Reunion: The Civil War in American Memory, 1863–1915* (2000).

Seymour Drescher teaches history at the University of Pittsburgh. He is the author of *Econocide: British Slavery in the Era of Abolition* (1977), and other studies dealing with slavery and abolition, including, co-edited with Stanley Engerman, *A Historical Guide to World Slavery* (1998).

Pieter Emmer is Professor of the History of the Expansion of Europe in the Department of History, Leiden University. Among his publications are *The Dutch in the Atlantic Economy, 1580–1890* (1990) and, edited, Vol. II of the *General History of the Caribbean* (1999).

Stanley L. Engerman is John H. Munro Professor of Economics and Professor of History at the University of Rochester, New York. His publications include *Time on the Cross: The Economics of American Negro Slavery* (1974), which he wrote in collaboration with Robert W. Fogel. He co-edited (with Seymour Drescher) *A Historical Guide to World Slavery* (1998).

Carolyn Fick teaches Caribbean and Latin American history at Concordia University in Montreal. She is the author of *The Making of Haiti: The Saint Domingue Revolution from Below* (1990).

Gad Heuman is Professor of History and Director of the Centre for Caribbean Studies at the University of Warwick. He is also co-editor of the journal *Slavery and Abolition*. His publications include *Between Black and White* (1981) and *The Killing Time* (1994), a study of the 1865 Morant Bay rebellion in Jamaica.

Suzanne Miers is Emerita Professor of African Studies at Ohio University. She is author of *Britain and the Ending of the Slave Trade* (1975) and numerous articles. She co-edited *Slavery in Africa: Historical and Anthropological Perspectives* with Igor Kopytoff, *The End of Slavery in Africa* (1988) with Richard Roberts, *Women and Chinese Patriarchy:*

Submission, Servitude and Escape (1994) with Maria Jaschok, and *Slavery and Colonial Rule in Africa* (1998) with Martin S. Klein.

Michael Naragon teaches American history at Winchester Thurston School in Pittsburgh. He recently completed a doctorate at the University of Pittsburgh with a thesis entitled 'Ballots, Bullets, and Blood: The Political Transformation of Richmond, Virginia, 1850–1874'.

Christopher Schmidt-Nowara teaches history at the Manhattan Campus of Fordham University in New York and is the author of *Empire and Antislavery: Spain, Cuba, and Puerto Rico, 1833–1874*. He received a doctorate from the University of Michigan in 1995.

David Seddon is Professor of Development Studies at the University of East Anglia. He has a doctorate in social anthropology from the London School of Economics based on his fieldwork in Morocco. He has travelled widely in North Africa as a research worker and consultant and speaks Arabic, Spanish and French.

Charles Swaisland has taught at the Universities of Birmingham and Mauritius. He received his doctorate from the University of Oxford in 1968 for a study of the work of the Aborigines Protection Society. Before that he served for many years in the provincial administration of eastern Nigeria.

Howard Temperley is Emeritus Professor of History at the University of East Anglia. His publications include *British Antislavery, 1833–1870* (1972) and *White Dreams, Black Africa: The Antislavery Expedition to the Niger, 1841–1842* (1991).

Index

Abdurahman, Abdullah 267
abolition: British sub-Saharan Africa 237,
    238, 242–3, 250–2, 253–4; Caribbean
    plantations 155; Egypt 215; 'Indian'
    model 239–40; Libya 227; Mauritania
    232–3; Morocco 223; Portuguese *libertos*
    244; Puerto Rico 194; speed of 1; Tunisia
    210; *see also* emancipation; neo-
    abolitionists
abolitionists: Aborigines Protection Society
    266; Antilles 188, 191–2, 193–4, 197, 198,
    203; economic issues 5, 290–1; Great
    Britain 41–66; Haiti 4; India 170, 172,
    173, 181–2, 184–5; Liberia 74, 75;
    pessimism 150; West Indies plantations 7
Aborigines Protection Society (APS)
    (*1837–1909*) 9, 265–80, 298
Adam, Revd William 173, 177
Africa: black separatism 73; British
    abolitionism 46, 47–8; emancipation 1;
    free labour 55; indigenous slavery 9,
    296–7; migrant labour 156, 158; Saharan
    208–36; sub-Saharan 217–21, 230–2,
    237–64; US slavery 173; *see also* West
    Africa
African Americans: Civil War 6–7, 121, 122;
    emancipation commemorations 123–4,
    125, 126–33; Liberia 67–92; political
    participation 101–7, 108–11, 112; the
    South 93–113
African Civilisation Society 266, 268
Afrikaners 238; *see also* Boers
Afro-Cubans 198, 201, 202
agriculture: Algeria 228–9; Caribbean
    foodstuff production 154; effect of
    emancipation 290; Egyptian slavery 214;
    Haiti 4, 17, 23–6, 27–8, 32–5, 283;
    indentureds vs freedmen 160–3; India 177;
    Liberia 86; sub-Saharan Africa 253;
    United States 290; West Indies 7; *see also*
    plantations; sugar production
Albania 213
Alexander, Archibald 73
Algeria 209, 210, 218, 220, 222–3, 226–9
Ali Pasha, Muhammad 214
amelioration 154
American Civil War 6–7, 58, 118–23, 124, 294
American Colonisation Society 5, 67, 69,
    70–1, 72, 78

American South 93–116; agriculture 290;
    Civil War memory 120–3; economic
    conditions 3, 153, 294, 295; political
    participation 101–7, 108–11, 112, 292–3
Americas: character of slavery 173–4;
    economic rationality of slavery 41;
    indentured labour 43
Anderson, Sally 93–4, 99, 111
Angola 244, 247, 248
anti-colonial movements, Antilles 188
anti-racism, Cuba 8, 201, 202
Anti-Slavery International 9–10
anti-slavery movements: Aborigines
    Protection Society 9, 265–80, 298; African
    slavery 245–6; Antilles 188; British and
    Foreign Anti-Slavery Society 9, 181–2,
    245, 265–6, 276, 298; economic
    predictions 295; expectations 284; Great
    Britain 42; India 173
Antigua 137
Antilles 4, 188–207
antiquarianism 127–8
Antrobus, R. 278
apprenticeship system: British abolitionism
    45, 54, 55, 56; Caribbean 7, 135–49, 157,
    291; Transvaal 272
APS *see* Aborigines Protection Society
Arabia 248–9
Ashmun, Jehudi 70–1, 79, 81
Asia: abolition 1; British free labour 55;
    labour migration to the Caribbean 151–2,
    153, 156, 158–64, 165
Association for the Study of Negro Life and
    History 119
Auckland, Lord 175–6, 180, 181
Azcárate, Nicholás 198

Baker, Ray Stannard 125
Baptists 145
Barbados 58, 60, 112, 288
Barbour, Neville 232
Barclay, Edwin 85
Barham, Joseph 48
Barkly, Sir Henry 267
Basutoland 277
Baynes, E.D 143
Bechuanaland 249, 277
Benedict, Samuel 69
Bergad, L. 196

Bey, Hassanein 217
BFASS *see* British and Foreign Anti-Slavery
    Society
Black, Major J.C.C. 120
Blackford, Abraham 76
Blight, David W. 6, 117–34, 294
Blyden, Edward Wilmot 73–4, 75, 86, 87, 89
Boers 88, 271–3, 274; *see also* Afrikaners
Bonaparte, Napoleon 11, 23, 28
Botts, John Minor 103, 104
Bovill, E.W. 212
Boyer, Jean-Pierre 34
Brazil 1, 57, 58, 290, 296
Bridge, Captain Horatio 77
British Caribbean: American South
    comparison 112; emancipation 52, 55,
    288; free labour 49, 60; indentured labour
    157; resistance to apprenticeship system
    135–49, 291; *see also* West Indies
British Empire: anti-slavery movements 265;
    citizenship 277
British and Foreign Anti-Slavery Society
    (BFASS) 9, 181–2, 245, 265–6, 276, 298
British Guiana 56, 140, 145–6, 157, 288, 293
British India Society 173, 265
Brougham, Henry 47
Brown, John 130
Brussels Act (*1890*) 245, 252
Buchanan, Thomas 80
Bundy, C.S. 93
Bushrod Island 80
Buxton, Sir Thomas Fowell 171, 267–8

Caldwell, Elias B. 72
Cameron, C.H. 174–5
Cameroon 248
Cape Colony 237–8, 271
capitalism: British abolitionism 62; Liberia
    81, 86; Western slavery 174
Caribbean: economic effects of emancipation
    288; indentured labour 151, 152, 156, 157,
    158–65, 288; post-emancipation 150–68;
    resistance to apprenticeship system
    135–49, 291; *see also* British Caribbean;
    French Caribbean; West Indies
Carnarvon, Lord 273, 277, 278
Cary, Revd Lott 70–1
Casement, Roger 275, 276
caste system 8, 169–70, 178–9, 180, 183, 185
Cayenne 269
Central Sahara 212–14
Céspedes, Carlos Manuel de 200
Chad: French rule 212, 218; heritage of
    slavery 209; independence 226; slave trade
    213, 217; social transformation 230–1
Chahoon, George 93, 110

Chesson, Frederick William 266, 267, 269,
    270, 276
children: African slavery 248, 259, 260;
    Caribbean apprenticeship system 145;
    Indian slavery 175, 176–7, 179–80, 185,
    186; Transvaal apprenticeship 272
China, migrant labour from 159–60, 165,
    188, 191, 268–9, 273–5
Christianity 84, 85, 277; *see also*
    missionaries
Christophe, Henri 16, 26, 30, 31, 32–3, 35
citizenship: American South 94, 100, 102,
    103; Antilles 189; British 277; Cuba
    196–7; Haiti 17; Liberia 78, 82, 83
civil war, Haiti 22–3, 31
Clarkson, Thomas 45
Clay, Henry 71–2
Code Noir (*1685*) 13
Colenso, Bishop John William 266–7
collective memories 117–18
colonialism: Antilles 188, 192; Haiti 4,
    11–12, 13; indigenous slavery 9; Saharan
    Africa 208, 222–7; slave systems 41; sub-
    Saharan Africa 249, 253, 254, 259–60;
    United States 69; West Indies 52
colonisation, Liberia 68, 71, 72, 73, 74, 77
comparative approaches 281–300
compensation 2–3, 281, 284; abolition in
    sub-Saharan Africa 238, 242, 250–1;
    Emancipation Act (*1833*) 54
concubines 254, 256
Confederacy 93, 94, 97, 100, 111, 119
Congo Free State 269, 275–6
Congo Independent State 247, 248
conservatism, India 170
Conservatives, American South 95, 101–2,
    103, 107–11, 123, 124
Conspiracy of La Escalera (*1843–4*) 191
constitutional arrangements: Haiti 23, 25;
    Liberia 69, 70, 82–3
consumerism 47, 56
contract labour *see* indentured labour
convict labour 44
Conway, Thomas 102
Corn Laws 57
corporal punishment 26, 271
Cox, Joseph 106
creoles: Antilles 190, 192; Caribbean
    agriculture 161, 162–3; Haiti 13
Cropper, James 55
Cuba 7–8, 57, 188–204; Aborigines
    Protection Society 269; plantations 58,
    288; productivity 60, 290
cult slavery 260
Cyprus 213

Daly, J.J. 270
Daniel, R.T. 101, 108
debt bondage 175, 184, 186
Delgado, Manuel Morúa 202
Dessalines, Jean-Jacques 15–16, 22, 26, 29, 30–1, 33
Dilke, Sir Charles 276
direct participation 103–6, 109
discrimination: African slavery 257; Liberia 86
Dixon, Thomas 123
domestic slaves, India 174, 177, 179
Dominica 112, 138–9
Dominican Republic 288
Douglass, Frederick 125, 127–8, 130
Drescher, Seymour 5, 41–66, 284
Du Bois, W.E.B. 120, 123–4, 125, 126–7, 130–3
Duke, John Halloway 140
Dulce, Domingo 192
Dunn, Ross 211, 222
Dutch Caribbean, indentured labour 157

East India Charter Act (1833) 169, 171
East India Company 169–71, 176, 181, 239; Act V 8, 183; free labour 47
economic development: Great Britain 5; Haiti 23, 27–8, 29, 32; slavery effect on 1–2
economics: abolitionism 41–4; African slavery 246; effects of emancipation 3, 55, 284–5, 287–92; free labour ideology 43–4, 45, 46, 49–50; Haitian economic decline 34–5, 51, 53, 283–4, 285, 287; plantation growth 153–5; post-emancipation Caribbean 165; Smith 43–4
education 259
Edwards, Thomas 125
Egypt 73, 214–15, 216, 227
Ellenborough, Earl of 170, 182, 183
Ellyson, Henry 110
emancipation: African-American commemorations 126–33; American South 94, 98–9, 101; Antilles 188, 192, 193, 194–6, 197, 203–4; arguments for and against 282–6; British abolitionists 44, 46, 47, 50, 51–9, 61; Caribbean 52, 55–6, 59, 61, 150–68; Cuba 7–8; East India Charter Bill (1833) 169; economic adjustment 3, 284–5, 287–92; failures of 281–2, 297–9; Haiti 4–5, 11, 15, 16–19, 21, 23–4; 'Indian' model 239–40; social/political effects of 292–6; sub-Saharan Africa 237; US semicentennial 118–19, 120, 121, 123–6; see also abolition
Emancipation Act (1833) 7, 53–4, 169, 177,

237–8, 265, 271
emigration: India 184–5; western Europe 267
Emmer, Pieter 7, 150–68, 185, 288
enfranchisement, African Americans 101
Engerman, Stanley 3, 281–300
England, Saharan Africa 208
Ethiopia 237, 248
Evans-Pritchard, Edward 218
exports: abolitionism effect 55–6; decline after emancipation 285, 290; Haiti 27–8, 29, 33, 283, 287
family structure, Indian immigrants to the Caribbean 163–4
Fergusson, Cutler 170
Ferrer, Ada 200
Fick, Carolyn 4, 11–40, 283
'fictive kin' slaves 259
Fiji 165, 277, 292
Finley, Revd Dr Robert 71
Fischer, David Hackett 117
Fitchett, John 106
Fitzgerald, Lord 183
Fitzpatrick, Sir Percy 275
Floyd, Silas X. 121
Foner, Eric 100
Forbes, Rosita 217
Foreign Abolition Bill (1806) 48
Fowler, R.N. 273
Fox Bourne, Henry Richard 266, 273, 274, 275–6, 277, 278
Fraenkel, Merran 89
France: conscription 247; Haiti 11, 12–13, 15, 16–17, 20–3, 28; Saharan Africa 208, 210–12, 215, 222, 223, 224–7; slave raiding 248; sub-Saharan Africa 217–21, 244, 252–3, 256
Franklin, John Hope 119
Frazier, E. Franklin 298–9
free labour ideology 42–50, 52, 57, 59–61, 284–5, 295
free-trade movement 54, 55, 56–8
Freedmen's Bureau 292
French Caribbean: decline in exports 285; indentured labour 157
French Revolution 4, 11, 12, 23, 297
French Soudan 212, 219–20, 252–3
Frere, Sir Bartle 177, 243
Froude, J.H. 273
Furbay, Elizabeth Dearmin 85

Galbaud, Thomas 16
Garrison, William Lloyd 74–5, 79, 89, 130
gerrymandering 111
Ghana 260
Gold Coast 237, 239, 242–3, 250, 277
Gomez, Juan Gualberto 198

Gordon, Sir Arthur 267, 269, 271
Great Britain: abolitionism 1, 9, 41–66;
    Aborigines Protection Society 9, 265–80,
    298; British and Foreign Anti-Slavery
    Society 9, 181–2, 245, 265–6, 276, 298;
    Cuba 189; free labour 285; Haiti 16, 22;
    India 8, 169–87; labour productivity 4–5;
    Master and Servant Acts 293; Saharan
    Africa 211–12, 214, 215, 216; Sierra
    Leone 68; sub-Saharan Africa 237–59; see
    also British Caribbean; British Empire;
    West Indies
Great Trek 238, 271
Greenleaf, Professor Samuel 69
Guadeloupe 48, 269
Guiness, Dr Grattan 275
Gurley, R.R. 71
Guyana 58, 112

Haiti 3–4, 11–40; British abolitionism 51;
    economic failure 34–5, 51, 53, 283–4, 285,
    287; pro-slavery arguments 285
Hargey, Taj 227, 233–4
Harris, Sion 76
Harris, Walter 211
Harvey, Thomas 146
Hennessy, Sir John Pope 267
Heuman, Gad 7, 135–49, 291
Hindu law 176, 178, 179
Hobsbawm, Eric 117–18, 144
Hodges, Tony 221
Hodgkin, Thomas 271
Holmboe, Knud 217
Holt, Thomas 135, 146
Howells, William Dean 120
Howick, Viscount 52
human rights abuses, Saharan Africa 233, 234
Humphreys, James 109
Hunnicutt, James 102, 103–5, 106, 109

ILO see International Labour Organization
indentured (contract) labour 289, 291–2, 299;
    America 44; British abolitionism 54, 58;
    Caribbean 151–2, 156, 157, 158–65, 288;
    Chinese in South Africa 273–5; Cuba 188,
    191; disguising slavery 249; Indians 55,
    151–2, 159–65, 184–5, 265, 268–71,
    274–5; superseded by slavery 43
indentured labour, see also migrant labour
independence struggles: Cuba 8; Haiti 3, 4,
    11, 28–9
India 8, 169–87, 293, 294; abolition 239–40;
    indentured labour from 55, 151–2, 159–65,
    184–5, 265, 268–71, 274–5
Indian Law Commission 172–3, 174–5, 176,
    178, 180, 181–3

indigenous peoples: Aborigines Protection
    Society 265–80; Egypt 215;
    Liberia/Monrovia 78, 79–80, 81–3, 85–6,
    87, 88–9; Western Sahara 221; see also
    Native Americans
Industrial Revolution 42, 153
integration, racial 286
International Labour Organization (ILO) 9,
    185
invented traditions 117–18
Islam 87, 210; see also Muslim law
Italy, Saharan Africa 216–17, 218

Jabavu, Tengo 267, 273
Jackson, Giles B. 123
Jamaica: 1831 uprising 52, 53, 137; 1865
    uprising 112, 298; apprenticeship system
    135, 136, 140–4, 145, 146, 147;
    emancipation 164; evictions of ex-slaves
    157; food production 154; low economic
    production 58, 288; slave labour
    production 2; women's role 146, 147
Jamaican Education Society 56
Java 55, 57, 160, 165
Jefferson, Thomas 165
Jews 77
Johnson, Andrew 95, 96, 98, 101
Johnson, Bishop James 267
Johnson, General Elijah 84
Johnson, James Weldon 121–2, 128–9, 133
Johnson, Marmaduke 101, 107, 108
Johnston, Sir Harry 85

Kammen, Michael 126
Keiley, A.M. 110
Kendall, Amos 68
Kenya 250, 256, 259

labour: Antillean ex-slaves 195; Haiti 24, 25;
    India 184, 185; Liberia 80–1; non-
    plantation 292; post-emancipation
    Caribbean 155, 156–8; US emancipation
    102; see also apprenticeship system;
    indentured labour; wage labour
labour movements, Antilles 198–9
Labra, Rafael María de 188, 197–8, 199
Lacroix, Pamphile de 26
Lamu 251
land issues: Caribbean freedmen 162; Haiti
    14, 18, 19–20, 21–2, 30–1, 32–5; see also
    property
landlords, debt bondage 184, 186
Lavigerie, Cardinal 245
Le Jeune, Nicolas 14
Lecky, W.E.H. 61
legal issues: Anderson court case 93–4;

delegalization of slavery 239, 242–3; emancipation in the American South 101 legislation: Act V (*1843*) 8, 183, 184; Brussels Act (*1890*) 245, 252; *Code Noir* (*1685*) 13–14; East India Charter Act (*1833*) 169, 171; Emancipation Act (*1833*) 7, 53–4, 169, 177, 237–8, 265, 271; Foreign Abolition Bill (*1806*) 48; Master and Servant Acts 293; Military Reconstruction Act (*1867*) 94–5, 101; Moret Law (*1870*) 193, 195, 203, 290; Pact of Zanjón (*1878*) 194, 195, 196; *patronato* (*1880*) 194–5, 196, 203, 290; racist 286; work/land codes in Haiti 24, 25, 32; Workman's Breach of Contract Act (*1859*) 184

Leopold II, King of Belgium 244, 245, 247, 248, 275

liberals, American South 122–3

Liberia 5–6, 67–92, 237, 249, 268, 286

libertos 244

libreta (workbook) system 191, 194, 198, 203

Libya 216–17, 218, 227

Lichtenberger, J.P. 125

Lincoln, Abraham 95, 130

Lindsay, Lewis 103, 106

Livingstone, David 244–5

Louverture, Toussaint 4, 15, 16, 21–8, 29, 31

Lowe, Richard 96

Lugard, Frederick 251, 252

Lundahl, Mats 27, 28

Lyons, A.M. 145, 146

Macaulay, T.B. 170–1, 172

McCurry, Stephanie 94

Maceo, Antonio 201

Macfarland, William 98, 101, 108

MacGregor, E.J. Murray 138

Madiou, Thomas 26

Maghreb 208, 210–11, 222

Mali 208–9, 218, 219, 222, 225–6, 230–1

Malthus, Thomas 51

manumission 15, 241, 251, 257, 258

Marshall, Woodville 145

Martí, José 201

Martin, Thomas 123

Martínez, Saturnino 198

Martinique 269

mass mobilization, American South 94, 96, 100, 103, 104, 105

Master and Servant Acts 293

Mauritania: abolitionism 208; contemporary slavery 223, 232–3; French rule 212, 218, 220–1, 224–5; Saharawi conflict 209, 224, 230

Mauritius 55, 165, 268, 269, 270–1

Maxwell, Sir Benson 267

Mayo, Joseph 96, 97, 98, 99, 100

Meacham, Carl 85–6

Mechlin, Dr Joseph 80

Merivale, Herman 60

Middle East 248–9

Miege, Jean-Louis 211

Miers, Suzanne 9, 183, 237–64, 296

migrant labour: British colonies 54, 58; Caribbean 7, 151–2, 153, 156, 157, 158–65; India 173, 185; *see also* indentured labour

militancy, American South 112–13

military, Haitian agricultural reform 26, 30, 33

Military Reconstruction Act (*1867*) 94–5, 101

Miller, Kelly 125

Minor, James Cephas 76, 80

missionaries 135, 163, 173, 245, 247

Moïse, General 26–7

Monrovia 67, 70, 79–80, 81, 84, 85

Montane, Lt-Col. 220

Moors 220, 225, 232

Morel, Edmund Dene 275, 276

Moret Law (*1870*) 193, 195, 203, 290

Moret y Prendergast, Segismundo 193

Morocco: heritage of slavery 223; resistance to Spanish 212, 221; Saharawi conflict 224, 230; slave trade 210–11, 222; 'white' Moors 225

Morrissey, James 106

Mozambique 244, 269

mulattos: Cuban conflicts 200, 201; Haiti 22, 31; Monrovia 81

Mulgrave, Lord 141

multiculturalism 118

Muslim law 240–1, 251, 254, 255, 256, 257

NAACP *see* National Association for the Advancement of Colored People

Nachtigal, Gustav 213

Naragon, Michael 6, 93–116, 286

Natal 292

National Association for the Advancement of Colored People (NAACP) 124, 126, 131

National Emancipation Exposition (Du Bois) 130–1

nationalism: black 127; Cuba 8, 197, 201–2

Native Americans 82, 88, 173

neo-abolitionists 124–5, 126

New England 2

Newport, Mary 84

Nietzsche, F.W. 117

Niger: African Civilisation Society venture

268; heritage of slavery 208, 209; slave trade 213, 222; social transformation 230–1; Tuareg 210, 218, 219, 226, 231–2
Nigeria 251–2, 254, 255, 256, 258–9
Nixon, J. Lyons 136–7
Northern Rhodesia 248
Northern Territories 250

O'Connell, Daniel 53
O'Connor, Owen 271
Odum, Howard 125
Oliver, John 102
Orange River State 271–2
Osborn, Melmoth 272
Ould Daddah, Mokhtar 224, 232
Ovington, Mary White 126–7

Page, John M. 76
Page, Solomon S. 76
pageantry 127, 130–1
Pan-Africanism 86, 127
patriarchy 256–7
patriotism, black memory 127, 128–9
patronato (1880) 194–5, 196, 203, 290
pawnship 241
Peggs, Revd James 173, 177
Pemba 238, 250, 256
Peru 269
Pétion, Alexandre 16, 31, 32, 33–4, 35
Pierpoint, Francis 95, 96, 97, 99
plantations: Antilles 189, 190, 194, 195, 203; Caribbean apprenticeship system 142–4, 145, 146; Cuba 7–8; decline of 34, 35, 284–5, 287, 290, 292; efficiency 151, 153–5; Haiti 4, 11–12, 17–28, 30, 32–5, 283; indentureds vs freedmen 156, 160, 161, 163; post-emancipation Caribbean 152, 156–8, 165, 288; West Indies 5, 7
planters see slave owners
Plevitz, Adolph de 271
POLISARIO see Popular Front for the Liberation of the Seguia el Hamra and the Rio de Oro
politics: American South 94–5, 96–7, 98, 99, 101–13; Antilles 189, 192, 196–202; British anti-slavery movements 182; Haiti 22–3; Liberia 83–5; participation of US ex-slaves 101–7, 108–11, 112, 292–3; Saharan Africa 208–9
Polverel, Etienne 16, 18–19, 20, 21
Popular Front for the Liberation of the Seguia el Hamra and the Rio de Oro (POLISARIO) 209, 227–8, 229–30, 232
Portugal 158, 244, 247, 249
poverty, India 175, 184, 186
Pretorius, Andries 272

Prim, Juan 192
Principe 244
property: Liberia 83; see also land issues
prostitution 176, 186
protectorates, Africa 210, 238–9, 244, 250
Puerto Rico 188–204
punishment: Haiti 13, 17–18, 25–6, 30; indentured labour 271; Indian slavery 176, 183; resistance to Caribbean apprenticeship system 136, 141, 142, 143, 144

Queensland 269, 292

race: American Civil War 120; Antillean conflicts 200–1, 204; British abolitionism 60; Cuba 199; integration 286; riots 293
racial segregation, United States 7, 125
racism: Cuba 201, 202; United States 74, 96, 119, 124; see also anti-racism; white supremacy
'Radicals', American South 123, 124
Ramsay, James 44, 45, 55
rebellions: Antilles 191, 192, 199, 200, 203; Conspiracy of La Escalera (1843-4) 191; French colonial Africa 219; Haiti 3–4, 11, 14–16, 21, 24, 26, 287; Jamaica 52, 137, 298; Liberia 5, 70–1, 88; Mali 225; Nigeria 258; see also resistance; riots
receptaves, United States 67, 68
Reconstruction 93, 98–101, 108, 123, 198, 299
redemption charges 251, 252, 257
religion: Liberia 85; see also Christianity
Republican Party, United States 94–5, 96, 97, 101–7, 108, 109–11
resistance, apprenticeship system 136–47, 291
Réunion 269, 270
revolts see rebellions
Richmond, Virginia 6, 93–116, 123, 286
Rigaud, André 22
rights: Antillean ex-slaves 197, 198; Haitian emancipation 12–13, 17; Indian society 179; Nigerian slaves 258; political 292–3, 294; US emancipation 94, 103, 109, 112, 113
riots: American South (1867) 99–100; British Caribbean 112; see also rebellions
Roberts, Joseph John 70, 80, 84
Rodgers, Daniel 124, 125
royal slaves 255
runaways: St. Kitts 138; sub-Saharan Africa 239, 250, 251, 252; United States 2

Saharan Africa 208–36

Saharawis 221, 224, 228, 229–30
St. Domingue 48, 51, 188, 189, 201
St. Kitts 136–9, 141
Saint Vincent 112
Sanussi Order 213–14, 218
Sâo Tomé 244
Saunders, D.J. 97–8
Schmidt-Nowara, Christopher 8, 173–4, 188–207, 290
Schoelcher, Victor 270
Schomberg, Charles 138–9
Scott, James 143
Scott, Rebecca 195, 196
Seddon, David 9, 183, 208–36, 296
segregation, racial 7, 125
Senegal 218, 219, 225, 226
separatism: Antilles 197, 199, 200; US black 73, 75, 86
serfdom 297
Serrano, Francisco 192
Sewell, William G. 164
Shaftesbury, Lord 272
Shaw, George Bernard 133
Sheller, Mimi 146, 147
Sierra Leone: British colonialism 68, 86, 237; economic weakness 286; free labour 47; indentured labour 159; problems of 89; 'sphere of influence' 249–50
Silber, Nina 119–20
slave owners (planters): anti-abolitionist arguments 50–1, 52; Antilles 191–2, 193, 196, 199; apprenticeship system 135, 136, 142, 146; attitudes 2; brutalization of 1; Caribbean emancipation 150, 151; compensation 2–3, 54, 238, 242, 250–1, 281, 284; demand for migrant labour 156, 157–8; fear of free blacks in the USA 74; free labour 58; Haiti 12, 13–14, 33–4; plantation economy 154–5; post-emancipation 295; power of 62; profits 44; sub-Saharan Africa 253–4
slave raiding 223, 224, 225, 245, 248
slave trade: Africa 296; British abolitionism 43, 45–6, 47, 48, 59; Central Sahara 212–14, 218; Cuba 189; Egypt 214–15; end of 191; indentured African labour 158–9; Libya 217; Morocco 211, 222; prices 154; Puerto Rico 190–1; sub-Saharan Africa 239, 244, 248; Sudan 227; West Africa 212
Sligo, Lord 135, 136, 140–1, 142, 143, 145
Smith, Adam 4–5, 41, 42–4, 49, 59
Smith, Sir Harry 271–2
Soga, Kirkland 267
Solomon, Saul 273
Sonthonax, Léger-Félicité 16, 17, 18, 19

South Africa 88, 165, 267, 271–5; see also Cape Colony
South Carolina 2
Southey, Sir Richard 273
Spain: Antilles 188–90, 191, 192, 194, 196–200, 203; Haiti 16, 22; Saharan Africa 212, 221, 223–4, 229–30; slave trade 7; sub-Saharan Africa 244
Spanish Caribbean, indentured labour 157
special magistrates, Caribbean apprenticeship system 136, 137, 143, 146
Stanley, H.M. 275
Stephen, James (Jnr) 52
Stephen, James (Snr) 48–9, 58
Steuart, Sir James 285
Steyn, G.W. 272
strikes, Caribbean apprenticeship system 136, 138, 139, 141
Sturdivant, N.A. 101, 102, 107, 108
Sturge, John 146
Sturge, Joseph 56
sub-Saharan Africa 217–21, 230–2, 237–64
Sudan 209, 213, 214, 215–16, 227, 230–1; contemporary slavery 233–4, 260; famine relief 265; freedmen 255
sugar production: abolitionism effect on prices 55; Antilles 189, 190, 194, 195–6, 199, 203; British abolitionist boycott 48; Caribbean 151, 153; Cuba 290; free trade 57–8; Haiti 27, 28, 33; indentured labour 292; West Indies 44, 48, 53–4, 61
Surinam 269
Swaisland, Charles 265–80, 298
Swettenham, Sir Frank 274
Swift, Jonathan 132, 133

Taylor, Henry 52
Taylor, Moses 106
Teague, Hilary 77
Temperley, Howard 67–92, 169–87, 286, 293
Ten Years' War, Cuba (1868-78) 199, 200, 203
Terry, General 97, 99
Tillman, Ben 123
tobacco, Richmond 95–6
Tobago 112
trade: Liberia 80; restrictions on Indian 185; see also exports
Trinidad 48, 58, 139–40, 157, 288, 293
Truth, Sojourner 130
Tubman, Harriet 128
Tucker, Dean 55
Tunisia 210
Turkey 213, 218

Turner, General John 97–8

Uganda 165
Underwood, John 93, 106
United Nations 9, 234
United States: agriculture 290; apology for
   slavery 118; black separatism 73, 75; civil
   rights 297; Civil War 6–7, 58, 118–23,
   124, 294; colonialism 87–8; Declaration of
   Independence 77–8; emancipation 118–19,
   120, 121, 123–33; free labour 60, 285;
   Freedmen's Bureau 292; government
   activism 198; historical changes 298–9;
   integration 286; Liberia 5, 6, 67, 68–71,
   83–4, 85; native-born slave plantations 57;
   racial prejudice 74; Richmond 6, 93–116,
   123, 286; runaways 2; see also American
   South

vagrancy: Antilles 194; Caribbean 158; Haiti
   18, 20; Mauritius 271; regulation 2
Vardaman, James 123
Villard, Fanny Garrison 125–6
Villard, Oswald Garrison 124
Virginia 6, 93–116, 123

wage labour: Africa 247, 253, 255, 260;
   Antillean ex-slaves 195; British
   abolitionism 43, 53; Haiti 19
wages, Caribbean plantations 153, 155
Walker, David 130
Wardwell, Burnham 105
Warner, Daniel B. 81, 85
Washington, Booker T. 124, 125, 127, 128
Watkis, Price 141
Wellington, Duke of 170
West Africa 211–12, 221, 238, 247, 252–3,
   256
West Indian Land Investment Company 56
West Indies: apprenticeship system 54, 55,
   56; British abolitionism 45–50, 53, 54,
   59–60, 61; emancipation 4–5, 7, 52, 55–6;

free trade 57–8; incomes 295; India
   comparison 169; Indian migrant labour
   268; integration 286; post-emancipation
   policy 293–4; Smith 43–4; see also British
   Caribbean; Caribbean
Western Sahara 212, 221, 229–30
Westmoreland, Earl of 42
Weyler, Valeriano 199
White, Frank 123
White, Frederic 145
white supremacy: American South 120, 123;
   emancipation commemoration 125; rise of
   119; US Conservatives 107, 108, 110, 111
Wilberforce, Samuel 58
Wilberforce, William 45–6, 48
Williamson, Joel 122–3, 124
Wilmot, Swithin 142
Wingfield, Sir Charles 269
women: African slavery 240–1, 254, 255–7,
   258; African-American political
   mobilization 104, 105, 106; Caribbean
   apprenticeship system 145–7; field labour
   288–90; Moroccan slavery 211;
   prostitution 176, 186
Woodruff, Philip 278
work see labour
Work, Monroe 125
working hours, Caribbean apprenticeship
   system 143, 145, 146
World Anti-Slavery Convention: 1840 173,
   177, 181; 1843 57
World Trade Organization 185
Wright, R.R. 125

Yaji, Hamman 248
Yoruba 252, 255
Young, Arthur 41

Zanjón, Pact of (1878) 194, 195, 196
Zanzibar 238, 247, 250, 256
Zulueta, Julián 192

Books of Related Interest

From Slavery to Emancipation in the Atlantic World

Sylvia R Frey, *Tulane University* and
Betty Wood, *University of Cambridge* (Eds)

This collection examines the effects of slavery and emancipation on race, class and gender in societies of the American South, the Caribbean, Latin America and West Africa. The contributors discuss what slavery has to teach us about patterns of adjustment and change, black identity, and the extent to which enslaved peoples succeeded in creating a dynamic world of interaction within the Americas. They examine how emancipation was defined, how it affected attitudes towards slavery, patterns of labour usage and relationships between workers as well as between workers and their former owners. To what extent were the work experiences of liberated slaves similar to and different from those of enslaved peoples? What can we say of the creative and political work of enslaved and free peoples? Viewed both from the African and the American side, how is slavery remembered? What is the link between remembering and forgetting the experiences of slavery and identity formation This volume addresses all of these questions in an attempt to elucidate the moral as well as the political dimensions of slavery and emancipation.

Contributors: *Sylvia R Frey, Betty Wood, Linda M Heywood, Daniel H Usner, Jr., Mary Turner, Rosanne Marion Adderley, Julie Saville, Rebecca J Scott, Lawrence N Powell* and *Theresa A Singleton.*

184 pages 5 photographs 1999
0 7146 4964 3 cloth
0 7146 8025 7 paper
A special issue of the journal Slavery and Abolition
Slave and Post-Slave Societies and Cultures Series No. 9

FRANK CASS PUBLISHERS
Newbury House, 900 Eastern Avenue, Ilford, Essex, IG2 7HH
Tel: +44 (0)20 8599 8866 Fax: +44 (0)20 8599 0984 E-mail: info@frankcass.com
NORTH AMERICA
5804 NE Hassalo Street, Portland, OR 97213 3644, USA
Tel: 800 944 6190 Fax: 503 280 8832 E-mail: cass@isbs.com
Website: www.frankcass.com

Slavery and Colonial Rule in Africa

Suzanne Miers, *Ohio University* and
Martin A. Klein, *University of Toronto* (Eds)

'I find this book a must for all who are interested in the question of slavery - especially those campaigning for reparations.'

West Africa

This book presents new case studies which enhance our understanding of the process of abolition at the grass-roots level. Some are on areas where there has been little research, such as the German colonies and the Algerian Sahara; others throw new light on questions already debated, such as emancipation on the Gold Coast, or discuss the impact of abolition on particular groups of slaves in their own emancipation, the immediate and lasting results of abolition, the role of the League of Nations, and the vestiges of slavery in Africa today, this volume adds considerably to our knowledge of an emerging field of African history.

Contributors: *Suzanne Miers, Martin A Klein, Dennis Cordell, Ahmad Sikainga, Andrew F Clark, Jan-Georg Deutsch, Andreas Eckert, Kwabena Opare-Akurang, Sean Stilwell, Don C Ohadike, Ismail Rashid, Toyin Falola and Taj Hargey.*

312 pages maps 1999
0 7146 4884 1 cloth
0 7146 4436 6 paper
A special issue of the journal Slavery and Abolition
Slave and Post-Slave Societies and Cultures Series No. 8

FRANK CASS PUBLISHERS
Newbury House, 900 Eastern Avenue, Ilford, Essex, IG2 7HH
Tel: +44 (0)20 8599 8866 Fax: +44 (0)20 8599 0984 E-mail: info@frankcass.com
NORTH AMERICA
5804 NE Hassalo Street, Portland, OR 97213 3644, USA
Tel: 800 944 6190 Fax: 503 280 8832 E-mail: cass@isbs.com
Website: www.frankcass.com

Popular Politics and British Anti-Slavery

The Mobilisation of Public Opinion against the Slave Trade 1787–1807

J R Oldfield, *University of Southampton*

> '*The campaign for the abolition of the slave trade has often been described but never better than by J R Oldfield in this account.*'
> **Times Literary Supplement**

In 1792, 400,000 people put their signature to petitions calling for the abolition of the slave trade. *Popular Politics and British Anti-Slavery* explains how this remarkable expression of support for black people was organized and orchestrated, and how it contributed to the growth of popular politics in Britain.

In particular, this study focuses on the growing assertiveness of the middle classes in the public sphere and their increasingly powerful role in influencing parliamentary politics from outside the confines of Westminster. The author also argues that abolitionists need to be understood not as 'Saints' but as practical men who knew all about the market and consumer choice. This pioneering book examines the opinion-building activities of the Society for the Abolition of the Slave Trade, the linkage between abolition, consumption and visual culture – cameos, trade tokens, prints, etc. – and the dynamics of abolition at the grass-roots level. A separate chapter on Thomas Clarkson reconsiders his role in the mobilisation of public opinion against the slave trade.

208 pages illus 1998
0 7146 4462 5 paper
Slave and Post-Slave Societies and Cultures Series No. 6

FRANK CASS PUBLISHERS
Newbury House, 900 Eastern Avenue, Ilford, Essex, IG2 7HH
Tel: +44 (0)20 8599 8866 Fax: +44 (0)20 8599 0984 E-mail: info@frankcass.com
NORTH AMERICA
5804 NE Hassalo Street, Portland, OR 97213 3644, USA
Tel: 800 944 6190 Fax: 503 280 8832 E-mail: cass@isbs.com
Website: www.frankcass.com

Classical Slavery

M I Finley (Ed)

The empires of Greece and Rome, two of the very few genuine slave societies in history, formed the core of the ancient world, and they have much to teach the student of recent slave systems. This volume was the final project of this century's leading expert on ancient slavery, Moses Finley, and much of the contemporary debate over ancient bondage bears witness to the power of his legacy. Designed to bring the contribution of ancient history to the attention of a wider audience, this collection discusses the classical definition of slavery, the relationship between war, piracy and slavery, early abolitionist movements as well as the supply and domestic aspects of slavery in antiquity.

176 pages 1987; repr. 1999
0 7146 3320 8 cloth
0 7146 4389 0 paper
A special issue of the journal Slavery and Abolition
Slave and Post-Slave Societies and Cultures Series No. 7

FRANK CASS PUBLISHERS
Newbury House, 900 Eastern Avenue, Ilford, Essex, IG2 7HH
Tel: +44 (0)20 8599 8866 Fax: +44 (0)20 8599 0984 E-mail: info@frankcass.com
NORTH AMERICA
5804 NE Hassalo Street, Portland, OR 97213 3644, USA
Tel: 800 944 6190 Fax: 503 280 8832 E-mail: cass@isbs.com
Website: www.frankcass.com